CEO

"Maybe the journey isn't so much about becoming anything. Maybe it's about un-becoming everything that isn't really you, so you can be who you were meant to be in the first place.

PAUL COELHO, Author of *The Alchemist*"

Printed in the United States of America

First Edition
ISBN: 978-0-578-61873-9
ISBN: 978-0-578-61874-6

Visit: **CEObook.com**

CEO

7 Secrets
To Unleash Your Inner Boss And Start Building Your MILLION DOLLAR FUTURE TODAY

Jeremy McGilvrey

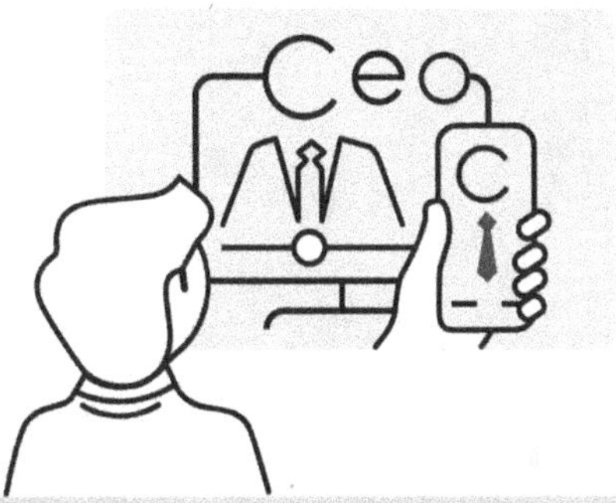

CEOs Reveal Their Secrets [100% Free]

In writing this book, the most mind-bending discovery I unearthed was: our subconscious regularly sabotages our conscious intentions. And the only way to reprogram our subconscious is through repetition. But what thoughts and actions should we be repeating?

This question and many more I ask CEOs from around the world. Get free access to my interviews here:

www.CEObook.com/Free

DEDICATION

To my sons Thomas and Tristan; I wrote this book for you. I have been through hell and back. I know what works and what doesn't. Implement what I teach in this book and you will always be the CEOs of your lives.

Contents

A Note from the Author

"Rock bottom became the solid foundation on which I rebuilt my life."

~J.K. Rowling

October 20, 2009, I shuffled into a criminal courtroom. My wrist and ankles were shackled together by a thick metal chain. I looked up at the judge and uttered – for me – three very difficult words: "I was wrong."

The judge looked over at the TV cameras, acknowledged them, then glanced down with a scorned look – and sentenced me to two 20-year prison terms (40 years).

Through an extraordinary sequence of events that was nothing short of a miracle (involving yet another judge), four years and one month later; I walked out of the front gates of a maximum-security penitentiary. After spending nearly half a decade in some of the most dangerous prisons the state of Texas has to offer, you'd think the hard part was behind me.

But it wasn't.

When I was released, I was handed a $300 check and told, "Good luck out there." With nothing left to my name other than an old box of clothes, my only option was to move in with my father at the age of 36. Through various jobs, I was able to earn about $600 a month. I was starting over, and doing it from the lowest level of the official poverty threshold.

If that wasn't challenging enough, I was also starting over as a convicted felon. And in today's society, that makes it extremely difficult to succeed. The statistics certainly aren't promising: more than half of Americans who are incarcerated return to jail within five years of being released (this rate of recidivism is significantly higher than any other developed nation). Facing such a daunting justice system makes my story all the more remarkable, especially when combined with the additional burdens I brought upon myself.

Although my father provided a home for me to live in temporarily, eventually I found myself homeless. There were numerous times when things were so bad that I was forced to shower in truck stops and find shelter in community centers. In the midst of my self-created hell, I quickly learned to embrace this life-saving philosophy:

The moment you stop fighting for what you want, what you don't want will automatically appear.

One employer after another rejected me because I was a convicted felon, even though I was more than qualified for every position I applied. The background check is the sentence that keeps you forever incarcerated. Eventually, I was able to get a job selling cars. I excelled and immediately became the number-one salesman every single month. Knowing that spending all my time at a car dealership, especially on weekends, was not going to fit into my long-term goals; I partnered with my brother, Jonathan, and attempted to start a company. That company quickly failed.

I continued to work my butt off and was finally offered a job from a business with whom I had a relationship with prior to going to prison. I would take my lunch and dinner to work with me because I spent so much time grinding, and trying to figure out solutions so that I could provide enough value to protect my job.

I share my personal story of struggle with you, not to invoke sympathy, but rather because I believe you may be going through significant challenges in your life as well. This book and the secrets inside will show you not only how I turned a major *setback* into a major *comeback*, but it will also show you how to gain complete control over your life and your current circumstances (whatever they may be).

The secrets I reveal in the seven chapters of this book are not theory. They are science-based strategies that worked for me under extraordinary circumstances, and I know will work for you regardless of the current situation you find yourself in.

I wrote *CEO* because I believe people want to learn from someone who has overcome extreme adversity. In fact, this book was born from adversity. When I initially attempted to write it from prison, I continued to face unexpected challenges. On multiple occasions, guards came into my prison cell through random shakedowns and threw away entire chapters of this book, chapters that took many, many months to write. I would get extremely frustrated, but I would always find a pen and go back to writing these words you are reading now. My relentless ability to persevere until I prevail and believe in the seemingly impossible is exactly what I am asking you to do.

Will implementing the secrets I reveal to you be difficult? Absolutely. But I promise it'll be worth it.

Looking back at the journey I've had since incarceration, it seems like there was one uphill battle after another. It seems like I've endured one struggle after another. But one of the most important lessons I've learned in life is that the roadblocks are not there to keep us out, they are there to see how bad we want it.

Now, the level of success I have achieved after being freed from a six-foot by eight-foot cage is something that's even baffling to me. Virtually every major publication from *Forbes* to *Entrepreneur* has written about my success. *The Huffington Post* even called me "a brilliant entrepreneur."

I wrote the number-one marketing book in the world (*Instagram Secrets*), and was recently accepted into Harvard's Marketing

Management Program. My hand-selected team and I created a website that earned the prestigious *Two Comma Club Award* for generating over $1,000,000 in sales. I was selected as one of the *Top 30 Internet Marketers* on the planet. And millions of people have been positively impacted by the heartfelt messages I regularly share.

How can all these achievements be possible with starting all over just a few short years ago, convicted, bankrupt, and in a dead-end job? The answers can be found in the seven secrets in this book. I cannot emphasize enough how much time and thought I have put into each word, into the science behind the strategies I reveal, and how much effort and attention I have poured into the exercises at the end of each chapter.

There are a lot of people giving advice these days. The problem is, very few have ever been through any real challenges. I know exactly what it's like to lose everything and start over from rock bottom. You may not be at rock bottom, and that will give you a distinct advantage. But wherever you are in life, take these secrets, implement them, and understand you're closer than you think you are. In fact, you're just seven secrets away.

Sincerely,

Jeremy McGilvrey

P.S. If there is anything I can do, if I can do anything to help you achieve your goals or overcome a challenge you're facing...I will do it. But you need to have the courage to make the request. You can do so by emailing me: Jeremy@CEObook.com or you can go here: www.CEObook.com/Help.

Introduction: You're Only 7 Secrets Away...

"If you are ready for the secret, you already possess one half of it, therefore, you will readily recognize the other half the moment it reaches your mind."

~NAPOLEON HILL

Before we get started, I would like to thank you for taking the initiative to pick up this book and start reading. I understand once your time is spent, it's gone forever. That is precisely why I want to be 100 percent certain you get nothing but mind-blowing ideas and strategies from the content you're about to consume.

If you trust me and continue to read each page that lies ahead, you'll be rewarded with a gift that is far more valuable than all the riches in the world. You will never have to dream about becoming the best possible version of yourself because you will know exactly *how* to develop the best possible version of yourself. Virtually everything you need to know about becoming successful at the game of life is contained in the blueprint that you will discover throughout these seven chapters.

In many ways, each chapter of this book was assembled, more than written. What do I mean? All the viable game-changing strategies I've ever read, heard, studied, and tried are contained within this book. Much of my knowledge came from spending nearly half a decade in a prison cell. That experience provided me with a unique opportunity to devour one book after another, written by some of the most prolific self-help experts to date.

But I also took the opportunity to read the works of brilliant neuroscientists and behavioral psychologists as well. As I was writing *CEO*, I couldn't stop at merely assuming you would accept what I had to offer. I felt it was important to explain *why* the secrets I'm sharing will allow you to achieve the success you desire.

Most self-help books simply say, "*Do it, do it, and more do it,*" and the really good ones also tell you *how* to do it. But I wanted to take it to another level. I wanted to present the science behind the *why*, because trying to do it – even when you know how – won't work unless you know *why* it works.

That's where the science comes in, and it's also why I invite you to read the first-ever "*do-how*-and-*why*" book that will finally allow you to make your dreams come true. You'll understand how most of your obstacles are mired in the entanglement of false beliefs, pessimism, and fear. These can all be eliminated when you know *why* your brain is holding you back and *why* it can change. The *how* is just an instruction manual, but the *why* is true knowledge; true understanding at the fundamental level, such that you become enlightened.

The *how* can be practiced over and over in your conscious brain, but the *why* will rewrite your subconscious. The *why* is truth, and truth is the undefeatable enemy of your false beliefs, unjustified pessimism, and fear. Truth is knowledge, and knowledge is enlightenment. That is why *this time* you will overcome your obstacles and finally break free from the roadblocks that have been holding you back.

If you know the *whys*, then it's far easier to believe you can achieve sustained success. If you believe you can, then...well, you know where I'm going with this, right?

The wisdom and scientific insights you will learn throughout this book will allow you to compress decades of knowledge into days. Contained in this book are nearly 25 years of my personal experience in regards to what works and what doesn't. Much of what I'm teaching has been refined over the decades, placed into a zip file, ready for you to open; one chapter at a time and one secret at a time.

There are several "asides" I've included to give you more detail and insight into the material. They are set aside for a reason: while they give you details behind the science, they may be more detail than you want. As asides, they can also be skipped without losing the importance of the book. However, I found it necessary to give you evidence – scientific proof – to back up the content in this book. I hope you will read them, simply because the science presented in this book is both fascinating and beautiful.

Throughout this book, you will also learn many of the life lessons I was taught from the school of hard knocks. I've made many, many mistakes trying to achieve success and live life on my own terms. I've paid the bonehead tax (faced two life prison sentences, ran several businesses into the ground, and had a failure so big it made the front page of the newspapers), so hopefully, you won't have to. As I will explain later in the content, mistakes are lessons; but the lessons are even sweeter if you can learn from someone else's mistakes.

> **"A smart person learns from their mistakes, but a wise person learns from the mistakes of other people."**
>
> ~UNKNOWN

My goal is for you to extract the maximum amount of learning possible from the exorbitant tuition payments I have made in life, both financially and emotionally. This is because I believe it is a cardinal sin not to share the lessons I've learned from the mistakes I've made.

The American industrialist and philanthropist, Andrew Carnegie, believed:

> *"As inconsistent as it may seem, you will learn more about how to succeed from the failures than you will from the so-called successes. They will teach you what not to do."*

Since there are certainly more ways to fail than succeed, I want you to learn the life lessons I've discovered from all of my missteps. It is important to me that you recognize and avoid the painful experiences I've endured. Additionally, I want to help accelerate your rate of progress and shorten the time it takes you to become the CEO of your life. After reading this book, you will have a roadmap so that hopefully your path to the life you seek will be much smoother than the grueling terrain I've had to plow.

Now, I invite you to plow through this book, and as you do, know that I am proud of you. I'm proud that you're the type of person who wants more out of life. I'm proud of you because you realize the person who is not willing to learn can't be helped, and, more importantly, the person who is willing to learn can't be stopped. I'm proud of you because you'd rather plan than party. I'm proud of you because you'd rather pick up a book than a beer. And that's why you are about to experience a profound change for the better in your life. You are going to learn seven secrets that are guaranteed to skyrocket your success. They work. Every. Single. Time. It's in the science. It's in this book. Which is why I can submit the following promise to you:

> **If you implement the strategies that are laid out in this book in the correct order and take action on the exercises at the end of each chapter, you will find yourself in a world full of prosperity, abundance, and happiness that you only thought was possible in your imagination.**

Let me be clear about something: the secrets I'm going to reveal to you aren't secrets because they are privileged information meant only for a lucky few. They are secrets because oftentimes they stay unknown, and they stay unknown because they're so deceivingly simple that they are unbelievable. Thus, their simplicity is so deceptive that the human mind will attempt to rationalize them away. Famous fictional detective Sherlock Holmes said it best, "There's nothing more deceptive than an obvious clue."

Many secrets I'll be revealing to you are lying right in front of you. All you need to do is acknowledge them, put them together, and use them every single day. Each secret on its own is powerful, but when you combine all seven of them, you will experience a radical transformation in how you act, and how you perceive the world (and how the world perceives *you*).

A lot of people reading this will dismiss the idea that the secrets to success could be this simple; surely, the answers are far more complex and grandiose. They must be hidden in an intricate web of riddles that only the genetically blessed will ever solve. The irony is complexity is an illusion. Just because something is complex and challenging does not necessarily make it effective. More often than not, the simple answer is usually the right one. Why? Because complexity is the enemy of execution.

"*Occam's razor*" is a principle first developed by the Franciscan friar philosopher William of Ockham, which stated that the simplest answer is most often the correct answer. The more accurate nature of this principle, however, is that you must not overcomplicate an explanation unnecessarily. If you're avoiding the simplest approach because it is just too simple to be right, then you are pushing it aside for alternatives that are more complicated. Thus, you are complicating your life, and such difficulties helps no one.

There is a Zen proverb that states, "Before enlightenment, chop wood and carry water. After enlightenment, chop wood and carry water." The secrets to success before you become successful are the same secrets to success *after* you become successful. The secrets to success that I'm going to reveal to you are timeless: they are always true and never-changing, no matter where you are in life. This is because becoming successful is like following a diet: you can't just sacrifice until you lose the weight and then go back to your old unhealthy eating habits.

Similarly, just like a successful diet won't work until you change your eating habits for the rest of your life; to have a successful life you also must make the necessary changes that you sustain and maintain, like the diet...for the rest of your life.

Once you make the commitment and adhere to your new lifestyle, momentum will begin to shift, and your life will get better and better. But this is more than just a ride because you're the one driving; you have chosen to take responsibility and commit to a new process. And the result of this newfound self-discipline is that momentum will remain in your favor and you continue to grow.

So, once you finally "make it," the journey does not end, and the strategies stay the same. In fact, the journey never ends, and the secrets continue to remain the same. That, in essence, is why success is not nearly as difficult as many gurus make it out to be.

Often times, our expectations about success in any area of life tend to be misguided. Because we operate under the false belief that success is burdensome and complicated, we choose not to pursue it. We look at the few people in life who manage to succeed and conclude that success must be out of reach for the average person.

Many people don't achieve success because they expect the path to be more difficult than it actually is before they even embark on it. These people allow their self-sabotaging beliefs to stop them far before the haters, naysayers, and obstacles have a chance to stop them.

We have been sold a story about ourselves that defines who

we are. Family, friends, educational institutions, mainstream media, personal experiences, social norms, and cultural expectations have shaped our worldview and created the self-image that we have today.

We believe that our lives are meant to go in a particular direction, but we also believe that we have real limits that hold us back and impair our potential. We blame our past and the way we were raised for the circumstances we currently find ourselves in. We accept the idea that success is something that is embedded in our genetics instead of molded into our actions.

What you need to understand and embrace is that you are the author of your life. You get to choose the characters that are in your life's story. You get to create the setting of your story. You get to determine what the plot is going to be. And most importantly, you get to decide what the outcome will be.

There are people in the world who have been brought up in far worse conditions than you and have many more mental and physical limitations. And yet, they've managed to achieve extraordinary levels of success that most people only dream of having.

You see, each one of us has something, a dream or a desire, that we want to see come true. But unfortunately, the majority of people never even take the first step to realize their dreams, and sadly, they never come close to living the life of their dreams. They lie on their deathbed in their final days wondering:

- "What if..."
- "Maybe I could have..."
- "If only I..."
- "I should have..."
- "I regret not doing..."

One of the most disheartening things I see in this world are people who so desperately want to make their lives better but never change a single thing. It reminds me of the quote by Eric Hoffer,

"Regret for the things we did can be tempered by time; it is regret for the things we did not do that is inconsolable."

~UNKNOWN

"People will cling to an unsatisfactory way of life rather than change in order to get something better, for fear of getting something worse."

But do you know what I know about you? I know that you're willing to make the trade-offs. You're willing to make the changes necessary to become the CEO of your life. That's why you picked up this book!

You're more than capable of making your dreams come true, right in front of your own two eyes. You deserve the happiness and success you want in life. All you need to do is believe in yourself and take action every day until you manifest your dreams into reality.

Regularly performing the correct activities (in the correct order), transforming your habitual thinking patterns, and implementing the secrets I reveal will finally allow you to permanently break free. That's why you are about to embark on a journey of overwhelmingly intense emotions and game-changing revelations. Every secret that you read will attempt to strip you bare of your old habits and old ways of thinking. Initially, this will be an extremely uncomfortable process.

If you stick with me and follow my guidance, however, you will be able to shed your old skin and emerge from your cocoon as an entirely new and different person. You will become stronger. You will become wiser. You will be better than ever before. You will finally be able to unleash your inner boss and start building that million-dollar future you deserve.

Every chapter in this book has one secret for you. Each chapter ends with a series of exercises for you to apply the secret to your life. If you actually perform the exercises and don't simply ignore them (like many people do when they read these kinds of books), you will start to make small yet noticeable advancements and changes.

Out of nowhere, random pieces of your life puzzle will begin to fall into place. It might not make sense to you immediately, and you might not fully comprehend what's happening until some time passes, but your inner world and your outer world will turn into something entirely different than what you see now. Your inner world and your outer world will be in sync, instead of fighting each other. Once that happens, almost like magic, you'll start attracting the very things in your life that you have always wanted.

How is that possible? It's possible because life has an interesting way of giving us what we seek and focus on. For example, the Bible teaches, "Ask and you shall receive"; and legendary personal growth expert Jim Rohn says, "Asking is the beginning of receiving." When you learn how to ask for success correctly, guess what happens? You'll find more success. It's really there for the asking. The same goes for having better relationships, improving your health, increasing the balance of your bank account, and achieving harmony in all aspects of life. If you learn how to ask for the things you want in life properly, then align your beliefs and actions, your conscious mind and your subconscious mind – over time, the Universe must deliver the things that you truly desire.

I cannot emphasize enough how important it is that you commit to taking action on all of the exercises at the end of each chapter. They are not there to fill the pages in this book (there are already plenty of pages). They are not there as a "summary" of the chapter. The exercises are there to help you begin connecting the dots and show you exactly how to do the right things in the right order. Think of the chapter before the exercises as the introduction to them, and the exercises as the introduction to the rest of your life, because they have a hidden agenda:

> The exercises, in connecting the dots, will insert the lessons into your intuitive (subconscious) activities of daily living. You will not only live these lessons, but you will become these lessons

in action. More importantly, on your journey to success, during the inevitable setbacks you encounter, the exercises will help rewire your brain and give you clarity, which will allow you to set your headlights to "high beam" and push through the dark and difficult times.

You must follow through with these exercises and consistently apply them if you want the secrets to work. You have to take a brutal and honest look at yourself, and promise that you will commit to following through on the insights I reveal throughout this book.

Do the work and you'll give birth to a version of yourself that is better and stronger than you ever thought possible. I can confidently tell you this because the seven secrets I'm about to share with you have the power to radically transform your life, as they did mine.

Now, buckle your seatbelt and hang on tight. Life is about to get very, very interesting.

CHAPTER ONE

Vision – Reverse Engineer Your Best Life

"All successful people, men and women, are big dreamers. They imagine what their future could be, ideal in every respect, and then they work every day toward their distant vision, that goal or purpose."

BRIAN TRACY, Canadian-American motivational public speaker and self-development author

What is *vision*? A vision can be defined as the image that your mind creates using the visual capabilities of your imagination. But this goes way beyond simple visual (eyesight) capabilities, way past the big "E" the eye doctor asks you to identify on the wall chart. The eyes of your imagination have no walls. They are unique in that they can see into the future. Thus, a vision is your "*mindsight*," not just your eyesight.

It sounds simple because it is intuitive, but within that simplicity lies great power. Every single thing that you see in the theater of your mind can manifest itself in your physical world. Everything must start as a vision before it becomes a physical and tangible reality, and perceiving a vision only means that your brain arrives at that place before your body does.

Keep in mind that your brain is your graphical user interface (GUI)

for the universe. Like a web browser, which renders images and sounds based on the code that is streamed to it, your brain receives the entire universe as mere data – vibrations, photons, temperature – and attempts to makes sense of it. Your brain is always interpreting and analyzing the data, and calling it like it "sees" it, whether right or wrong. This is why you see an elephant in a cloud, the man in the moon, or a person's profile in the veins of marble. It's why optical illusions succeed until we reason through them.

The things that simply *occur* to you, cloud elephants and whatnot are simply the ruminations of your brain without a filter. Your brain is almost always working on autopilot, trying to make sense out of things; what you *create* in your mind's eye is your brain working *for* you. Like the clouds themselves, their accidental elephants come and go; but rather than wait for such ruminations to strike, you can proactively create a universe for your brain, the universe you want. A universe to which you can go.

> **If the universe through which you navigate is exactly as your brain interprets it, why shouldn't your self-created vision define the universe in which you want to live? If you can envision it, you can create it and bring it into reality.**

Professional athletes who *envision* (imagine) themselves doing their exercises and routines use the same neurons as when they are actually *doing* them. This is not just identifying exercises and routines as "things" they think about, like a to-do list; they actually *visualize* themselves executing the physical activities, mentally going through the motions. In fact, the benefits of exercising have even been realized in test subjects who merely visualized exercising instead of engaging in any physical activity at all. A study published in the *Journal of Neurophysiology* revealed, "Simply imagining exercise can tone muscle, delay atrophy, and even make your muscles stronger."

This is quite a discovery, and it speaks volumes about our mind/body connection. Research reported in the *Journal of Open Neuroimaging*, in which fMRI imaging was used, expounded on the above study by demonstrating that the same parts of the brain were active whether a person was imagining an action or performing an action:

> *"The results argue for a functional equivalence between execution and imagery."*

According to Katrina Chen, a contributor to Northeastern University's science magazine *Nu Sci*, rehearsing a detailed mental image can allow athletes to improve their physical performance. Repeated visualizations can train the subconscious mind, which can then guide the body during the performance of those actions. There are two theories as to how this occurs:

1. By imagining movements, the subconscious creates neuromuscular patterns similar to those created during the actual physical movements. So when a tennis player visualizes a serve, electrical activity in the brain recreates the same electrical activity as when the tennis player actually serves the ball.
2. Alternatively, the mental imagery creates an instruction set for the upcoming motions, a blueprint that contains the goals, motions, and sequences needed to execute the activity.

Scientists have proven that by rehearsing a mental image of a physical action, we can actually improve the physical execution of the action. Therefore, through the power of mental rehearsal, our brain no longer is a record of the past, but rather becomes a map to the future. Imagine what such visualizations can do to help create the life of your dreams. This scientific breakthrough in visualization is a key insight because it proves we all possess the power to engineer the life we want simply by imagining it.

Rehearsals for designing your dream life will begin immediately!

A neurological aside:

Recent research in neuroscience has revealed that what we imagine and the manifestations of that vision can literally change our brains. Yes, we can alter the connections and the structures in our brains. Meditation has been shown to shrink the amygdala, the brain structure responsible for the interpretations of emotions. Thus, there is the benefit of less emotion used in decision-making. In another study, musicians who play stringed instruments grew the areas of their brains responsible for fine motor movement.

However, here might be one of the most amazing displays of neuroplasticity: Daniel Kish was blind by two years of age. For some reason, he started to make clicking sounds with his mouth and from the echoes he got back, he had a picture of the physical environment around him. Daniel Kish taught himself echolocation. He was so good at this, that he could ride a bike safely and fearlessly without vision. Hey, if bats and dolphins can do it, why can't humans?

When Daniel's brain was studied, something quite remarkable showed up. The visual areas of his brain, that would normally be dormant in a blind person had grown connections with the auditory part of his brain. He had literally created the hardware needed so that his hearing would allow him to see! Daniel Kish is now an expert in human echolocation and the President of *World Access for the Blind.*

BESPOKE VISION

Bespoke: a British term that refers to custom-made or tailor-made clothing. Thus, a bespoke garment or suit has been customized to the uniqueness of the customer.

From the car you drive to the house you live in, as well as the clothes you wear, these were all someone's vision before you drove in, lived in, or wore them. These visionaries visualized the finished product, and their vision even included you eventually purchasing their product. This is a continuum, and it is why you must understand that you can become what you visualize and you can create the things you envision. You, however, are the necessary ingredient; you cannot visualize your vision without you in it. (The car without you driving it is the vision unrealized!) You must visualize yourself as part of your vision. I know that sounds like something from a fantasy novel, so let's dive deeper and see how we learned to develop our visions from the moment we were born.

You arrived on this earth as a blank canvas and were thrust into a world created by other people. Your intellectual neurons (i.e., brain cells) were all disconnected, waiting to be wired together. At the beginning of your life, the visions you saw were profoundly influenced by others. As a child, you were only able to see and understand what your caregivers were capable of showing you. They influenced what you saw and how you perceived the world, e.g., happiness with a smile or discord with the raising of one's voice. And those concepts you grasped became the connections of your brain cells that gave you your world view. But there is a lot of possibility in a blank canvas, and a child's world view is a dynamic process, not necessarily painted on a canvas in permanent ink.

As you grew older, more influences arrived in your life: peers, your neighborhood, your formal education, and the media you consumed. The interactions you had with others, along with your environment, began to paint a vision in your mind of who you *thought* you were: the combination of the world and your place within it (and *with* it). This vision could have been true or false, but nevertheless, as a child, you only saw the world through a lens that others created for you, as well as by the way others viewed you.

You may not realize this, but the environment in which you were raised – and the way others viewed you – directly correlated with how they saw themselves as they raised you. This is because the desire to "belong" and "feel included" is part of human nature, but their including you required molding you in their own image and likeness. As a result, "who" you are is likely just a version of yourself painted through a lens of other people's own expectations, experiences, and definitions. However, this possibly has nothing to do with who you truly are. Other people have literally corralled you along their paths as a captive audience.

The more you aged, the more you began to take control of your visions; however, even as you ventured beyond your caregivers' and peers' definitions, the images that were instilled in your mind from childhood still existed. They served as your template. Even today, the home you live in, along with the person you have become and everything else in your life are all a result of what you've visualized up to this point. You may have allowed pictures to pop into your mind unconsciously, or perhaps you purposefully painted them. But either way, they are alive and sitting in your mind right now, dormant but with the potential to be actualized.

While it sounds dismal to hear that other people painted your visions for you, there is a silver lining to all of this: you are a creative human being who is the architect of your visions, so you can create yourself into anything you want to become. The template manufactured for you in the early years of your life is not a set of constraints but can serve as a springboard that gives you the capacity to develop a new blueprint, one that energizes you and allows you to create the life you truly want.

You should not settle for the vision others painted for you. You have a vote, too, and are entitled to provide the input that can improve and transform your life. You just have to summon the courage to follow your vision.

As a creative and visionary person, you can see things not as they are, but as they can be. You can learn how to see things better than they are and manifest that vision into reality. You can have a bespoke vision, tailor-made just for you. Bespoke visions not only fit better, they also look amazing on you!

You must gain control of your visions to gain control of your life. You are a creator, and therefore you can create the person you want to become, the environment in which you want to spend time, the relationships you want to be a part of, and the life you truly want to live by merely using the power of your mind – by purposefully incorporating mental rehearsal.

Accepting the idea that we can visualize ourselves into anything that we want can be exhilarating, yet intimidating all at the same time. Part of the template you've inherited is to be skeptical and dismiss this notion as, *"That's not the way the world is."* The power of visualization and creating your visions comes from realizing that you – not the way the world is – are responsible for who you currently are and that you did not get this way by pure happenstance.

Over time, through experiences, through surprising windfalls and lessons from the school of hard knocks, **you created you**, so you should no longer blame other people and windblown circumstances for the person that you are right now. It's called ownership, and if you try to bring your visions to fulfillment without it, you're fooling yourself. Subsequently, you are in absolute control of your destiny, missteps and all, but the missteps need to be corrected (ownership), not just skipped over (explained away).

You have the power to visualize yourself as a loser or a winner. You can visualize yourself into wealth, success, and abundance, or you can visualize yourself into lack, misery, and poverty.

When you live paycheck-to-paycheck, you also live "emotionally" paycheck-to-paycheck. Both impact your happiness and fulfillment.

Likely, your mindset about money came from the template you inherited from your upbringing. Bestselling author and personal finance expert Suze Orman believes, "Messages about money are passed down from generation to generation, worn and chipped like the family dishes. Your own memories about money will tell you a lot, if you take that step back and see what those memories taught you about who you were – and whether those memories are still telling you who you are today."

Often times the visions we play in the movie screen in our mind about money are handed down from our family. And the only way to break free from the generational poverty consciousness so many people fall victim to, is by deliberately changing the channel, by digging down deep and embedding new beliefs. When new beliefs, ones that vividly illustrate prosperity begin to play in your mind – things start to shift. You begin to move your life in a new direction. This is the catalyst to change.

You see, the way you imagine your future playing out on your inner screen is a determining factor in how bright (or gloomy) your future will be. You must learn how to focus on visualizing the activities that will yield sustainable results, because what you see in your mind's eye is what you become. It's completely up to you: poverty or prosperity?

With the power of visualization, you can begin changing at this very moment. Mental rehearsals, take two!

BIG VISION EQUALS BIG LIFE

> "Whether you think you can, or you think you can't – you're right."
>
> ~HENRY FORD, American industrialist and the founder of Ford Motor Company

I'm a huge believer in the fact that we are absolutely, 100 percent responsible for our decisions and the life we create. However, not everyone begins the game of life at the same starting point. Some people are born into homes and families that have no concept of success, achievement, or goals. Certainly, without these concepts, an inspiring vision is non-existent. On top of that, many people receive a big dose of dream-crushing negativity at an early age.

For some individuals, all they saw growing up was negativity – cautionary tales, negative reinforcement and dependency at the hands of those who called the shots. Because of that, they chose not to pursue their dreams. If you grew up in a home where nobody chased their dreams, you might have come to believe that this behavior is the norm. You are not alone because sadly, hundreds of millions of adults all around the world think that this kind of behavior is perfectly normal.

> When people spend their childhood around others who have no hope, zero motivation, and low self-esteem, they have to

fight viciously against those negative influences all their lives. Oftentimes, when you see the wrong thing consistently, you come to accept the wrong thing, and unfortunately, you produce the wrong thing. Consistently.

It's not impossible for a child who comes from a negative environment to have a completely different life, but it typically takes a defining moment such as a caring adult or a life-altering event that repaints the visions which have been created in a young person's mind.

Maybe you were told during your childhood to stop imagining and dreaming, but it's time to start again. We all have a picture in our mind about who we are and who we want to be. We all see ourselves in a certain way. That's why it's crucial for you to understand: if your vision is limited, your life will be limited.

Limiting your life (by having a limited vision) goes against the grain of what we are as human beings. In 1942, psychologist Abraham Maslow published his paper on the hierarchy of needs. His *Theory of Human Motivation* was envisioned as a pyramid of stages of growth. The bottom tier of the pyramid of his hierarchy of needs is physiological needs: water, air, etc. The next tier is one of safety – being safe via a roof over one's head, law and order, and living life without fear of harm. Next up is a tier for love, brotherhood, belonging, and camaraderie. After that is esteem (***self***-esteem).

As we move up Maslow's pyramid of the hierarchy of needs, the needs become more focused (represented by serially narrowing tiers as you climb to the pinnacle of the pyramid) and loftier, as you approach the pinnacle. So what happens when we reach the very top: self-actualization.

This pyramid's pinnacle represents fulfillment, and the infrastructure below supports the pinnacle. But the climb up the pyramid is the march of civilization, from the basic animal to the sophistication that comes from the full realization of our potential

– our true selves as it was meant to be. And the full realization of our potential, to achieve our visions, and to become the best possible version of what we can be, is what this book is all about.

Some people are stuck well below the pinnacle of the pyramid. They have never risen above a particular level. Because of this, they never question why they choose to live in their present location, work at their current job, or eat the foods that they do every day because it's all they've ever known. The types of people who wander aimlessly through life stuck on a lower level aren't putting much thought into their everyday decisions. They simply go through life by merely going through the motions. Therefore, they fail to realize: who you are exposed to, both inside and outside of your home, both inside and outside of your genes, along with the information you choose to consume affects how you create your visions and the quality of them.

Those stuck at the bottom of the pyramid – physiological needs – are cavemen. The very talent that humans have for improving society, that is, a rational codification of laws and innovative progress, makes for something we call "civilization" which raises us above animals that live only on instinct. Thus, civilization has meant achieving higher tiers on Maslow's pyramid, above the animal needs of merely satisfying physiological necessities, upward toward self-esteem and self-actualization.

Above the lowermost physiological needs is the next tier: safety. And those who choose to remain there are the ones who follow the rules and rarely take any chances to pursue their vision. These would be the people who do nothing to get out of a dead-end job because their status quo is a "known", which is safer than venturing into the "unknown" that comes from taking chances – the chances that allow people to climb higher.

The next tier is the "belonging-and-love" tier. Those who stop there are satisfied with life by just those things: belonging and love.

> For the record, staying at the belonging-and-love layer is not a failure, but it is also noteworthy that climbing even higher to follow your vision won't negatively impact a strong foundation of belonging and love. The upper tiers, however, may not be stable unless firmly supported by the underlying foundation. A pyramid can become a house of cards with any of its foundation layers missing. Skip or remove a layer at your own peril, like a game of Jenga.

Keep in mind that Maslow's strategy of thinking of your road to self-actualization follows the pyramid structure I've just described, with the lower foundations supporting the higher achievements above.

One of the most significant impediments to climbing your own pyramid is the expectations of others. Your pyramid, seen through the prism of other people's expectations, may be quite different from how you see it. While your vision may make perfect sense to you, it may not make sense to others; but this is based on how they see themselves. This is where resilience becomes crucial, which I discuss in detail in Chapter Three.

For example, I remember reading Arnold Schwarzenegger's biography and Arnold's defiance against his father, Gustav, stood out to me. When Gustav noticed that Arnold was getting bigger and spending countless hours in the gym, he wanted to know why Arnold was so obsessed with lifting weights. Arnold proudly told his father that he wanted to become the world's greatest bodybuilding champion in Europe, and then use that success to become a prominent movie star in Hollywood.

Arnold's father, who was a very disciplined police chief at the time, thought his son had gone completely insane when he verbalized his vision of dominating the bodybuilding world. Arnold's mother nearly fainted when she heard what her son wanted to do with his life. Fearing the worst, Arnold's parents decided to take him to a psychiatrist to help break him from his vision. Clearly, Arnold's pyramid was significantly different from the one his parents had envisioned for him. But nothing could stop Arnold, not even the psychiatrist. As a result, Arnold's father forbid him from visiting the gym more than three times a week. But this didn't faze Arnold one bit. He would improvise weightlifting workouts using random items in his home so he could continue working out six days a week.

Arnold's vision was so strong and unbreakable that his father eventually relented and gave in to his demands. There was clearly no stopping Arnold Schwarzenegger from achieving the vision that was ingrained into his mind, so he was eventually allowed to go to the gym as many times as he liked.

It was Arnold's vision that allowed him to tap into the natural potential that was lying dormant inside of him (the same potential that's inside of you). The relentless dedication he had toward his vision, even against his own family's wishes, was only possible because of the images he saw in the movie screen in his mind. Nothing in the world was more important to Arnold than becoming the greatest bodybuilder of all-time.

True to his vision, Arnold attained self-actualization, his own pinnacle on his own pyramid. But it was his pyramid, not the one constructed in the minds of his parents. Like Arnold, those who attain self-actualization have a clear vision of self-esteem, belonging/love, safety, and even physiological needs, long before arriving at the top of Maslow's pyramid.

STRONG VISIONS SAVE LIVES

> "When you have a vision that is strong enough and powerful enough, nothing can stand in your way."
>
> ~LEWIS HOWES, Author and entrepreneur

The moment your vision becomes the primary focus of your life, you unlock the extraordinary potential that you didn't even realize existed inside of you. All of a sudden, you start seeing connections between things that previously didn't exist in your mind. Your confidence in your ability to persevere through difficult situations will soar. But most importantly, you start manifesting your dreams and your vision into existence.

People do the most incredible things when their vision overrides their fears. They solve seemingly hopeless problems when they are "shown" a path to the solution. And one of the most beautiful things about our envisioning "muscle" is that it's incredibly powerful, especially when we are young.

To demonstrate this life-changing power that our limitless abilities possess, even in our early years, let me share an incredible story I recently heard about two young boys.

> While two boys were ice skating, one fell through the ice and was trapped under it. The young boy remaining on the ice started punching at the ice to break it and rescue his friend, but he could not get through. Help was on the way, but the rescuers were moving very slowly on the ice, tentatively, fearing the same fate.
>
> Before waiting for anyone else to reach the spot where the young boy fell through, the other boy climbed a tree and in desperation, tore off a large branch with nothing but his strength and sheer determination then came back down the tree. Before help arrived from the shore, the young boy had already smashed the ice with the branch, breaking it and miraculously saving his friend.
>
> Everyone along the shoreline who saw what had happened was in complete shock and awe. Even the emergency paramedics who by this time had arrived at the scene couldn't believe what had just taken place. How on earth did this child summon the strength to rip off a tree branch, smash it through thick ice, and

save his friend from imminent death?

While this serves as an exciting story in its own right, there's an important takeaway I want to illuminate. The young boy was able to rip off a tree branch and break the thick ice because:

1. First, it had to be done;
2. Second, no one told him he couldn't.

Regardless of age, gender, or educational background, a person with a strong vision believes not only that what they envision *can* be done, but also that it *must* be done. The young boy saving his friend had a powerful vision driving his actions: my friend *can* be saved and he *must* be saved – no ifs, ands, or buts about it.

VISION IS LIFE

> "Create the highest, grandest vision possible for your life, because you become what you believe."
>
> ~OPRAH WINFREY, American media executive, actress, talk show host, television producer and philanthropist

Viktor Frankl, author of *Man's Search for Meaning*, was asked how he survived the concentration camps during World War II. When giving lectures years later, Frankl would say the following:

> *"There is only one reason why I'm here today: what kept me alive was you. Others gave up hope. I dreamed that someday I would be here telling you how I, Viktor Frankl, had survived the Nazi concentration camps. I've never before been here, I've never seen any of you before, I've never given this speech before. But in my dreams, I have stood before you and said these words a thousand times."*

Viktor Frankl's vision allowed him to survive Nazi concentration camps. If that doesn't show the real power of vision, I don't know what does.

Let me ask you: What kind of vision do you need to create to get you through the current challenges you're facing?

No matter how bad things may be, understand that a strong vision allows you to see even in the darkest places of your life. In some cases, it can even mean the difference between life and death.

For obvious reasons, I love this short poem that sums up the power of our vision and how it impacts how we see the world around us:

> *"Two men stare from prison bars; one sees mud, the other sees stars."*

You may not be looking through prison bars, but what do you see when you look at your outside world? If you want to take complete control of your life (and the direction it's going), it is critical to examine the visions you have in your mind and ask yourself why you have them.

The pictures that play in the movie inside your mind are a result of everything from your past. But these pictures can be changed. However, until you actively start to create new pictures of what you want, you will always be living out the old (uninspiring) visions that were created by your past or by other people you've had in your life. New scenes for the movie that plays inside your mind can end up on the cutting room floor; you just need the right scissors, and proactively changing your vision is the first editing step that determines what makes it to the final reel.

For many of us, we've been handed a script for reciting, no questions asked. But this is unacceptable. Simply reciting is nothing more than going through the motions. That script reads only according to the things other people have seen throughout their lives, a plotline according to the way they believe life should go. Following such an unedited script, tragically, leads to following what has been accepted by many as the natural course of life:

1. birth,
2. schooling,
3. job,
4. marriage,
5. kids,
6. retirement,
7. death.

The reason many people believe this is the correct way to live is that this all-too-common vision has been created for you "to recite" by family, friends, media, religion, and society as a whole. These people and institutions have put you on a two-dimensional number line, limiting you in your ability to rise above it into other dimensions, or even to see what's above your line which progresses along steps 1 through 7. A two-dimensional number line has no forks in the road – left or right – above or below. A vision like that is myopic in only one direction along the journey toward step 7, and it's beset with pit stops which typically leads to an unfulfilled life.

A neurological aside:

Those who have vision disturbances in early childhood (such as trauma, the need for repeated eye surgeries, retinal detachment, etc.) have impairments that go beyond the eye as a visual organ. There is another visual organ which is called the "associative visual cortex" in the brain. Whereas the eyes collect light waves and photons and then transmit this data, it is the associative visual cortex where the data lands in the brain and actual "seeing" takes place.

This specialized brain area associates the data with what is known to it about the universe. It assigns recognition to what we see. It gives us our thoughts on what we see. It turns the "noise" of unfiltered data into the visual universe to which we can relate.

> If this area isn't used, as in children who tragically have visual disturbances early in their lives, their eyes can be perfect but they won't see a thing due to the atrophy of function, i.e. the "use it or lose it" principle. This is referred to as "central blindness" or being "brain-blind."

Many people will never question their limited vision because they perceive it as the norm. They are "brain blind" to their full vision potential. They get stuck in a particular tier of Maslow's pyramid. The reality is that you can actively choose to change your vision so that it matches the lifestyle of your dreams. You have the right to veer off the predestined number line. You can climb the pyramid. And most importantly, you can retrain your central vision.

You can design your life just as you want by painting the correct pictures in your mind. Your life cannot create itself. It must be created by someone, and it is up to you to decide whether you're going to create your life or let the world do it for you. That blank canvas you began with is waiting for the artist in you. Will it end up hanging in the Louvre or at the bottom of a birdcage?

After you make the deliberate and conscious decision to create your vision, then after you have played that vision over and over again in your mind like you did with the very first song you fell in love with, neurons begin to wire together, and your actions and daily routines begin to draw your vision to you. Now you've let the genie out of the bottle. Once that happens, everything else begins to fall into place: how you live your life, what friends you choose to hang around, what you eat, what you do for fun. Vision is purpose, and when your purpose is clear, so are your priorities and your life choices.

Clarity of vision creates clarity of priorities. When your priorities are clear, it's only a matter of time before your vision becomes a reality.

VISION IS A COMPASS

> "Vision is the art of seeing what is invisible to others."
>
> ~JONATHAN SWIFT, Essayist, political pamphleteer, poet and cleric who became Dean of St Patrick's Cathedral, Dublin

A vision that gets superior results includes a clearly-articulated mental picture of the future you intend to create. In essence, it's a dream with direction. Once you paint the picture of who you want to become, you should be able to see that picture each time you make a decision. Forget about your present surroundings, because they are the result of your old thinking (i.e. your obsolete vision). As you start visualizing what you want, you will begin making decisions that align with the new vision of yourself you see in your mind's eye.

Let's say you are someone who gives in to temptation easily. And one day a friend suggests the idea of putting off your plans to work on your goals by spending your weekend at a music fest. In this case, you need to think about the vision of your future self and what such a person would do in this situation. Would the new "you" spend two days partying, or would the new "you" have better things to do? If you want to be the *future you*, you've got to start thinking like the future "you" to *become* the future "you." You can't wait until you're in the future to think like the "future you."

Once you've created your vision, when you replay your vision routinely in your mind, you begin to walk down the road toward manifesting it as your reality. It's a new number line for you. However, each thing that takes you away from that ultimate vision is the equivalent of making a pit stop on a road trip. The more pit stops you make and the more time you spend on them, the longer it's going to take to get to your destination. And if you take too many pit stops along the way, or if a particular pit stop snares you with pretty poison, you may decide to give up on your vision altogether.

You always have the choice to decide which number line you'll travel: the predestined one the world has made for you, or the one that allows you to climb to the top of Maslow's pyramid. Your path – imagined, envisioned, and engaged – is the new number line, and it's imperative you do not get derailed or succumb to obstructions along the way.

Your vision is your guide, your crow's nest even in life's strongest storms. You need to always keep your vision in front of you, especially when times get tough and self-doubt begins to seep in. Write your vision down, review it often, keep developing it, and your vision will allow you to move mountains.

When Alexander the Great had a vision, he conquered the world. But when he lost his vision, he couldn't conquer a liquor bottle. When David had a vision, he conquered Goliath. But when he lost his vision, he couldn't conquer his own lust. History contains many examples of people who achieved extraordinary feats with a single vision, yet lost it all when that vision faded into nothingness.

When your vision becomes an authoritative guide in your life, you won't be making any more pit stops, and you won't make the grave mistakes many well-known successful people have made in the past. As long as your vision is clear in your mind and you are replaying it day-in and day-out, you will make the right decisions that will help you become – and remain – the CEO of your life.

It's time for you to start visualizing the things that your eyes cannot currently see so that you can finally become the person you've always wanted to be. Embrace and pursue your vision with your mind's eye wide open.

OWN YOUR VISION

> "The vision, this dream, this goal is invisible to everyone except the person holding it. It is responsible for every great advance and achievement in our lives. It is the underlying motive for just about everything we see about us. It is a beautiful building where before there was an empty lot. It is the bridge spanning the bay. It is the landing on the moon. For if you want it badly enough, you will go get it."
>
> ~NAPOLEON HILL, Author of *Think and Grow Rich*, one of the top 10 bestselling self-help books of all-time

Sometimes the most significant obstacles we face in realizing our dreams are our family and friends. Motivational speaker Les Brown says, "Someone's opinion of you doesn't have to become your reality." The same thing can be said about other people's opinions of your vision.

You must remember that other people don't have the capabilities you have or the knowledge you have, nor can they see the picture in your mind. Everyone is on a unique wavelength. Your vision is *your* vision. You own it, and it's your empowering and driving force. Anyone that dissuades you from your vision isn't telling you that you can't do it. They are actually telling you not to do it because they would never be able to do it themselves.

While you should respect the limitations other people impose upon themselves, never let people impose their limitations upon you.

You have to accept the fact that other people won't be able to see your vision even when you physically present it to them on a silver platter. Therefore, forgive them in advance and keep moving forward toward your vision. It's okay if nobody else sees your vision as long as you can see it.

STUBBORNLY HOLD ON TO YOUR VISION

"If you can dream it, you can do it."

~WALT DISNEY, American entrepreneur, animator, voice actor and film producer

Did you know Walt Disney was fired from a newspaper job for not having enough creativity? That seems like an absurd story, even laughable when you first hear it, but it's true. Disney's inspirational journey of moving from being a business failure to a beloved cartoon creator is a shining example of how you should never stop believing in yourself just because no one else does.

In fact, when Disney World opened for the first time, Walt had passed away several months earlier. Mrs. Disney, his wife, was asked to speak at the grand opening in Walt's place. The gentleman who introduced Mrs. Disney said, "I just wish Walt could have seen this." Mrs. Disney stood up, walked to the podium, and confidently said, "He did."

History shows us that the only people in this world who left legacies behind are those who had a unique vision they stubbornly held onto in the face of many difficulties. The Wright brothers are another excellent example of people hanging on to their vision, even when times got tough. Orville and Wilber Wright had a vision of a flying vehicle being used to transport people all over the world, a radical concept at the time that involved vehicles heavier than air.

Initially, everyone laughed at the Wright brothers, but they persisted in bringing their vision to reality, and with the laws of physics on their side, they created the world's first airplane. Because of their persistence in realizing their grand vision, they left a legacy that has stood the test of time. Even today, the North Carolina license plate has an image of their airplane and proudly reads: First in Flight.

The Wright brothers had very little resources when they started. They did not have a college education, connections with influential people, or any funding for their project. The only thing they had was a laser-focused vision based on the simple concept of *lift*, a vision that gave them a meaningful purpose greater than themselves. It didn't matter if no one else was around to see them or help fund their audacious vision. What mattered is that what they saw on paper and in their mind's eye – that *lift overcoming gravity* – outshined what people saw in the conventional wisdom limited by the weight of air.

> **"Vision doesn't follow resources – it happens the other way around."**
>
> ~UNKNOWN

On its own, the vision of changing the course of the world with a flying machine made of bicycle parts was enough for the Wright brothers to put blood, sweat, and tears into their work. They would go out into the fields every day with multiple spare parts, relentlessly fail to build a working flying machine, and then go home to rethink their plans and try a different approach the next day.

Compare this to Samuel Pierpont Langley, a gentleman who worked on creating a flying machine at the same time as the Wright brothers. Langley was well-connected and armed with the brightest minds at Harvard, a War Department $50,000 grant, and everyone in the media rooting for him to succeed. Langley, however, failed.

Langley didn't have a vision as the Wright brothers did. All he had was the pursuit of fame and riches that the end result would give him. What he had was a job, not a meaningful vision to guide and drive his efforts, so it's no surprise that he came up short.

What can we learn from the Wright brothers about the importance of having a vision?

We can learn that a strong vision is more powerful than money. A strong vision is more powerful than education. And a strong vision can overcome virtually any obstacles life throws in your way.

You and you alone are blessed with what you can see in your mind's eye. You can take a vision from nothing to something. This is why visionaries leave legacies: they envision something that did not exist and then they make it happen! Ready or not, the world must make room.

Visionaries bring the vision they stubbornly held onto into everyone's reality, and it stays in reality long after they're gone. When they face turmoil, it's their burning desire and passion for their vision that keeps them going. It's never about the money. It's always about the difference they make. Unlike Langley's "job," the Wright brothers' vision was a quest, what the French call a *raison d'être* (reason to be).

I believe many people would soar to new heights and see their dreams come true, just like the Wright brothers did if they would just start seeing themselves differently and create a new vision for who they want to become. But unfortunately, many people don't, and therefore, act as their own judges and juries. They choose to sentence themselves to a life of suffering and/or mediocrity from the unimaginative pictures they have created in their minds. They deny their *raison d'être* and replace it with *Que sera, sera* ("whatever will be, will be"*)*. And although *Que Sera, Sera* became a hit song for Doris Day in 1956, accepting what the world gives you is surrender – giving up.

Sorry, Doris, but when you sang,

> *"Que será, será*
> *Whatever will be, will be*
> *The future's not ours to see*
> *Que será, será*
> *What will be, will be,"*

This is the opposite of what I'm teaching. This book urges you to make the future something for you to see now, that is, visualize your future and bring the vision to your present.

Resigning yourself to "*what will be, will be*" is a poverty consciousness, but it isn't just in those who don't even try; it is also in those who give up. If you find yourself continually replaying past failures over and over in your mind, snap out of it. Change the channel. Intentionally start visualizing all the extraordinary things you can do with your life. It may seem impossible now, but I promise that you'll look back one day and be awestruck at how far you have come. Envisioning possibilities and solutions (not problems) is a prosperity consciousness you must develop if you want to leave your mark on this world, just like the Wright brothers did!

VISION IS POWER

> "If you are working on something exciting that you really care about, you don't have to be pushed. The vision pulls you."
>
> ~STEVE JOBS, Co-founder of Apple, industrial designer, investor, and media proprietor

When you begin envisioning the future "you" (that extraordinary person you will become), it is crucial to attach strong emotions and feelings to your vision. As you do this, you will need to have your heart set on building your perfect life in your mind with real intensity and focus. This will allow you to clearly see yourself succeeding even if others can't see such promise. You will see it so clearly that you will wake up to your vision with a smile on your face, invigorated with the extra motivation and energy that will push you to achieve your vision.

For that reason, I always tell people to create a vision that makes them want to jump out of bed in the morning. Your vision will ignite a fire of passion, which fuels your commitment to do whatever it takes to achieve it. A truly captivating vision wakes you up long before any alarm clock ever will, with a wake-up call out of the deepest sleep, and pushing you out of your bed.

As your mind begins to see your vision as *fait accompli*, so will your heart. You start to feel that what you are envisioning in your mind is real, and that it's within your grasp, waiting for you to take ownership. Your vision will allow you to transfer dreams of greatness into the reality of achievement through your daily actions.

As you begin to work on your vision, it will slowly accumulate power. Once your vision is powerful enough, you will start to see everything else begin to fall into place. You will start to attract people into your life who will assist you in bringing your vision to reality. You will begin to behave in a manner that helps you achieve your vision. Everything that you do will be in complete alignment with the vision of the person that you see yourself becoming – the *future you* – and the things you see yourself having.

As you're reading these words, it's crucial for you to truly believe in your vision regardless of how far-fetched you may think it is. Even today, it is hard to believe that humans can blast out of the Earth's gravitational pull and spend time in outer space. Not all that long ago the idea of going into space would have been met with the same reluctance of acceptance as one would give to a child who says they are going to be a mermaid when they grow up.

Something important I want you to embrace:

The vision you create for your life has no boundaries and knows no limits. That's why your vision gives you the power to become anything you want to be in life.

VISION IS SEEING YOUR TRUE SELF

> "The Universe must deliver the picture you have in your mind about who you are, and what you deserve to have – no matter how impossible the situation might seem."
>
> ~RHONDA BYRNE, Author of *The Secret* and Australian television writer and producer

Have you ever known someone who's acquired a massive fortune, lost it all and got it back within a relatively short amount of time? I remember reading an article in *Inc. Magazine* titled, *11 Inspiring People Who Lost It All And Came Back Stronger*. This article profiled examples of extremely successful people who lost their money and then acquired it back very quickly.

There was one common pattern, one common element I saw among people who went bankrupt, losing all their money, yet made a rapid comeback: they just couldn't picture themselves as being poor. They had a reference point in their mind about being rich. And nothing was going to stop them from getting rich again. The past hadn't defined their vision; instead, their vision had defined their future. This is congruent with Rhonda Byrne's quote about the universe. And this is precisely why it's vitally important you understand that the way you truly see yourself is the person you will become...or, sadly, remain.

> **"Everyone in showbiz is driven by ego, so how do you go from having loads of fame to working at 7-11? You can't do it!"**
>
> ~RYAN SEACREST

When people see themselves as poor, they remain poor. That's why it's said, "If you took all the money in the world and divided it equally among everybody, it would soon be back in the same pockets as it was before."

A great example of people lacking the vision of seeing themselves as wealthy is lottery winners. A large portion of people who win the lottery or come into any large sum of money eventually end up right where they started – or worse. Why? They lack the vision of wealth. Even when all this money has literally dropped on them from out of nowhere, they lose it. They cannot see themselves being rich, nor do they have the actions and mindset to support it.

WHY IT'S IMPORTANT TO CREATE YOUR OWN VISION

> "Have a vision and create your own reality. Otherwise, someone else may create it for you."
>
> ~TONY DICICCO, U.S. soccer player and coach, won two Olympic gold medals

Most people's visions are a combination of their current circumstances, the information/media they choose to focus on, and how the people closest to them see themselves. Sometimes this works to your advantage. Other times, it works toward your disadvantage.

What I have discovered is when people lack vision and clarity, and when they surround themselves with others who lack vision and clarity, their lives turn into a vicious cycle of replaying all the reasons why things won't work out. This mindset keeps them trapped because even when spoon-fed how to solve their problems, they have an additional problem for every solution.

They continually *focus* on the wrong thing and, in turn, continually *get* the wrong thing. They cannot see themselves any different and settle for a life filled with only mediocrity and poverty as a result. What little self-esteem they have defends their lot in life by explaining how it's everyone else's fault; there is always an undercurrent of not taking responsibility. Vision, on the other hand, is fully owned!

Every single human being on this planet has limitless potential to achieve extraordinary feats and create the life they want. Not the life they are living currently, but their real, authentic ideal life.

However, the reason why I believe so many people are not living up to their full potential and not enjoying the life they envision is because they have allowed other people to create their vision for them. They are living somebody else's vision. You may wonder how that's even possible. It happens when you go through life without paying attention. You follow the path of least resistance, sucked into the vacuum left by someone else's vision of you. Without even realizing it, it happens to you.

You find yourself living where you don't want to live. You're eating what you don't want to eat. You're driving a car you don't want to drive. But are you doing anything about it? Are you angry? Are you fighting to make a change? No, many people are not. They've been lulled into thinking this is okay. Vacuums, by nature, are unstable, and there is no shortage of vacuums on your path. They're easier to fill with others' expectations, so it all seems okay. You can't get into trouble, or so you think.

But other people's expectations blind your mind's eye, so it's not okay! You may not get into trouble with the people who push their expectations on you, but you will with your future self! It's time to snap out of it because it is a real disservice to yourself (and the world) to not develop the best possible version of you. You cannot accept – as your own vision – the vision of those with whom you choose to surround yourself. If you do, you will continue to live your life without exploring all of your own, unique, full, and limitless potential.

To demonstrate why it's important to create your own vision instead of allowing others to create it for you, I'd like to share a powerful story about a dog named Bella.

One day while walking across the street from her house, Bella, who was pregnant with puppies, was hit by a car. The accident crushed both of Bella's rear legs. Despite experiencing severe pain and injuries, Bella was able to drag herself back home.

It took several weeks for Bella to recover and begin walking again. But due to the accident, Bella's rear legs never properly healed. As a result, when Bella walked, she drug her back legs on the ground behind her.

The time came for Bella to give birth to her puppies. All the puppies were healthy without any complications or deformities, and fortunately, there were no consequences from the car accident.

A few weeks later, Bella's owner started noticing something very strange: all of the puppies walked the same way as their mother. That's right – when the puppies learned to walk, they also started dragging their rear legs behind them.

The owner was shocked to see this and immediately took the puppies to a veterinarian. Every test under the sun was run several times to ensure that nothing had been missed. It turned out that there was absolutely nothing wrong with the puppies' rear legs. They were just walking in the same way their mother walked simply because that's what they were used to seeing. In their mind's eye, that's just the way it was. They copied what their mother did, assuming that was the way dogs were supposed to walk.

Unfortunately, this same thing happens to a lot of adults. Growing up, the only thing they saw were people "dragging their rear legs" so to speak. Now, as they age and begin living their lives, they're repeating this *learned* behavior. This is why people accept inferior results from themselves and expect that things will never change: it's all they have ever known. In their mind's eye, that's just the way it is.

If your dad had a dead-end job his entire life and your mother had little to no vision for her life, there is a good chance you'll fall right in line with this kind of mindset and lifestyle. That's the bad news.

The good news is, just like those puppies, there is nothing wrong with your hind legs. In other words, you can be so much more than you are right now and you already have the potential that is waiting for you to unleash it – you just need to foster the courage to dig down deep and bring it to life.

A psychology aside:

Psychologist Martin Seligman's classic work on "learned helplessness" showed how a negative mindset can lead not only to helplessness but brain changes that only increase fear and negativity. In Seligman's original studies, dogs who had been helpless to avoid electric shocks in a previous trial failed to recognize an easy escape route that simply required jumping over a barrier to avoid shocks in a subsequent trial.

On the other hand, the dogs who did have some control over the shocks in the first trial quickly spotted the escape route in the second trial and used it to avoid further shocks. Even when the "helpless" dogs were shown the escape route in the second trial, it took several attempts in which they were physically helped over the barrier, for them to realize that they could actually use this route to escape further shocks.

Regrettably, a lot of people get stuck in helpless behaviors driven by the labels they created for themselves in their childhood, then continue to cling to these same false labels in their adulthood. They wander through life without ever taking a moment to think about who they want to be. You can, in fact, create yourself and – even more importantly – ***recreate yourself***. You can choose the type of person you truly want to be. You can choose the aura that you want to radiate to the world. All you need to do is stop dragging your hind legs and start visualizing the right thing.

You can be virtually anything you want to be if you'll just visualize it as if it is already in existence. If you do, it is; if you don't, it will never be.

A cosmic aside:

We are creatures trapped in time. But time is a dimension – like length, width, and depth. As 3-dimensional beings (not 4-dimensional), we cannot perceive time in its entirety, like we can a measure of ribbon. We can only experience ourselves in cross-sections of time, moment by moment. However, that ribbon exists throughout time.

Therefore, what you truly are is made up of the *you* over time. Outside of time, what you are...*is*, has always been, and will always be. Our past certainly has an impact on our present, but outside of time, our future impacts us just as much in the present. We just don't have the sense-perception to appreciate it. Nevertheless, this is why it is important to visualize what you want to be as if it is already in existence: It is, or it isn't: if you don't visualize what you want to get out of life, it never will be.

Paint a bright picture of your true self in your mind's eye and begin to craft a reality of your new life right where you are. You can start with something as simple as sitting up straight, chin tucked, and your crown pointed to the sky. You are the ruler of your new vision because you are the creator of your (new) life.

While you cannot change your life overnight, you can change it over time. And right this very moment, you can completely *shift* the direction of your life by embracing and implementing what you are reading in this chapter. Take action now, and change the vision of who you truly are and start living according to that new vision.

Mental rehearsals, take three!

HOW CAN YOU USE VISION?

> "Always remember there are only two kinds of people in this world: the realists and the dreamers. The realists know where they're going. The dreamers have already been there."
>
> ~ROBERT ORBEN, Magician and American writer

Have you ever thought about what you are replaying over and over in your mind? Have you ever consciously thought about what you're allowing yourself to think about? Many people spend a lot of time thinking about what has happened in the past. Yet, if we are blessed with the power of visualization to create our future, then thinking about the past is no different than running on a treadmill. All you're doing is wearing yourself out and going nowhere.

The past provides us with lessons that can help in making future decisions, and there is nothing wrong with referencing your past. The problem comes in when you regurgitate past negative events in your mind and the feelings that come with them. This only keeps you in the exact same spot when you need to be moving forward.

> **"When you're always looking back you can't see what's coming."**
>
> ~UNKNOWN

You can't create your future while reliving your past at the same time. Focusing on the past will keep you in the past. If you want to change your current circumstances, you must change your current thinking. You need to move on. Your life can only be what you visualize it to be. Some people live the same day over and over in their minds and in their lives. This is a horrible place to be because it is a cycle of never-ending self-destruction.

It is not easy, but you can break free from thinking about the past and start thinking about the present, which, of course, is your gateway to the future. Each time your mind wanders into the past, catch yourself, stop doing it, bring your mind to the present, then take your mind to the imagination stage in which you visualize your bright future.

In the imagination stage, start thinking about the things you want in your life. It can be a better relationship with your family, a luxurious mansion, a thinner waistline, a multimillion-dollar business, becoming a bestselling author – whatever you want. Remember, this is your vision. Just make sure the things you are visualizing are new and that they energize you and make you feel happy when you visualize them.

Don't let these visualizations be interrupted by the profitless thoughts of anger or jealousy over what you don't have or why you don't already have it. And remember: you're not in it to keep up with the Joneses (or the Kardashians). They're not your reference point. Developing the best version of yourself is your reference point. Your imagined future is your reference point. Stay centered in the present (as the gateway to your future) and imagine yourself into the future you want with the power of visualization.

We always get what we focus on in life. Therefore, if you want to move forward, you cannot allow your mind to continue hanging out in the past. Start creating your visions right now, and discard the old movies that have been replaying in your mind so you can create a new, bestselling blockbuster.

IMAGINE SUCCESS INTO YOUR LIFE

> "Imagination is everything. It is the preview of life's coming attractions."
>
> ~ALBERT EINSTEIN, Theoretical physicist who developed the theory of relativity

Now that you know how visualization can help you gain control of your life, you must purposefully engineer your visions into reality. Engineering your life as you see fit requires a precise form of imagination known as *imagineering*. Imagineering is the process of using mental images to build factual results. Rather than allow random pictures to pop into your head, imagineering forces you to create the pictures that you want to bring to life.

You cannot create something in your life that you have not first created in your mind. Many people devote zero time to imagineering, yet expect their circumstances to change. It won't happen. The first step toward achieving your vision and your dreams is to visualize them. Making them before you imagine them is putting the cart before the horse and just can't be done. It reminds me of a tagline from Sony, the Japanese electronics company, which said, *"Make. Believe."* Sony had it backwards though. Because until you believe... you will never *make*.

You must build your perfect life in your mind before you can begin to lay its foundation in the physical world. Somebody first imagined everything that we see here on this planet, and then it was created. It cannot happen the other way around.

As children, our imagination muscles are remarkably strong. We imagine fantasies of flying cars, castles, dragons, and more. Children have sipped imaginary tea from toy cups, fought imaginary monsters, and built forts to protect themselves from imaginary enemies. Sadly, as we grow up, the outside world starts to affect what we imagine, and the quality of the images in our imagination decreases over time.

What's the difference between the imaginations of children and those of adults? Could it be fun? Fun releases dopamine, the "reward" neurotransmitter. Could it be that many adults have lost their sense of fun? Of wonder?

Wonder and the fun that comes with it is part of learning, so it is a tragedy when people stop imagining altogether. No fun, no wonder, and no learning. Think about visualizing what your life can be; that's really fun. However, without visualizing what your life can be, you cannot move it in the direction you want it to go.

When you stop imagining, you'll find that your brain continues to create pictures in your subconscious on complete autopilot. However, these pictures are based on images you've imagined in the past or perhaps images that come from your current environment. These images may not be any fun at all, so if you want to grow with a renewed sense of wonder, you need to get to work creating the new vision from your future that will eventually become your new reality.

Whether you choose to practice visualization or not, your life will continue to move in a particular direction. However, without focused visualization (imagineering), you are nothing more than a backstage actor in somebody else's play.

Take some time now and allow yourself to dream. Dream about who you wanted to become when you were a child. Dream about the things you told yourself you would do when you grew up. Dream about the life you just knew you would live when you were a child. It was fun, remember? Go ahead. I'll wait.

I really want you to do this now. Why? Because this is an important step to begin strengthening your imagination muscle and enticing your neurons to fire differently which will help create a new neural pathway – one that connects your current life with your dream life.

Honestly, when was the last time you allowed yourself to dream (like hopefully you just did)? For many of us, it's been too long. Every day you should take time to imagine all the things you want to do with the one and only shot you get on this earth. Don't allow logic or reason to stifle your thoughts. Don't allow your "inner adult" to hold you back. Your imagination is your personal creative place where you can build, destroy, rebuild, adjust, edit, and delete things as you see fit. Let your inner child come up with the goods, and let your inner adult sort them out. In other words: **Imagine like a child, then plan and execute like an adult.**

Imagine as far as your mind's eye can see. Eventually, the dots will connect and you will see the life that you know is rightfully yours. This is how you, "Begin with the end in mind," as Stephen Covey puts it in his bestselling book, *The 7 Habits of Highly Effective People*. You picture the end result so vividly that it eventually appears.

> **"Look, if you had one shot, or one opportunity. To seize everything you ever wanted in one moment. Would you capture it or just let it slip?"**
>
> ~MARSHALL BRUCE MATHERS

When you embrace visualization and harness the power of imagineering your creative juices will begin to flow, you'll hone in on your ideal life, and construct the pictures in your mind to bring them to fruition. Once your vision is constructed with great detail, you will be able to visualize it over and over again until it becomes a deep desire. Once it becomes a deep desire, you will put everything you have into making it happen, and, eventually, it will happen.

MAKE THE DECISION AND IT IS DONE

> "All men dream: but not equally. Those who dream by night in the dusty recesses of their minds wake up in the day to find it was vanity, but the dreamers of the day are dangerous men, for they may act on their dreams with open eyes, to make it possible."
>
> ~T.E. LAWRENCE, British archaeologist, army officer, military theorist, diplomat, and writer

There are two important things you must do before you can begin to engage in the visualization process which will lead you in the pursuit of your dreams. First, you must decide exactly what it is that you want and you must be specific. Second, you must make a decision to fully commit, i.e., do whatever it takes to achieve your vision.

It is not enough to say that you want to be successful – you must describe in detail what success means to you. For one person, success is having a billion dollars, and for another, it is ending world hunger. Planning has to be based on getting a clear vision of what you want because without a vision; you don't know which goals to set along the way. Without goals, you have no targets. Without targets, you have nothing to aim at, or by which to measure your progress to determine if you are moving toward your vision – *the* vision.

A word about *goals* vs. *vision*:

> Your "goals" and your "vision" as I use them in this book, are two different things. Yes, they can be synonymous on the surface, but I want to make an important distinction between the two: ***vision*** is your future self, where you want to be. Your first billion, solving world hunger. ***Goals*** are the stepping stones, and creating interval goals toward your vision is how you map out the path, as you will see in the next chapter.

Let's say you have a vision of starting your own business. That's great, but that's not nearly enough. You must decide what kind of business you want to begin before you can engineer a specific vision about it. For the sake of simplicity, let's say you want to develop an app.

To truly visualize and achieve the dream of developing an app, you have to get down to figuring out the nitty-gritty details. You have to find out if your app is marketable enough to make a recurring profit. If so, you have to figure out a business model that will achieve that. This will involve intensive research. You need to figure out how much it's going to cost to develop this app, and the most important thing you need to discover is who are your competitors. Who is currently doing what you want to do? Buy all the apps similar to the one you want to create, and model their process and structure.

If you're not a coder, now you have to figure out the cost of hiring one, along with all the other ancillary costs, e.g., the cost of launching your app and marketing it to your target audience. There are many details you could think about, but the point is to start thinking about the little things. The more detailed your vision is, the easier it is going to be to visualize it as a real, living thing.

Just thinking about your vision of creating an app isn't enough. You must write it down. Write everything down on paper or in a Google document, do some more research, check out the websites and forums in your niche, contact people who might know about making apps; in other words, find real information in order to help your vision become a reality. The more thorough you are, the more you can envision it coming to life – the easier it will be to have your subconscious working on it in the background.

Don't forget to ask yourself why you created your vision. Think about what the motivating force was for creating your vision in the first place, as it will help push you through the tough times when things don't seem to be going as well as you would like. Envision yourself on the cover of an influential magazine, touting how much your app has changed people's lives for the better and allowed them to become more productive.

Never underestimate the power of vision, as the person who has a clear and passionate reason for "why" they are doing something will always outperform the very best in the world at doing the "how" (i.e. logistics). It's the age-old tale of brains-over-brawn.

MAP OUT YOUR VISION

"The vision that you glorify in your mind, the ideal that you enthrone in your heart, this you will be built by, this you will become."

~JAMES ALLEN

Now that you've gathered all the information, it's time to make your vision real. For it to be real, you've got to believe in it. You must believe your vision is possible, even if it defies logic. This is crucial! And the best way to really believe in your vision is to map out a plan that is believable in your mind.

Let me explain. People have all sorts of things they want to accomplish in their lives, but more often than not, such visions rarely come with a plan. The most common misguided vision I hear people say is, *"I'm going to be rich one day";* however, that is not a vision. It's merely a random thought. A wish. It would be nice if money would fall out of thin air or start growing on trees, but even if it did, the exact same people would end up with all the money anyway. The distribution of wealth would end up the same: it would end up right back in the people's bank accounts who have an abundance consciousness.

However, since money will not begin growing on trees any time soon, and winning the lottery is a long shot, at best. In order to turn the random thought of becoming wealthy into your vision, you need to make it real. You need to write it down and map out a plan for attaining wealth that your mind will believe.

RICH PEOPLE SEE DIFFERENTLY THAN POOR PEOPLE

"Too many people spend money they earned to buy things they don't want, to impress people that they don't like."

~WILL ROGERS, American stage and motion-picture actor, vaudeville performer, cowboy, humorist

Remember a few paragraphs ago when I talked about lottery winners going broke? The Consumer Financial Protection Bureau states: "Nearly one-third of lottery winners eventually declare bankruptcy." Many people find themselves scratching their heads in confusion when they hear someone who has claimed bankruptcy after winning the lottery.

What could explain this phenomenon of poor people amassing large sums of money, and then losing it all? Steve Siebold, a self-made millionaire and author of *How Rich People Think,* discovered the answer after 26 years of interviewing the world's wealthiest people. Siebold wasn't surprised to see that rich people perceive the world far differently than poor people, but he was shocked at how rich people viewed *themselves*.

He learned that wealthy people don't see themselves as broke. In fact, even if they are low on money, they understand that being poor is permanent, but being broke is only temporary. Siebold discovered that wealthy people always envision themselves living a life of abundance and see themselves making the right business decisions. They see themselves as dominant individuals, and therefore, they become (and remain) dominant.

Poor people, on the other hand, don't see themselves as wealthy. They don't see themselves making the right decisions. Usually, they're second-guessing themselves, then allow self-doubt to set in after they finally make a decision. Poor people believe life happens to them, and that they are the product of their circumstances. *Que sera, sera.* They see their problems as permanent, and they struggle to see the light at the end of the tunnel. And if they do eventually see the light, they think it's a train coming.

The result of this faulty thinking – of having a poverty consciousness – is that money cannot stay with a person who does not *see* themselves (in their mind's eye) as wealthy. And by the same logic, money cannot stay away from the person who possesses a prosperity consciousness, and cannot see themselves (in their mind's eye) as poor. While being broke is a temporary situation, being poor is a permanent state of mind – a mental condition that may even be a mental illness.

Mental illness? Is that really a stretch? According to Mental Health America:

> *"A mental illness is a disease that causes mild to severe disturbances in thought and/or behavior, resulting in an inability to cope with life's ordinary demands and routines."*

Reading this definition, can a poverty consciousness be viewed as a type of mental illness? There isn't much difference between struggling with "life's ordinary demands and routines" and an inability to cope with them due to a poverty mindset.

"You cannot outperform your self-image."

~DAN LOK

The primary difference between wealthy people and poor people is nothing more than how they *see* their future unfolding. It all comes down to the vision they have for themselves. For you, this is where the fundamental shift must take place for you to change the direction of your life and create a new road map that you can clearly see leading you to the destination you desire.

Think about it like this: if you're driving to a distant city and you've never made that trip before, you'll consult a map to see how you're going to get to where you want to go. The same process is true for the journey you will take to achieve your vision, except that you get to design the map yourself. Wealthy people achieve tremendous success in life because they've mapped out their vision and maintained the discipline to hold on to their vision when the going got tough.

Decide on the first thing you need to do to achieve your vision, then the second, third, fourth, and so on. Map it out. Write everything down using numbered steps with headings that indicate the order. These steps, when followed sequentially, will bring your vision to life, and in turn, will allow you to live a life full of prosperity.

A mapped out plan with well-defined steps is intensely powerful. Your vision will become tangible, and that will help your mind believe it is real. This will improve your faith in your vision. With great faith, the intensity to attain your vision is even more significant because you know and believe with every fiber of your being that it is possible.

> **Always remember: you plan your tomorrows by the visions you have today.**

NEGATIVE VISIONS CAN INSPIRE

> "Hustle isn't just working on the things you like. It means doing the things you don't enjoy so you can do the things you love."
>
> ~UNKNOWN

For some people, picturing what they do not want in their mind is a profoundly motivating factor. For me, picturing one of my children getting sick and not being able to afford to provide the best medical treatment possible is something that pushes me when I'm not engaging in high productive activities (spending major time on minor stuff).

There have been times I've lain in bed in the morning not wanting to get up and go to work, but then the picture would pop in my mind of something happening to one of my boys and me not being able to deploy every resource under the sun to help them. This energizes me to leap out of bed and get moving. It provides the kick in the pants I sometimes need to focus and dominate.

Billions of dollars of life insurance are purchased because

people have a negative vision that if they are not around, their families will suffer financial hardships. Negative visions have propelled people to do amazing things. This is not the same as the negative reinforcement and naysaying that I discussed previously, which poisons a child or an adult into a life of mediocrity and underachievement.

Instead, it's a reasoned proactive stance against negative consequences that can arise from failing to regularly perform positive and productive tasks.

Some people are so terrified of not being able to build their own business and be a slave to build someone else's business that they go to extraordinary measures to produce. Take the average startup entrepreneur for instance. Initially, they work an exorbitant amount of hours and receive a depressingly small amount of money in return. They are fueled by their negative vision, hating the fact that if they fail, they will have to go to work building someone else's dream.

> **"Why are you prepared to risk everything for that dream that no one can see but you? Why would you prefer to put in 80 hours a week for your own dream just so you don't have to put in 40 for someone else's? Answer: freedom."**
>
> ~UNKNOWN

Dying without leaving this world a better place may be a negative vision that drives you. Whatever your negative vision is, I don't want you to focus on the negative as a limitation, but rather as motivation to sidestep it, avoid it, and leave it behind. I want you to do whatever it takes to force yourself to take action because it will be a very sad day if someone you love really needs you and you can't help them because you spent days, months, or even years engaging in unproductive activities.

HELP YOUR VISION

> "Your mind must first create a picture, and your training must be in sync with the visualization."
>
> ~ARNOLD SCHWARZENEGGER, Austrian-American politician, actor, filmmaker, businessman, author, and former professional bodybuilder, 38th Governor of California

You can visualize in a prison cell, under a bridge, on a mountaintop, during a walk, or floating on your back in the ocean. That is the power of your mind: visualization works anywhere. However, one of the best ways I've discovered to help the visualization process is by surrounding yourself with people who also believe in the power of visualization.

When you choose to associate with people who inspire you and challenge the status quo, they will assist you in expanding your vision and help you achieve the life you desire. Spending time with the right people helps fill in the missing details of your vision. Their ebb-and-flow will interface with your own ebb-and-flow. The combined momentum you can create when you get the right people in your life ends up being more than the mere sum of the parts (as I will cover in detail in Chapter Six). In fact, the combined ebb-and-flow that results from the passion forged among synergistic partners becomes an unstoppable tsunami.

The right people will show you a lifestyle that is better connected to the one you want. This will help guide you toward living in the environment you truly desire. The right people will show you different ways of doing things and different ways of thinking. From this, you can model their actions, habits and behaviors while adding your own innovations.

What you see in your mind is what you will eventually get in your physical reality, so it is imperative that you monitor who gets access to your mind. The people you choose to surround yourself with will either enhance your visions or place limits on them.

Visualizing yourself into the future you desire requires constantly monitoring the people you associate with, along with the character traits of self-discipline, patience, focus, and relentless determination. Once you have done the work to create a clear vision, it's the discipline and effort to maintain the vision that will make it come true. The moment you create the vision, you're on your way, but you get there by diligently and stubbornly sticking with your vision. *"Stay on message"* meaning: always stay focused on your vision should be your mantra. For you, the reader, this book is my message to you.

THE VISION IS THE MESSAGE

> "The most pathetic person in the world is someone who has sight but no vision."
>
> ~HELEN KELLER, American author, political activist, and lecturer, Keller was the first deaf-blind person to earn a Bachelor of Arts degree

I ended the last paragraph by stating that this book is meant to be the message. In 1964, however, Canadian philosopher Marshall McLuhan coined his famous phrase, "The medium is the message," to mean that the media (TV, movies, books, etc.) are themselves more of the message than what they are providing in the way of content. That is, the way content is delivered (i.e., the medium) is more powerful in affecting our thinking and visualizing the message than the actual information portrayed, simply because it is purposely designed to do just that – affect our thinking.

A cognitive bias aside:

One of the common cognitive biases is the "framing effect". This refers to the fact that how information or an idea is presented influences how it is perceived. For example, in a study conducted at Stanford University, when crime was framed metaphorically as "a virus," subjects proposed social reform initiatives, but when crime was described as a "beast," subjects' solutions were more aggressive, like focusing on jailing criminals. The medium is indeed the message.

Today, news shows are produced with animated segues and dramatic sound effects between segments; they are attention-getting hooks that usher us into some inner circle of *breaking news* and *what you need to know*. They make us wait, though, until after the commercial break. News anchors portray faces of concern, pathos, or gravity when reporting danger, tragedy, or important developments. Then, immediately after they are done, they dismiss these stories to go home to their own lives, leaving us with the emotional baggage. Such baggage is made up of negative images that implants and anchors themselves into our subconscious. This identification between the media and what they plant into our minds is just another strategy to have us continue tuning in. Meanwhile, we've had negative visions put into our minds without even realizing it. Again, this is another key reason why it's crucial to monitor who (and what) gets access to your mind – to continuously guard venomously what you allow your mind to see.

Such media and mediums become extensions of ourselves and for this reason, become part of our lives. An example of this is Facebook, which offers content that tells us what our friends are eating, where they are, and what they're buying. The message, however, is not what they're eating or where they are, but that we can keep track of them and compare our lives to theirs.

Tiffany Gee Lewis cited Shauna Niequist (*Relevant* magazine) in the *Deseret News*:

> *"Everyone's life looks better on the Internet than it does in real life. The Internet is partial truths – we get to decide what people see and what they don't."*

Lewis then added:

"Social media offers us a form of escape – I can look at a friend's bathroom redo instead of cleaning my own. I can read the latest tweets from my favorite authors instead of ever tackling that book idea in my own head. And because I'm doing something, I still feel more productive than I would sitting on the couch watching game shows. The medium is still the message."

An uglier example is the act of burning books. The book-burning is the message, not the content within them. Historically, this act has been used politically to teach people what is unacceptable to a state, religion, or group of people, the irony being that burning the books burns a vision into people's minds. The takeaway message is not only that some ideology is unacceptable, but that "*we*" (the book-burners) control what *you* (the readers) are to read and think. "*We*" control what you are allowed to visualize.

Anytime you allow someone (or something) to control or restrict what you are allowed to see and/or think warning bells should go off – red flags should surface. This is because your own vision should always be your message; your belief in your ability to achieve your vision should be the medium. And you should never allow others or "mediums" to talk you out of your vision. Sometimes staying on message is more akin to staying true to yourself – true to your vision.

STAYING ON MESSAGE: STAYING ON VISION

"A river cuts through rock, not because of its power, but because of its persistence."

~UNKNOWN

In a prison cell, I started with an intense dedication to my vision of writing a book that would act as a cautionary tale as well as a success guide. Initially, I began by reading one book after another, searching for answers to my burning question: *how did I go so wrong?*

There were five lessons (I'll explain in greater detail in Chapter Three, "*Resilience*") that served as my answers, five nearly fatal flaws that reared their ugly heads:

1. I focused on my image more than my integrity;
2. I constantly sought instant gratification;
3. I took any advice that would be self-serving, no matter how suspect;
4. I became arrogant and saw my success as an entitlement which lead me to believe I was better than others; and
5. I made exceptions in my core life-values when it suited me.

However, in my comprehensive self-appraisal; I was relieved to discover that I had done many more things right than I had done wrong. This discovery helped rejuvenate my vision.

What I did right as well as what I did wrong revealed invaluable lessons I felt obligated to share. So after I identified my mistakes as well as my successes; I began taking notes. There were lots of successes and lots of mistakes, so...lots of notes. So many notes you could wallpaper the Sistine Chapel with them.

Out of this tome of notes arose the outline for this book, the secrets to success, as well as the pitfalls that lurk on the path to success. When I decided to write *CEO*, its secrets, and document what I did right as well as what I did wrong; I saw that it would reveal not only the *what* and *how*, but the *why* (science), too, for success.

My excitement caught fire and with my new passion ignited; I began seeking feedback from friends and family. This, sadly, was when I failed to stay on message. I was discouraged because much of the feedback was not positive. I heard things like, *"How can someone who has failed as badly as you teach people how to become successful?" "Your best thinking got you a 40-year prison term, why would someone take advice from you?*

This negativity planted self-doubt in my mind. Were they right? When it came to my vision of writing this book for you, I panicked: *what do I do?* After all, this book was supposed to champion against the idea of negativity. So, what if the feedback on my advice to fight negativity...was negative itself?

In my mind, this paradox caused my vision (writing a book about failure and success) and my passion for it to dissipate. I began to believe that what my critics (i.e. friends and family) offered was valid when it should have been an emergency and a greater call to action to complete and publish this book. Instead, though, I didn't even hear the sirens as they passed me by.

I put this book off for years. Sure, I continued to work on it periodically, but I allowed the negativity of others to make me feel like I needed to become successful before I was "qualified" to publish a book about success. I betrayed my own vision for the "anti-vision" of others.

That's why I wrote and published *Instagram Secrets* prior to publishing this book, even though I began working on this book (*CEO*) long before *Instagram Secrets* was even a thought. While my Instagram book proved to be extremely successful (an international number-one bestseller), my mistake – and what delayed this book unnecessarily – was the vision of myself in the present (the convicted felon, the *bad* person, others' vision of me). I mistakenly felt compelled to expunge this vision of me in the minds of others, the naysayers, before I published this book.

> **"No matter how much you change, you still got to pay the price for the things you've done."**
>
> ~BEN AFFLECK

This mistake also meant that others defined my vision of who I believed I was, not me. That's why I said I *betrayed* my own vision. Their classification of me was based firmly on the mistakes I had made in the past, where I *was* a convicted felon and judged to be a bad person. What would have served my vision better and proven loyalty to it was to realize that my past was *their present* version of me, which had nothing to do with my *future* version of me; that is, my vision.

My future self eventually came to the rescue. Plucked from my vision of the future was the act of designing the cover of this book before I wrote a single word. It's true. (Marshall McLuhan would have approved!) I didn't have any exceptional writing skills, a deal with a publisher, or any media outlet helping me. But I did have a cover. And this was a major part of my envisioning process. I had the vision of creating this book for you etched deep into my mind and regularly looking at the cover helped me stay on message.

But that only took me so far in my envisioning process of creating this book. I needed to see the future, make it tangible, and bring it into the present. To take my visualization to the next level, I started regularly envisioning people emailing me every day and telling me how much this book has changed their lives. I envisioned being one of the world's top authorities at helping people break free from a life of mediocrity and achieve greatness.

I saw mothers and fathers requiring their children to read this book. I envisioned parents reading *CEO*, then taping a $100 bill to the refrigerator, quizzing their children about the strategies I reveal, and then giving them the money after they answered the questions correctly. (Yes, $100 is a lot of money, but "strong reasons create strong actions," Shakespeare.)

I did not just fantasize about writing this book for you. I purposefully envisioned it. There is a distinct (and massive!) difference between *fantasizing* and *envisioning*. Fantasizing is *"What if?"* while envisioning is "*What I will be is what I say I will be.*" Fantasizing is *"Que sera, sera" (*"the future's not ours to see"*)*; envisioning is *raison d'etre (*destiny*)*.

Day after day I disciplined myself to conjure up visions about how this book could potentially change the world. That's why my mission for *CEO* is: to make a billion lives better. Envisioning people sharing this book with their friends and family prompted me to acquire a simple domain, CEObook.com.

> The title says it all: here is the blueprint for becoming a CEO and everything that it means, as both a leader – and the dreamer seeking to become a leader. But it also says that even CEOs can learn, all achievements open the doors to more achievements. So, when you're a CEO, you're not finished. You owe it to yourself to act on the next vision!

After I created the cover and envisioned the profound impact this book would have on people's lives; I outlined the chapters. With my grand vision set in stone, I mapped out everything and broke down exactly what it would look like once everything was completed. I arrived at seven secrets. In what order would they be presented? Why seven? Why not more...or even less? I kept asking myself questions until I had a crystal-clear picture of what the end result would look like.

Then I started writing.

I worked on finishing this book, day after day, one page at a time. Initially, I began writing in a prison cell. (I was the guy looking to the stars.) When I was released, I continuously refined the content. It was slow and difficult, and at times those treasonous doubts about whether I was qualified to write this book would resurface. This time, however, I stayed loyal to my vision; I never allowed myself to get derailed.

Stay on message. When I would get frustrated about how long it was taking me to complete this book; I envisioned all the people I knew I could help and then I stared at the cover. *Stay on message.* I even printed the cover out and taped it to another book, so my mind would see it as real. The cover was my way of helping my mind believe this book would be published (and in your hands, like it is now) one day. It firmly planted the finished product in my mind (i.e. my vision of the future being realized).

No matter what was happening in my life, my vision of creating a book – this book – for you was always a top priority. I regularly replayed in my mind how this book would help people embrace their struggles and overcome their challenges. When I would see someone enduring a difficult situation, I'd get motivated and think to myself, "Gotta finish this book so I can give it to them and help them."

CONCLUSION

> "Be brave enough to live the life of your dreams according to your vision and purpose instead of the expectations and opinions of others."
>
> ~ROY T. BENNETT, Author of *The Light in the Heart*

It would be impossible for me to close a chapter on vision without telling you the story about the four-minute mile. This story changed the way I viewed what was possible in life.

On May 6, 1954, Roger Bannister broke the four-minute barrier when he ran the mile in three minutes and 54 seconds. Prior to Bannister breaking the record, known throughout history as an impossible feat, no one had ever run a mile in less than four minutes. But many people wondered just how long his "impossible feat" record would stand.

Just 46 days later, Bannister's world record was shattered. Since then, more than 1,400 athletes have run the mile in less than the once-unbreachable four minutes, with the current record being a whopping seventeen seconds (3:43) faster than Bannister's historic magic mile.

Why does this make the hairs on the back of my neck stand up? Because it proves – let me repeat, it *proves* – how we impose self-limiting beliefs on ourselves, simply because we see (in our mind's eye), believe, and accept these limits.

As part of Roger Bannister's training, he relentlessly visualized himself breaking the four-minute mile barrier. This created the sense of certainty he needed to make his dreams come true. He didn't let the four-minute mile come to him; he went after it. Otherwise, he would have been waiting for a long time.

Just like the legendary athlete Bannister, you too can realize that what you see in your mind is what you will either remain or become. (Letting life happen versus making life happen.) That's why you need to be fired up about what you envision, because:

1. What goes into your mind will affect the way you think;
2. the way you think will affect the way you perform, and
3. the way you perform will affect the type of lifestyle you live.

This is why it's never enough to, proverbially, *do your best*. "Your best" may be entangled with constraints which you've come to accept – conventional wisdom which is a lie that imposes self-induced limits. You must have the vision, the energy, and the persistence to prevail – to do whatever it takes to *make things happen* (regardless of what others believe or what you previously believed).

> **"Every man dies. Not every man really lives."**
>
> ~WILLIAM WALLACE

Even the Bible teaches us, "Where there is no vision the people perish." Having an inspiring vision for your life is literally a life-or-death matter. Listen for the sirens! When I heard them is when I chose to begin this book – my vision – and handle the emergency. It is why I made the subject of vision the entire first chapter of this book.

Don't unnecessarily delay bringing your vision to pass because of profitless self-sabotaging thoughts (like I initially did). Take action now on what you know you need to do. Do whatever it takes to make your vision visible, make it tangible, and take action so it will become a reality.

When you have a strong vision, you can see the invisible, feel the intangible, and achieve the impossible.

A printed out cover taped onto another book to stand proudly on the to-read shelf? Sounds crazy, but your vision gives you the persistence to do whatever it takes to get things done in life. Your vision is the inspiring picture of the future that energizes your mind and empowers you to do whatever it takes to achieve it.

If you can picture your vision in your mind as if it has already been completed, it will become effortless for you to take the actions necessary to get you to where you want to be. You've visualized your final outcome hundreds of times in your mind by replaying it over and over again. Now, it's only a matter of time before it becomes a reality.

By now, you can clearly see that you possess the power to create the life that you want and that everything you need has been lying dormant inside of you. Don't get discouraged because it's just a seed right now. Some of the largest and mightiest things on Earth came from nothing more than a seed.

Don't get hung up on the fact that you may not currently have all the resources required to achieve your vision. Because the only real resources you need in this world are your heart and your mind, as everything else stems from those two vital things. Once you understand that, you'll realize you had the key in your hand and in your heart all along.

You now have the ability to unlock the treasure chest that contains your dream life. But it's up to you to decide whether you want to open the vault and unleash your greatness by tapping into the power deep within you, or...remain average.

EXERCISE NO. 1: UNCLUTTER YOUR MIND

Before you begin visualizing or imagineering, I need you to clear your mind, because you cannot begin picturing the life you want or the things you want if your mind is a mess. Look at the images below and tell me which image your mind most identifies with (be honest with yourself).

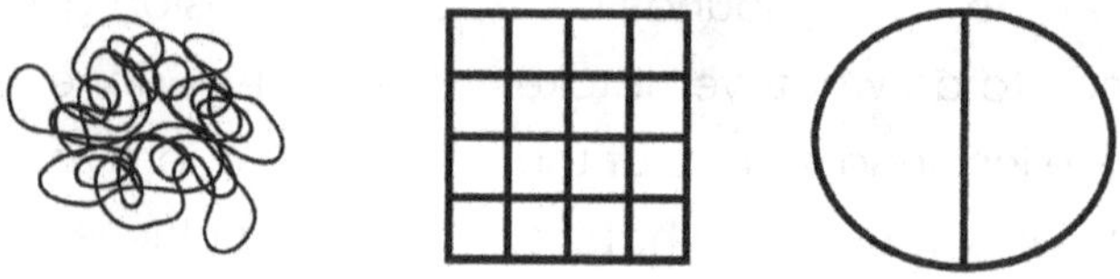

A **B** **C**

I'm guessing in this chaotic world that we live in, there is a strong chance you chose A. If you did, this means your mind is not at ease. Therefore, I want you to do a simple meditation exercise before you begin picturing the life you are going to create. Why meditation? Meditation has proven to help us untangle the mental mess we engineer in our minds.

> **"Meditation teaches you how to disengage yourself from the thought process. It's the mental art of stepping out of your own way."**
>
> ~BHANTE HENEPOLA GUNARATANA

First, set a timer on your phone for five minutes. Next, if possible, turn off all external noises around you (trust me, I understand as a father – for some strange reason children do not have an "off" button). If it is not possible to silence the room you are in, do the best you can to only focus on tranquility.

Now I want you to lie flat on the floor with your back to the ground. You can close your eyes or keep them open, whichever you prefer. You can also do this sitting up in a chair facing forward but do not focus on anything in particular (if you keep your eyes open). Try to relax every muscle in your body. Begin with your head, then your neck. Move to your arms and fingers, then chest, followed by your legs.

Once you feel completely relaxed, I want you to only focus on your breathing. Breathe in through your nose, counting silently to yourself to four as you breathe in, hold that breath for one second, then use four more seconds to breathe out through your nose. It's important that your stomach rises when you're breathing in and not your chest.

Repeat this process until the timer goes off on your phone. If negative thoughts arise, do the best you can to take your mind back to only focusing on the routine:

1. breathing in for four seconds through your nose,
2. pausing for one second, then
3. breathing out through your nose for four seconds.

Disease is caused from dis-ease.

Meditation is key to relaxing your mind. It enables you to unclutter your thoughts and focus on the things that are truly important to you in life. I urge you to make meditation an essential part of your daily routine because, without a clear mind, your visions will be drowned out with all the negativity we are exposed to throughout our lives.

EXERCISE NO. 2: ENVISION THE FUTURE YOU

Now that your mind is clear, take some time in a quiet place to visualize yourself as you want to be. You must be certain about your future self, and you must be precise about who you want to become and what you want to have. Imagine in vivid detail the person you want to become. Imagine the home you want to live in, the clothes you want to wear, the people with whom you want to spend time with, and the environment you deserve to be in.

Make your vision as detailed as possible and make it inspiring, because when reality hits and your vision is finally real, it's going to blow your mind, because – after all – it's always been *real*, right?

Once you've done the visualization in vivid detail, it's time to decide what parts of your vision you want to manifest in your life. After you've made that decision, you need to do the research. Find out what the actual cost of your dream house would be. Find out what your investment will need to be for you to start that business or charitable foundation. Be as detailed as possible and write everything down. "Tabulate" your vision; this will confirm the reality you need to incorporate. There's nothing wrong with adding the reality to it because you will be able to understand – then conquer – that reality.

After you have figured out the details for what you want, it's time to make sure you visualize those details in your mind as frequently as possible, with the minimum being at least twice a day (right before you go to sleep at night is ideal, because it helps your subconscious work on your vision while you sleep, talk about maximizing every minute).

You need to become obsessed with your vision. Once you do, your vision will start to pop into your mind without you having to think about it. Without even trying you will dream about your vision. This is the initial phase of you *becoming* your vision. Eventually, your vision will become your reality. And you'll be in it, live it, and become one with it.

EXERCISE NO. 3: INVEST IN YOUR VISION

Christian award-winning music artist and fashion mogul Kanye West said, "Before I had it, I closed my eyes and imagined." When I was released from prison; I was completely broke. But every now and again I'd still go to the most expensive restaurants in Houston. I'd only order a glass of tap water and a happy hour special appetizer. The bill would total less than $20 including the tip.

But I needed to put myself in that environment even though I couldn't afford a single thing that was full price on the menu. I needed to *see* myself eating there. I needed to *see* myself taking my family to this opulent restaurant and all of us ordering from the left side of the menu, ignoring the prices on the right side.

Now, guess what? My son Tristan and I frequently eat at high-end restaurants. And we order whatever we want (Tristan likes his steak well done, hopefully, that changes as he ages). I honestly believe this has a lot to do with me visualizing this experience. When I was broke, I saw it. Then my actions matched my vision. I knew I couldn't waste hours of time searching for the bottom of my Facebook newsfeed if I was going to regularly eat at the best restaurants and order whatever I wanted.

Something else I did to help my vision: when I was a teenager; I'd go look at multi-million dollar homes, even though I lived in a house that was valued less than $45,000. What was I doing back then? Was I setting my vision too high? Was I overreaching? Heck no! I was planting seeds in my mind. And sure enough, with time those seeds sprouted and blossomed.

Do like I did. Go to the most expensive restaurant you can find within an hour's drive. If you don't have the money to eat there – trust me I've been there, too – just order an appetizer and a glass of water. Then, envision yourself frequenting places like this. Go to the most expensive neighborhoods you can get into and vividly picture yourself buying the home of your dreams. And if you're really serious about living in a multi-million dollar home and regularly eating at fancy restaurants make absolutely certain you envision yourself doing the work it takes to get there.

Your actions must match your visions.

Now when I was looking at my dream houses or going to expensive restaurants I was doing more than just visualizing. I was actually living in the vision and through my actions, I was bringing my vision closer to reality. This is key because a vision without emotion and manifestation isn't nearly as powerful. What I am talking about here is the mind-body connection.

Imagine a coach trying to fire his team up before a game. Would he stand there and just get his players to visualize winning the game? No emotion, no movement, just a quiet exercise in imagery? Or would he accompany the image with fiery talk, high fives, fists colliding violently with each other, people jumping up and down in a frenzy of optimism?

There's a role for both of course, but when you embody your vision through action and emotion, it becomes extremely powerful. It becomes programmed into the body and that physical programming feeds back to the brain, empowering the vision. In other words, you have to be doing, and link deep emotions to the achievement of your vision because it is action and emotional ties that ultimately rewires your brain and gives your vision power.

EXERCISE NO. 4: MAKE A VISION BOARD

Similar to the book cover (this book cover) I taped onto another book, allowing my vision to sit on the shelf as if it were already published, why stop there? A vision board allows you to display an assortment of images associated with your vision. You can use a corkboard, a bulletin board, a scrapbook, a collage on a large piece of cardboard, your wall, or even the LED "desktop" from an old outdated computer collecting dust in a closet.

Whether you paste or copy-and-paste, it doesn't matter, just as long as you can easily change out the images as your vision approaches you or is fine-tuned along your journey. Remember, this is a morphing reality as you make your journey – a living, breathing memorial to your future (although "memorial" is the wrong word; a better word is "promise"). It is important to consider your vision board as a crystal ball in which you see your future, and not just a wish list.

Decide whether you want just one display or several that can represent parallel themes. For example, you could have one for your dream car, one for your dream home, one for your dream family, another for your dream trip abroad, even one for acts of philanthropy...there simply are no limits if you trust your vision.

Focus tightly in on what you truly want, because this exercise is so important. Choose the images that exactly render your vision, and give you the emotional feelings you expect to have when you achieve your vision; smell it, feel it, get into it. Remember that your timeline is just cross-sections of you, therefore, look at it from outside of your timeline so that you and your future become one and the same.

You should aim for a vision board that provides strong positive emotions associated with your future. If it doesn't then it may be tempting to think you did the vision board wrong, but this is incorrect; what you've probably depicted is not really what you dream of doing, creating, or having in your future. But if it isn't, it can be changed or as I like to say, *perfected*. Focus very deeply and bring your heart's desire for your future to the forefront of your life here and now.

Always keep your eyes open for the images that will represent your future and your heart's desires. They can be in books, magazines, advertisements, and even calendars. They can be images (or sounds) you find on the Internet. Sound is a great way to foster excitement because it causes electrical signals from our brain cells to fire in a way that arouses our emotions. The roar of a high-end car engine, waves splashing, the sound of the Wall Street opening bell...anything. These are easy to loop with even rudimentary audio software.

You can even cruise the streets and go on road trips to take your own photos. Have some fun – take selfies in front of your future house or in your future car!

It's okay to include pictures that are not directly related to your vision, but just make you feel good. Such is the role of puppies and babies and their ability to release dopamine in your brain. Memories of family and friends during happy times do the same and are more relevant. A peaceful sunset or a natural wonder can make you feel part of something special just by being alive. Life is a gift, so include scenes from it.

Keep your vision board in a place where it is always in your field of view. Let your eyes drift to it from time to time. If a particular part of your vision board loses its punch, make the changes necessary to bring back the spark – to rekindle the emotional ties. Something as simple as a different camera angle can do this. If you're out of your house or office, a photo of your vision board on your smartphone or tablet allows you to take your vision with you where ever you go. The more you "consult" your vision board, the more your vision will draw close. It will come to your mind at first, then to your life later. Visions like this just do that; they just fit.

Every day, you should set some time aside to concentrate on your vision board. Move from image to image, thinking about each one. Make a full sweep. Envision your future self in those images, feel the emotions they evoke as you see yourself in the pictures. While you're looking at your vision board check yourself and make certain your daily activities are leading you to achieve all that you see.

Each day you should look forward to the time you get to focus on your vision board. You should enjoy the process of seeing yourself accomplish what you set your heart to achieve because the journey is the most beautiful part. You are in complete control of your life. You are plucking yourself off of your number line and dropping yourself further down toward your destiny. But it's all the same number line, remember? It's as if you are one and the same with everything on that board.

You and your future will strike the same chord, instead of playing discordant notes that have no harmony or render no melody. It's your song, and it's a song worth singing. When the "fat lady" finally sings it, it'll be about you and what you were able to achieve because of the visions you took action to manifest into your life and bring to pass.

EXERCISE NO. 5: YOUR PERFECT DAY (MENTAL REHEARSAL IN WRITTEN FORM)

The final exercise I want you to do in this chapter – and this is extremely important – I want you to write down, in this book, what your perfect day would look like in one year.

> **"Backcasting is a planning method that starts with defining a desirable future and then working backwards to identify policies and programs that will connect that specified future to the present."**
>
> ~WIKIPEDIA

This will not only give you direction for the current actions you must take to get to your perfect day but more importantly, it will give you hope. This exercise has gotten me through one of the darkest periods in my life, and it can do the same for you.

In other words, "reverse engineer" your perfect day. (I talk more about the value of reverse engineering in Chapter Six.) Please write out in as much detail as possible what your perfect day would look like one year from today. The more detailed you can make this, the more real it will become in your mind's eye, and the more it will increase synaptic activity as your brain begins creating new neural connections that result from repeated visualization.

It's imperative you write this out, not just think it. It's also imperative that you review it at least once a month (preferably more than that) to make certain your actions and priorities are aligned with what you truly want in life.

Today's date: ______________________

(If you need more space see the Notes section in the back of this book.)

CHAPTER TWO

Goal Setting – Write It Down, Make It Happen

"To put away aimlessness and weakness, and to begin to think with purpose, is to enter the ranks of those strong ones who only recognize failure as one of the pathways to attainment; who make all conditions serve them, and who think strongly, attempt fearlessly, and accomplish masterfully."

~JAMES ALLEN, British philosophical writer, pioneer of the self-help movement, author of *As A Man Thinketh*

Some people create their own reality, while others accept whatever role the world has given them. As I mentioned in the previous chapter, being a character in someone else's play is no way for you to live your life because you may not like how the play ends!

My mission in this chapter is to not only help you make your way through the maze of life successfully, but excel by accomplishing the things in this world that you were meant to do.

We spent a lot of time talking about the importance of creating your vision. Now we are going to crystallize that vision in written form. Through goal-setting, you can take visualization to the next level and improve the probability of manifesting your vision into reality.

When people first hear or think about goal-setting, they often experience this invisible shield or subconscious resistance because they assume the process is something extremely complicated and time-consuming. This type of negativity holds many people back. On top of this faulty thinking, there's the false belief in the difficulty of setting goals for the vision of your future when you're mired in the distractions of the present. But press on, you must.

VISION VS. GOALS

> "Ye can not see the wood for trees."
>
> ~JOHN HEYWOOD, Prov. II. iv, *The Proverbs and Epigrams of John Heywood* (1562 AD)

To be successful, it's not enough to see the forest for the trees; you must also be able to see the trees for the forest, for the forest is crossed one tree at a time. Similarly, the path to your vision is best made one goal at a time.

You wouldn't use the word "trees" (individual objects seen as multiple) in place of "forest" (one object made up of multiple individual objects). This is an interesting analogy for the distinction I make between your vision (the *forest*) and your goals (the *trees*). Your vision may be your destiny, but the goals to get there are your destiny-making steps. Therefore, it is crucial to uncover an important divergence between both goals and vision.

Many books equivalate goals with vision, using them interchangeably. But these are distinctly different concepts; hence, they comprise two separate chapters in this book (Chapters One and Two, respectively). In stark contrast to the book you're reading now, those who equate goals with vision distort the distinction between them with two equally misleading strategies that live at two equally incompatible extremes:

1. They will either provide you with a lot of vague advice that gives little to no direction (i.e. too much vision with no discrete goals); or
2. They provide so much detail that you end up spending an outrageous amount of time filling out the 20-page worksheets before getting a chance to take action. (Thus, too many goals to result in a laser-targeted vision.) You become frustrated, exhausted, and find yourself running to stand still.

Which begs the questions: What is a goal? How is it different from your vision?

In the previous chapter, I explained the difference between goals and your vision. Your goals are the interval steps – even baby steps – on the journey to your vision. Be practical! You can only bite off what you can chew, and seldom can you swallow a vision all in one gulp. (Warning: choking hazard!) At the risk of overusing a metaphor, I submit that taking smaller bites means better digestion. Thus, the entire vision becomes more palatable when you can enjoy the simpler satisfaction of tasting one goal at a time. You can savor the flavor, making the journey itself as satisfying as the vision you attain when the time comes. This hopefully clarifies the difference between goals (the journey) and vision (the destination); clarification is necessary, because what I offer you here is a happy medium between some books' vague advice (vision-centered at the expense of goals – #1) and the opposite extreme in other books' self-defeating micromanagement (goal-centered, at the expense of vision – #2).

Taking the best of both worlds, I want to offer enough direction to provide you with a starting point. (I say "starting point," but your vision is really the "ending point" that you reverse-engineer.) I also want to include enough flexibility in the protocol to allow you to adapt as plans change and new circumstances arrive out of nowhere. Because they will!

My perfect balance for you is to explore both your vision and the interval goals to achieve the results you desire in life while resisting the temptation to equate the two. In this chapter, I'll discuss goals as they relate to your vision because they are intimately connected, but they are not the same. You don't climb a forest; you climb a tree. Likewise, you don't go through a tree; you go through a forest. You must understand the difference between the two.

This chapter is going to be part workbook and part science-based formulas that have been thoroughly researched and proven to produce results. You will learn *how,* and you will also understand the explanation as to *why* you should approach your vision in a goal-setting way. You should also expect to do exercises as you read through this chapter, so I'd like to recommend that you recall all of your visions from the previous chapter and have a pen handy so you can execute the exercises that will assist you in connecting the dots as you pursue your vision.

SIMPLE TO DO, BUT SIMPLE NOT TO DO

> "The simple things are also the most extraordinary things, and only the wise can see them."
>
> ~PAULO COELHO, Brazilian lyricist and novelist, author of *The Alchemist*

When it comes to setting goals that will become the journey toward your vision, I see far too many people doing the right things but doing them in the wrong order. You don't achieve your goals by doing certain things; you achieve your goals by doing certain things, in a certain way, in a specific order. You could find two people doing exactly the same things, and you might not see much difference except that one succeeds and one fails. However, on closer examination, you'll find that one does a series of things a certain way, and the other – doing those exact same things – does them in another way. The difference here is that you have to do them in the right order. Why is this distinction so crucial? Because it's the repetition of doing the right things, the right way, in the right order that produces success. Thus, just having goals is not nearly enough (this is where many people go wrong): you have to set them properly and approach them in an orderly fashion that helps you build momentum.

> **"You don't get rich by doing certain things, you get rich by doing things in a certain way."**
> ~BOB PROCTOR

Many people lack the organization required to set goals properly. This leads them to shoot at many targets but not hit a single one. As a result, they shimmy in multiple directions that cancel each other out, instead of their goals invoking a single net vector force toward their vision.

That's why in this chapter, I will help you create a solid foundational blueprint so your goals are organized and laid out in an easy to follow step-by-step plan. Let me warn you though: do not be fooled by the simplicity of merely setting goals. (*Simple to do, but simple not to do.*) You must also execute and take action in order to achieve your goals.

Before we dive into my goal-setting techniques and principles, however, I want to share a short story with you that illustrates how straightforward goal-setting can be.

> A group of young entrepreneurs were having lunch at an upscale restaurant in downtown Los Angeles, California, when an old man approached their table and said, "The secret to success is written on this piece of paper I have in my hand. I'll sell it to you for $10,000."
>
> The businessmen quickly blew off the old man. But one of them

found it odd that the man simply walked away without bothering to barter. Before long, he got a strange feeling that maybe, just maybe, this man actually cracked the code to success.

With curiosity getting the best of him, he stood up, excused himself from the table and rushed toward the front door, catching a glimpse of the white-haired man just as he was about to exit. "Wait!" the young entrepreneur shouted, swiftly moving closer to the old man. "I'll make you a deal. You let me read what's on the paper, and if I like what I see, I'll give you $10,000."

Confident that he did indeed crack the code, the old man agreed and handed over the paper. After examining it for what seemed like a very long time, the entrepreneur shook his head in amazement. Then, he pulled out his checkbook and wrote the wise man a check for $10,000.

He went on to outperform all the other businessmen who were at the table that day by tenfold, achieving great prosperity and extraordinary success by implementing the strategy the wise man revealed to him.

Do you want to know what was written on the paper? Do you want to know what the secret to success was? What was written on the paper was very simple, yet profound. It read:

Every morning when you wake up do two things:

No. 1: Make a list of the things that need to be done that day.
No. 2: Do them.

Simple, right? Perhaps too simple? Sometimes in life, the simplest things to do are also the simplest things not to do. This introduces the concept of "*self-regulation*", a skill all leaders and successful people have developed.

Let me expand on the story a bit by suggesting that before you go to bed at night, make a list of the things that need to be done the following day. Why should you do this? Because a research study from the Proceedings of the National Academy of Sciences revealed that rapid eye movement (REM) sleep substantially increases our creative process.

You can put this strategy to good use by sleeping on the tasks/goals you intend to accomplish the following day. I always try to determine what I'm going to work on the next day before I go to bed. This allows my mind (my more powerful brain: subconscious) to begin engaging with what I need to accomplish while I sleep. Several times I have woken up with solutions to problems I spent hours trying to figure out the previous day. It's almost like putting a roast in the crockpot and letting it simmer overnight.

An important note: when creating your list, do not overwhelm yourself. Stick to the three most crucial things/goals that will have the most significant impact on your ultimate vision, or even on the interval goals that you have set on your path to your vision. This will force you to remove trivial, unimportant tasks and allow you to focus on the vital few tasks that make a difference.

Something new I recently started implementing was giving myself a quick win. I try to begin my day with a super simple task. This would not be on my list, but it would create confidence and momentum. Call it "destiny candy."

A neurological aside:

What happens when you sleep? While sleep is considered a respite from life, that's a myth. Your brain is just as busy (if not more so) during sleep as when you are awake. In fact, your brain never sleeps. Sleep is when your brain organizes everything that has accrued during the day, e.g., memories, actions, and emotions. Your limbic system, especially your hippocampus, is actively preening the events to determine which will be assigned from short-term to long-term memory. This is referred to as "*memory consolidation*."

It is why you may forget what you had for lunch one day, but never forget – as long as you live – a kid who slugged you on the playground when you were in grade school. Thus, your hippocampus prioritizes your life – its events and memories. You can only imagine the jumpstart you get by making your three-item to-do list before retiring for the day when your subconscious assists you in uncovering solutions while you sleep.

When you're prioritizing your tasks/goals (to-do list) the night before it's important you know which ones need to be done first – which ones are the most important or most difficult to accomplish. This is key because behavioral scientists have proven that our willpower is the strongest when we first begin the day. This will help you pursue accomplishing the day's most difficult tasks when you are at your strongest.

But there's a little Jedi mind trick at work the night before: the very act of making a list and designating each item according to importance will allow you to assign them corresponding "weight" in your mind as you sleep. According to the *Journal of Consumer Psychology*:

"Unconscious thought leads to an automatic weighting process whereby important decision attributes receive more weight, and unimportant decision attributes receive less weight."

Let's put this new knowledge to work now. Take a moment and turn to page 547 in the back of this book. Write down the three most important things/goals you want to achieve by the end of the day tomorrow. Then, before you go to bed tonight, review what you wrote so your subconscious can begin going to work on the tasks while you sleep.

Okay, with that quick lesson in personal productivity out of the way, let's return to the subject of setting and achieving your goals.

The first step in goal-setting is to clarify precisely what you want for yourself. What do you want to achieve? What do you stay up at night thinking about? We talked about these questions in the previous chapter focusing on your vision. Now I'm going to double down and ensure that you are certain about what things you want to get out of life because you begin "getting them" with the goals you set toward your vision.

THE PASSION QUOTIENT

> "The most powerful weapon on earth is the human soul on fire."
>
> ~FERDINAND FOCH, French general and military theorist

Some things in life make your heart beat a little faster than usual. Some things are so important that you are willing to lose sleep, skip meals, sacrifice comfort, and even temporarily lose your sanity over. In an ideal world, your goals and the vision they achieve should evoke all those things combined. You must become obsessed with your goals if you expect to achieve your vision.

It is imperative that you are extraordinarily passionate about your goals because extreme passion is the key ingredient that is going to help you become (and remain) the CEO of your life. Without passion, none of the goal-setting strategies I am going to teach you will work.

> A neurological aside: passion engaged is dopamine released!
>
> Dopamine is the main "feel-good" reward neurotransmitter in our brain. It is positive reinforcement for doing things that benefit us. This positive reinforcement, released in love, success, victory and accomplishment is so powerful that it is also what drives addiction.

Thus, dopamine is not just associated with pleasure but is also the neurotransmitter behind motivation and reward-seeking.

You may have heard about the power of passion through headlines such as *Mother Lifts Car To Save Child* or *Man Survives 6 Days In Desert Without Water By Eating Ants*. For the mother, she was passionate about saving her child; for the man, he was passionate about living. It reminds us of the story in the last chapter in which the boy was able to rip off a tree limb to save his friend drowning in the icy water:

"Two reasons: the boy was able to do it because, first, it had to be done and, second, no one told him he couldn't."

That's the romantic explanation. However, there's actually scientific research that shows how important of a role passion plays in the achievement of your goals. Researchers describe the significance of passion through a formula called: *The Passion Quotient.*

The Passion Quotient formula comes from a famous *New York Times* and Pulitzer Prize-winning author, Thomas Friedman. According to Friedman, passion and curiosity:

"...are key components for education in a world where information is readily available to everyone and where global markets reward those who have learned how to learn and are self-motivated to learn."

Friedman believes: The Curiosity Quotient plus The Passion Quotient, combined, are greater than The Intelligence Quotient (IQ). He states:

"Give me the kid with a passion to learn and a curiosity to discover and I will take him or her over the less passionate kid with a huge IQ every day of the week."

INTENSE PASSION HELPS ACHIEVE GOALS

"Passion is oxygen of the soul."

~BILL BUTLER, American cinematographer, shot *The Conversation*, *Jaws*, and three *Rocky* sequels

Personally, when I think of passion, I think of watching the late great legend Michael Jackson perform. Jackson's passion oozed from his pores when he was on stage performing. Go to YouTube and search *"Michael Jackson live performances"* and you'll see the insane amount of passion he possessed. Seriously, stop reading now and watch one of Michael's live performances.

You'll instantly notice the passion. You'll also notice how contagious it is (watch the audience's reaction to Jackson). You may even get goosebumps just watching this icon perform (like I do). That level of passion is exactly what it's going to take for you to achieve your goals.

A "Michael Jackson-level" of passion intertwined with extreme feelings and emotion is the fuel that will help you stay on track during the tough times. If you have a burning-hot passion behind your goal, it won't matter when you face rejection because you'll shake it off and try again. **You'll be able to persist and persevere until you prevail.**

You can achieve almost any goal you commit your heart and mind to, and I firmly believe that it's never too late to set your goals toward becoming that person you have always wanted to be. You just have to want it bad enough.

I remember hearing Eric Thomas, author of *The Secret To Success*, describe what it takes to achieve your goals:

"You've got to want to achieve your goal like you want to breathe, like when you're underwater and can't hold your breath anymore. When you can't breathe, there is nothing else you're thinking about – nothing else but breathing."

That's the level of obsession you must have with your goals. When you want to reach your goals as badly as a drowning person wants oxygen, you will do whatever it takes to achieve them, no matter what.

Now, if you already have those kinds of goals, the ones you *have* to accomplish, not just *want* to accomplish, then you're already substantially ahead of the people who "kind of, sort of" want to succeed. "Kind of, sort of" is not passion. "Must have, will have" is passion. That's why individuals who most consider to be extraordinary have a white-hot desire for their goals and are willing to do whatever it takes to make things happen.

FALL IN LOVE WITH YOUR GOALS

> "We are most alive when we're in love."
>
> ~JOHN UPDIKE, American novelist, poet, short-story writer, art and literary critic

As much as I made a distinction between your vision and your goals, there should be no difference in the passion you bring to each. You should feel as passionate about your goals as you did the first time you fell in love. Remember that lovey-dovey obsession where you could not get your mind to think about anything else but that one person?

It's not just that you couldn't get your mind to think of something else – you didn't *want* to think of anything else. This is the same kind of obsession you should feel when thinking about your goals. If your goals make you feel that way, I'm confident you will achieve them.

WARNING: Do not have so much passion that you let the end (your vision) justify the means (your goals). Two of the five flaws that I identified in Chapter One and revisit in Chapter Three apply to this caveat: I took any advice that would be self-serving, no matter how suspect; and I made exceptions in life-values when it suited me.

Never forget: **your values should always dictate your goals; your goals should never dictate your values.**

With that said, deciding upon which goals you should pursue toward your vision is not a matter to be taken lightly. That is why you must make your decisions carefully, and the *Be, Have, Do* exercise will help you do precisely that. We're going to go through this simple exercise right now, so turn to page 548. You'll see ***Be, Have, Do*** at the top.

The *BE*:

On the first page under the subtitle, *What type of person do you want to be?,* I want you and your pen to go no-holds-barred. Write down, in as much detail as possible, the type of person you want to be. This can be about your personality traits, your physical appearance, your relationship with others, whatever type of person your heart desires. Do you want to be a great mother or father? Do you want to be better educated on subjects that you're passionate about? If so, write it down. If you have writer's block, think about how you would want someone to describe you. Write all those things down now, please.

The *HAVE*:

After you complete the *BE* part of this equation, move on to the next section under the subtitle, *What do you want to have?* Once again, don't hold back. Do not limit yourself. Go no-holds-barred again and think about all the things you want to have in life. Don't be shy about it. If there were no limits to what you could have in your possession, what would you want?

Would you want a diamond bezel Rolex? What about your own private island? Perhaps a Lamborghini? A luxurious mansion? Do you want to live in a home so large that it requires an intercom to tell the family dinner is ready? Do you see yourself owning a yacht with your name etched on the side of it? How about cutting the ribbon on that charitable foundation building wing you donated?

Whatever you can think of, write it down now in the *HAVE* section. Again, this is not the time to hold anything back. Completely deconstruct your idea of what "impossible" means; **if someone else has done it, you can too.**

The *DO*:

No doubt you have noticed some similarities here between *vision* (Chapter One) and *goals* (Chapter Two), but it's the DO exercise that bridges the gap between them.

Now, with the *BE* and *HAVE* sections filled out, you should be getting inspired by all the possibilities life has in store for you and be anxious to complete the final part of this exercise: the *DO* section. Think about all the things you want to do in your life. Where do you want to go? What do you want to see? Do not focus on your current circumstances. Do not focus on restrictions.

If you've always wanted to backpack through Europe, write that down under the subtitle, *What do you want to do?* If you want to get married and have nine kids, write that down, although *Eight is Enough*. If you want to start your own business, write it down. If you want to write a book, write it down. Writing an entire book can start with writing down "Write a book." That's what I did!

I dare you to come up with 25 things you want to do. The key here is to allow your mind to think and dream big. That's why I keep reminding you to ignore limitations: think about the infinite possibilities the universe has made available to you.

Take a few minutes now and write down everything you want

to do. Let me know how serious you are about living a full life by committing it to paper.

Did you stop and do the exercise? I really hope you did, because it's phenomenal what takes place when you write out what you want. I can't explain exactly what happens that helps bring you closer to your dream life. But what I can explain with complete conviction is this: if you're serious about success, if you're serious about providing for the people you love, then you will do the exercise. The individuals who do this exercise will have a far better chance at success than the ones who skip this short task. Do the exercise and I promise your future self will thank you.

You may recall what I said in the previous chapter: imagining yourself doing exercises uses the same brain cells as actually doing them. Your brain cannot help but imagine you achieving what you just wrote down when you commit your intentions to paper. This simple procedure of committing your ideas to paper sparkes the imagination process that's vital to help your brain begin setting in motion what is necessary for you to achieve what you have just written down.

The beauty of what you wrote is that everything on your lists is possible. The only question that remains is this: how much effort are you willing to put in?

Now go back and examine your lists. Which goals did you write down that would really bring happiness and a sense of accomplishment after you achieve them? I want you to select one specific goal that you wrote down. Your biggest dopamine-magnet. Choose something you can visualize yourself achieving; something that you're exponentially passionate about.

The key here is that you are selecting one goal and one goal only. This is because you're more likely to achieve a single goal with an all-out effort directed toward that one goal than ten separate goals with your effort spread thin.

One goal: one vector force; too many goals: shimmying.

Go to the back of the book where you just wrote everything down and circle that one goal that would really set your heart on fire when you achieve it. Later in this chapter, we'll get into the planning phase of goal-setting. For now, I just want you to circle that one specific goal so your subconscious can begin working on it.

THE HARVARD TEST

"Strong reasons make strong actions."

~SHAKESPEARE, English poet, playwright, and actor

Harvard Business School professor Rosabeth Moss Kanter suggests that you test yourself to see if you're genuinely committed to reaching your goals, simply by seeing if you can answer "yes" to the following questions. Even though the questions refer to multiple goals, each crucial to achieving your ultimate vision, answer all these questions in the context of the single goal that you just circled:

- Do you feel strongly about the importance of your goals?
- Do you have a burning desire to achieve your goals?
- Do your goals match your values and beliefs?
- Are your goals something you continuously dream about?
- Do your goals get you excited when you think of them and when you share them with others?
- Are your goals realistic – in other words, are you sincerely convinced your goals will be achieved?
- Are your goals vital to the future of the people you care about?
- Are you committed to the long-term as you work toward your goals?

- Are you willing to put your credibility on the line for your goals?
- Can you make your goals the primary focus of your activities?
- Are you willing to devote your personal time, evenings, weekends, and vacations to bring your goals to reality?
- Will you be able to fight through rejection, criticism, and negativity when advancing toward your goals?

If you were able to answer "yes" to these questions, the likelihood of seeing the goal you circled come to pass is virtually guaranteed. See it as another rung ascended on your vision ladder. But you must sincerely believe in the yes answers and allow your beliefs along with your actions to synchronize. Simply saying yes for the sake of yes is kind of like the flawed technique of a salesman getting his prospect to say yes three times then asking for the sale. **Yes is useless without how**. And the how manifests itself when you truly and genuinely believe you can and will do whatever it takes to accomplish what you set your mind and heart to achieve.

WRITE DOWN WHAT YOU ARE COMMITTED TO

> "Until you commit your goals to paper you have intentions that are seeds without soil."
>
> ~ZIG ZIGLAR, American author, salesman, and motivational speaker

Now that you know exactly what your primary goal is – and hopefully you have already committed it to paper – you are on the right path. In case you skipped over the *Be, Have, Do* exercise (that was my way of seducing you into committing your goals to paper), I want to attempt to sell you again on the importance of writing down your goals.

This is not to lecture those who skipped the exercise (you know who you are!). Rather, it's to emphasize that as long as your goals are merely hanging out in your head, you cannot even call them goals. At best, you can only call them ideas. I really want to drive home the point that when you write down your goals, you transform them from a thought – to something physical...to something real. From pie-in-the-sky to concrete.

The simple act of writing your goals creates a link between you and your goals, and it helps keep you loyal to what you say you're going to do. Writing down an idea to make it stand out as real invokes electrical signals from a different part of your brain, so when your goals are put in writing, they become ingrained in your mind. On top of that, studies have consistently shown that written goals strengthen your resolve to achieve them. Writing down your goals acts as an internal contract that you have signed with yourself. **If your vision is your quest, your goals become its manifesto.**

Too many people nod their heads, merely humoring the importance of writing down their goals but never actually do it. Therefore, let me share a quick study with you to reinforce my airtight argument about the significance of committing your goals to paper (or digital paper, i.e., the notes section of your phone or computer).

Psychology professor Dr. Gail Matthews of Dominican University divided 267 people into two groups: those who regularly wrote out their goals and those who didn't. These were men and women of different occupations, living in different parts of the world.

The result of the study? The people who wrote down their goals were 42 percent more likely to achieve them. The research revealed that this happens because writing accelerates your brain's "encoding" process, which is responsible for taking in new information and storing it into long-term memory. As the written material is in your own words, you're recreating the image of the goal in sync with your mind as you write it down. Creating something in your "own image and likeness" is indeed divine!

Don't be misled to think this is make-a-wish mentality: write down stuff and good things will happen. Writing down your goals is much more than simply making a to-do list for yourself. It's not merely writing down random items on a piece of paper or on an online document. No, this "list" of goals, as I stated previously, is a contract, and that is a crucial key to its success. It is affirmation in a support group of one.

When you write your goals down and design intelligent plans to achieve them you are mapping out your manifesto. You are providing your dream with direction. And when you write out these goals along with plans to achieve them – you are giving yourself an opportunity to pivot when the obstacles come.

As another pertinent example to the benefits of committing your goals to paper, let's look at the world of orthopedic medicine to present scientific evidence that expands on the benefits of writing down your goals. This study demonstrates how written goals expedited the recovery process for patients who had undergone hip or knee replacement surgery.

> In a 1992 Scottish study on the rehabilitation of joint replacement (hip and knee), patients were all given a booklet that detailed their rehab schedule. But here's the twist: in the back of each booklet were 13 additional pages – one for each week of rehab – with blank spaces and instructions. The scientist conducting the study wrote the following in the back of each booklet:
>
> > *My goals for this week are ________? Write down exactly what you are going to do. For example, if you are going to go for a walk this week, write down where and when you are going for a walk.*

Researchers conducting the study discovered some patients chose to use the blank pages in the back of their booklet to write out goals, while others chose not to:

1. Some patients wrote down specific goals (e.g. "I will walk to the bus stop by Thursday to meet my wife from work"), and
2. Some patients chose not to write out their goals.

The results were astonishing. The patients who wrote specific goals in their booklets began walking in half the time it took those who didn't, and they were getting into or rising out of chairs three times faster. In general, they were performing all of their activities of daily living significantly sooner after their surgeries.

You have to understand that recovery from this type of surgery is excruciating. These operations involve sawing through bones and cutting through muscles. It takes effort, will power, and motivation to recover from such an arduous medical procedure. For all patients, the surgeries were the same and, except for the written-down goals, the rehab was the same. In essence, it was the same pain for both groups, yet the patients who wrote their daily goals out on paper did considerably better. Why?

When you write down your goals, it signals something pertinent to your subconscious mind that can partner with your conscious mind. Call it a *meeting of the minds* if you will. You're using several parts of your brain toward your goals that reinforce your will – and your *ability* – to succeed. No longer are the hopes for accomplishing your goals vague. They're standing out for your memory consolidation, your subconscious, and your executive decision-making brain, and they even help regulate which neurons will fire when you begin to take action and pursue your goals. The hammer's been cocked, so to speak.

An infectious aside:

The analogy to a vaccine (to stay in the clinical realm for the moment) is apt here. A vaccine delivers molecules similar to sickness-causing germs so that when the virus invades your body, your immune system has already been "locked and loaded" to quash the invader. Similarly, when goals are written and the other parts of your mind are on "standby," ready for action, the action proceeds more quickly, efficiently, and – here's the payoff – happens at all!

That meeting of the minds goes from idea to committee to a movement to a whole revolution. And when you do the exercise of circling that one special goal – call it "your primary goal" – your subconscious understands that out of all the ideas you have, this one is different because it qualifies as a bullet point; this one means it's go-time. Once your subconscious embraces your goal, it will pull you toward your goal just like gravity pulls us down to the earth. Written goals, thus, ground you to your vision.

A narrative psychology aside:

Dr. James Pennebaker has spent a career researching the impact of journaling and found it to be incredibly valuable, especially in healing. Numerous studies such as *Writing to Heal: A Guided Journal for Recovering from Trauma and Emotional Upheaval* have shown when people write about their stressful experiences they improve immune function and heal quicker than those who don't journal.

Scientific research has proven there's a huge difference between just thinking about something and writing about it. The writing becomes an embodiment of the idea. There is evidence that beyond the actual embodiment involved in the physical act of writing, the consideration of key life and health issues leads to a re-evaluation of them and how they are perceived, often creating a more positive narrative.

Summarizing the findings of Pennebaker and Seagal in a 1999 research paper:

> *"Writing about important personal experiences in an emotional way for as little as 15 minutes over the course of three days brings about improvements in mental and physical health. This finding has been replicated across age, gender, culture, social class, and personality type."*

SIMPLIFY YOUR PRIMARY GOAL

"Simplicity is the ultimate sophistication."

~LEONARDO DA VINCI, World-renowned artist

You should be able to sum up your primary goal in a single sentence. Sure, there will be smaller goals along with this primary goal, but the primary one – even though overarching – should be simple and straightforward. (*Simple to do…*) A single sentence is easy to remember, and it allows you to get crystal clear on what your goal is without having to ramble.

Here's an example: *"I am going to easily make $13,750 in passive monthly income through my online business by March 9th of next year."* Notice how specific the goal is? You have to make it specific because our minds can't process general wishy-washy things, and neither can the Universe. (Remember from Chapter One, *the* universe is the one you construct.)

It's beneficial to write down your primary goal on a piece of paper that fits into your wallet so you can look at it and read it several times throughout the day. When you're stopped at a street light, waiting in a line, or have some spare time, take out your goal and read it out loud. The more you engrave this goal into your mind, the better.

Sounds easy enough, right? Of course it does. But sadly, most people do not and will not write their goals down. Personal development legend Jim Rohn said that the things in life that are easy to do are also easy *not to do*. So don't allow yourself to skip the crucial step of writing down your goals and keeping them on you at all times.

Writing down a goal brings it to life. After you have clearly defined your goal and written it down, the way you experience the world and easily attract people, ideas, and opportunities into your life is profound. It will seem as if everything you need to achieve your goals is suddenly materializing before you.

"So let it be written, so let it be done."

~MOSES

I don't claim to know the exact ins and outs of everything that takes place when you commit your goals to paper, but what I do know is that it is part of an intricate set of laws that govern what takes place in your universe. Once your goal is decided upon and written down, the probability of it becoming a reality substantially increases because it becomes a part of your universe, and your universe is *the* universe as you construct and create it.

YOU SEE WHAT YOU SEEK

> "Speak what you seek until you see what you said."
>
> ~MARSHAWN EVANS DANIELS, TV personality, creator of the Godfidence movement and founder of SHE Profits

Have you ever noticed when you start thinking about something new, something different than what you usually think about, you begin seeing that new thing everywhere you go? A common example of this is when you purchase a new car and now it appears as if there is a sudden influx of that car in your town. It's almost like everyone has one.

Well, it wasn't that everyone went out and bought the same car as you, on the same day as you. Instead, those cars were there all along. You weren't able to see them before because your mind wasn't actively seeking them. Before you made the decision to purchase this new car, your brain had been filtering any thoughts of similar vehicles out of your conscious mind because it was unnecessary information – irrelevant.

Our brains naturally do this because we are bombarded with millions of sensory bytes of information every day (visual, audio, physical, etc.). To keep ourselves from going insane, we ignore 99.9 percent of the information that is sent our way. Through all the "noise," we only see, hear, or experience the things that we choose to think about constantly.

Whatever you are thinking about most is what you're going to start seeing in your physical world. Something that may have been in the 99.99 percent of the things you previously ignored will now move over to the 0.01 percent of things you see, merely because you consciously chose to focus your attention on it.

I had a client who once told me now when he goes to the mall, he sees baby strollers everywhere. These baby strollers did not suddenly appear. They were there all along. What changed was the fact that my client had recently had a baby.

This phenomenon is similar to what will happen when you decide on your goal and the plan you will implement to accomplish it. Once you write down your goal and create an outline for achieving your goal, you will see the things and the people who are going to help you reach your goal.

This is precisely how the *Law of Attraction* works. This law is not some mysterious, esoteric voodoo concept that people make it out to be when it is explained, typically, incorrectly. Much like the *Law of Gravity*, the Law of Attraction is quite practical and straightforward, and its correct explanation makes sense (in fact, more sense than the Law of Gravity, which really has never been fully explained).

The Law of Attraction works because our brain is constantly trying to align what we perceive in our outer world with the things we see and experience in our inner world. So when you instruct your brain to look for the things you want, you'll not only be attracted to them, but begin *to attract* them, and in turn, you will *see* them. The most amazing thing you're going to experience is realizing that the thing, person, or opportunity, has been in plain sight all along. It's like you finally tuned in to the right wavelength.

That's why the Law of Attraction can make things appear as if you're miraculously drawing something into your life by simply thinking about it. In reality, you are now just seeing what was already there. You are truly "attracting" it into your life. It was only accessible once you focused your thoughts and your mind on it, and now you can see it. That, in essence, is how the Law of Attraction works.

When you focus on something new, it is almost as though you're giving your mind a new pair of eyes with which to see the world. These new eyes are able to detect the right people, situations, conversations, ideas, resources, and opportunities at your disposal. With this new perspective, your mind is better equipped to match up the outside world with what you want most on the inside: your goals. It's really that simple.

THE EYES LOOK, BUT THE BRAIN SEES

"I have three eyes. Two to look, one to see."

~BELLAMOR

When it comes to attracting what we want into our lives, there's actually a lot more at work than just the Law of Attraction. There's a network of neurons located at the base of our brains that regulate and dictate what our eyes are allowed to see. This part of our brain is known as our *reticular activating system* (RAS), and its function is to only allow us to see the things we agree with. The RAS connects the spinal cord, brainstem, cerebral hemispheres, and the cerebellum, and it allows us to navigate our universe as our brain sees *the* Universe. In other words, it determines our consciousness and how we relate to what our consciousness calls our universe: a universe filtered by the fine-mesh screen of expectation (and bias) that has built up in each of us. This is why the confirmation bias exists.

> **"The eye sees only what the mind is prepared to comprehend."**
> ~ROBERTSON DAVIES

The confirmation bias is our brains' tendency to cherry-pick information that confirms (and conforms to) our current beliefs. Confirmation bias explains why two people with opposite views on a subject can see the same evidence and come away with different opinions. This happens because our RAS interprets *what* we see and *how* we see it. Our RAS creates the definitions by which we live our lives.

> This is why, for example, the abortion controversy will never be actually settled – legally, politically, or ethically. The different factions – whether they fall into pro-life or pro-choice groups – use different definitions. One says life begins at conception; another at implantation; another at closure of the neural tube; yet another at the presence of a heartbeat; and beyond. Who's right? Each knows they are right, right?

Different definitions (starkly different) are what actually define the disagreeing groups. Guess who programs the definitions, the system in your brain that dictates what you're allowed to see? You do. You program your RAS. You tell your RAS what is important and what is not important. Therefore, it blocks the unimportant things out of sight.

When you picked up this book, if you said to yourself, "Another guru trying to tell me how to live my life – I doubt any of his strategies will work," it's unlikely you will learn much from the content I spent decades assembling for you. However, I'm hoping you picked up this book and said, "Holy cow, this guy has been through hell and back and somehow made it to the top – I bet he can teach me a lot about success." With this mindset (and highlighter in hand), your RAS will go into overdrive searching for ideas in this content to help you live your dream life. In other words, just the way you reacted when you picked up this book would have determined whether I was to be part of your universe or not. But, of course, here you are, so...well done!

Think about people who say there's just not enough time in the day. These people are always running late because their RAS confirms their belief. The same goes for people who say if it weren't for bad luck, they'd have no luck at all. Their RAS goes to work, finding all the ways they can be unlucky.

Have you ever met someone who says all the good men/women are taken? Well, their RAS makes certain they are right. As they go through each day, their reticular activating system is pointing out every single piece of evidence that confirms their negative belief that their chances to find that "special someone" has come and gone. Each person with whom they cross paths has at least one thing about them that qualifies for a line-item veto. This is why many people need to get busy reprogramming their RASs. Because if they don't, they are going to go through life without ever finding happiness. Nothing they encounter will ever meet their definition of happiness.

One of my favorite quotes comes from Bob Marley, "Some people feel the rain. Others just get wet." I love this quote because it reminds me that life is an interpretation. Reality is an interpretation. Your universe – the vibrations, photons, etc. – is constructed by the three pounds of brain contained in your skull. The way we act when we fail is an interpretation of the setback – which can be either positive or negative. If we perceive something to be life-altering – in either a good way or a bad way – guess what happens? We allow it to alter our lives in either a good or bad way.

If your life alterations are unfavorable, you more than likely programmed your RAS unconsciously to see them that way. You allowed false beliefs to infiltrate your mind without even realizing the damage that you were doing. So how do you fix it? How do you reprogram your RAS? How do you train your RAS to avoid the "dark side" of the force? It's actually quite simple.

Based on research, the more you visualize what you want, the more you reprogram your brain through your RAS to seek out what you want instead of constantly replaying over in your mind what you don't want. You change the network of neurons that act as a filter. The more you believe in yourself, the more you start visualizing yourself being on time, getting lucky breaks, and finding true love – the more your RAS will go to work in your favor confirming these new beliefs. And this also applies to getting something positive from a mistake.

> **"Men are developed the same way gold is mined. Several tons of dirt must be moved to get an ounce of gold. But you don't go into the mine looking for dirt. You go in looking for gold."**
>
> ~ANDREW CARNEGIE

This is why the adage of "you get what you focus on" has tremendous wisdom behind it. What you focus on is extremely powerful in life. It can actually become your entire universe, so what you focus on can be the difference in achieving your goals or not achieving them. It all really comes down to the interpretations and perceptions you decide to give your life.

Fortunately, you do not have to fall victim to a faulty RAS. The good news is that you can completely reprogram and train your brain to adjust what it filters and blocks out. And the most effective way for you to rewire your RAS is through the practice of visualization.

A neurological aside:

Neuroplasticity is the concept that we can change our brains – that the structure is "*plastic*", that is, malleable and able to be changed. Less than just one generation ago doctors-in-training were taught that the brain was "*static*"; that it couldn't be changed; that if a part of the nervous system died or was impaired, this was a permanent situation.

Today we know different. The concept of neuroplasticity has allowed those with strokes to regain the use of a limb by rerouting the brain circuits for this movement. How? By thinking. Like the motor circuitry that controls muscle movement, your RAS is also made up of neurons and they, too, can be rerouted to give you a different mind's eye on your universe.

Visualize things differently and they soon become different for your universe. And the more you do; the more your new, tailor-made RAS will "set".

In 1949, neuropsychologist Donald Hebb introduced his oft-cited maxim, *"Neurons that fire together, wire together,"* and thus ignited the then-radical but now well-established concept of neuroplasticity.

As you read this very sentence, you are creating new synapses between/among neurons in your brain. Read it again and the same synapses fire, which strengthens this bond, making them "stick" together more firmly. Next, recall the sentence out loud and/or write it down, and it's likely to make it to long-term memory tonight while you sleep, saved from the trash heap of worthless minutia on which your hippocampus has passed judgment and discarded.

It's not, "*You are what you eat,*" but, "*You are what you keep.*"

Keeping your RAS set properly will allow you to bring your goals to fruition. And incorporating visualization regularly into your daily life will help keep your RAS focused on the opportunities and people who will assist you along your journey.

The more you visualize becoming the CEO of your life, the more you rewire your RAS. Five minutes a day of visualization, consistently repeated over time, will allow you to completely change your previous false beliefs and create the successful lifestyle you've always dreamed of.

When you visualize yourself achieving your goals, don't just focus on the end result. Focus on everything that comes with it: the new beliefs you want to install, the feel-good emotions that come with achieving the goal, the actions that you will take every day toward achieving the goals to your ultimate vision, and the steps you will take when obstacles come your way. This is called "mindfulness", an existential form of paying attention. The more of your vision that you picture and see in your mind, the more it will become part of your universe.

Why does visualization work so well in reprograming your RAS, you may ask? It's because your brain cannot tell the difference between something that you have vividly imagined happening in your mind, and something that actually happened to you in real life. Remember in the previous chapter how I explained that an athlete who envisions doing their exercises uses the same neurons as when he/she actually does them? With each successive visualization, you are slowly re-firing – and thus rewiring – your RAS to become a machine that focuses on anything and everything it's going to take for you to achieve your goals.

Mental rehearsals, take four!

THE "F" EXERCISE AND SMOKE RINGS

> "Sometimes what you want is right in front of you. All you have to do is open your eyes and see it."
>
> ~MEG CABOT, American author

Often I do the "F" Exercise during my speaking engagements and most people are shocked at the outcome. This short exercise will help you understand how the things we need in order to achieve our goals are often directly in front of us. Unfortunately, our mind is just not open to seeing them.

Let's see if this simple exercise helps open your mind to all the possibilities the world has to offer you. This will be a real eye-opener.

Read the following sentence below and count how many times you see the letter "*F*." Cover the rest of the page below or beside the sentence and do not peek. Otherwise, you will ruin the experience and insight this exercise provides.

FINISHED FILES ARE THE RE
SULT OF YEARS OF SCIENTI
FIC STUDY COMBINED WITH
THE EXPERIENCE OF YEARS

How many "*F*s" did you count? If you counted three, you would be in the company of most people who read that sentence. And like most people who read this sentence, you would be wrong. The correct answer is six. Go back up and read it again. See if you can find all six.

Many people don't find all six because they don't count the letter "*F*" in the word "*of*." This happens because our brain has the ability to go on autopilot and skip right over things it doesn't consider to be of great importance. It can easily skip over words like "*a*", "*to*", and "*of*". Alternatively, our brains can insert a word when it's missing in a sentence. (Alternatively, our brains can *insrt* a *lettr* when it's *missng* in a word.")

At the 1964-1965 New York World's Fair, the General Cigar exhibit handed out buttons that touted its attraction: an outdoor fountain that blew rings of mist into the air as if they were smoke rings. It's unknown whether this was a proofreading mistake in manufacturing or a brilliant marketing hook, but without exception, everyone who read the button out loud said, "Meet me at the smoke ring," when it was actually, "Meet me at *the* ***the*** smoke ring."

It's indeed a little unnerving to think about how many things we may skip over in life because our brain has decided they aren't all that important. The good news, however, is that you can start to actively direct what your brain allows you to "see" by giving it the right instructions and directions. With all this refiring and rewiring of brain cells and neuronal networks, your RAS will have no choice but to change its filtration process.

Reprogramming your brain and teaching it what it needs to be on the lookout for is precisely why it's so important that you write down your goals and the steps required to achieve them. These steps are short-term goals that make up your overall plan. They will carry you toward the achievement of your primary goal and ultimately your vision. There is a lot of talk in this chapter about steps and breaking down your goals. But for now, I just want you to understand that if you're truly serious about reaching your goals you will write them down and create a step-by-step action plan for achieving them.

This step-by-step plan is crucial because goals without plans are worthless wishes. Therefore, a plan to reach your goals is key because it helps keep you focused when self-doubt creeps into your mind and you start to lose hope of accomplishing them. The plan reinforces your belief that achieving your goal is yours for the taking. It also gives you direction, and progression is what will get one goal realized, then the next, and so on. Additionally, as stated before, writing your goals down ignites new electrical signals from a different part of your brain, so when your goals are put into writing, they become fixed in your mind. This helps program your reticular activating system to open up new opportunities for you to achieve your goals.

DON'T BE A CIRCLE-WALKER

> "Direction is more important than speed. Many people are going nowhere fast."
>
> ~UNKNOWN

Dr. Jan Souman from The Max Planck Institute for Biological Cybernetics conducted an interesting study to examine what happens to people when they're left in an unknown location without a map, light, a compass, or any way to determine landmarks.

Study participants were placed in random locations in the Sahara Desert and in a German forest. They were instructed to find their way out. Scientists discovered that as soon as people could no longer determine what a straight line was, they began to walk in circles.

The participants sometimes veered a little to the left or a little to the right, but ultimately ended up walking in circles, and relatively small ones at that. The participants assumed they were heading in a particular direction, but without the assistance of a positioning device or a fixed point, they were hopelessly lost.

"The results from these experiments show that even though people may be convinced that they are walking in a straight line, their perception is not always reliable," said Dr. Souman. She recommends we avoid trusting our senses because we can trick ourselves into thinking we are walking in a straight line when the exact opposite is true.

What is the main takeaway from Dr. Souman's study? People without written goals and a written plan for reaching them are no different from the circle-walkers. You may think you're headed in the direction of your destination, but without having a map or plan to determine whether you're on the right path or not, it is impossible to know where you are going.

The process of reaching your goals is similar to using a GPS (global positioning satellite) device to get to your destination. If the GPS knows where you are and where you want to go, it can create a route to help you get there.

Let's say you and I are going to make a bet. We're going to bet on who of two subjects will reach their destination (goal) first. Let's raise the stakes on this bet; let's make it life or death.

Person A will get a physical address (a goal) and we'll tell them to get to that address as soon as possible. Person B will also get a physical address, but we're going to give them a GPS to lock in the address (the goal). Now, you and I are going to bet who's going to get to the goal first. Who are you going to bet your life on? The answer is simple: the person who has the GPS. This is why goals and the plans that accompany them are so important because they give us direction.

Similarly, if your mind and subconscious know where you want to go and how you want to get there, they will work in unison. The only difference between you and a GPS is that you get to create your own turn-by-turn directions. You get to map out the steps to reach your goal. And just like a GPS, you can reroute around obstacles, slow traffic, and road work because having your goal planted firmly in your mind will help render a satellite view toward it.

Former General Electric CEO Jack Welch gives some guidance about how to map out your plan:

> *"Strategy is first trying to understand where you fit in today's world. Not where you wish you were or where you hoped you would be, but where you are. Then it's trying to understand where you want to be five years out. Finally, it's assessing the realistic chances of getting from here to there."*

While this quote, on first reading, seems to slightly conflict with what I'm teaching (i.e., that even the impossible is achievable when you envision it), it perfectly aligns with what I've been talking about so far. Here's the message in the bottle: a lot of people aren't honest with themselves about where they are now, and then they try to map out a plan without a valid starting point. So besides having a vision and goals toward that vision, you must have a reliable starting point because a reliable starting point is a valid point of reference that allows you to embark on your journey unambiguously. Any GPS device requires not only a destination, but a viable starting point, and the road toward your vision is no exception.

The beautiful thing about assessing your chances of seeing your goals come to pass is that the more detailed your plan is, the more your mind will believe in it. If Jack Welch's caution against "realistic chances" seems to inhibit your vision, then ensure that your starting point is valid and use your GPS-like abilities to reroute around the obstacles, traffic, and road work. You can employ your newly reprogrammed RAS to help execute your plan.

This is really the missing link between people who have goals and don't achieve them and the people who have goals and crush them: the ones who win have a plan – a smart GPS route from a valid (i.e., honest and realistic) starting point. And it's a detailed plan with the goals written down, contractually obligating them within themselves, which is powerful enough to positively impact even the excruciating rehabilitation of post-op joint replacement patients!

The same goes for "rehab for your life." There is no difference. The ones who lose don't have a plan, or if they do, it is incomplete and lacking the details needed to achieve their goals. And while it's not imperative (but it is desirable) that your vision doesn't seem realistic on the surface, as I explain in the next section, your starting point must be the first step of a thousand that will lead you to your desired destination; then, at that point your goals will align properly.

WHY UNREALISTIC GOALS ARE KEY

> "I don't think anything is unrealistic if you believe you can do it."
>
> ~RICHARD L. EVANS, President of Rotary International, writer, producer, and announcer

Before we jump into breaking down your primary vision into goals, I want to suggest that your vision be something that sounds unreasonable and unrealistic. After all, it's a result of the imagineering I discussed in Chapter One. Your vision should make you stretch past your limits – you know, the very limits many of us self-impose on ourselves.

Why is it so crucial to have an awe-inspiring vision? Because having an enormous vision is an adrenaline booster. It fuels you with the fire and passion required to overcome the inevitable setbacks that accompany any vision and the goals that take you there. And fire and passion makes dopamine, so it feels good, and that's positive reinforcement for our brains.

On the other hand, a "realistic" vision is uninspiring and will only push you through the first few goals and the obstacles that accompany them. Don't forget all that passion we discussed before!

Without the passion that only a mind-blowing vision evokes, you may end up giving up and deciding that your vision is no longer worth your time and effort after only a few setbacks. Many people get caught in this self-sabotaging cycle because they believe if the end result (vision) is mediocre, their effort and action (that is, each interval goal) is mediocre as well.

Think about it. Are you going to really pour it on, are you going to leap out of bed in the morning, are you going to make sacrifices to pay off old credit card debt? Probably not. That's not a very inspiring vision. But what if you searched on the Internet and printed out a picture of a mammoth-sized eleven-bedroom house with an extraordinary view that had a nine-car garage filled with exotic vehicles (again, like children, *Eight is Enough*)? And what if when you looked at that picture, you thought about all the people who doubted you, all the people who didn't believe in you or give you a chance? Would that vision provide the fuel to run through brick walls and do whatever it takes to achieve it? I bet it would.

"Never lower your target; increase your actions."
~GRANT CARDONE

Another reason why you want an unreasonable vision is so you can prove to yourself how great you really are. This allows you to shatter your self-imposed limitations. Everyone has their own four-minute mile – find yours!

It's more rewarding to stretch and fall short of achieving an unrealistic vision than to achieve an easy one. In the former situation, you end up being much further ahead in achievement than the latter. That's why I often say:

The problem with most people's vision is not that it's too significant and they miss it, but it's too insignificant and they achieve it.

I love the way John Maxwell describes our limits in his book, *The*

15 Invaluable Laws of Growth:

> *"A rubber band is of no use unless it's stretched. In turn, neither are we as humans. Stretching makes us stronger and allows us to grow."*

SMALL STEPS TO BIG ACHIEVEMENTS: SMALL GOALS TO YOUR BIG VISION

> "By the yard it's hard, but inch by inch, anything's a cinch."
>
> ~LES BROWN, American motivational speaker, author, former television host

Breaking your vision down into small bites can turn the impossible into the possible. It's similar to the frequently used metaphor about eating an elephant. So how on Earth do you eat a giant five-ton elephant? Answer: one bite at a time. (And maybe a little Tabasco.)

Your vision is likely something that is rather large in scope and will take quite a while to achieve. Therefore, it is wise for you to break it down into a step-by-step blueprint so that you have an action plan for getting there. Your plan might change as you start working toward your vision, but you need a plan to get started, and that's where the goals come in.

Another crucial ingredient to any plan is a deadline. Having an endpoint allows you to reverse engineer your plan and work backwards. If your primary goal takes a year, for example, then create an action plan for the overall year. After that, break the year down on a month-by-month basis. Break down each month on a week-by-week basis. Break down each week on a day-by-day basis. The day-by-day part can be revised each month, which gives you the flexibility to adapt to changing circumstances. That is, rerouting around the obstacles, traffic, and road work.

Once you have created your plan, you'll have a clear, personal map for getting from point A to B to C and so on until you reach your vision. This process is essential because, without it, you will lack direction and lose focus; simply, you won't be able to notice your progress, and that will be demotivating.

If you want to write a book, for example, you might simply write out all the steps that you need to take, and then arrange them in the correct order so that each step is completed at the appropriate time. This planning phase is the difference between you becoming an author, and you simply wishing you were an author. (Remember from Chapter One: the difference between fantasizing and envisioning?) Many times when people say they want to write a book, they quickly retreat when they realize they need to write 200 pages. But if they broke their plan down and realized they only need to write one page a day for six and a half months, they would likely see their vision of becoming an author come true, instead of six and a half months later seeing nothing except unwritten goals toward their unwritten book!

No matter how you break down your ultimate vision, the main point is that you have a series of smaller, manageable goals that you can get started on right away. It's when people don't break down their vision into goals that they get overwhelmed by the complexity and the magnitude of what needs to be completed in order to achieve their vision. Unfortunately, this leads to them giving up and living a life without purpose or meaning.

HOW TO WIN A MARATHON

> "The secret of getting ahead is getting started. The secret of getting started is breaking your complex, overwhelming tasks into small, manageable tasks, and then starting on the first one."
>
> ~MARK TWAIN, American writer, humorist, entrepreneur, publisher, and lecturer

It was 1984. Thousands of marathon runners from around the

world were gathered for the Tokyo International Marathon when an unknown runner came in and stole the show. The Japanese athlete, known as Yamada, easily left behind all the runners in the race and finished the marathon in first place. After the race, Yamada was bombarded with questions by the media about who he was and what strategy he used to win.

"Use wisdom to defeat opponent," was Yamada's puzzling but straightforward answer. No one seemed to understand his response, as it appeared to be more about mental strength and endurance than physical tenacity.

Two years later, everyone was shocked again when Yamada scooped up another international marathon win in Italy. Reporters swarmed Yamada the moment he finished the race, asking Yamada what his secret to success was.

"Use wisdom to defeat opponent," repeated Yamada, echoing his sentiments from his win in Tokyo. Marathon competitors were understandably baffled by this so-called *wisdom* he was touting. It wasn't until a decade later, in his autobiography, that Yamada finally disclosed the mystery behind his answer.

Yamada revealed his initial attempts to win marathons failed because he always became exhausted around the seventh mile. His mind would play over and over again how much farther he needed to run to complete the entire race. This was intimidating, and out of fear, his mind would defeat him. However, in those past attempts, his vision was the *mythical* finish line (one he could not see himself crossing), and this daunting distance made reaching it tentative at best.

Yamada eventually discovered that he was in a self-destructive loop and decided to try something different. His new approach involved traveling the entire marathon route in advance and marking important landmarks along the course until he reached the finish line. Each landmark was considered a goal.

That way, when he ran the race, he would focus on running as fast as he could toward the first goal, and once he got there, he would strive to reach the second goal. With the entire marathon route broken down into several smaller goals, he could easily finish all of them – one at a time – and cross the finish line before anyone else.

With this new strategy of breaking his vision (winning the marathon) down into manageable goals: *Tentative* became *definite*.

Previously in this chapter, I compared goals to rungs on a ladder. In a way, achieving your grand vision is like climbing a ladder. Where you're climbing to may be high – even inconceivably high – dangerously and ridiculously high, but each rung, a firm, sure step at a time, assures your safety. Each rung ascended with a firm footstep that is solid and secure keeps you safely on your way, regardless of the height involved. It's not the ladder that gets you there, just like it's not the vision that gets you to your destination; it's each rung, a solid step at a time, a goal at a time, that gets you there. You can rise to your vision – even one that is inconceivable, dangerous, and ridiculous – with one firmly secured, firmly planted goal at a time.

When it comes to your vision and the goals you need to set on your journey to achieve your vision, the interval goal-setting I recommend models Yamada's strategy.

> **Set your ultimate vision, then break it down into small goals; write down both your vision and your goals, then break your goals down into manageable steps. Now design a detailed plan to achieve your goals. Lastly, take action. It's really just a variation of the *Be, Have, Do* exercise.**

If breaking down a vision into step-by-step goals works for marathon runners that have to perform grueling feats of endurance, it will undoubtedly work for you as well.

ACTION FUELS SUCCESS

> "If you go to work on your goals, your goals will go to work on you. If you go to work on your plan, your plan will go to work on you. Whatever good things we build end up building us."
>
> ~JIM ROHN, American entrepreneur, author and motivational speaker

A goal-setting analogy I often share is that the Space Shuttle takes 80 percent of its rocket fuel to get one inch off the ground, while the remaining 20 percent takes it to the moon and back. That's why it's important to understand that getting started and finding initial traction is always the most difficult part. It's called "escape velocity", and once you get going and start accomplishing tasks that are on your plan, the momentum shifts in your favor and your rate of progress speeds up exponentially.

Progress begets progress.

All of us have the ability to achieve the vision that is in our hearts. But it's our goals and the step-by-step plan that provides the rocket fuel which creates the continued thrust for climbing successfully to our vision. Your plan provides the step-by-step blueprint, but it's the action (the *do* of the *be, have, do*) that gets you to your vision when you're shooting for the moon.

The faster you take action on your short-term goals, the sooner you will see your ultimate vision achieved. As you act to reach each goal, your vision will begin to move toward you. But you must take action! You cannot simply write a plan and leave it there, hoping that it will manifest itself.

Are you an action taker? Do you think you have what it takes to become the CEO of your life? If so, act now instead of waiting. One of the biggest mistakes people commonly make with setting goals is they think the perfect time will arrive for them to get started. But let me make this abundantly clear:

There is no such thing as the perfect time a'comin'. The only perfect time is right now.

I've learned that the sooner you start taking action, the sooner you can make the necessary adjustments. But you cannot make adjustments if you never get started. Waiting for the perfect time or the perfect plan wastes both time and plans, that is, perfection leads to procrastination and is your enemy when it comes to goal-setting.

That's why it's said perfectionists are often the ultimate losers in the game of life because they never start anything and use perfectionism as an excuse for procrastination. The ultimate winners strive for excellence – step-by-step – instead of striving for perfection as a singular target. Like Yamada's mythical finish line before he made his step-by-step strategy, perfection – as your vision – is a myth; ethereal. The finish line can only be earned step-by-step, goal-by-goal.

The metaphor of the Space Shuttle also serves to remind us that perfection is never "in the can" from the beginning, but requires continual mid-course corrections. Expecting to accomplish something without fine-tuning as you go is using perfection as an excuse to never even start. In pursuing your goals, such perfection is not only seductive, but irrelevant; what's relevant is *not* putting off what you know you need to do.

A black hole aside: where physics meets psychology at the law of procrastination.

In physics, graphing something such as gravity will demonstrate that the force of attraction is inversely proportional to the distance between two objects. The farther away an object is from another, the less the gravitational attraction between the two; inversely, the closer, the stronger the force.

Applied to psychology, the farther away you are from a deadline

– your goals – the less pressure there is to begin pursuing them. This also means that the farthest you are from your deadline is the time when your goals are actually the easiest to pursue because you can approach them in a methodical, predictable manner.

Just as fighting gravity becomes more difficult along the rising curve of force as the distance shortens, so, too, is it harder to accomplish your goals if you procrastinate, because the difficulty rises as you get closer to a deadline. When a graph plots a measurement over time, you will see a point, where your goals are plotted, become less likely (harder to accomplish). When they become impossible, you've fallen into the black hole of procrastination.

Parkinson's law states, "work expands so as to fill the time available for its completion." It's important that you create a sense of urgency for the completion of your goals and adhere to the deadline you put in place. Because if you're waiting until you "get around to it" the likelihood of you achieving your goals diminishes with each passing day and the gravitational force of the black hole becomes increasingly powerful.

Never forget: If you don't take action, you automatically fail by default; and taking action is always the easiest way to proceed and then succeed. It's not just a good idea – it's the law!

A WARNING

"Permanence, perseverance, and persistence, in spite of all obstacles, discouragements and impossibilities: it is this that, in all things, distinguishes the strong soul from the weak."

~THOMAS CARLYLE, Scottish philosopher, satirical writer, essayist, translator, historian, and mathematician

Before we continue, I have to warn you about the one thing that causes people with the best of intentions to fail at reaching their vision. Let's say your vision has been decided, your plan has been worked out, and you start attacking that plan step-by-step according to the interval goals you have set. Then, the unthinkable happens: you fail at one of your short-term goals and you are unable to see past it.

The first sign of difficulty is often the point where many people abandon their grand plan and give up. If you are serious about achieving your vision and each goal toward it, you must accept this reality: there are going to be mistakes, failures, and setbacks between the day you wrote down your vision and the day you plan to achieve it.

Seth Godin, a bestselling author and one of the most popular bloggers on the planet, refers to the time gap between when we set out to do something and when we actually begin to see results as "*The Dip*". (He even wrote a book by that name.)

Godin says we must all go through the dip in order to become the best at what we're doing. The good news, however, is that after the dip comes an awesome peak:

> *"The peak is what we must climb if we're ever going to become world-class at our craft."*

According to Godin, the greater the dip, the greater the reward, since a larger dip just makes it more difficult for most people to succeed.

Unfortunately, a lot of us fall into the dip. We struggle to make any real movement or progress toward our goals. I want to make sure you don't become one of those people who wash out in the dip, so let me give you five tips that I discovered that will help take you from the inception stage of your plan and pull you up through the dips that inevitably follow. That way, you can ascend to the achievement stage.

Tip No. 1: Discipline is superior to motivation.

Self-discipline assists you in keeping your progress consistent with your efforts when you don't feel like working toward your goals. If you are serious about achieving your goals, you have to maintain discipline over your thoughts and actions. You are both the boss and the worker. Check yourself daily. Understand that self-discipline is when you tell yourself what to do and you don't talk back.

Tip No. 2: Take 100 percent responsibility for your results.

When your excuses are more numerous than your goals, it will be extremely difficult to succeed. Things like chance, luck, divine intervention, or – as Shakespeare called them, the "slings and arrows of outrageous fortune" – are nothing more than rationalizations for why you're not putting the work in. Whether you achieve each goal or not is 100 percent on you. Take consistent action, and own it completely, and the results will come if you continue to believe in the process.

Tip No. 3: Take care of yourself because you're the only "you" you've got.

Without a proper amount of sleep, you will be fatigued. With less energy, you are likely to make poorer food choices and feel less like exercising. You have to exercise and eat properly in order to get yourself into the best physical and mental shape possible.

Sleep deprivation is the most effective form of torture. Therefore, get seven to eight hours a night of deep sleep so that you show up recharged and ready to conquer the day (notice I did not say seven to eight hours of bedtime, it's crucial to get seven to eight hours of sleep routinely each night). Prepare your meals on Sunday evening so you have food ready for the week ahead. Follow an exercise routine to keep yourself in excellent shape. Make your health a top priority. And don't forget to meditate to help unclutter your mind.

Tip No. 4: Constantly ask yourself, *"Are my daily activities getting me closer to achieving my goals? My vision?"*

Are your daily activities moving you measurably closer toward achieving your vision, and the goals that are on your roadmap? If not, you're wasting your time. Immediately eliminate any activities from your life that are not assisting you in making progress on your plan. If you are dead-serious about accomplishing your goals, your minute-by-minute actions count and will add up to either give you broken dreams or an accomplished vision.

Tip No. 5: Embrace your failures.

Some of the most important lessons in life come from failure. Make sure you examine the root causes of your failures to understand precisely how they happen. Investigate where you slipped, not necessarily where you fell. Understand that successful people see failure as a valuable learning lesson, instead of something defeating and final. If you are someone who finds failure unbearable, begin to restructure your RAS by consciously envisioning positive outcomes from your *learning experiences*.

Don't run away from failure. Failure will give you an opportunity to adapt and restructure your plan. Become the type of person who sees failure as a valuable lesson. Use your missteps to evaluate what you could have done better and what needs to be fixed. Never perceive failure as an indictment of your character. Instead, perceive failure as the midcourse correction that allows you to alter your plan to achieve your goals.

A domestic aside:

I understand that this all reads as a very tidy way to proceed if the only person you have to take care of is yourself, but many of us have a significant other and/or children. You can still implement everything within the pages of this book in the framework of an entire household, but it will require an extra step or two to include the important priorities of others. Extra considerations may make it more difficult, but it's not unreasonably difficult, and it will be a skill you will need outside the home as well – and with less friendly people!

In Chapter Six, I will discuss how you should choose your "right" circle of friends and even how your family should be "all in" for your vision and your goals – that is, unified as a family on the same plan with you. This goes both ways, of course. Everyone has their own "hierarchy of needs" pyramid to climb, and a good provider will make sure everyone is on the right track. Every successful man and woman learns time management, diplomacy, and inclusion in today's competitive world; these skills are no different than what's expected of you in the non-competitive world, i.e., your home. Make the time for others who need you and your time. It pays back in dividends later.

CONCLUSION

> "Small wins are the steady application of a small advantage. Once a small win has become accomplished, forces are set in motion that favor another small win. Small wins fuel transformative changes by leveraging tiny advantages into patterns that convince people that bigger achievements are within reach."
>
> ~CHARLES DUHIGG, Pulitzer-prize winning American journalist and non-fiction author

One of the main reasons why I wanted you to focus – step-by-step – on each goal was so you could make your vision the finish line, the payoff. You will find that such goals, to use a math term, are *recursive*; that is, in achieving each goal – step-by-step – the next goal comes more easily because of the input that the previously achieved goal provides. Then, all you have to do is follow the same formula to achieve any other goal; that is, serially accomplish the remaining goals to achieve your vision.

It's a breeder reactor. Accomplishments accrue; success amasses! Momentum breeds momentum. The finish line, your vision, is no longer a myth. Like Yamada, you are using wisdom to finish your race, and his wisdom was a formula.

Using a formula is one of the main reasons why the people who write books...write many books. It's the same reason why people who become wealthy and lose their money reacquire their wealth. It's just a simple formula you follow over and over again. But the key here is that you must have complete confidence and faith in your formula.

> **"Decide what you want. Write it down. Make a plan. And work on it every single day."**
> ~UNKNOWN

It all comes down to deciding what you want, making a written plan to get there, breaking your plan down into manageable tasks, and then starting. Maybe you think you can't write an entire book, but I bet you can write just one word. So if you can write one word, you probably can write two. After that, I'm sure you can find the confidence to write a sentence. Then, as you already know, a book is just a combination of sentences. It's really that simple. It's just a formula for combining words, sentences, and paragraphs to write a book.

The same goes for money. Maybe you think you can't become a millionaire. But I bet you can find a way to earn one dollar. If you can find a way to earn one dollar, you can probably find a way to earn two. After you earn two dollars, you can find the confidence to earn ten. Now you have a way to go to get to a million, but it's really just a rinse-and-repeat formula. Sure, you'll need to find ways to become more efficient if you're going to complete a book or become a millionaire, but my point is once you break your vision down into manageable steps, maintain focus and discipline, and consistently complete the goals on your plan, you will achieve your vision.

Nothing significant is ever easy; but usually, it's very simple. Remember in Chapter One when I said:

"Two reasons: the boy was able to do it because, first, it had to be done and, second, no one told him he couldn't"?

Simple; not easy.

Remember this?

Every morning when you wake up do two things:

No. 1: Make a list of the things that need to be done that day.
No. 2: Do them.

Again, simple; not easy.

If you were to read nothing else on goal-setting except for the information in this chapter, you would be well on your way to achieving the vision you've set. Really, there is no need to over-complicate this process. You don't need a $5,000 seminar or a complex program to set goals and achieve them. People have been achieving goals for hundreds of years before goal-setting books or gurus ever existed; so don't think that you need anything special.

You now have all of the foundational goal-setting principles in your hands, so all you need to do at this point is to follow the instructions in this chapter and achieve the vision of your dreams. If you create your vision and set your goals, your vision will be waiting for you. As you make your way stepwise, conquering each goal, your vision will be calling you louder and louder. Even from the beginning, if you have a plan you should be able to hear it in the distance. Listen up, because it's "personal and confidential" and meant only for you.

EXERCISE NO. 1: WRITE DOWN YOUR TOP 5 ACCOMPLISHMENTS

Write down the top five things you've completed in your life that you are most proud of. It could be graduating high school or completing a college degree. It could be honorably serving in the military or raising your children to be assets to society. Whatever they are, write them down.

This is so important because successful people invest more time reflecting on what they've already accomplished, rather than on what they need to achieve. This gives them a boost of confidence that helps them believe in themselves and their ability to achieve any goals they set in the future.

My Top 5 Accomplishments Are:

1. ______________________________

2. ______________________________

3. ______________________________

4. ______________________________

5. ______________________________

Do you want to take documenting your achievements to the next level? Write a letter to yourself telling yourself how proud you are of your accomplishments. Call it a brag sheet. Then, when you find yourself going through a challenge in life, pull out your brag sheet and read it. This will give you encouragement and help you persist until you prevail.

EXERCISE NO. 2: WRITE DOWN 3 OF THE GOALS THAT WILL MOVE YOU CLOSER TO YOUR VISION

With your three primary goals written down and a plan in place to take action on them, you have everything you need to get started on achieving your ultimate vision. However, here are a few creative ideas I'd like to encourage you to consider including in your plan:

- The obstacles that you will face (internal and external) and how you plan to overcome them
- Educational resources (seminars, books, websites, mentors/coaches, etc.)
- New habits and behaviors that you need to start
- Existing habits and behaviors that you need to stop doing altogether
- Existing habits and behaviors you want to do more of (or less of)
- How you plan to put your new habits in place while eliminating the old ones

In Chapter Five, I will go into extensive detail about how to ingrain new habits into your daily routine. For now, just recognize which habits need to be eliminated and which ones you believe you need to develop to achieve your goals.

EXERCISE NO. 3: CREATE A BATTLE BOARD

It's said that nobody plans to fail. They just fail to plan. Creating a battle board (different than a vision board) will assist you in mapping out your overall plan to achieve your goals and ultimately your vision. How is a battle board different from a vision board? Your battle board is your plan written out.

You can use a whiteboard or simple free software on the Internet that emulates this mind-mapping strategy. You could tape roll out paper on your wall. The key is just to write out in as much detail as possible your plan of attack. Whiteboarding my ideas out is without question one of my secrets to success.

High-performance coach Brendon Burchard states:

> *"I really believe that if you're going to do any major projects in your life or if you're trying to achieve your dreams, you need one of these Battle Boards."*

The first time I created a battle board was in 2006. Guess what happened in 2007? I made my first million. Clearly outlining the activities that illustrate your battle plan is key because a visual representation of your plan will help keep you focused. The repetition of constantly examining your battle board will reprogram your brain and allow your subconscious to work on your plan without you even realizing it. You'll be in the shower and a brilliant idea will pop in your head because your subconscious has been working on it in the background of your mind.

There are entire war rooms in the military dedicated to the process of mapping out there battle plans utilizing battle boards. If the armed forces believes this is the best strategy to achieve their goals (win a war) then it would be wise for you to model their method and win the fight to achieve the goals that lead you to your ultimate vision.

EXERCISE NO. 4: REVIEW YOUR PROGRESS MADE TOWARD YOUR VISION ONCE PER WEEK

At least once a week, refine the initial plan (your battle board) you had written down for your vision – goal-by-goal. Perhaps there are some new things that you need to start doing or some old things that you should stop doing. Remember to make the best use of the obstacles you may have encountered. Maybe there are some adjustments you will have to make with your plan now that you have access to new information. Use the GPS of your new RAS to reroute around the setbacks, traffic, and roadwork.

Setting a time in your phone's calendar (or any time management tool) for regular weekly meetings with yourself where you can sit down for a few minutes and see the progress that you are making is crucial to ensure that you stay on track. You can note the things that went right, the things that went wrong, and what adjustments you plan to implement for the coming week ahead. Although your vision stays the same, the plan of sequential goals may change each week as you pass them in review.

EXERCISE NO. 5. SHARE YOUR GOALS WITH SOMEONE YOU TRUST

A study by The American Society of Training and Development (ASTD) revealed that you are 65 percent more likely to achieve a goal if you share it with someone you trust. The study further shows that your chances of succeeding go up by nearly 95 percent if you have specific accountability meetups with the person with whom you shared your goal.

Now, this is your big step to committing to your success: by sharing your goal and your "why" with someone you trust and having regular accountability meetings with them. It can be your significant other, a trusted friend, or even a blog post with your audience.

When you verbalize and share your goal, it not only increases your desire and dedication to accomplish it, but you're also inviting support from others which adds gasoline to the fire of your passion. Verbalizing your goal *partners* you with others, engenders accountability, and strengthens your commitment to the goal.

EXERCISE NO. 6: MAKE A NOT-TO-DO LIST

You can't mow your yard, change the oil in your car, or binge-watch that mystery TV series if you have enormous goals to chase.

Temporarily, you may be forced or lured into doing these tasks/things. After all, you can't let your house or car be destroyed by neglect. (And you really need to know whether the butler did it.) But you also have to understand that your time must be spent on more important activities, and time management is a duty that comes with the territory of achieving your goals. That's why I want you to make a *Not-to-Do* list.

Consider this: if you save $50 on changing your own oil, which will take you an hour, compare that in "*vision-hour*" dollars. If your vision is to make a million dollars a year, then on a 40-hour week your hour taken for that oil change – delaying your vision by an hour – really costs you nearly $350. Or, as another example, if you take an hour for the round trip back to the store that double-charged you for a gallon of milk, the dollars you get refunded back really cost you many times that in the vision-dollar exchange rate. Also, that hour today will never be realized in your future. It's like trying to make the baby steps of your *today* fill the giant steps in your future. The shoes just don't fit, which is why that sort of thinking makes you trip.

List the tasks that you spend time on:	Circle one of the following:		
1.	Automate	Delegate	Eliminate
2.	Automate	Delegate	Eliminate
3.	Automate	Delegate	Eliminate
4.	Automate	Delegate	Eliminate
5.	Automate	Delegate	Eliminate

EXERCISE NO. 7: TRACK YOUR TIME AND MONEY

Where you spend your money and time will paint a crystal clear picture of your priorities. Too many people talk a big game when it comes to their goals and their vision, but, unfortunately, many of their actions never match their words. And I have always believed if there is ever a discrepancy between what someone says and does, always believe what they *do*. Actions do not lie.

Track Your Money:

Start by logging into your bank account and make a simple pie graph for your expenses. Here's an example:

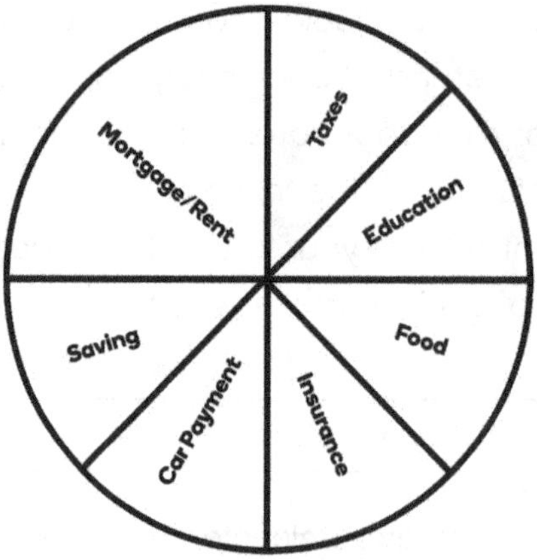

Let me tell you what you're looking for when you break down the percentages of where you're spending your money. If you say that you want to start your own business, but 38 percent of your money is going toward your rent or mortgage, and 25 percent is going toward a car payment, you really *don't* want to start your own business. How do I know this to be true? Because your actions don't match your words.

If you truly wanted to start your own business, you'd be saving more money to market your business and spending less money on your home and car. Achieving your goals requires that sacrifices be made. These sacrifices will be painful temporarily, but over the long-term, you will look back and thank yourself for being mature enough to make them. Remember that your "vision dollars" are worth significantly more than your present dollars.

Turn to page 551 in this book, then login to your bank account.

Write down your last 30 days of expenses. Put percentages next to each. Then fill out the pie graph.

Track Your Time:

For the next six days, track where you're spending your time. The most successful people on the planet do this, from Warren Buffett to Jeff Bezos. See the timesheets on page 552 of this book along with instructions on how to fill them out.

This may be one of the most powerful exercises in this book. Why? Because it astounds me how much time people waste. According to a study by Nielsen:

> *American Adults Spend Over 11 Hours Per Day Listening To, Watching, Reading Or Generally Interacting With Media.*

Holy cow! Eleven hours per day? Let's break this down. Let's say you live until age 80. So from 18 to 80 (let me find a calculator)...62 years, spending 11 hours per day, equals 682 hours or, 28.5 ***years*** "*listening to, watching, reading, or generally interacting with media*"!

When you review the timesheets, pay close attention to where you're spending your time. If one of your goals is to form a better relationship with your significant other or get in better shape, but your timesheet reveals you're not dedicating any time to invest *in* your relationship or *into* your health – you really don't want to achieve those goals. You're only pretending you do (in other words, lying to yourself). And your Maslow's pyramid will fall like a house of cards.

CHAPTER THREE

Resilience – Turning Setbacks Into Success

"The ultimate measure of a man is not where he stands in moments of comfort and convenience, but where he stands at times of challenge."

~DR. MARTIN LUTHER KING, JR., American Christian minister and activist who became the most visible spokesperson and leader in the Civil Rights Movement

Resilience is a person's ability to recover from setbacks, stress, misfortune, or catastrophe. A resilient person is not emotionless, but rather someone who is able to experience a failure or a setback and bounce back and move on. Resilience is the mother of survival and the sibling of perseverance. Together, they allow you to "stay on message" for your vision, pit stop after pit stop, speed bump after speed bump.

So, how resilient are you? The answer to that question isn't quite as simple as you might think. The amount of resilience you have involves your genetics and your past experiences. It also involves, a little thing called "grit".

In this chapter, I'm going to use a lot of stories to demonstrate the power of resilience because I've discovered that the best way to explain resilience isn't with a formula, but rather, with stories.

Why stories? Because as the saying goes, facts tell and stories sell, and I really need to sell you on the importance of developing your resilience muscles.

For me personally, resilience saved my life. If you haven't read the story when I was at rock bottom and seconds away from suicide, turn to the back of the book and read the Acknowledgement. This will help you see precisely why I have chosen resilience as one of the seven secrets.

A PICTURE OF RESILIENCE

"Throw dirt on me and grow a wildflower."

~DWAYNE MICHAEL CARTER JR., known professionally as Lil Wayne, American rapper, singer, songwriter, record executive, entrepreneur, and actor

A man owned a farm deep in the heart of Iowa. He had a very hard-working mule to help him haul supplies. One scorching summer day, the mule was exhausted from all the work he did, and the hot rays from the sun were painfully stinging his back. As soon as the farmer released his harness, the parched mule ran over to a nearby well to satisfy his thirst with a drink of water.

Upon getting there, the mule quickly discovered that the well was dry. Desperate for water, he leaned too far forward and fell in. In a panic, the mule tried climbing out of the well, but he was not able to. From a distance, the farmer heard the mule's cries for help, and when he reached the well, he realized what a misfortune his farm animal was in.

Standing there, weighing the costs of pulling the poor mule out of the well and evaluating the value that the mule brought to the farm, the farmer decided it wasn't worth the time and effort to get the mule out of the well. Therefore, he decided to call his farmer friends from nearby and have them help shovel dirt into the dry well to bury the mule and put it out of its misery.

The dirt dropping down on the trapped mule made him hysterical. Realizing what was happening (the farmers were trying to bury him alive), he attempted to kick the dirt away. However, the mule also quickly realized that no matter how hard and how much he kicked, the dirt kept coming. He just had to figure something out – but what could the mule possibly do?

Inch by inch, the dirt began to rise around the doomed mule. Each shovelful of dirt was painful for the mule to withstand as it came down, hitting his sun-baked back. All the mule could do was shake the dirt off and try to stand back up again. It seemed as if there was no escape for the mule and death was imminent.

Fortunately, as the dirt continued to pile up, the mule suddenly realized that he could step up on the dirt and rise higher and higher in the well with each pile shoveled at him. That gave the mule a life-saving idea: as long as he could step up over and over again, and withstand the hard and fast blows from the falling dirt, there was a way out!

The farmers eventually realized this too, and they started to shovel dirt even faster. Eventually, the dirt was so high that the mule, though exhausted beyond belief, was able to jump out of the dry well.

What seemed to be the end for that poor mule actually turned out to be his salvation as he climbed out of the well into freedom again. The dirt that was meant to bury him had saved his life because of how he had *responded to the situation.*

This is a picture of resilience. It's forcing ourselves to find a solution, or at the very least, recognize a solution that emerges from the most unlikely places. It's realizing that everything thrown at you, or

> **"A successful man is one who can lay a foundation with the bricks others have thrown at him."**
>
> ~DAVID BRINKLEY

on you, is something you can use to climb higher. This realization (or lack, thereof) can literally mean the difference between life and death for some people, and underscores the importance that it's not necessarily the conundrum we find ourselves in that is fatal, but the way we react to the cataclysmic circumstances. It all comes down to our perception of the events in our lives. If we perceive something as life-altering and in turn life-ending, unfortunately...it becomes just that – a personal apocalypse.

THE SCIENCE OF STRESS

> "Most people spend 70 percent of their life living in survival and living in stress, they're always anticipating the worst-case scenario based on a past experience and they're literally, out of the infinite potentials in the quantum field selecting the worst possible outcome."
>
> ~DR. JOE DISPENZA, Neuroscientist, international lecturer, researcher, corporate consultant, author, and educator

In the previous chapter, I discussed how achieving step-by-step goals are *recursive*; that is, each goal achieved will inject fuel for momentum toward the next one. It is an ironic realization that failure can also be recursive, fueling an alternate approach that puts that failure behind you. Each failure can become either a dead end or a mid-course correction, depending on how resilient you are.

When famous psychologist Angela Duckworth studied an incoming class of cadets at West Point, she measured their grade point averages, physical aptitude, military abilities, and self-discipline. After she correlated these factors with whether students quit or graduated, she discovered that nothing mattered as much as grit.

Duckworth and her co-workers defined grit as the tendency to work:

> *"...strenuously toward challenges, maintaining effort and interest over years despite failure, adversity, and plateaus in progress."*

In this chapter, grit and resilience are interchangeable terms. And there's a science to how grit (resilience) plays a role when large amounts of stress appear in our lives.

Stress is our bodies' and minds' reaction to a challenge or obstacle, so unless we learn to handle stress effectively, it's likely the challenge or obstacle will remain – as well as the stress from it – stopping us from achieving our goals. Because stress is the brain's biochemical reaction that makes you feel unpleasant until that challenge or obstacle is addressed, effectively handling stress goes hand-in-hand with overcoming the very things that stand in your way. People who do not learn to handle stress will see the stress, itself, become an obstacle, too. Grit to the rescue.

With grit, stress to your system does not go unchallenged. Your body, however, gives you an immediate advantage with the two adrenal gland hormones, adrenaline and cortisol. When you understand the role of each of these important hormones, you will understand how to use stress to your advantage as well as how to defuse it so that you won't suffer from its disadvantages.

Stress kills. And failing to understand how to cope with it properly will kill your chances of success in life.

Adrenaline, cortisol, and serotonin: your adrenal glands and immune system are both protective systems in the face of all types of stressful experiences. The production of adrenaline and cortisol by our adrenal gland protects us from threats outside of our bodies and our immune systems protect us from threats inside of our bodies. Adrenaline and cortisol work in tandem, as a phased reactant to stress: adrenaline first, quick and potent; cortisol second, slow and sustained. Serotonin, made from nerve cells, also plays an important role in your resilience to stress.

When we experience stress, our adrenal glands begin to secrete the two primary stress hormones, adrenaline and cortisol, through a complex series of responses within our body.

- **Adrenaline is what prepares us for "fight or flight".**

  It causes dilation of the pupils for a better view of a dangerous environment; diverts (re-routes) blood away from the gastrointestinal (GI) tract toward your muscles for action, and to those parts of your brain responsible for coordination and the physiological adjustments needed for sudden increased activity and thus, causes the small muscles in your skin to raise your hair (originally a scare tactic to make us look bigger to an adversary); raises pulse rate and blood pressure to help deliver the re-routed blood more efficiently, as oxygenation will be consumed more quickly during the stressful circumstances and increased activity; boosts energy supplies by releasing and raising the level of glucose; and that increases your perspiration.

  As adrenaline rises quickly, it also fades quickly – that "adrenaline rush" is fleeting.

- **Cortisol, on the other hand, rises slowly but more of it remains in your system, and for a longer time. The more stress we feel and the longer we feel it, the more cortisol is released.**

  Cortisol also further suppresses the digestive system and other non-essential systems in a crisis, enhances your brain's use of glucose, and promotes healing (should the need arise).

  Cortisol begins as an anti-inflammatory, acting as the governor of your immune system to make sure it doesn't overreact. That's a good thing. (You don't need to be itching from hives in a crisis.) However, if you are unsuccessful at addressing your stress, cortisol can remain, and over time, it becomes "pro-inflammatory" which brings about many undesirable inflammatory effects. That's a bad thing – a good hormone gone bad. Since cortisol can potentially double-cross you, the right strategy is to learn how to successfully deal with stress so that you can prevent the long-term effects of cortisol, which may come later.

- **Serotonin**: while the neurotransmitter serotonin isn't an adrenal hormone (it is secreted by nerves), it figures prominently with stress. Stress can cause wild fluctuations in our serotonin levels, which is responsible for the fatigue we feel with any type of exertion that exceeds our ability to tolerate it. Thus, the stress you don't train yourself to address can be fatiguing, making it less likely you will rise to the occasion to fight it.

Both the amount and frequency of cortisol released are directly related to the amount of stress you have experienced in your life. However, the more stressors a person has successfully addressed (painful events, abnormal responses to events in life, negative people, etc.), the less likely stress will cause the body to engage in adrenaline's "fight or flight" response. This happens because *defusing* cortisol by *diffusing* stress directly affects how adrenaline is released and then metabolized away, or how cortisol rises and falls over a longer period of time.

There is no better way to defeat stress than to embrace Duckworth's definition of "tendency to work," that is, *work strenuously toward challenges, maintaining effort and interest over years despite failure, adversity, and plateaus in progress.* This is in essence your stress-management protocol. Jumping to seize control of a problem is the grit that people use to rise up against what is causing their stress, and in doing so they are taking care of the problem and stress simultaneously. Doing nothing leaves both the stress and the problem, often in a vicious cycle.

Problem → stress → inactivity → bigger problem → more stress.
Problem → stress → grit (resilience) → solve problem → less stress.

And...

Less stress → new problems → no stress.

In the book, *Athletic Development*, by Vern Gambetta, he explores the concept of "*supercompensation training,*" described as the "adaptive rebound above the baseline" when applied to increasing one's demands and stamina to athletic training. His four phases of supercompensation include not only ratcheting up one's efforts as training continues, but interspersing periods of wind-down (i.e., recovery).

Training ourselves to adapt to episodes of stress is no different. (Of course, there's no doubt that athletic training includes stress.) In other words, people accustomed to successfully defusing high-stress levels accomplish this by working on their response to stress and thereby the entire biochemistry of stress. This results in their secreting less cortisol over time; the fatigue (physical as well as psychological) becomes less than when there is no rational plan of stress management. It's not that they don't feel stress, but that stress becomes increasingly manageable and can be dealt with.

If you were to train without the give-and-take of alternating exertion with strategic wind-downs for recovery, however, this is what is called "over-training"; this can alter the brain's neurotransmitter, serotonin, whose fluctuations can cause fatigue that dooms such a training regimen to failure. Without the recovery phase, it's one step forward but two steps backward. How can recovery be applied to stress training? Simply by dealing with little stresses that don't involve substantial risk. Work on the little things first, e.g., traffic frustrations, listening when you really want to talk, negating any negative acts perpetrated against you by insisting to yourself you will do some positive act for another.

Like in Gambetta's application of supercompensation to athletics, people who work on their stress succeed in creating a stress-adaptive rebound above their baseline. Thus – and this is the important part – they have increased their resilience. And if the effects of stress become less damaging, there is a diminished need for a rise in adrenaline or cortisol; and serotonin levels remain stable.

Without deliberate self-training applied to stress, people who have experienced minimal stress in life will have a far stronger reaction to stressors, simply because they are untrained. Large stressors, such as losing a significant amount of money on a business venture or going through any major setback in life will overwhelm their low threshold for their adrenal glands to kick in and become actively involved.

If stressful events were to happen to a person with little history of stress (or without deliberately and systematically managing the stress), his/her adrenaline would peak, then fade, and their cortisol levels would skyrocket and then persist. This could potentially lead that person into debilitating depression and overwhelming anxiety. Even small amounts of stress have the potential to become major events in this kind of person's life.

"Don't worry about anything; instead, pray about everything. Tell God what you need, and thank him for all he has done. Then you will experience God's peace, which exceeds anything we can understand. His peace will guard your hearts and minds as you live in Christ Jesus."

~PHILIPPIANS 4:6-7

In addition to the experiences that we have had over our lives, our genetic makeup can also affect our stress levels. We are naturally inclined to either be easily stressed out or more resilient to stress. Unfortunately, there's not much you can do to change your genetic makeup. But don't worry. The good news is that you can build up your tolerance to stress, and it's all thanks to the amazing plasticity of your brain and the extraordinary power of your mind.

Such plasticity can remold your brain over time, but before understanding how to use your brain's plasticity to undo the damage from stress, it is helpful to understand the damage stress does to us. While your stress hormones take the energy of the body and use it all for the task of fighting or running, they also shut off the functions of bodily processes that will not be needed during fight or flight. However, remaining in this state of preparedness for lengthy periods of time taxes our system heavily:

- Adrenaline, which acts first, makes you "brawn-over-brain" instead of "brain-over-brawn," the latter of which distinguishes us from cavemen. It shifts blood flow from your stomach and the thinking part of your brain to your muscles and the part of your brain important for reflexive coordination. Thus, without thinking, you fight or flee with better coordination, strength, and speed.

  Another way of looking at it is that when you are under stress, you are less intelligent because your body is taking you out of conscious thinking and putting you into reflex or a state of unconscious action. At some point, however, you need to convert from brawn-over-brain back to brain-over-brawn so that you'll be able to design and implement intelligent strategies. For engaging in strategy, the caveman in you is simply out of his/her league.

- As mentioned a few paragraphs ago, cortisol is initially anti-inflammatory, dampening any immune overreaction so that things like hives or shortness of breath don't interfere with your ability to address a crisis. Over time, however, cortisol exaggerates your physiological responses at the cellular level,

which interferes with your ability to synapse your neurons efficiently, think clearly and implement the strategies that will provide your best outcomes.

When you're under outside threats, your brain's amygdala (via fear and anger) and hippocampus (via aggression) immediately perceive these emotions as stress and signal your adrenal glands to crank out adrenaline and cortisol. Stress is your brain's cue to direct your adrenal glands and ready your body for immediate action while reducing interference from your immune system.

But the prolongation of this process (suppression of your immunity) is why stressed-out people often get sick much more easily than people who are under less stress in their lives.

Those under less stress have become that way by successfully dealing with stress each time it arose, while those who have not "trained" their response to stress are constantly under the initial effects of stress and a dysfunctional immune system. These "*stress-naïve*" people will continue to stumble on in this way, falling victim to the pro-inflammatory effects of chronic stress. There are some researchers who extrapolate this point by claiming that up to 90 percent of all doctor visits stem from stress!

The grit you muster, therefore, creates the action to remedy problems, and the stress "rheostat" becomes much less sensitive. Stress is replaced by success. So how can you summon this "grit" that will allow you to replace your stress with success? By harnessing the potential of your own brain. Studies have proven that our brains are forever changing, even as we move into adulthood. Our brains create new neural pathways and connections among neurons in response to what we feed it. Our knowledge and our experiences help our brain create those pathways and connections. This means that as you put yourself out there, on your journey of goals toward your vision, and as you experience higher levels of stress, your brain will gradually adjust to the stress. You only have to be ready to adjust to it first, and the rest will work itself out.

A neurological aside:

> Your brain does not become impervious to stress. What happens is that as you learn to deal with stress, you make it harder to become discombobulated during stressful situations. You're resetting your stress rheostat when you successfully handle stressful incidents. That is, you become *adept* (not "*adapted*") at dealing with larger issues. When you begin to navigate stress better, your neurons synapse more efficiently. Solutions become easier for you because you have conditioned your brain to handle challenging times; you've learned to surf the waves of uncertainty that stress causes and have learned to put yourself at ease, which can only help the actions you undertake to become more efficient and achieve your goals.

People who go through extremely stressful situations or traumatic events, such as a divorce, a health scare, or bankruptcy, don't change the way they are because of what adrenaline or cortisol does to them. They change because they've been woken forcefully out of a hypnotic slumber – the drone of their routines and patterns that have had them merely existing along a path of least resistance.

So awakened, in fact, that they have climbed out of their subconscious automated programming to become consciously more engaged and ingrain new strategies, habits, and routines in this new world that has been heaped upon them. While a divorce, heart attack, or bankruptcy are certainly stressful situations in life, more importantly, these life-altering events demand change, the effect is a new level of urgency that can re-write their subconscious patterns, habits, and routines.

The wake-up call has been placed and those who answer it are resilient. Those who don't will only see such setbacks and disappointments as a cause for further deterioration because now they cannot construct a new path of least resistance. They are shoved, battered, and punched around by their circumstances. Stress and the adverse effects it has on their nervous system will set in and likely induce a self-imposed downhill spiral – a meltdown.

Resilient people, however, successfully handle large amounts of stress. For you to be in this group, you will have to learn how to deliberately exercise calmness and seize control in chaotic situations. Both the avoidance of overreaction and resisting the temptation for rash knee-jerk decisions during times of extreme stress are crucial to sustained success in life. Fostering a tranquil mindset during challenges helps prepare you to experience temporary setbacks, handle them, and then position yourself favorably to handle more stress in the future. Eventually, stress will have less impact on you and how you perform.

A self-control aside:

Taking deliberate calm in chaotic situations may be one of the most important self-regulating skills we can acquire. This is because **rushing to solve a problem has the potential to make the problem worse.** That's why I want to share a concept with you known as *The Power of the Pause*. During stressful situations in life, many of us are prone to make brash decisions that lead to poor outcomes. We often make these impulsive decisions because our irrational emotions are controlling our (irrational) behavior.

When adverse events happen in life, pause, reflect, breathe deeply – then after you have calmed down act. Do not simply act without thinking through the consequences. Daniel Kahneman writes in his game-changing book *Thinking, Fast and Slow*, "An inability to be guided by a healthy fear of negative consequences is a disastrous flaw." When we are overwhelmed with emotions often times we're unable to employ proper forward-thinking that will bring about the best long-term outcomes. Pausing is certainly a self-control character trait that takes work along with patience. But if you are able to harness The Power of the Pause in your life stress will become significantly easier to manage during the turbulent times.

The Japanese have mastered The Power of the Pause. It's said they always have a translator, even when they don't need one when engaging in business negotiations. This gives them the opportunity to listen, digest the information and frame a response that does not come from an emotional reaction.

Your ability to bounce back from setbacks under extreme stress is a determining factor in how high you climb your ladder to success. Everyone goes through stressful moments, but the key is to embrace the struggle, deal with the difficult situation head-on, and remain calm so you can find solutions. Keep learning. If failures add to your wisdom, and they do when they result in mid-course corrections, you must accept that failures always come with stress. It's a package deal. And oftentimes, this package is gift-wrapped!

A Harvard medical study revealed stress-resistant people embodied the following characteristics:

1. They took charge of their lives and refused to be the victim.
2. They knew what they wanted; they had meaning, direction, and purpose in their lives. Their goals were well-defined; their course was well-charted. These were people who were fixed on specific points and followed a path that would get them there.
3. They maintained healthy lifestyles. They exercised daily and watched what they ate. They took advantage of the mind-body connection, understanding that the mind affects the body and the body affects the mind.

4. They had friends they could trust and talk to. Being human means engagement with our fellow humans. Without it, we're mostly bags of water, some chemicals, and electricity.

Stressful situations will show up in your life regardless of how safe or cautious you are. This is because it's impossible to control how other people behave. (Heck, we haven't even learned how to control the weather yet!) In spite of this upstream swim, you must learn how to handle stressful experiences and build up your tolerance to these challenging times; because the way you respond will make all the difference.

HUMAN ENGAGEMENT AND SELF-CONTROL

"For fools rush in where angels fear to tread."

~ALEXANDER POPE, English poet

Alexander Pope was wrong. Fools play it safe; fools play "not to lose". This is the antithesis to everything I'm trying to teach. But it goes deeper than that because arguing against the late English poet also can be applied to the fourth characteristic of the Harvard study I just shared (*4. stress-resistant people had friends they could trust and talk to*).

In other words, venturing ahead (where angels fear to tread) is not foolhardy, and it also need not be done alone. Further reflecting on Pope's angels and fools evokes another proverbial insight:

"No one's fool is no one's friend." ~Raoul Hebert

While Pope's phrase goes against the lessons of this chapter, being no one's fool by trusting no one and always going it alone distorts it to an exaggerated degree: you've got to trust someone.

Human engagement is good for your brain and certainly your heart (both romantically, as well as cardiovascularly). Sure, there are those who will hoodwink you, but like the person who never treads where angels won't, someone who doesn't trust *anyone* will be deprived of the nurturing power of human engagement. When I teach how to become the best version of yourself, it's no darn good without human engagement. You don't need a degree from Harvard to know that.

While close friends are part of the formula for becoming stress-resistant, know that one of the crucial ingredients to sustained success is learning how to become your own best friend – learning how to always bet on yourself. In Robert Greens book *The 50th Law* he points this out beautifully:

> *"You must always be prepared to bet on yourself, on your future, by heading in the direction others fear. This means you believe that (should) you fail, you have the inner resources to recover. This belief acts as a mental safety net."*

No matter what happens along the road to success, you are always in control because you choose how you will react to any given situation. Invoking the first Harvard characteristic of stress-resistant people, your sense of who you are will determine your actions, reactions, and how successful you become in life.

Here's a quick parable that proves we are always in complete control of how we behave:

> A Zen student said to his teacher, "Master, I have an ungovernable temper. Help me get rid of it."
>
> "You have something very strange," replied the teacher. "Show it to me," he continued.
>
> "Right now? I cannot show it to you," the student replied.
>
> "Why not?" asked the Zen master.
>
> The student replied, "Because it arises suddenly."
>
> "Then it cannot be your own true nature," said the teacher, "If it

were, you would be able to show it to me at any time. Why are you allowing something that is not yours to trouble your life?"

After that, whenever the student felt his temper rising, he remembered his teacher's words and checked his anger. In time, he developed a calm and cool temperament.

One of my favorite Chinese proverbs is this:

"If you are patient in one moment of anger, you will escape one hundred days of sorrow."

It's crucial that we understand we are always in complete control of how we behave and react. Too many people make poor choices out of anger and fear – the overreactions and rash decisions I mentioned previously (remember the Power of the Pause). The temporary feeling of lack of control can leave behind permanent damage.

Also, this can lead to how others respond to you. A spontaneous, fleeting, regrettable incident can be forgotten and usually is – by you. The victim of the incident, however, may very well remember it forever. Although forgiveness is possible, forgetting is not if the pain is sufficient enough. When the victim of your indiscretion sleeps at night, his or her hippocampus is busy filing the incident into long-term memory. For you, however, the incident may very well get discarded like last week's news.

FAILURE EVOKES PAIN; PAIN EVOKES FEAR – THE FORMER IS NOT YOUR FAULT; THE LATTER IS

"The signature of the truly great versus the merely successful is not the absence of difficulty, but the ability to come back from setbacks, even cataclysmic catastrophes, stronger than before. Great nations can decline and recover. Great companies can fall and recover. Great social institutions can fall and recover. And great individuals can fall and recover. As long as you never get entirely knocked out of the game, there always remains hope."

~JIM COLLINS, *How The Mighty Fall*

Failure is painful, no doubt. When you have learned to defuse the stress from your setbacks, however, the pain diffuses, as will the fear that accompanies the pain. In Chapter Seven, you will learn about something called the *"Confidence-Competence Loop"* in which overcoming your fear to do something will lead to competence in doing it, and from that, more confidence, etc. The cycle I'm discussing here is similar: defusing stress from setbacks lessens the fear to try again.

Unfortunately, many people fear the pain of failure so much that they render themselves powerless and stay down when life knocks them down. This is why if you ever feel like your control over your circumstances is limited, that you are mostly helpless in the face of difficulties, so it's best to keep your ambitions low – you will always react to stressful situations out of fear. A fearful reaction is an emotional one and has no place in your vision or goals. Such reactions will maintain your low self-esteem by pushing you toward failure, and it's not the kind of failure you can learn from. In other words, you will receive exactly what you expect in life. Tragically, it also will be what you deserve as you make yourself your own victim.

If acting out of fear only attracts more fear, you must train yourself for the exact opposite by viewing yourself as confident and courageous; you must see yourself as someone who deserves all that is good in life. When you think in a positive manner about yourself, a simple failure will be unable to hold you back. Regardless of how many curve balls life throws at you, you'll continue to aim high and believe that you are truly destined for greatness.

No different from creating the universe you want (discussed in Chapter One), you are what you think and say you are. Therefore, you must develop a picture of yourself as the kind of person that conquers fear and failure. Do whatever it takes to create this picture; you can see yourself as a number-one bestselling author or a savvy and influential business person.

Mental rehearsals, take five!

Whatever you want your self-image to be, purposefully create the picture in your mind that gives you inner power and strength. This image of yourself is crucial to how you truly see yourself and how you see yourself overcoming obstacles. Understand that your self-image and your sense of self-worth comes from you, and only you. It certainly does not come from the opinions of others, who have their own agendas, i.e., their own self-image and sense of self-worth which may be in conflict with yours. Once you realize that you call the shots, your confidence will soar, and you will become more comfortable with taking the necessary risks that increase your chances of success.

Even when you feel weak, tell yourself you are strong. Even when you feel like you don't have the power to walk another step, tell yourself that there's only one more step left to success. The self-talk that goes on in your head is very important for building resilience. You must be both the cheerleader and the player in your own game of life.

Always stay positive, no matter the situation. Nobody is asking you to be happy about a mistake or failure, but the instant something bad happens, you must force yourself to find the positives in the situation and envision yourself overcoming the setback.

As I stated before, failure can either be a dead-end or a mid-course correction depending on your **perception** of it, so you should always think about what lessons you can learn from the bad thing that happened and add this new wisdom to your toolkit. If you can shift your thinking away from the negativity of the failure, you're already one step closer to becoming a more resilient person.

With that said, avoid over-analyzing any single failure. It is sad to see that some people harbor the disappointment of a single failure for the rest of their lives and never get over it. In fact, many people who never see the success they hope for will tell you about a single failure in their life that sent them on a completely different track. Thus, regurgitating past thoughts of failure in your mind is a dangerous thing because you can easily get stuck in a place of constant negativity. Don't let that happen to you. It's both profitless and unattractive.

> **"Every success I know has been reached because the person was able to analyze defeat and actually profit from it in the next undertaking."**
> ~WILLIAM MOULTON MARSTON

Constantly I remind people during my speaking engagements that when we fall down, we grow. When we stay down, we die. Zig Ziglar points out in his extraordinary book, *See You At the Top,* that getting knocked down in life is a given, but getting up, resuming from where you are, and moving forward is a choice.

My hope is that you will make the choice to develop your resilience muscles and never allow the obstacles life throws in your way to hold you back. I know sometimes it's hard. I know sometimes you want to quit. I've been there, too. But allowing myself to pause and regroup rather than give up has made all of the difference.

Temporarily taking a break, regrouping, then training your mind to make the shift from running away from problems to running toward them is one of the most crucial secrets to becoming the CEO of your life. When you develop the habit of forging through obstacles without even realizing you're going through a struggle, you know your resilience muscles are getting stronger.

What truly separates the resilient people from the non-resilient ones is their ability to keep moving forward after they encounter a setback and find a solution.

YOU CHOOSE YOUR ATTITUDE

> "The longer I live, the more I realize the impact of attitude on life. Attitude, to me, is more important than facts. It is more important than the past, the education, the money, than circumstances, than failure, than successes, than what other people think or say or do. It is more important than appearance, giftedness or skill. It will make or break a company, a church, or a home. The remarkable thing is we have a choice every day regarding the attitude we will embrace for that day. We cannot change our past; we cannot change the fact that people will act in a certain way. We cannot change the inevitable. The only thing we can do is play on the one string we have, and that is our attitude. I am convinced that life is 10% what happens to me and 90% of how I react to it. And so it is with you, we are in charge of our Attitudes."
>
> ~CHARLES R. SWINDOLL, Christian pastor, author, educator, and radio preacher

In Chapter One I talked about a "bespoke" vision, one which is tailor-made for you, by you. The same can be said about your attitude. Sure, there might be a few things that are out of your control when it comes to chasing your dreams, but the one thing you can always control is your attitude. Like a flat tire, you can't get anywhere with a bad attitude. But in the same way, you can change a tire, you can change your attitude.

One of the major differences between people who succeed and people who come up short is their attitude toward the obstacles and setbacks life throws their way. Your attitude has the power to shape your reality. That's why I believe one of the first steps toward success is taken when you refuse to be the victim of a setback. (Harvard first characteristic.)

Remember your personal constructed universe, your consciousness, and your reticular activating system (RAS)? Attitude is a part of all of them, serving as an executive report or summary for them. As such, it's a call to action for a remedy based on the facts, not an emotional plea for what coulda/woulda/shoulda been! Answering that call to action is resilience, is it not? It's like having a spare to fix your flat tire. With a bespoke attitude, you can overcome any challenges life brings your way.

Too many people try to avoid challenging times by doing very little with their lives, that is, just playing it safe. However, this is a doomed strategy because obstacles and setbacks are inevitable, even in the dullest, safest, most inert lives. Even in these most inactive lives, setbacks will appear. It will be on a much smaller scale, like getting a flat tire or burning the toast, but you can't avoid them.

The difference between resilient and non-resilient people is that resilient people are accustomed to significant setbacks; they find things like getting a flat tire to be only a minor inconvenience. It may bug them, but it won't bugger them. Stressed out people who have very little resilience, on the other hand, are only accustomed to small setbacks. Therefore, things like getting a flat tire can ruin their entire day or even their entire week.

People who strengthen their resilience muscles, foster a steadfast positive attitude, and who have readjusted their stress rheostat can overcome almost any obstacle and create an opportunity out of it – regardless of how significant or insignificant the challenge they are facing may be.

People who choose not to strengthen their resilience muscles eventually allow adversity to win. They convince themselves that they have to accept their current circumstances because they are unable to see a way out. They refuse to look for solutions that will allow them to move forward. Some even champion their "poor me" persona, having a problem for every solution that could help or which has been offered to them.

We've all seen these people; in fact, we've all *been* these people at one point. But some of us find a way to emerge from the chrysalis of self-imposed impotence. The thicker the cocoon for moths or the chrysalis for butterflies, the more resilience is needed. But make no mistake, neither is impenetrable from the inside!

And no donkey's well, no matter how deep, is inescapable. It just takes some repurposing, which is best accomplished by using your next failure as your next lesson. Recall, if you will, the story I told earlier about the mule who fell into the dry well and was about to be buried alive: you must never give up. The very thing that was sent to end the mule's life, the dirt, was actually what saved his life. As a matter of fact, it wasn't really about the dirt at all. It was about how he was able to see the situation and control how he responded to it. **That's why it is our decisions, not our conditions, that determine our destiny.**

Never feel your destiny is out of your control (regardless of your current circumstances). Never give up hope. And never be a prisoner of your past, because it's your own personal book of lessons. Like the seemingly doomed mule, the 40-year prison term I was given was a stepping stone, an opportunity to prove just how resilient I truly was. It was a chance to earn the right to pen these words you're reading now. Because of my perception of the problem, I was able to overcome this enormous obstacle and achieve extraordinary levels of success by adopting the right attitude, rather than be buried permanently with the wrong attitude. Sure, it was a difficult prison sentence, but I did not allow it to become a life sentence. Instead, I made it a life *sentience,* a perception, a feeling, and a new attitude I used to climb out of the well (my prison cell).

> **For nearly half a decade, I sat in a prison cell. And instead of counting time, I chose to make time count. Every day I became smarter. Every day I became stronger. Every day I survived better. And every day, I got closer to turning a major setback into a major comeback.**

Understand that when you are at the end of your rope and feel you can no longer move forward, that's when you must dig deep and find the extra ingredient that can be summoned only during a time of desperation...and then grasp firmly. This is your "fight or flight" mode, and you must choose to fight. You must fight the part of you that wants to quit by tapping into the power of resilience so you can prove to the world (and yourself) how great you truly are.

You must learn to view your downtimes in life as great opportunities for growth. You have to learn that when life has you down on your knees and strips you of your resources, that's when you have to become resourceful; these are the times when you have to really pour it on and look "fight or flight" mode directly in the eye and choose *beast mode*: claws out and ready, pupils dilated for distant vision, hair on end to project your prowess. That's adrenaline, and its synthesis is catalyzed by resilience.

"The good times keep you going; the bad times keep you growing."
~UNKNOWN

Life's challenges are there to strengthen you. Setbacks plant seeds for future success. Downtimes have the potential to develop your character. But you have to consciously direct your mind to focus on the positive regardless of how challenging the situation may be. You have to win from within. Because the real battle always takes place in your mind.

That's why the major determining factor in whether you become a victim or a victor derives from the mindset you foster during challenges. You, in essence, are either your own worst enemy or your own best friend, because what you allow your mind to focus on – whether lack and limitations or resilience and resolve – is what you will get. The choice is completely up to you. Choose wisely, your future self (and perhaps your family) is counting on you to make the right decision.

RESILIENCE TAKES ORDINARY PEOPLE AND MAKES THEM EXTRAORDINARY

> "Hardships often prepare ordinary people for an extraordinary destiny."
>
> ~C.S. LEWIS, British writer and theologian

When it comes to facing setbacks in life, there are two types of people:

- those who choose to embrace their *extraordinary* potential and rise to the occasion, and
- those who decide to embrace *ordinary* and give up.

It's easy to keep moving forward when life works in your favor, but an extra ingredient, something extraordinary, is needed to maintain a fighting spirit when it seems that everyone and everything is going against you.

Which type of person are you currently? What type of person are you going to become? Before you decide, remember that there is a reason that this world is filled with billions of ordinary people and just a handful of extraordinary ones. So what's the difference between these types of people, you might ask? Without question, resilience is what separates the two groups.

> **"A gem cannot be polished without friction, nor people perfected without trials."**
>
> ~CHINESE PROVERB

The end result of being extraordinary is glamorous, sexy, beautiful, exciting, and amazing. But a lot of difficult work leads to that moment. Just like a diamond has to be cut and polished to create the perfect finish, humans have to be roughed up a little by life before they can reach their extraordinary potential. To stretch the analogy even more, consider the pressure placed on ordinary coal that is required to create an extraordinary diamond.

People who have achieved phenomenal success have dealt with many challenges along the way, challenges that would have otherwise defeated a lesser person, and resulted in failure. However, those who are committed to becoming extraordinary don't even have the possibility of failure in their minds. They have such a high degree of confidence that they are not frightened by taking risks and acting boldly. That's why they view obstacles as opportunities. These are the people who realize that tough times don't last, but tough people do.

Delete the word "failure" from your life, and you will thank yourself in the future for doing so. Teach your children a life lesson by cutting the word "failure" out of the dictionary you have in your home. Then ask your child to go look up the word "failure" and tell you the definition. When your child returns and reports to you that the word is not in there, smile and look at them and say, "Failure is not in you either."

Believe it or not, you can actually reach a mental level in life where failure does not exist. It would take up too much valuable real estate in your constructed universe. What you used to define as failure is now nothing more than a valuable life lesson. It won't matter how difficult something is or how many mistakes you make: you will find a way to learn the lesson and move on. This is why people who are afraid to learn from their mistakes keep repeating them. It is also why the hard lessons in life are actually blessings in disguise if you know what you're doing.

Only the road to success that takes you to your desired destination should exist in your mind. (Harvard second characteristic.) It would be naïve to think there won't be potholes, dark spots, and overhanging trees on this road. But you must convince your mind to forge through any obstacles because your dream is at the end of that road. Furthermore, the only way you're going to achieve it is by going through whatever life has decided to toss in your way to prevent you from getting there.

Randy Pausch, a former professor at Carnegie Mellon believed:

"The brick walls are not there to keep us out. The brick walls are there to give us a chance to show how badly we want something."

Let me ask you: How bad do you want it?

Do you want it bad enough to break through the brick walls that stand between you and your dream? You can't simply say you do; your actions must prove it. And the proof is in the perseverance. That's why giving up is always easier than climbing up, and giving in usually looks more attractive than digging in, however, you must ignite your resilience muscle and tell yourself that you won't back down despite being knocked down.

Instead, you will rise up and prosper. You will keep moving forward no matter what and break through any and all brick walls that get in your way. It is your resilience which shouts, "Make way!"

As long as you stay on the road heading in the direction of your dreams, you will get there. Just like when you get on the road to head home in the evening, it doesn't matter if you get pulled over by a police officer, experience heavy rain, encounter malfunctioning traffic lights, or get a flat tire – none of that matters. You can deal with everything because you know that once you get through it all, you'll be home.

THE BIO-DOME EXPERIMENT

"When everything seems to be going against you, remember that the airplane takes off against the wind, not with it."

~HENRY FORD

The Bio-Dome experiment was an attempt to create a perfect environment in the harsh deserts of Arizona. Researchers constructed a huge glass dome around an artificially "controlled" environment.

The dome provided purified air, clean water, and even filtered light for everything that was under it. Scientists believed that they created the perfect growing conditions for trees, fruits, vegetables, and even human beings.

Everything that lived under the dome seemed to be doing well, with one exception. When trees grew to a certain height, they would topple over. This baffled researchers for the longest time until one day they realized the one natural element they had forgotten to recreate in the Bio-Dome: wind!

When trees are forced to fight against the wind, their roots grow deep into the soil which makes the trees stronger as they grow taller. Without the strength created by the resistance of wind, the trees couldn't stand on their own.

People are not so different from trees. When we experience trials and get (grow) through them, we are strengthened. If we could hear trees in the forest talking, I doubt we would hear them curse the wind each time they encountered a storm. Instead, I believe we'd hear them thank the wind for assisting them in deepening their roots, which enables them to grow stronger and taller while being able to dig in for the stormier times ahead.

When you face a storm in life, know that you are being strengthened. It is resistance training. Resistance grows our muscles, and it is also what grows our character. Understand that few traits gain more results over time than persisting through trials and tribulations. Resilient individuals possess the ability to spring back from setbacks, and therefore their roots are deep. In the words of wise King Solomon:

"If you faint in the day of adversity, your strength is small."

You have a natural resilience built into you that has come from the challenges you have faced in the past. At the very start – *from* the very start – you were challenged by the very struggle to be born, and you didn't overcome that by your wits, by strategy, or even ambition. No, you overcame that with innate resilience. From the get-go – your very birth – you came into this world stronger than you think. That first challenge and the many other challenges that followed have honed you into the resilient person you are today, augmented – certainly – by your wits, strategies, and ambitions you've been able to pick up along your journey.

This augmentation is, collectively, your abilities, and now it's time to believe in them and in yourself and find the confidence to overcome any obstacles, any setbacks – any storms life blows your way. Know that the more difficult your life has been, the stronger you genuinely are. Never discount the hardships you have experienced and think, "Poor me." Instead, look back on your hardships and be thankful for them, because they have deepened your roots so you can make a difference and go out and do extraordinary things with your life.

> **"You should never view your challenges as a disadvantage. Instead, it's important for you to understand that your experience facing and overcoming adversity is actually one of your biggest advantages."**
>
> ~MICHELLE OBAMA

Without question, when going through challenging times, it can be difficult to appreciate the value of the struggle. I remember when I was a young financial advisor at Merrill Lynch, one of the largest investment banking companies in the world, many of the people who I worked with had grown up with privilege. They had been given the keys to the kingdom by birthright of growing up in the right circumstances, family environment, and world order decreed to them merely by which umbilical cord they hung from. For many, the struggle to be born was their last real struggle, because the umbilical cords in such families seldom gets fully severed.

Frequently I overheard my colleagues at Merrill Lynch talking about the lavish lifestyle they had when they were kids and the elitist traditions that seemed amazing to me, the common man who grew up in severe poverty. At our office they flaunted all the connections they had, simply because of the environment in which they grew up, surrounded by the jump-start benefits that come from inner circle camaraderie with the "right" people.

I found myself feeling sorry for myself. Of course I did. "Poor me" had no such connections. Poor me enjoyed no camaraderie with the right people, no red carpets, no "get-out-of-my-dismal-life-free" card. Poor me had to hustle and grind for every client I acquired. I found myself seriously looking back at all of my hardships, and regurgitating all the poor me malnourishment for having to go through these struggles – struggles as mythical to my colleagues and removed from their world as unicorns.

I thought about the paper route poor me had when I was a kid and about having to get up ridiculously early in the mornings to deliver newspapers in the harsh Iowa winters, massive snow drifts covering the roads because I was out even before the snowplows. I thought about my grandmother dropping poor me off so early in the morning that it was still dark at the park where the farmers picked me up to take me to their farms and tend to their crops for ten to twelve hours a day. I started my poor me days in the dark, and I ended my poor me days in the dark.

Poor me, indeed.

Now I see that the struggles I went through in life, before I was even a teenager, are the primary ingredients in my adult life that have catapulted me ahead of many people who had grown up privileged. Poor me?

Think again!

Beginning in my early childhood, my roots were being strengthened and were growing deeper with each challenge and ill wind I braved. Those struggles are what made me into the resilient person I am today. Those struggles I endured early in life are what allowed me to have a breakthrough rather than a breakdown when I was given a 40-year prison term. And today, those struggles are what keep me obsessed with getting better – and hungrier – at each opportunity for growth. My struggles are now my greatest asset.

Privilege, it seems, is in the mind of the beholder. This connection or that connection pales in comparison to the connection I have with myself.

Looking back, I can clearly see that the work ethic I developed early in life is one of the fundamental driving forces to the success and freedom I enjoy now. To this day, while there may be people I can't outsmart, there are very few who I can't outwork. Hard work, resilience, a burning desire to make things happen, and the will to never give up has provided amazing results in my adult life. Resilient me!

SUCCESS DOESN'T HELP YOU GROW – FAILURE DOES

> "Good people are good because they've come to wisdom through failure. We get very little wisdom from success."
>
> ~WILLIAM SAROYAN, Awarded the Pulitzer Prize for Drama in 1940, and in 1943 won the Academy Award for Best Story for the film adaptation of his novel *The Human Comedy*

You should expect resistance and walls on your journey to success, but you should always expect to win. A life that doesn't push you, frustrate you, make your heart pound, your tears drop, your sweat shine, your lips smile, or make your head spin is a life that can't teach you anything. A life without adrenaline is a life without success.

Do you have the ability to get knocked flat on your backside by life and get up again? This is an important question because if you are serious about becoming the CEO of your life, you should expect to be knocked down many, many times.

Most people start working on their dream with a heart full of confidence in their ability to succeed. In their mind, they have envisioned a dream (*vision*, from Chapter One), and they've mapped out the steps (interval *goals*, from Chapter Two) to reach that dream. But then comes that dreadful day where one of those steps leads them into a ditch. It's at that very point that the difference between those who have resilience and those who don't becomes abundantly clear.

Successful people fall into the ditch just as much as unsuccessful people do, but they discover the way out and start working on the plan for the new next step. The unsuccessful person sits in the ditch and does little to get back up again, doomed by the additional dirt being shoveled from above. They don't analyze and adjust their plan. They feel broken, disappointed, and have convinced themselves that this first setback is a definitive sign that they cannot succeed.

Failures and setbacks happen (even to the best of us). And without question, failure is just as prominent in life as success, if not more so because there are certainly more ways to fail than succeed. However, failure gives you the strength to handle success, along with the knowledge and the ability to do whatever it will take to accomplish what you set your mind to.

You have to prepare yourself for failure. Admit to yourself right now that you are going to encounter failure in the form of setbacks. You must also acknowledge that it's okay to fail when you know you can forge through all that comes your way. Your challenges and mistakes will become your lessons – your stepping stones to success. Bad times keep you growing (and deepen your roots).

Cofounder of Rich Dad Company, Kim Kiyosaki made an insightful observation about the importance of making mistakes:

> *"Most of us are taught, beginning in kindergarten, that mistakes are bad. How often did you hear, 'Don't make a mistake!' In reality, the way we learn is by making mistakes. A mistake simply shows you something you didn't know. Once you make a mistake, then you know it. Think about the first time you touched a hot stove (the mistake). For making that mistake, you learned that if you touch a hot stove, you get burned (the lesson). A mistake isn't bad; it's there to teach you something."*

Scientists have conducted numerous studies to understand what gives people the ability to withstand hardships, make countless mistakes and still move forward. Although the definitive answer is still a bit of a mystery, they have discovered that resilience is an essential ingredient to overcoming adversity and it's a characteristic that can be built up over time. On the other hand, hopelessness is the common denominator in people others consider to be failures. It is not poverty, ill health, depression, or laziness. Hope may be the final layer that keeps resilience alive and sometimes the last thing you can dig down deep for in desperate times. A person with resilience never, ever, gives up hope.

That's great news for every hopeful person trying to chase a dream. Isn't that the definition of a hopeful person – someone who chases a dream? It means that each failure and setback you face is going to give you greater resilience while preparing you to face life's next test. A test will arrive just as you are about to taste your dream, and you must be ready to learn the lesson it is attempting to teach you so you can forge ahead. Right when you're about to have a breakthrough is when you'll be tested the most.

"Just before you break through the sound barrier is when the cockpit shakes the most," replied legendary pilot Chuck Yeager when a reporter asked him what it felt like to break the sound barrier.

Captain Yeager was the first person to break through the sound barrier and he didn't allow turbulence to shake him (nor should you). Lessons from your failures and mistakes can be rather turbulent. Eventually, the lessons disappear, and your path smooths out. School's out when the wisdom becomes intuitive and prosperity shows its face. But you must keep the machine fueled. You must keep going, you must believe in your dream, and you must believe in your plan and the steps you have mapped out to get there. Will it be easy? Absolutely not. Will there be lessons? Will there be turbulence? Of course. But I can promise you this: when the blue sky of prosperity shines brilliantly, you'll look back on the journey and realize the challenge was the real reward.

THE NO. 1 ENEMY TO RESILIENCE: FAILURE

"Failure is the price we must pay to achieve success."

~JOHN MAXWELL, *New York Times* bestselling author, speaker, and pastor

Failure and resilience are natural enemies, but that doesn't mean they coexist; it means one must defeat the other. As I've explained before, how you react to failure can be one of your greatest assets.

Here's a list of people who have made a career out of failing: Donald Trump, Beyoncé, Stephen King, Carlos Slim, Steve Jobs, Barack and Michelle Obama...I didn't have to do much research to come up with this list of household names. I just wrote down the names of a bunch of famous, respected, and successful people. I know for certain that each of them has faced failures and setbacks. How do I know? Because in life, the more you do, the more you will fail.

While doing more and failing sounds like a bad recipe for success, remember that the priceless gift from this cycle is the accrued wisdom from your mistakes. Lessons learned always correlates with more success to come. If there are far more failures than successes in your life, this is only to be expected, because this is a numbers game and it's rigged for volume: but doing more will give you the successes that are special and life-changing.

The majority of people who have left their mark on this world will have a history of failure. That's why I believe the difference between people who lose and people who win comes down to how resilient they are.

No matter how hard we try, no matter how talented we may be, we will fail. None of us are immune from making mistakes. Why? Because people aren't perfect. Also, because we're human, and in turn, we're at the mercy of the interactions with all the other humans. No one is infallible, and when we have bad experiences, we must allow these experiences to remind us that we need to accept our imperfections and not allow them to define us.

Years ago, I was giving a speech at a mastermind event when a news reporter rushed at me and stuck a TV camera in my face. He asked, "How do you have the nerve to get up on stage and give people advice after you were sent to prison?" I looked directly into the TV camera, not at the reporter, and said, "I'm not going to allow a failure from my past to dictate my future."

This is the exact mindset you must have. I understand that you have failed before and it is terrifying to try again. I know the fear that sets in when you want to be bold and chase your dreams. I'm no hypocrite. I practice what I teach, and what I teach is that you cannot allow whatever happened years ago, months ago, or even weeks ago to limit you from reaching your full potential and sharing with the world the gifts you were blessed with.

FAILING FORWARD

> "Recently, I was asked if I was going to fire an employee who made a mistake that cost the company $600,000. No, I replied, I just spent $600,000 training him."
>
> ~THOMAS J. WATSON, American businessman, former chairman and CEO of IBM

Some people shrink from failure, while others embrace it. So does that mean one person is sane and the other is insane? Certainly not. People who embrace failure are those who have learned to see it through a different lens than the one that the average person uses. The RAS from Chapter Two comes to mind as a different way to see your universe.

Thomas J. Watson, the founder of IBM, is a strong proponent of what he calls failing forward. He has always said that the formula for success involves massive failure. Watson believed if you aren't doubling your rate of failure, then you aren't going to go far in life. Watson and many other successful people in the world see failure as a sign of progress (your higher education) and a necessary step to achieving greatness. This is essentially the same as saying that trial-and-error will always trump wait-and-see.

If trial brings error, then successful people learn to see failure as a stepping stone. Unsuccessful people only see failure as a tombstone. It all boils down to your perception of the disappointments in life. This is why it's said where your focus goes is where the energy flows. Are you dispersing (i.e. wasting) energy toward doom and gloom, or are you instilling (i.e. investing) energy toward finding solutions?

DISCOVERING WHAT DOES NOT WORK IS PART OF THE PROCESS

> "An expert is a person who has made all the mistakes that can be made in a very narrow field."
>
> ~NIELS BOHR, Danish physicist and Nobel Prize winner

> "Now only an expert can deal with the problem
> Because half the problem is seeing the problem."
>
> ~LAURIE ANDERSON, *Only an Expert*, from the *Homeland* album

Jonas Salk worked for years trying to develop a vaccine that would save millions of lives from the devastating Polio disease. During that time he experienced many failures, but he always said he viewed everything as a form of success:

> *"As I look upon the experience of an experimentalist, everything that you do is, in a sense, succeeding. It's telling you what not to do, as well as what to do. Not infrequently, I go into the laboratory, and people would say something did not work, and I think, great, we've made a great discovery. If you thought it was going to work, and it didn't, that tells you as much as if it did."*

Failure is not a curse, but a gift. Each failure is indeed a lesson for you; there is a nugget of knowledge somewhere in the middle of that failure. The key is not to allow your emotions to override your senses to the point that you don't see or learn the lesson. *"Half the problem is seeing the problem."*

Failure is simply part of the process, and the only way to avoid failure is if you were to come up with the perfect plan from the get-go. If you're able to do this, it's likely that the problem you are trying to solve must be a rather simple one. Let's be more practical and put aside the idea that the perfect plan exists, and instead, accept that through experimentation and failure you will develop the perfect plan. Then, and only then, will you discover your desired destination.

Now that we've established that failure is an essential component of success, we can also look further into the mystery of what a failure is. Say that you try something and the end result isn't what you anticipated – what most would call a failure. This is the point where you have to figure out why, when you thought A plus B would equal C, that it actually didn't. Clearly, there was something wrong with your mathematics. And right there is your golden nugget: your lesson is in your failure. You can always learn from your failures.

The key is to avoid being so consumed by the fact that you failed to the point where you forget about the lesson you're supposed to take away from the failure. Whatever the lesson is, it is designed to help you course-correct as you travel down your road toward success.

If you fail and choose to stop, the lesson will remain hidden; you will just accept such a failure as a given, like a law of physics. But for the person who is determined to succeed at all costs, there is always a lesson that will help them move on to the next step and defy the false physics of failure.

It's almost like a game of Clue. You learn one new fact which gives you a new clue. One clue leads to the next one and the next one until you finally win the game. Each failure will push you toward the next failure until you eventually succeed.

The most important thing is to learn the lesson that the failure is trying to teach you; otherwise, you'll be doomed to fail in the same way again and again. And if there is any rule about a "right" way to fail, then it has to be this: don't fail in the same way twice.

FAILURE IS FEEDBACK

"May God bless you with discomfort at easy answers, half-truths, and superficial relationships, so that you may live deep within your heart. May God bless you with anger and injustice, oppression, and exploitation of people, so that you may work for justice, freedom and peace. May God bless you with tears to shed for those who suffer from pain, rejection, starvation, and war, so that you may reach out your hand to comfort them and turn their pain to joy. And may God bless you with enough foolishness to believe that you can make a difference in this world so that you can do what others claim cannot be done."

~FRANCISCAN BLESSING

Nobody is immune to failure. Nobody is so perfect and all-knowing that they will never make a mistake in life. I'm not perfect, you're not perfect, and neither is any person on this planet, even those whom you may look up to.

John Maxwell is one of my all-time favorite personal development authors. He's reached *New York Times* bestselling status multiple times for his extraordinary personal growth and leadership books. Maxwell sums up one of his personal missteps beautifully with the following story:

"On March 12, 2009, I made the mother of all stupid mistakes. I tried to go through security at a major airport with a forgotten handgun in my briefcase. That is a federal offense. It was by far the dumbest thing I've ever done. I'm convinced that we are all just one step away from stupid."

Making mistakes certainly does not make us stupid (not learning from them does). There's a big difference between looking stupid and being stupid by not acknowledging mistakes, and thus failing to learn from them. We have been conditioned from birth that mistakes are horrible things, and that we should avoid all forms of failure. We are shamed and conditioned to feel guilty for making mistakes. We are scolded by parents and teachers when we don't get straight A's across all the subjects in school. As a result, we have become machines of constant avoidance in a rapidly changing society. Even the thought of taking a small yet imperfect risk to do something that will benefit us long-term has become unthinkable.

We avoid taking beneficial risks out of the fear of a potentially dangerous unknown. We avoid a big payoff to safeguard what we have. In Tennis 101, the coaching truism is *"Don't play not to lose; play to win."* Maybe you fear looking stupid in front of a group of people judging you. Maybe you *will* end up looking stupid in front of that group of people judging you. Perhaps you don't want to deal with the discomfort that comes with feeling "stupid" for not understanding something the very first time you come across it. You may even fear the loss of something – such as your status in society – that you deem to be precious and essential to your very survival.

> **"A mistake which makes you humble has more value than an achievement which makes you arrogant."**
> ~UNKNOWN

So what is it that many of us do in response to the fear of making mistakes and failing? We procrastinate on the things that we know we're supposed to be doing to achieve our goals. We moan and complain about why everything in life has to be so stressful and overwhelming. We choose to retreat toward easy behaviors like sleeping in, scrolling through our social media feeds, and watching TV instead of doing the work that is necessary to succeed.

Above all else, we seek out comfort in what is familiar and known, rather than explore the unknown in which our dreams and desires lie. We play *not to lose*. Our minds make up hundreds of rationalizations (rational lies) for all the reasons why something will not work, while arrogantly predicting with 100 percent certainty exactly how the future is going to play out. "*Never try, never fail*" is the motto that dictates how many people choose to live out their lives.

I remember watching a video on YouTube from sales trainer Matthew Ferry that accurately describes the irony behind our attempts to avoid failures and mistakes. He said that because the future is uncertain by its very nature, two things must be true:

1. You have absolutely no way of knowing if you are going to fail, and
2. you also have no way of knowing if you are going to succeed.

Ferry goes on to say that trying to claim otherwise is blatantly lying since you have not done the thing that you currently are avoiding. And even in a situation where you have done something similar in the past, the conditions and circumstances you face right now are entirely different. Therefore, the odds of succeeding have drastically changed as well. The past stays the same, but the present is always changing, no longer applicable to what worked in the past. And your future will prove it!

So what can you do, with full conviction and commitment, to overcome the fear of making mistakes or facing the possibility of failure?

The first thing to do is: recognize that by trying something new in your life, you are inherently creating chaos and disorder. You are breaking free from your many years of repeated (and profitless) behaviors and habits. In doing so, you are telling your mind to abandon what feels comfortable and familiar and take a leap of faith into something that has an infinite number of unknown outcomes.

Price Pritchett writes in his book, *You²*:

> *"You deliberately destabilize yourself when you break out of the habit patterns that represent the status quo. You create some inner chaos for yourself. So be prepared for the possibility of confusion, anxiety, and failure. That's part of opening yourself up to a new methodology that has the potential to deliver exponential performance gains."*

When you make the deliberate choice to pursue your dreams and head down an unknown path, your mind will start screaming, "Danger! Danger!" and you'll begin to experience that scary feeling in your stomach that comes with taking a new and unfamiliar risk. To make matters worse, even when you make it to the halfway point, your mind will attempt to convince you that everything you've done so far is a catastrophic failure and the amount of time and money you have invested up to this point has been wasted, and that you should seriously consider cutting your losses.

The second thing to do: conduct a mindset shift on how it is you perceive mistakes. The best learners – and the most successful people – are those who don't see their mistakes, losses, and failures as permanent. They also don't see these mistakes as proof that they should quit and throw in the towel. Instead, they choose to see them as temporary setbacks. Patricia Seller, in an article for CNN titled, *So You Failed. Now Bounce Back*, wrote:

> *"The most successful people at bouncing back view failure not like a cancer but, rather, like puberty: awkward and uncomfortable, but a transforming experience that precedes maturity."*

How do you perceive mistakes as temporary? You make the conscious decision to reframe each mistake as another stepping stone toward your inevitable success. Every new mistake you make is proof that you're trying, that you're making progress and learning something new. That you are venturing where no "*you*" has gone before. A mistake is merely a guiding compass – the aforementioned mid-course correction – that tells you one of three important things:

1. What you should start doing
2. What you should continue doing
3. What you should stop doing

With this mental reframe in mind, you are now in a better position to approach your mistakes in a way that is both healthy and constructive. You can analyze what you did and reflect on what you've learned from the experience. On top of the new knowledge you've gained, you also have conscious awareness of why mistakes and failures are not death sentences. Like I illustrated previously, it makes them life *sentience*.

As a result of this new thinking pattern, you are in a powerful position to change the direction you're headed and make the necessary adjustments. You can get up and persevere and try new and different approaches to reach your goal. In an interesting twist of fate, failure has transformed you into a resourceful person who can rely on his/her intuition and gut feeling to make effective decisions with greater speed and less hesitation. This mindset shift puts you in an authoritative position because now you're better equipped with the supreme self-confidence to head in the direction toward achieving your goals and vision.

On the other hand, if you choose to give up and quit, allowing your mind to sabotage your success, you will find it very hard to make any measurable progress in life. You will be unable to figure out why you are moving in a never-ending circle, doomed to endlessly repeat the same mistakes over and over again. You'll *know* what lessons you're supposed to be learning, but you'll never actually end up *learning* them.

> **"No, you're not perfect, but you're not your mistakes."**
> ~KANYE WEST

Failing and making mistakes gives you an opportunity to turn your wounds into wisdom because failures, like wounds, will heal. When you approach your missteps with the intention of extracting the maximum value possible out of them, you avoid the common trap of repeating your mistakes. *Wound me once, shame on you; wound me twice, shame on me.*

Responding the right way to failure – whether it comes in the form of mistakes you make or adversities you face – transforms it from an arduous experience into something that can help you become better than you were before.

I read a poem years ago by James Casey called *Climb the Steep*. John Maxwell cited it in his book; *Sometimes You Win--Sometimes You Learn: Life's Greatest Lessons Are Gained from Our Losses*:

"For every hill I've had to climb
For every rock that bruised my feet
For all the blood and sweat and grime
For blinding storms and burning heat
My heart sings but a grateful song
These were the things that made me strong."

Looking at this theme from another point of view, from the 19th Century poem, *Maud Muller*, John Greenleaf Whittier writes:

"For of all sad words of tongue or pen,
The saddest are these: 'It might have been!'"

While we can choose to learn from our wounds and let them heal into valuable nuggets of wisdom, it's equally important that we practice discernment. What do I mean? Not all mistakes are positive learning experiences. While it's true that we learn our lessons from the mistakes we make, we also need to determine if the mistake we made was due to ignorance or stupidity. Ignorance means we didn't have the necessary information at the time, but stupidity means we had the necessary information but misused it or chose to ignore it. Being ignorant merely means you haven't learned...*yet*; being stupid means you don't learn...*ever*.

Ignorance, however, does not grant you a license to be reckless. I am not advocating that you abandon all sense of self-responsibility and personal integrity. I am also not saying you should take action irresponsibly and impulsively. I'm saying:

Any perception of your own limitations and any level of belief in them is preventing you from taking action toward your goal and

potentially experiencing a transformational breakthrough.

Failing and making mistakes have the potential to become the "map" that helps you perfect your plan and guide you toward becoming the CEO of your life. But you can only tap into their potential if you choose to perceive and use failures as learning opportunities for changing your game plan, adapting, and continuing to move forward.

CEOs EMBRACE FAILURE AND SURGEONS DO NECESSARY SURGERIES THAT STILL FAIL

> "Experience is what you get when you didn't get what you wanted. And experience is often the most valuable thing you have to offer. It's a reminder that failure is not just acceptable, it's often essential."
>
> ~JOHN MAXWELL

In the days before sophisticated CT and MRI imaging, the decision to operate for suspected appendicitis was based on seat-of-your-pants clinical judgment. The conventional thinking was that if you, as a training doctor, called it appendicitis and then operated and was wrong, you did a needless surgery on someone, usually a child. Alternatively, if you said it wasn't appendicitis and did not operate and were wrong, the patient died. No pressure on the doctor, right?

Certainly, a surgery for nothing is concerning. A "negative app" is what the training doctors called an appendectomy whose pathology report came back reading "normal appendix", meaning that with nothing wrong with the appendix, the diagnosis was wrong and the surgery was for nothing. The pathology report might just as well read, "completely, totally, way normal appendix! What were you thinking when you decided to operate and remove it?"

In those days, a doctor justifying a needless surgery to parents of a child who had only a bellyache required courage. Therefore, it seemed that the budding surgeon who had the fewest negative apps was the one who correctly made the appendicitis diagnosis more often than his colleagues.

This, however, is quite misleading, because the fewest negative apps also meant the most missed cases of appendicitis, prompting Dr. Isadore Cohn, LSU professor of surgery in the 1970s (before everyday CT scans), to say:

> *"If you don't have a lot of negative apps, you're not doing enough appendectomies!"*

Are CEOs much different from surgeons? I'm confident that if you interviewed a handful of extremely successful CEOs, they would tell you that their success was right around the corner from their last failure and that the next "operation" would be life-saving. And they would go on to explain that had they stopped, none of their success and impact on the world would have been possible. A doctor, after a surgery to remove a normal appendix, could just as easily say, "but the next surgery could save a life."

This is why wallowing in the depths of depression when life throws you a curveball is wasting valuable time because there is a good chance you are on the cusp of something big (don't get rattled by the cockpit shaking). You need to persist and go out and get it. I love the way Shark Tank star Barbara Corcoran puts it:

> *"The difference between successful people and others is how long they spend time feeling sorry for themselves."*

Even startup companies prefer to hire a CEO with a failed business venture in their background. Why? Because a person who failed often knows how to avoid future failures. A person who has experienced business failure is often more aware of the pitfalls that lurk in the corporate world. This is more valuable than a complacent mindset that people often get when they only experience success. To succeed, you have to take the good and the bad, the "negative apps" along with the life-saving operations.

Using the cliché, "Nothing ventured nothing gained" is tempting to assume as the take-home message here, but what I'm discussing goes way beyond "nothing tried, nothing done."

What that cliché misses is this: "nothing ventured, nothing gained" is just as applicable to betting on red or black at the roulette table. CEOs who embrace challenges understand that mistakes are not failures, but pieces of proof that show an effort was made. Mistakes also yield information that can be applied to the equation for their next foray. They're not just flipping coins here and calling heads or tails. They understand that their mistakes, different from betting on the wrong color or the wrong side of the coin, give them the ability to apply the new lessons so that they can unleash their creative juices and go from bad to great. When you simply bet wrong, you lose; but when a setback takes place in a CEO's company, he/she assesses it, revises the plan, and moves on. Still a win.

Taking another "gamble" based on what went wrong last time is not really a gamble. It's a strategy based on knowns – utilizing the lessons learned from the previous mistake. On the other hand, making another luck-o'-the-draw bet is just the same gamble as the last bet.

> **"I would never promote a person into a high-level job who was not making mistakes, otherwise he is sure to be mediocre."**
>
> ~PETER DRUCKER

Gambling oftentimes is based on emotion; being a CEO needs to be based on facts and intelligent execution. A CEO who knows little about failure has a natural inclination to allow their emotions to paralyze them, which only makes a setback worse. Gambling is a game of chance; being a CEO is taking chances. Gambling is mindless; being a CEO is mindful.

When you come to the realization that failure is essential to success, you can move out of your comfort zone, try new things, and make the adjustments necessary to your plan without sulking or getting lost in your own self-created pity party. Poor me has left the building! That is why a key tenet to resilience is literally snapping yourself back into shape, no matter what has happened. And as soon as you do, you've got to get back to the plan (your Battle Board, as discussed in the exercise section of the previous chapter) and figure out what needs to be changed.

Often times, our disappointments in life exist because of the gap between our expectations and reality, as anyone who has attempted to fly off of a tall building (expectation) will tell you, should he survive (*not* the reality). On the other hand, resilience allows you to close that gap as quickly as possible and move on. (*Wouldn't the elevator get me to the ground better, while being more agreeable with the laws of physics?*) Getting to the ground is the expectation. How to do it safely because of the formidable height is the reality.

Your failure should provide you with clues about what went wrong and how you can make things right. Take the time to find the lesson your failure is attempting to teach you and make the required adjustments to your action plan. If you find yourself in the aftermath of a bad experience, try to remember that you're still breathing, so it could have been much worse.

One failure – just a single one – is the reason millions of people in the world end up living a life they don't want. You are allowed to be disappointed over a failure, you also are entitled to step back and take a little time to figure out what went wrong. What you are not allowed to do, however, is hold onto the failure as a permission slip for never having to try again. It's like Rocky Balboa famously said:

> *"It's not how hard you hit. It's how hard you get hit. And keep moving forward."*

Attaboy, Rocky...resilience. There's the bell again, so now get back in that ring!

ELEPHANTS NEVER FORGET

> "The mind is the limit. As long as the mind can envision the fact that you can do something, you can do it, as long as you really believe 100 percent."
>
> ~ARNOLD SCHWARZENEGGER

If you've ever been to a circus or a zoo and have seen animal trainers working with elephants, you must have wondered how on earth a tiny person can control a five-ton animal. There's a simple reason behind this that will probably make you feel sorry for the elephants and even sorrier for the humans who have assigned themselves the same fate. With that said, there is a powerful truth in the process.

Animal trainers don't control the elephant's physical movements as much as they control the elephant's thinking. When a baby elephant is being trained, one of its ankles is tied with a rope to a wooden stake placed in the ground.

The baby elephant is not that strong, and so when it pulls on the rope, it's unable to get away. After numerous attempts of breaking free from the rope that is tied to the baby elephant's ankle, it gives up and stops trying to escape. This exercise becomes a part of the elephant's normal training.

When the elephant gets older and has enough power to easily drag anything it's tied to, the elephant doesn't even attempt to move because it *believes* it can't get away. Even though it's fully capable of escaping and has been for a long time, it remains stuck to both the spot on the ground and the confinement in its mind.

The elephant remembers the struggle from its younger years

and believes it is forever a prisoner. That past experience limits the enormous power it holds. The elephant remembers this struggle forever, that's why people say that elephants never forget.

Just like the elephant conditioned to be controlled by a human, a lot of people have allowed past failures to control them and create self-imposed limitations that hold them back. The important thing to remember here is that failures from your past may have knocked you down or kept a leg staked to the ground, but you are more than capable of getting back up. You've got a dream to chase! Chase it. It's time to let go of the limiting beliefs you have been fostering and stand on all your legs, not just the ones unstaked. It must be all legs; otherwise, it might as well be none.

Don't allow failures of the past to keep you from your destiny. Don't allow faulty thinking to replay over and over in your mind. Because oftentimes, the line between failure and success is so fine that we are on the cusp of greatness without realizing it. With a little more effort and with the mindset that anything is possible, what seemed like a hopeless failure could easily turn into a magnificent success. Too many people have thrown up their hands and quit when a little more effort, a little more patience and a mindset of endless possibilities would have led them to success had they kept trying. That is, more resilience.

For me personally, right when the straw was about to break the camel's back, when I was at the end of my rope – it was that small additional effort that ended up making all the difference for me. And I believe that small additional effort will make all the difference for you as well.

You owe it to yourself, as your responsibility, to forbid past failures to stop you from unleashing the power inside of you. Your failure will be limited to nothing more than a one-time occurrence as long as you learn the lessons that come with it. You may have another failure, but it will be a different kind of failure that will provide you with more knowledge. This knowledge may be the final lesson you need to learn so you can see your dreams come true.

No matter how badly the cockpit shakes, find the inner courage to give it that one extra pound of thrust.

YOU ARE YOUR OWN LIMITS

> "Success is to be measured not so much by the position that one has reached in life as by the obstacles which he has overcome."
>
> ~BOOKER T. WASHINGTON, American educator, author, orator, and former advisor to presidents of the United States

I've seen many people embarrass themselves out of success. What does that mean? It means if you've ever attempted to do something that the average person doesn't do, then you will surely have experienced some pushback from others in your life. A lot of people have family members and friends who are naysayers. You might have an idea you think is brilliant, but they can provide you with an endless list of reasons why it won't work.

During the difficult moments on your journey to success, when things might not be going exactly the way you want, the same naysayers will definitely be the first ones to remind you, *"I told you so."* What naysayers fail to realize is that success lies in having made an effort, and failure lies in never having tried or in giving up. People who have tried and failed, then gave up, never grasp the fact that the bad experiences life throws at us are only bad if we fail to learn from them.

It might sound crazy, but the fear of failing in front of other people, along with the fear of how people might change their perception about us, holds many people back from diving straight into the very thing they've wanted to do their entire lives.

You may have people in your life now who you are extremely

close to. And perhaps at one point in these people's lives, they may have tried something outside of their comfort zone, failed, became fearful, and given up. They remember the disappointment, the hurt, and the laughs they received from others. So in turn, they are attempting to save you from following in their footsteps. Their intentions are good, but they fail to understand that your drive and determination, your skill and will, are not only different from theirs but, unlike theirs, are alive and well and kicking and screaming.

When people like this see you trying to do something great with your life, they think they are "protecting" you. Many times they will go to extraordinary measures to stop you from being bold and trying to do something that they have failed to accomplish. You must forgive them and move on. Your future is too bright to be sacrificed because someone else is attempting to impose their limitations on you. If you allow someone to hold you back, you might just as well go live with them in the uninspiring universe they've created.

TOUGH LOVE

> "Tough love may be tough to give, but it is a necessity of life and assurance of positive growth."
>
> ~T.F. HODGE, Writer, blogger, commentator, and graphic designer

People who love us and want to protect us sometimes make a grave mistake, quite unintentionally, when we are experiencing failure. The mistake they make is that they help too much. Wait! What? How can too much help be a mistake?

Too much help is a massive mistake because we won't learn the lessons life is attempting to teach us when we fall. And when we don't learn how to get up on our own, it impairs us from strengthening our resilience muscles. Often times, too much help early in life leads to learned helplessness, which negatively impacts the development of our resilience.

Let me share an example with you of how I'm attempting to strengthen my son Tristan's resilience muscles from early on in his life. When my son began walking, he regularly fell down. And never (or at least rarely) did I rush to pick him up. As my boy grew older and he would run as fast as he could on the playground, he'd still occasionally fall, and even then I still would not hurry over and help him up.

Now you may be thinking that I'm a horrible parent. I know for a fact many of the other parents that would watch me stand there when my son fell would look at me in disgust and think the same thing. It was not uncommon that other parents would run over and try to help my son up as I stood there and watched Tristan lying on the ground. I would politely tell these parents to leave my son alone and let him get up by himself.

What was I doing, besides dying on the inside? My heart would break each time I saw my son fall. I always wanted to rush over and help him up. However, I knew that I would not always be there. And I knew that from day one, my son needed to learn how to get up on his own. I was preparing Tristan for the times when life would knock him down – a preparation right in my own household, from the moment he began to take his first steps.

Too many parents don't allow their children to strengthen their resilience muscles. Then when life throws them a curveball, they think it's the end of the world. It's crucial to let the people we love build their tolerance to adversity early in life because just as night follows day, challenges will regularly appear. And it's our duty to allow the people we love to develop courage, confidence, and resilience so they can overcome these inevitable setbacks.

PARENT LIKE A GIRAFFE

> "The worst mistake a parent can make with their children is allowing them to feel entitled, to teach them that just because you asked for it you should get it, and that other people have a responsibility to give it to you. Nothing is free in this world and nothing is promised. Teach them if you want something, work for it, believe in it, and when you get it, celebrate it, but do not run people over in the process."
>
> ~UNKNOWN

Without question, the greatest example of teaching their young to get up from an early age comes from a mother giraffe. Giraffes give birth standing up. When a new baby is born, the first thing in its life is a fall of about five feet. What a way to enter into the world! No loving cuddle. No smiles. Just a giant drop. The stuff Child Protection Services loves to condemn.

It gets worse. When the baby giraffe tries to shake off the initial shock and stand up on its four legs, you would think the mother would try to help her baby out. Nope. The mother actually does the exact opposite: the mother gives the baby a kick, which knocks it right back down. The baby giraffe again tries to get up, but the mother kicks the baby's legs out from under it, knocking the giraffe back down again.

The mother continues repeating this strange behavior until the newborn giraffe is too exhausted to get up. Then, at this point, the mother giraffe leaves the baby alone for a moment before nudging it to get up.

From first glance, this looks like a very cruel relationship between the mother and her newly born baby, but the explanation is simple: to survive predators, the first lesson a baby giraffe must learn is to get up to its feet quickly. This is key to a giraffe's survival.

The mother is teaching her baby from its first seconds of being alive one of the most important lessons to staying alive: get up even when you can't. Strangely enough, the mother giraffe's behavior is also supported by an Arabic proverb which states:

> *"Sometimes, in order to teach something good, you have to be a little rough."*

FEAR OF FALLING AND FEAR OF FAILING

> "Don't let your fear of falling keep your dreams from taking flight."
>
> ~UNKNOWN

Whether a toddler, a teenager, or an adult in the December years of life, we have certain and sometimes specific fears that we face. Although the topic of fear can be broad, the origin of fear began the moment we realized we could fall. Immediately we tense up, clench our fists and brace for impact. Fear triggers a natural protection response so we can avoid potential injury and pain. As we experience adverse events throughout our lives, we develop ways about how we choose to respond to fear.

While fear might be triggered by a variety of things such as people, events, or circumstances, it's up to you to choose how you will respond to it. The adrenaline from your adrenal glands prepares you for either running away or standing your ground. It's really your call. Will you collapse or run, or will you face your fear and rise to the occasion?

Think of children for a second. They are often much better at handling fear than adults. Kids don't allow pain or fear of failure to stop them. Fear of failure really doesn't exist to a child. For example, kids learning to ride a bike: they try, fall down over and over again, hurt their knees and elbows, and get bruises. But each time they fall, kids rise and keep trying until they achieve their goal of riding a bike. They don't stop or give up until they figure it out. To children, the reward of being able to ride a bike is much greater than the pain they may experience during the learning process.

When we're young, we're fearless. But for some odd reason as we age, our fears become more profound. However, if you really think about it, dig deeper, and analyze fear, you will realize that fear is more imagined in your mind than it is real.

All of us have different fears in our lives. Everyone is afraid of something. However, it is not necessarily the fear that we have to overcome, but rather what our fear is masking. For the majority of people, it is masking pain; pain of disappointment, pain from what others will say (or think), and pain of loss; of course, the pain of failure is one of the main things hiding behind fear.

While our natural and subconscious reactions to fear have been developed based on how we chose to handle fear all along (from when we first realized we had the potential of experiencing pain), we have the power to change the way we interpret and handle fear. Overcoming your fears is a critical factor in whether or not you become the CEO of your life. And it's what separates high achievers from those stuck in mediocrity. We either submit to fear or we dominate it, like with the two natural enemies of failure and resilience.

"I never feared death or dying. I only fear never trying."
~WIZ KHALIFA

People who defy logic and achieve extraordinary things in life are the ones who chose to break free from their fears, develop resilience, and overcome the obstacles they face. They do this because they know the reward is greater than the false peace of giving in to fear. They allow their drive and ambition to override their fear.

"God placed the best things in your life on the other side of your fears."
~WILL SMITH

One of the ways I've discovered to

help overcome our fears is to surround ourselves with fearless people, with people who have developed the exceptional ability to face fear and dominate. This will allow you to feed off of their energy and use their strength to rise to the occasion.

Dorothy: *Weren't you frightened?*

Wizard: *Frightened? You are talking to a man who has laughed in the face of death, sneered at doom, and chuckled at catastrophe.*

It is critical to realize that in reality, failure doesn't exist, so in essence, there is no reason to be fearful of failing. Laugh at it, sneer at it, chuckle at it. Failure simply means that you have found a way that something doesn't work, or that you made a mistake. This mistake can be a setback, and it may force you to shift your path slightly, but it's just that: a simple mid-course correction. It may slow you down, but you shouldn't end up in the proverbial ditch.

When you make a mistake, the sooner you own it, the sooner you overcome it. A mistake itself is not who you are, but simply something you did. You do not need to fear that a simple error on your road to your dream will define who you are unless you allow it to. Additionally, one of the best decisions you can ever make when it comes to challenges is to extract the lesson from the mistake and move forward. Your ability to choose to learn from your mistakes or not is based on – first – your acceptance that obstacles present opportunities to learn and grow, and – second – that you treat them as stepping stones toward your path to success.

The difference between average people and those who have reached unimaginable levels of success is their perception of their mistakes, challenges, and setbacks, as well as their response to them. High achievers are those who grow and develop themselves so that they can see failure in a positive light and as a sign of progress. They expect to feel discomfort – bruised elbows and knees – but they've acquired the solid mental capacity to manage disappointments and losses, and they know that setbacks present them with the knowledge they need to get to the next level.

While it is perfectly natural for our emotions to temporarily hold us back when we experience hardships, we must never allow our emotions to control us permanently. Emotions have a way of blinding us of reality until all that's left is a fear of fear.

Allowing fear and negative experiences of the past to destroy your future is like living in a coffin. It slams a lid on your potential and keeps your life locked in a box. It shows that you are unwilling to allow adversity to be your teacher. And if that's the case, then you will repeatedly fail to learn from your losses. And in turn, it is unlikely you will ever achieve sustained success. Don't put yourself in a coffin; people in coffins are dead.

> **"The only thing we have to fear is fear itself."**
>
> ~FRANKLIN D. ROOSEVELT

Emmet Fox, one of the most influential spiritual leaders of the early 20th Century, observed:

> *"It is the law that any difficulties that can come to you, at any time, must be exactly what you need most, at the moment, to enable you to take the next step forward by overcoming them." Fox then adds, "The only real misfortune, the only real tragedy, comes when we suffer without learning the lesson."*

KEEP GOING AND KEEP GROWING

> "Whether adversity is self-imposed, attracted, or swiftly delivered by God himself, know that you are being battle-tested...and strengthened for a purpose greater than you can understand. With each successive hardship comes the endurance to overcome even bigger storms. God knows what battle I'll have to fight next in my life, but I know I'll be ready."
>
> ~RYAN BLAIR, American entrepreneur and author

Recently, I was on an airplane and heard the pilot say, "This is your captain speaking. There are quite a bit of storms heading into the Washington, DC, area. We're going to go around a few of them, but some we'll have to go through. It's going to get pretty bumpy, but we'll have you safely to your destination in about thirty minutes."

What a fantastic metaphor for describing the obstacles you'll encounter while trying to achieve your goals! The pilot doesn't give up and quit because there are storms between him and his goal. Instead, he chooses to take persistent action, alter his plan slightly, and continue to fly toward his desired destination. He also, like Chuck Yeager, doesn't allow himself to get rattled even if everything else is rattling.

Achieving your goals is a lot like trying to fly a plane through harsh weather conditions. If you consistently take action on your goals and refuse to retreat or become discouraged from setbacks (turbulence), you will achieve exactly what you set your mind to. And when you do encounter a setback, whether professional or personal, it's not the end of the world. It's an opportunity to turn a loss into a potential gain and keep moving forward. That's the kind of mindset you need to have if you want to be successful in any area of life.

An additional take away from the point I'm attempting to make: the pilot doesn't wait for the perfect conditions to arrive before flying. He starts immediately and gives himself permission to make adjustments along the way.

Brian Tracy expands on my point in his book, *Flight Plan - The Real Secret of Success*. In Tracy's book he explains:

> *"Life is like an airplane journey. From the time you take off you will be off course 99% of the time. All airplanes are off course 99% of the time. The purpose and role of the pilot and the avionics is to continually bring the plane back on course so that it arrives on schedule at its destination."*

Your goals are the same way: the sooner you start taking action and the sooner you stop over-analyzing potential "what if" scenarios, the faster you can make the necessary adjustments. But if you never get started, you won't be able to make those adjustments. Allow yourself to extract the lessons from each of the setbacks you face in pursuit of your goals, and then move on.

Remember the lessons and footnote the mistakes. There's nothing worse than moping around over a failure for a long period of time because all you're doing is slowing down the potential progress you could be making instead. High achievers understand this, which is why they maintain a positive mental attitude in the face of losses and setbacks. Likewise, unsuccessful people cower away in fear when they encounter setbacks in their lives because their minds make the situation far more significant and worse than it actually is. That's why I've discovered that how we think when we lose determines how long it will be until we win. You get to choose whether you magnify the struggle or crucify the struggle.

The best way I know to train our minds to seek out positive outcomes in the face of adversity is to consistently take action and intentionally program ourselves to win. During our down times, it can be difficult to persevere when our minds keep telling us that what we're trying to do will not work. This is precisely why I often tell people, "Listen to your heart and tell your mind to be quiet." I give this advice because our brains are always trying to talk us out of what we know we need to do.

FOLLOW YOUR HEART, YOUR BRAIN IS STUPID

> "The cost of not following your heart is spending the rest of your life wishing you had."
>
> ~UNKNOWN

Why do our brains try to talk us out of what we know we need to do? This happens because of our amygdala, an almond-shaped (*amugdalē*, Greek: "almond") set of nerve cell clusters in each temporal lobe of our brains that is responsible for keeping us safe. The amygdala is the caution light that goes off when we encounter danger. It does this by its association with emotion – specifically, fear.

Therefore, when setbacks arrive in our lives, our amygdalas light up. In connection with our adrenal glands, our brains become hyperalert: our pupils dilate, our heart rates increase and glucose spreads through our bodies to make adjustments for the best defense. Successful people use this reaction to fight; unsuccessful people fall victim to this reaction by fleeing.

There was an interesting article in the *Neuroskeptic* section of *Discover Magazine* in 2018 titled, *Can I Have My Amygdala Removed?* It discussed the pros and cons of this part of our brain, pointing out many reasons why our amygdala is crucial to our survival, notably its ability to strike fear in us. We have survived from the caveman days because of our amygdalas become hyper-active when fearing things like fire, large-toothed predators, and pointed sticks served us well. So I certainly agree with the experts on the benefits of this vital part of our brain, but I think too many of us take this too far. After all, we're not cavemen anymore.

Becoming a slave to our amygdalas can result in crippling phobias. Phobias, by definition, are not reasonable fears like fire, predators, or pointy sticks, but unreasonable fears such as spiders, clowns, or taking that next step toward our goals and vision.

To answer the question posed by the article title, the removal of amygdaloid tissue, once used to treat aggressive behavior, crippling fear and anxiety, and epilepsy is not really a legitimate option in today's society now that pharmaceutical progress has allowed us to replace such an invasive and destructive procedure.

We've come a long way since the caveman days. We've evolved a lot of brain matter around the primitive areas, such as the amygdala and the rest of the ancient limbic system, so our minds are a balance of sensible caution (primitive brain) and also intellectual speculation and ambition (modern brain).

Unfortunately, many people allow their primitive brains to sabotage their success, ignoring the ambitions that come from the higher executive brain portions (modern brain). Their primitive brain is the part that says, "Run!" when their executive/modern brain is trying to say, "Take your shot."

A neurological aside:

The amygdala is part of the limbic system, an ancient part of our brains we share evolutionarily with reptiles. The limbic system knows fear and escape, like that lizard on the fence eyeing you suspiciously. Thus, the primitive part of your brain is not the human mind. When we as humans say we are acting or speaking "from our hearts," it is simply a romantic phrase that says we are actually acting or speaking from our minds, which is the neurological reality. We have spent millennia wrapping complex convolutions of neurons around our limbic system just to be able to line-item veto anything which our intellect (or, "heart") says the lizard in us all is wrong about.

A romantic aside:

Just to be clear, the many references in this book about "following your heart" – which I'll continue to do (because I'm a romantic) – are really referring to following the partnership of your gut instinct and intellectual ambitions, all of which are in your higher mind. Your heart doesn't contribute to the momentum of moving forward, except that it might beat a little faster when you do.

Now that I've made the distinction between the romantic

notion of following your heart and the heart as a mere pump, I can confidently say you should listen to your heart and follow your dreams. You should do so even when the odds are stacked against you because the odds are always stacked against you when you're attempting to do something great with your life. If more of us would follow our heart (combined with our modern executive mind) more of us would make the impact on this world that we were put here to make.

> **"Follow your heart" needs to be the mission-critical battle cry we tell ourselves. Translated: "Follow your ambitions and intellect, for your primitive brain is stupid," or, "Follow your human mind, not your lizard!"**

We should follow our human, evolved minds, not the survival part – the ancient part – of the brain. A 100 percent reliance on the cautions from your amygdala to make decisions often ends up leading to an unfulfilled life. Constantly choosing the options that are "safe" and "practical" prevents you from taking on riskier choices that can lead to long-term fulfillment. It may make for a sweet life for your cowardly amygdala, but it's an insult to your mind – and to your "heart's desires." This is because sooner or later people who live overly cautious lives often experience depression, anxiety, and disappointment when they look back at all the opportunities they missed out on. That's your mind's revenge on your amygdala for its bad advice.

> **"The best and most beautiful things in the world cannot be seen or even touched. They must be felt with the heart."**
> ~HELEN KELLER

You will come across countless people who will caution you with the question, "Why take a chance?" This will happen, especially if they feel your current situation is good enough. This book is all about encouraging you to take a chance (to bet on yourself) because I believe if you don't take a chance, then you don't have a chance.

That's why I want to encourage you to listen to your heart. Whether you want to call it your "heart," your "gut," or your "evolved mind" doesn't matter: it's really just acting on what truly inspires you and following your intuition. Learn to follow what you "feel" is right, instead of suppressing your desires and passions. When you do, you'll be expressing your possibilities as probabilities and sowing "definites" for your future reaping. This will allow your authentic self to come to life, and when it does, you'll realize that the answers you need are always inside of you.

I'm not suggesting that you should never use *all* of your brain when it comes to making difficult decisions. What I'm saying is that you should recognize the wisdom which lies within you. Don't only listen to the primitive voices in your head; allow your heart to guide you toward taking the first step, rather than needlessly over-calculating all your available options before getting started. Checking, rechecking, and checking again before you take your shot is your amygdala talking. Sometimes it's perfectly okay to tell that lizard, "Thanks, but no thanks."

PRESSURE PRODUCES DIAMONDS

> "A fumble, an interception, or a bad decision that costs the team does not mark him for his career – unless he allows it to."
>
> ~JIM TRESSEL, American college football coach, five national championship victories

Maybe you've dropped the ball a couple of times in life, but it does not define you unless you choose to allow those negative experiences to dictate who you are. Successful people will not allow what happened in their past to define them, and they are able to quickly shift their focus from the setback they experienced toward staying positive and experiencing the reward in front of them. This shift in focus allows them to defuse the negativity that temporarily infiltrates their minds from past failures.

Successful people have a short-term memory when it comes to their failures. Unsuccessful people file their hardships deep in their mind and hold on to the painful memory for eternity. Successful people don't regurgitate past failures in their minds whereas unsuccessful people often do. The result of this faulty thinking (negative self-talk from regurgitating past failures) is performing poorly when the pressure's on.

One of the primary reasons why successful people can perform under pressure, while unsuccessful people end up choking in the same situation, is their mental perception of the problem. But there's something else going on beneath the surface that allows successful people to truly thrive when the odds are stacked against them. To explain what I mean, let me tell you where the word "choke" comes from.

The dictionary defines "choke" as "difficulty in breathing, swallowing, or speaking." Its anatomical connotation is the disconnect between your airway and your esophagus, in which food risks obstructing your windpipe (trachea). However, in the context of failing to execute under pressure (when your amygdala is hyperactive and running on overdrive), choking's slang connotation means "to fail to perform effectively because of nervous agitation or tension, especially in an athletic contest." Translated, "you blew it."

When you're under tremendous pressure, and you fail to achieve something, your heart starts pounding and your mind starts racing. (Adrenaline, like the mind, is a terrible thing to waste.) With that, you lose the ability to breathe regularly and think normally. As a result, you also lose the ability to maintain your composure and perform properly.

If someone has a lot on the line – their reputation, a large audience scrutinizing their every move, one single chance to make something happen – they are a lot more likely to choke and exhibit worse performance than what you can normally expect of them.

There was an interesting study done in which golfers were instructed to hit their ball to a nearby area where a flag was placed in the middle of the green. When nobody was watching and the golfers were free to focus on the shot, they were almost always able to hit the green. But when they had a money incentive set in place for landing their ball on the green, and they had a large audience watching, their shots were 20 percent less accurate than when they were alone.

The only thing that changed between the two scenarios was the pressure. The combination of the monetary benefit of hitting the ball on the green, along with the additional stress of people watching them, weighed heavily on the golfers. This caused tension in their mind, which ignited the pressure the golfers experienced and further caused a self-induced meltdown. It's abundantly clear that the golfers didn't have the right mental response when it came to this self-induced pressure. Otherwise, they would have performed the same in both scenarios.

Pressure may bust pipes, but I believe it strengthens people. I love the metaphor about coal being transformed into a diamond (that's why I touched on it previously): a diamond was nothing more than a chunk of coal that changed under pressure. Pressure produces diamonds. Or as Joel Osteen puts it:

> *"Pressure: it can turn a lump of coal into a flawless diamond, or a person into the champion they were meant to be."*
>
> *"Or, an average person into a perfect basket case."*

Understand that when the pressure is on and you're dealing with stressful situations, these times in life will allow you to emerge better because of the amount of resilience you have developed.

I could give you many examples of people choking under pressure. I'm sure you know someone who has choked or perhaps you've experienced it first-hand. But rather than focus on the problem, let's look for some inspiration and find a solution. Let me share this quick poem I read from Jim Tressel's book, *The Winners Manual:*

How do you act when the pressure's on,
When the chance for victory is almost gone.
When Fortune's star has refused to shine,
When the ball is on your five-yard line?

How do you act when the going's rough,
Does your spirit lag when the breaks are tough?
Or, is there in you a flame that glows
Brighter as fiercer the battle grows?

How hard, how long will you fight the foe?
That's what the world would like to know!

Cowards can fight when they're out ahead.
The uphill grind shows a thoroughbred!
You wish for success? Then tell me son,
How do you act when the pressure's on?

What do you do when the pressure is on and you need to rapidly come up with a solution to your problem? The best thing to do is relax and let go. This might sound counter-intuitive, so the best way to explain it is by telling you how to throw a powerful punch.

The world's greatest boxers know that if your body is too tense, you will not be able to throw a punch that knocks out your opponent. On the contrary, if you are loose and relaxed, you will be able to hit the other person with tremendous speed and power. This same principle is used by baseball pitchers to throw baseballs at near 100 miles per hour. It's also the explanation behind the controversial opinion that drunk drivers are less injured than sober ones when in the same type of car accidents because they're too loose to brace for impact. (Of course, that is more than made up for by alcohol causing much more severe accidents than the types sober drivers are in.)

You were born with the ability for smoothness of action, which your body uses for the most efficient kinetics of action; hence, the most speed or power, depending on the need. This ability is because of your *cerebellum* (*"little brain"*), the part of your brain that manages coordination all in the background without overtly thinking – thinking, that is, like the golfer about the money on the line or the audience who may be watching. Tensing up, due to overthinking what your background "little" brain is already on top of, overrides the smoothness that is courtesy of your cerebellum. Choke!

While your cerebellum – when there is no interference from overthinking – controls the smoothness of physical action, there is another, vaguer, control in your mind that works similarly toward the speed or power of your ability to think clearly and effectively. However, this ability isn't limited to modern-day sports. Relaxing your mind and body for peak performance is an ancient strategy that's been used for hundreds of years by the world's greatest philosophers and scientists.

Let's take a look at how one of the most brilliant people in history was able to relax his mind and solve complex problems effortlessly.

ALBERT EINSTEIN'S PROBLEM-SOLVING METHOD

> "Your mind will answer most questions if you learn to relax and wait for the answer."
>
> ~WILLIAM S. BURROUGHS, American writer and visual artist

Albert Einstein came up with his famous $E=mc^2$ equation

through relaxation. He had an unusual yet effective way of relaxing that allowed him to tap into his creative problem-solving abilities.

Einstein had the habit of drifting off into sleep a few times a day. He always rested in his work chair, held a pencil in one hand and placed a glass plate below the hand holding the pencil. When Einstein was in this position, he would start to fall asleep. He would get sleepy to the point where the pencil would fall out of his hand and make a loud clanking noise upon hitting the plate, waking him up.

Einstein swore by this unorthodox napping method, insisting that these micro-naps were key to relaxing his mind and allowing him to tap into his genius. He would intensely focus on a subject for many hours, take his small nap, and repeat this cycle over and over again until he solved the problem he was facing.

During these short naps, Einstein was allowing his subconscious mind to work on the problem while giving his conscious mind a chance to recharge its batteries.

> Your subconscious mind is the source of your most creative insights and is far more powerful (exponentially more powerful) than your conscious mind in developing innovative ideas. Your conscious mind is your brain making sense out of your universe. Therefore, it is rational. Your subconscious, however, is the random firing and misfiring of thoughts; it doesn't forbid tangential thinking or kooky connections between concepts.
>
> Think about how your dreams go. While nonsensical musings allow a trial-and-error for many things that cannot work, occasionally things will – and yield a novel solution for a problem that has been extremely difficult to solve.
>
> When your conscious and subconscious are used together for learning, this becomes a "super-learning experience", which we will take a deep-dive into in Chapter Seven. And in the previous

chapter (Chapter Two), this was the rationale behind the exercise of writing down goals (conscious) for you to "sleep on" (subconscious) overnight.

Einstein discovered (long before neuroscientists did) the immense power of our subconscious. And he frequently tapped into his subconscious mind to solve the most important problems in physics. In other words, he left *his* universe to come up with solutions for *the real* Universe!

Einstein's problem-solving method worked for two specific reasons. First, he had complete faith in his ability to solve the problem. In conjunction with his naps, he did everything he could in his waking hours to find solutions. That included viewing the problem from all possible angles, doing his research and sharing his ideas with colleagues to get valuable feedback. Then, as he napped, as I discussed in Chapter Two, his subconscious could dwell on the problems he wrote down (as I instructed you to do in the exercise).

Second, Einstein did not allow his self-worth to become tied to his ability to solve the problem. Instead, he practiced patience and allowed the solution to come to him when the time was right: the problem was so important to solve that he was willing to wait.

A neurological aside:

Researchers in the journal *Brain Mapping,* have proven through fMRI imaging studies of the brain that creative and non-creative thinking in the brain each uses different areas. This was determined by which parts of the brain "lit up" in two groups of people: freestyle rappers and poets as they created poems. This sheds some light on why our best ideas may come to us while we're in the shower, riding the bus/subway, or just before drifting off to sleep.

Apparently, the "busy" areas of the brain involved with our busy lives dominate these creative areas, but when there just isn't enough "busy-ness" going on, the creative areas can be heard. It is very similar to dreaming, but with a slight twist. Dreams are random firings of collected "thought debris" from one's day; creativeness is a dopamine-driven interconnection of neural networks that are otherwise out-shouted by the conscious brain when busy.

Something else the researchers discovered was that after the creation process, reviewing or refining the very things that were created used different parts of the brain than those responsible for the "creations." Some areas were active in both the creation and the refining activities, but in the creation process, specific areas were more isolated in their activation.

What this means to someone pursuing a vision, and the goals that will take him/her there is that simple relaxing (which you intuitively do occasionally without even knowing it: crossing your legs is a relaxation method because it induces unity between your left and right brain hemispheres, automatically establishing calmness in the nervous system) of the mind and body allows for creativity. In other words, the rational brain gets out of the way.

Calmness of the mind certainly has implications in learning, which is the whole point of failing and resumption through resilience. In Chapter Seven, I will detail the types of learning the brain does, from the empty sponge of the infant to someone seasoned and already educated heaping more data into his or her brain. However, for now, it's just important to know that there are different types of brain waves associated with different types of learning.

For instance, Delta and Theta waves, in the first six years of life, corresponding to passive learning, which while unfocused,

> produces an amazing opportunity to instantly memorize information. This is why children in multilingual households speak two or more languages when exposed to them during this phase of learning. It is "super-learning" because it is subconscious learning, not unlike the creative juices of the creative brain that stand out when we relax.
>
> This makes for very exciting insights, from being creative in the shower to learning from our mistakes, when the normally suppressed creative neural networks can make even the improbable associations that can solve the problems in our conscious world.

Einstein was wise enough to realize that your failing today does not mean you will fail forever. It is only when you choose to quit for good that failure is permanent. If Albert Einstein didn't solve a problem one day, it didn't faze him. He would simply try the next day and had faith he was eventually going to find the answer. A day of failure did not mean a lifetime of failure for Einstein. It only meant another day of napping with his pencil in his hand.

You would exponentially increase your probability of achieving your goals if you employ the same approach Einstein did toward solving the challenges life throws your way; that is, relaxing your mind and harnessing the creativity and super learning that comes with relaxation (i.e. an "unbusy" mind). Perhaps you have failed at doing something once, or even several times, but it doesn't mean that you'll fail again the next time you try. There are so many opportunities and ways to go about solving problems in modern-day society that it's almost heartbreaking to see people attempt great things, fail early, then quit permanently.

Take things one step at a time. Pause, but don't give up. Relax, but don't go comatose. Maybe you didn't make millions of dollars with that invention you finally patented and put on the market, but that doesn't mean your invention is bad. Perhaps one potential customer slams the door in your face, but that doesn't mean your product (or app) can't help countless others.

Learn to view each failure in its entirety but in its *segregated* entirety. Put it on a shelf. Look at it from different angles. What could you do better, and how can you do it better? Figure it out. Then ask yourself: do you have a problem or an opportunity for a solution? Sleep on it. Take a shower. Or take a bus/subway. And have the patience to allow the answers to come to you.

CONCLUSION

> "It is not the critic who counts; not the man who points out how the strong man stumbles, or where the doer of deeds could have done them better. The credit belongs to the man who is actually in the arena, whose face is marred by dust and sweat and blood; who strives valiantly; who errs, who comes short again and again, because there is no effort without error and shortcoming; but who does actually strive to do the deeds; who knows great enthusiasms, the great devotions; who spends himself in a worthy cause; who at the best knows in the end the triumph of high achievement, and who at the worst, if he fails, at least fails while daring greatly, so that his place shall never be with those cold and timid souls who neither know victory nor defeat."
>
> ~TEDDY ROOSEVELT, 26th president of the United States

Many people can craft a vision of what they want in life (Chapter One). And writing out interval goals along with plans that will help achieve the vision is fairly straightforward as well (Chapter Two). But when it comes to facing adversity and challenges along the way, this seems to be the element that holds most people back. That's why I spent some additional time in this chapter really drilling down the importance of strengthening your resilience muscles and attacking this vital character trait from as many angles as possible.

Strengthening your resilience muscles is one thing, keeping them strong however is another. That's why it's beneficial to recognize that one of the key tenets to maintaining strong resilience muscles is having a short-term memory on your losses. The quicker you are able to extract the lessons from your setbacks and forget the negative experiences – the less you give the opportunity for your resilience muscles to atrophy. This is certainly easier said than done.

When my financial planning firm failed – and that failure was put on the front page of the newspapers – I had a very difficult time erasing my massive mistakes from my mind. My mind wanted to replay my failure over and over. My self-talk kept a voice in my head, constantly reminding me of what a failure I was. But I had to force myself to shift my focus away from my colossal screw-up and toward extracting the lessons.

If you can make your mistakes irrelevant, it doesn't matter if you can forget them or not. In fact, it'll be hard if they are part of the lessons learned. The takeaway here is just not to allow your mistakes (or failures) to keep you from learning the lessons, making the necessary adjustments (in your plan, behavior and beliefs) and being bold and trying again.

> **"While we are free to choose our actions, we are not free to choose the consequences of our actions."**
> ~STEPHEN R. COVEY

During my prison term, I spent a tremendous amount of time figuring out exactly where I went wrong. Here's what I discovered:

1. **I worked harder on my image than on my integrity:** As a young financial advisor, my first instinct was to work on my image. I thought if prospects saw me driving a certain

car or wearing an expensive suit, they would want to do business with me. Now, I have learned that was wrong. I have also learned that when we spend too much time polishing our image, we tarnish our character.

2. I looked for instant gratification:
   Seeking instant gratification played a significant role in my imprisonment. And my greed and impatience caused me to lose everything. I learned that the chief cause of failure occurs when we trade what we want most for what we want now. My prison experience taught me that long-term happiness requires short-term sacrifices, and that the best shortcut is usually disguised as the long way.

3. I did not mix the advice I was given with common sense:
   I trusted the advice my corporate attorney gave me with regard to the stock repurchase contracts, and I was sold when my president thought it was a "marvelous idea." But I was so wrong. I learned that I must do a better job of mixing the advice I receive with common sense, and not let my emotions sabotage my better judgment.

4. I became arrogant and saw my success as an entitlement:
   The more successful I became, the more invincible I thought I was. Prison was a tremendous ego-busting experience and one that I was in great need of. I learned that arrogance is easy to rationalize and difficult to recognize. I also learned to find ways to check myself.

5. I made exceptions:
   When I made an exception once, it made it all that much easier to do again and again, greasing an already slippery slope. Then, before I realized exactly what was taking place, behavior, which at one time seemed completely unacceptable, began to seem normal. The most important

lesson I have learned is that exceptions are the most dangerous things we have to deal with in life. I know that this is precisely how I got off track, but most importantly, I know I will never make that mistake again.

I share the lessons I learned with you because I want to emphasize that I'm constantly practicing what I teach. And also, because I believe other people can learn an awful lot from my mistakes. Richard Dawkins, author of *The Selfish Gene,* stated:

"Organisms that only learn through trial and error, lose to organisms that learn from other's trials and errors."

The amount of trial-and-error I have experienced in life is what provided me with the wisdom to write this book. And the number one reason why you are reading these words is because of my ability to bounce back from failure. It all boils down to the amount of resilience I've developed throughout the difficult times in my life. Having a vision is necessary, and setting goals is necessary, but resilience saves the day for them every time.

I've done the best I can to try to illustrate the importance of resilience, the impact it can have on your life and how you can go about building it. Unfortunately, resilience isn't something you can simply study, memorize, and have automatically appear. You can comprehend it in theory, but the character trait is developed through the conscious choice of continuously withstanding challenges regardless of what life throws at you.

"Life is truly known only to those who suffer, lose, endure adversity, and stumble from defeat to defeat."

~ANAIS NIN

When you start taking action in pursuit of achieving your goals, without question, you'll encounter setbacks. And it is at those defining moments you'll have a choice to make. Will you tap into resilience and persevere until you prevail, or will you accept defeat? My hope is that you will press on – that you'll deny the temptation to accept defeat as your reality, and instead, think that no matter how long it takes or how impossible something may seem, you are in it for the long haul.

Some people just can't be defeated. You just have to decide if you're one of them.

Instead of looking for the easy way out (the sure path to defeat), you need to face every problem, challenge, loss, and difficulty with the intention of gaining something beneficial out of the experience. When you approach setbacks with this mindset you'll quickly realize that your worst days can end up becoming your best days because you end up learning some very powerful life lessons from the hard times. Thus, your setbacks become important investments into your resilience development.

When you overcome your setbacks (and I promise you will), you will be able to look back at those pivotal moments and bask in the vast amounts of resilience you have developed. Sure, you may have felt frustrated and depressed when you first encountered them, but as you go further along on your journey to success, overcoming the challenges will become proud moments in your life. You'll discover that the resilience you built from experiencing setbacks and conquering them was one of the greatest gifts you could have ever acquired.

Remember Captain Yeager's words, "Just before you break the sound barrier is when the cockpit shakes the most." That's the way it works for all of us when we're about to have a breakthrough. So let the cockpit shake; you cannot stop it. But stay focused on the journey until you achieve your goals.

EXERCISE NO. 1: COMMIT THE QUOTE BELOW TO MEMORY

You need to be able to recite this to yourself when times get tough:

"We are all faced with a series of extraordinary opportunities brilliantly disguised as impossible situations."

~CHARLES R. SWINDOLL

EXERCISE NO. 2: GET SOME SUN

When exposed to the sun, your skin manufactures vitamin D. This vitamin acts as a mood stabilizer and releases pleasurable hormones in your brain. Ten minutes of sunlight can literally and figuratively brighten up your world. It is also a way to engage your mind-body connection (Harvard 3rd characteristic).

EXERCISE NO. 3: LISTEN TO POSITIVE MESSAGES

Your brain works 31 percent better when it has a positive mindset, according to Shawn Achor, author of the *New York Times* bestselling book, *The Happiness Advantage.* Achor's research has shown we become 31 percent more intelligent just by being in a positive state of mind. Therefore, during difficult times it's essential to have positive, encouraging, and uplifting messages infused in your mind. You can do this in your car, in your office, in your home – any environment you find yourself.

During times of adversity, your mind is your biggest problem. When you lock into positive messages, when you continuously imbue your mind with encouragement, it will increase the probability of you coming up with solutions.

Alternatively, when your mind is focused on the negative – when fear has overtaken you – it is nearly impossible to come up with solutions during difficult times. This is just your mind focusing only on the negative at the expense of the creative process required to come up with new ideas that will put your troubles behind you. Negative thinking blinds you from discovering opportunities to overcome your obstacles.

As explained in this chapter, when your scheming mind (any negative attitude desperate to escape consequences) overcomes the creative mind (and it's powerful partner, your subconscious), you're dead in the water.

There are many life-preservers you can grab hold of. You can simply go to iTunes or YouTube and search for motivational speeches, where you will discover several albums and playlists. You will find countless hours of motivational messages for free that will inspire and encourage you.

It's important to understand that you do not listen to these messages only when you have time; you do not listen to these messages only when you feel like it. You force yourself to constantly hear motivational talks over and over and over again. This is one of the best ways to overcome a negative mindset because there's nothing worse than being alone with your own thoughts when negative things are happening around you. That's a defective lens that can only distort and destroy your universe.

There are people in the world who have spent a tremendous amount of time listening to the most positive and encouraging messages ever published, taken those messages and combined them all together. They have spent endless hours so that you can listen to all of their hard work for free. If you're reading this and you're one of those people who have put together motivational speeches to help encourage others, I want to personally thank you because you've gotten me through some extremely difficult times in my life.

EXERCISE NO. 4: GET YOUR HAIR CUT

Why is this important to strengthening your resilience muscle? It is crucial for you to feel good about yourself when you're going through challenging times. A positive self-image will do wonders for your ability to bounce back from setbacks. A polished reflection will end up making you smile more, and smiles have a way of reverse engineering themselves back to those parts of your brain that feel the things that make you smile. And, if you remember from Chapter One, the "imagining" neurons are the same ones that fire as the "doing" neurons. Thus, smiles mean more smiles.

But wait. Know that this isn't the same thing as polishing your image at the expense of your integrity. As I stated previously, that's a huge mistake and one I made and learned from. Instead, you must polish your self-image for self-esteem, and this must partner with your integrity. When you do that, the smiles are genuine. Otherwise, you're taking a good thing and turning it bad.

EXERCISE NO. 5: VOLUNTEER

"*Well, that's an hour I'll never get back,*" no volunteer has ever said. "Goodness is its own reward," explained New Orleans Charity Hospital surgeon John L. DiLeo, M.D., having done many surgeries on the medically underserved.

When you volunteer, you release a trifecta of happiness hormones into your brain: dopamine, oxytocin, and serotonin – or, reward, bonding, and feel-good, respectively. A happy mind is a positive mind, and a positive mindset will help you find the solutions you need to overcome the difficult situation you're facing.

Another benefit of volunteering is swimming in someone else's pond. Whether you're the proverbial big fish or a small fish, getting into someone else's pond will shatter the insulating (and segregating!) bubble that keeps you involved with only like-minded people. Volunteering exposes you to *un*like-minded people. Like Einstein leaving his universe to solve the problems of the real universe, engaging with others from totally alien walks of life can sometimes add insight you can bring back to your own pond. You'll be the bigger fish for it!

Finding ways to volunteer is simple. Go to Google, type the city you live in, followed by the word "volunteer." Look through the search results and find an organization that aligns with the things you are passionate about in life.

EXERCISE NO. 6: MEDITATE

The facts don't lie. Numerous scientific studies have proven that meditation can mitigate stress, increase memory retention, and strengthen our problem-solving skills.

Some of the wealthiest executives in the world make time to meditate every day. Meditation allows us to focus our minds and to declutter and untangle our thoughts, which results in calmness in our lives. This calmness allows us to step out of our conscious mind and tap into our subconscious mind. Our subconscious mind is where the real magic is. It's also why Albert Einstein famously said:

> *"We cannot solve our problems with the same thinking...(that)... created them."*

Below is a simple yet effective strategy to make the most out of meditating. Start with just five minutes and try to work your way up to twenty minutes daily. And remember that consistency is the key to successful meditation. (Refer to page 66 in this book for previous guidance on meditating.)

1. **Rhythmic breathing**
   The right way: four seconds in and four seconds out, followed by four seconds in and four seconds out. Or five seconds in and three seconds out, followed by five seconds in and three

seconds out.

The wrong way: five seconds in and three seconds out, followed by four seconds in and four seconds out. See how your breathing is out of sync? The key here is to maintain the exact same amount of time you inhale-and-exhale throughout your entire meditation session. Rhythmic is smooth; non-rhythmic is choppy and inconsistent.

2. Smooth breathing

   When you're breathing in for five seconds and out for three seconds – if that is the breathing pattern you want to follow throughout your meditation session – make sure you don't take several choppy breaths when you breathe in for five seconds or out for three seconds. Each cycle of 4 + 4 or 5 + 3 should take the same amount of time (eight seconds). Sporadic breathing will yield poor results in calming your mind.

3. Location of your attention

   Remain mindful of every time your thoughts begin to wonder and, if they do, gently refocus your mind on nothingness (peace and tranquility). When you're breathing, focus on the center of your chest, right where your heart is. I know this is contrary to how the vast majority of gurus teach meditation, but it makes perfect sense.

   Here are three reasons why:

   1. Your heart generates more electrical power than any other part of your system. In fact, that's the whole basis behind the science of ECG recordings. The heart generates fifty times more electrical output than the brain and 5000 times more energy.

   2. Breathing through the center of your chest helps get you outside of your mind. Or more specifically...outside of your *conscious* mind.

3. You feel the awareness in your heart; you say *I love my son with all my heart*, not, *I love my son with all my mind*.

Below is a great acronym to remember when you meditate:

Breathe
Rhythmically
Evenly
And
Through
Heart
Every day

Personally, when I meditate, I like to repeat silently to myself, "*I am here now*," to help my mind stay in the present.

EXERCISE NO. 7: CREATE A SENSE OF URGENCY; MAKE LIFE ITSELF AN EMERGENCY

At this very moment, someone in the world is taking their last breath. Regularly, I'm reminding myself that my time is running out. I believe we all have proverbial hourglasses above our heads, and each moment of each day we have less time. That's why I need you to do this quick exercise.

This short exercise will help paint a picture illustrating that you have less time than you think, which I hope encourages you to take action on the things you want to do with your life:

365 days in a year (fact)
80-year life expectancy (hopefully)
365 X 80 = 29,200 total days you have to work with
Now take your current age: let's say you're 30
30 X 365 = 10,950 days that you have already used up
29,200 – 10,950 = 18,250 days left

That's it.

That's all the days you've got to make a difference. To share love with the people you care about. And to leave your mark on this world. You have no time to waste worrying about all the reasons why things won't work or worry about past happenings. Worry is profitless, but assigning importance to something you have to change is profitable. The time is now to get started. Because once this day is spent, it's gone forever.

Create your own sense of urgency...

_________ X 365 = _______ days that you have already used up
(your age here)

29,200 – _________ = _________ days left

CHAPTER FOUR

Instant Gratification – Sacrifice A Moment for A Life

"Choose well; your choice is brief, and yet endless."

~JOHANN WOLFGANG VON GOETHE, German writer and statesman

"...and lead us not into temptation..."

~THE LORD'S PRAYER

Several years ago, I read a book by a famous self-help author. And I'll never forget what I discovered when I opened it and started reading. In the introduction, the author wrote that we are the way we are because that's the way we want to be – otherwise we would be in the process of changing the way we are.

When I read that, I set the book down and took a moment to reflect. Recalling the von Goethe quote above, I thought about what it was that interferes the most with wanting to change the way we are, and it is a very important concept that doesn't get much attention in the self-help industry: *Instant Gratification* (a.k.a. *Immediate Gratification*). Thus, one of the biggest obstacles to change – even when we intellectually reason that changing ourselves is the right decision – is instant gratification. That is, the "*gimmes*" come and go (von Goethe's "*brief*"), but their repercussions can weave a permanent pattern in the fabric of our lives (von Goethe's "*...yet endless*"); sadly, such quickly and sloppily woven patterns clash with our true fiber.

History is riddled with instances of people's capacity to chase instant gratification above all else. You'd be hard-pressed to find a greater human desire than the one for immediate results, and you'd be hard-pressed to find a more frequent cautionary tale in literature (and politics).

Instant gratification can be defined as something that pleases or satisfies you immediately. Instant gratification can be given or received. However, it only exists as a pleasure-seeking mechanism. Humans tend to pursue pleasure at all costs, so it's no surprise that people tend to seek immediate pleasure. The other side of the coin is that we also do whatever it takes to avoid pain, and the line between these two drives can often blur.

This means that we are primarily governed by our desire to experience pleasure and avoid pain. No matter the cost or the consequences, the vast majority of people in the world make decisions based upon how much pleasure they can attain while avoiding as much pain as possible. Various schools of psychoanalysis describe this phenomenon as the *Pleasure Principle*.

As children, we operate exclusively on the pleasure principle. We have no concept of waiting for anything; it simply doesn't exist. We want everything *now*. As we grow older, we learn how to delay the gratification of our pleasure as we come face-to-face with what psychoanalyst Sigmund Freud called the *Reality Principle*.

We learn to understand that we can't have everything we want right away, no matter how much we may want it. This is called "delaying gratification". Given that humans are hardwired to seek out pleasure, learning to delay gratification can be challenging.

And sadly, many people never learn to master this vital skill. They never learn how to delay gratification.

According to Jerry S. Wiggins and Krista K. Trobst, in *Comprehensive Clinical Psychology*, 1998:

> *"The psychoanalytic model of primary (pleasure principle) and secondary (reality principle) modes of thought is meant to account for both a developmental sequence and characteristics of the mature adult (Rapaport, 1951)."*

This means that we mature from infancy's primary drive of seeking pleasure and avoiding pain to the secondary mode of thinking that comes with maturity (based on reality). However, all adults mature differently.

An evolutionary aside:

Primitive man operated primarily on his/her limbic system, which proved valuable in survival by using benefits derived from emotions, fear, aggression, hunger, and sex drive. Such a primitive system had little restraint: if something was desired – food, mate, etc. – it was simply seized and taken. *(So simple, even a caveman could do it.)* Since then, the emergence of a higher intellect to suppress unacceptable behavior has led to the rise of civilization. However, like the little devil on your shoulder, your caveman's hardwiring for immediate gratification is always there to tempt you.

Leading behavioral psychologists have concluded that the level of control we have over our desire for instant gratification directly determines how successful we will become in life. According to *Psychology Today*, studies regularly show that delaying gratification is one of the top character traits of successful people and that over time, suppressing immediate gratification will improve self-control and ultimately help achieve long-term goals. This means that the ability to postpone gratification is a major predictor of success in people's lives.

Each time you make a decision, you need to calculate the value of immediate gratification versus the value (i.e. *investment*) of delayed gratification. Because we tend to do this subconsciously and without much conscious thought, often we have no clue that we are evaluating all of life's decisions on the simple basis of gratification.

Shocking, isn't it? Now you might be wondering: what's wrong with that? What's wrong with wanting to constantly seek out pleasure?

If you are continuously feeding your desire for pleasure instead of delaying gratification, it is impossible for you to achieve great things. How can I say that with so much confidence? Easy: virtually all great things require time and preparation, and anything that comes easy and fast typically leaves you the same way.

Look at Maslow's pyramid. The things that will give you real pleasure in life – that is, fulfillment and self-actualization – are the things that take time to build and grow. So as you absorb these words, I would like you to think about the principle of delayed gratification and how it can serve you when you learn to trade what you want now, for what you want most in life.

THE MARSHMALLOW EXPERIMENT

> "If you study the root causes of business disasters, over and over you'll find [a] predisposition towards endeavors that offer immediate gratification."
>
> ~CLAYTON CHRISTENSEN, American academic, business consultant, Harvard Business School Professor

There is a proven connection between success and a person's willingness to make sacrifices in delaying gratification. In an op-ed column for *The Wall Street Journal,* Arthur C. Brooks argued that people who are unable to delay gratification ultimately end up failing in their endeavors, as sacrifice is an essential part of becoming a successful entrepreneur.

Much of the material in Brooks' article was based on a study that was conducted in 1972 by Stanford psychologist Walter Mischel. In the study, small children sat at a table and were given a marshmallow. These children were told if they waited fifteen minutes to eat the marshmallow, they would get not only that first marshmallow but a second one as well. However, if they were unable to wait, they would not get a second marshmallow.

The researcher would then leave the room, giving the child the chance to decide whether to give in to immediate gratification and eat the first marshmallow right away, or delay gratification and choose to wait fifteen minutes to get a double marshmallow payoff.

It's important to remember that children behave in accordance with the pleasure principle, so the results shouldn't be shocking to anyone who reads this. Two-thirds of the kids were not able to delay gratification. This result was expected, but that's not the part of the study that the researchers were interested in. What they wanted to know was how these children would end up doing in their later years. They followed up with the same kids after some time had passed.

Since two-thirds of the children gave in, obviously there is the one-third that managed to defer gratification. More than a decade later, the researchers followed up on their study, and here's what they discovered about the children who were able to delay gratification with the marshmallow test. Those children:

- Scored on average 210 points higher on their SATs than the kids who did not delay gratification
- Were less likely to drop out of college than the kids who did not delay gratification

- Earned more money than the kids who did not delay gratification
- Suffered fewer problems with drugs and alcohol than the kids who did not delay gratification

The evidence is clear: success in life hinges on whether or not we can discipline ourselves and defer seeking instant gratification which will, in turn, set us up for future sustained success. It really doesn't matter if we're a college student or a CEO, having the foresight to sacrifice now for later will always produce the best long-term results.

Brooks elaborates on some of the implications of his research into delayed gratification and explains how it plays a major role throughout our lives, along with how it can even make or break an entrepreneur's career:

> *"But the evidence goes beyond a finding that people who can defer gratification tend to turn out well in general. When we hear about successful entrepreneurs, it is always as if they have the Midas touch. A pimply college kid cooks up an Internet company during a boring lecture at Harvard, and before lunch he's a billionaire. In real life, that's not how it works.*
>
> *"Northwestern University professor Stephen Rodgers has shown that the average entrepreneur fails about four times before succeeding. When asked about their ultimate success, entrepreneurs often talk instead about the importance of their hardships...*
>
> *"When I asked the legendary investment company founder Charles Schwab about the success of the $15 billion corporation that bears his name, he told me the story about taking out a second mortgage on his home just to make payroll in the early years. Why this emphasis on the struggle?*
>
> *"Entrepreneurs know that when they sacrifice, they are learning and improving, exactly what they need to do to earn success through*

their merit. Every sacrifice and deferred gratification makes them wiser and better, showing them that they're not getting anything for free. When success ultimately comes, they wouldn't trade away the early days for anything, even if they felt wretched at the time."

So, again...people who are unable to delay gratification ultimately end up failing in their endeavors, as sacrifice is an essential part of becoming a successful CEO. Successful people realize early on that they must master the mental skill of delaying pleasure if they want to achieve their goals. What exactly does that mean? It means not being distracted every time they get a notification on their smartphone. It also means giving up on going out to parties on the weekends and, instead, choosing to stay home (or go to their local coffee shop) to work on their dreams. It means instead of relaxing and having fun after their 9-to-5 job is over, they schedule 6 p.m. to 11 p.m. as their "hustle" hours for building their business.

Sure, everyone has the desire to have fun right now. But everyone also has the ability to delay their gratification for the better things that will come to them in the future if they are serious about achieving success in their lives.

A self-discipline aside:

In her book *The Willpower Instinct*, Kelly McGonigal claims there are three keys to self-discipline: the ability to do what has to be done; the ability to avoid temptation, and the ability to remember the big picture of your life.

It's critical that you learn to sacrifice and fight for what you want in life. Because I have found that if you're not willing to fight for what you want; eventually, you'll be forced to fight against the things you don't want later on. It other words: sacrifice for what you want, or what you want will become the sacrifice.

COMMAS INSTEAD OF PERIODS

"An undisciplined life is an insane life."

~SOCRATES, Greek philosopher

Let me share an example with you that illustrates two things:

1. Successful people "get it" about delaying gratification.
2. They also have a written plan.

The *Two Comma Club* is an award individuals receive after they produce over $1,000,000 on a website. I'm proud to say I'm a member. What's more, I became a member just four years after being released from prison, after I had lost everything.

This led to my invitation, as part of a group of the world's top 30 Internet entrepreneurs, to participate in contributing a chapter to a book on Internet marketing. (This speaks well for a topic I cover in Chapter Six, centered on choosing your friends wisely.) If I would have continued hanging out with people who were not growing themselves and allowed their negative habits to impact the way I behaved, it is unlikely that Russell Brunson, co-founder of ClickFunnels, a $100,000,000-plus software company, would have reached out and asked me to contribute a chapter to one of his books.

Russell did not recruit me because I drive a fancy foreign car (I don't) or have a watch that doesn't tick (it does). He reached out to me because I spent a tremendous amount of time developing the best possible version of myself, and that would have been impossible had I given in to instant gratification. Because of that, I had something to bring to the table – something of value to offer.

The idea behind Brunson's book was that the top online marketers would share their expertise in regards to the following scenario:

You suddenly lose all your money, along with your name and reputation, and only have your marketing know-how left. You're unknown, unfinanced, and unconnected. You have nothing. You're a nobody. What would you do from Day 1 to Day 30 to save yourself and get back on top?

In other words, you no longer have your big guru name, your social media following, or joint venture partners (affiliates). Other than your vast marketing experience, you're an unknown newbie. You have bills piled high and people harassing you for money over the phone. But in this scenario, you also have an Internet connection. What would you do, from day 1 to day 30, to save yourself? What would be your plan?

My plan became a chapter in Russell's book (*30 Days*) and had two things in common with the other experts' 30-day plans. Of course, one thing in common was the written plan itself, which constituted the actual assignment. But the other thing is the takeaway message here:

Every one of these experts' calendar countdown (including mine) for rising out of the ashes to glory was fundamentally dependent on delaying instant gratification.

We all, thereby, avoided the biggest mistake that will stop the countdown to success like no other. It is a mistake that is easily made when your goals are not written down (see Chapter Two). Without a written plan, your crystal ball to see your vision gets very cloudy and you get caught up in the present, which is begging for the shiny object syndrome: the new car, new house, new opportunity and many other extravagances. For example, many flourishing business owners, when they finally catch their breath and make some money, go get that new (shiny) car. This down payment – along with the large monthly note – is a sure sign of someone who is undisciplined and unable to delay gratification.

Practicing what I teach (and learning from my past mistakes): for many years while I was in the re-building phase of my life (after prison), I drove a Kia, even though I could have easily afforded a brand new BMW, Mercedes, Tesla, Range Rover – you name it. But I knew my short-term sacrifice (denying a status-driven car) was guided by my merely needing something on wheels that took me from point A to point B. This was all I really needed while I was making my comeback. I knew this translated into more money I could use for growing my business.

That's just one example of delay now and profit later. Looking into the strategies implemented by all the members of the *Two Comma Club*, the same logic permeates their entire mindset. What was the overriding theme of their logic? What did these successful entrepreneurs do? All of them, without exception, took their returns – small initially, then larger as the 30 days progressed – and immediately re-invested the money they made right back into their businesses (back into *themselves*). This means the business comes first, not the trip to the new car dealership. Not the new house. Not the season tickets. The successful business owners know they need to keep **re**-investing in their business until they have a stable, repeatable, and predictable process for generating revenue.

> **"My proceeds from the PayPal acquisition were $180 million. I put $100 million in SpaceX, $70 million in Tesla, and $10m in Solar City. I had to borrow money for rent."**
>
> ~ELON MUSK

Do we all want a shiny new car? Sure. But, more than the car, we want to be able to live life on our own terms, we want the freedom that only discipline and sacrifice can provide. We demand to be the CEOs of our lives! This is a beautiful example of delaying gratification, and I thought it was awe-inspiring that all the top Internet entrepreneur interviews I watched (at https://www.30days.com) confirmed unanimously that they would immediately reinvest all their profits back into their business.

Delay that shiny new car for your shiny new life!

In a way, the *Two Comma Club* contains a parable in its very title. A comma, either in a number (hopefully, a large number) or in a sentence, means to keep on counting...or keep on reading. In other words, it's ongoing. Not stopped. You want more commas in your life than periods, which end sentences. The period is final. Period.

CHOICE AND GRATIFICATION

> "The first principle is that you must not fool yourself, and you are the easiest person to fool."
>
> ~RICHARD P. FEYNMAN, Nobel prize-winning physicist

It's a sad but true fact that many people sleepwalk through their decisions. They simply live without putting much thought into why they do what they do. If you're one of those people who have been going through the motions, it's time for you to wake up and start thinking about the decisions that you make and why you make them. If some of them stink, it's time to wake up and smell your decisions!

People who don't strive to change for the better are often unsuccessful because everything stays the same for them. Their horizons are the status quo. There are no ventures, but also no failures, and that's okay with them. Doing the same things over and over is what makes their lives sleepwalks.

Have you ever gotten home and realized you don't exactly remember a turn you know you made to get there? This is called "*muscle memory*." Individuals who are not making deliberate decisions, who go through their lives sleepwalking with only muscle memory, often confuse the subtle difference between the words *want* and *need*. An example: if someone says that they need new shoes, take a look in their closet and you will likely find dozens of pairs of shoes. What they really meant to say is that they *want* a new pair of shoes. See the difference? The inability to distinguish between *want* and *need* is one of the things that allowed us to graduate above our caveman brains.

Let's look at another example: when someone says, "I need to take a break this weekend," what they really mean to say is that they *want* a break this weekend. They don't actually need the break because they aren't going to die if they don't get it. No bones will break, no blood clot will cause a stroke, and no gaskets will "blow."

The human body and mind are incredible in their potential and their endurance. As long as you are passionately chasing your dreams, they will support you so well that you won't even need a break.

> There are schools for children who don't have recess. Imagine that! There are no field trips. The only time away from didactic efforts is during physical fitness. Yet these children are happy. Why? Because a school that thinks children need a break is admitting that things are so bad that breaks are necessary. The truth is that children respond best to regimental education, with known limits and a predictable day. Such children achieve, and achieving children are happy children. As stated in the last paragraph, they "won't even need a break."
>
> This is not to say that this is the best way to establish a school schedule for children, as it is well known that play for them is extremely important. The point I'm making is that if you enjoy what you're doing, it won't be psychologically taxing.
>
> As adults, of course, things at times can seem overwhelming,

but the phrase "I need a break" is a sneaky little lie that we tell ourselves in order to feel good about not going after our dreams with everything that we can muster. If people like Elon Musk and Steve Jobs said, "I need a break," whenever they felt like straying off the path of success, I can guarantee you that companies like Tesla and Apple would not exist today.

I completely understand that there are times you get burned out. But there's a big difference between taking a break for a few hours, and then getting back on track, and taking days or even weeks off. Sometimes all you need is a good night's rest, and then you can wake up fresh in the morning and get back on point.

It's vitally important for you to distinguish the difference between your needs and your wants. When you are able to do that, you can stop sleepwalking through your decisions and you can also more easily tell the difference between immediate gratification and delayed gratification, and you will know when something is optional (wants) and when something is mandatory (needs).

To learn this difference requires alertness; that is, the first requirement to start learning delayed gratification is self-awareness. If you want to get from where you are right now to where you want to arrive in the future, you have to start becoming aware of the choices that you make and how they will slowly lead you away from (or toward) your desired destination over time.

Awareness allows you to be fully conscious of your decisions, especially the bad ones. It helps you recognize that your bad decisions are fueled by your brain telling you, "I need to experience pleasure and feel good *right now*, even if that means sabotaging important long-term goals." Do this often enough, and your brain won't even remember the *"even if that means sabotaging important long-term goals"* part but will jump-start at the "right now" part.

Above all, awareness helps you avoid the trap of "Oh, it's just this one time." Ask anybody who has struggled for years to break any bad habit, and they'll tell you that an exception is a slippery slope toward ruining all the hard work you've already done. Remember not to grease that slippery slope.

> **"99% commitment is a bitch, 100% is a breeze."**
>
> ~JACK CANFIELD

In the next chapter, I tackle habits in detail, but for now, make no mistake about it: exceptions will derail you in life. They may not do so immediately, but they always find a way to steer you off course. That's why I believe exceptions, especially made for instant gratification, are the most dangerous things we have to deal with in life. They become habits very easily. And the biggest chapter in the forbidden book of exceptions is the one on instant gratification.

HOW GRATIFICATION CHANGES THE SHORT-TERM AND IMPACTS THE LONG-TERM

> "One thing I learnt early in my career is that personal gratification takes second place."
>
> ~BRIAN O'DRISCOLL, Irish professional rugby union player

Every decision you make affects your life for better or worse. This means there is no such thing as an insignificant decision, and there is no such thing as a middle ground. (Heck, even "doing nothing" is something because you're choosing not to do something!). From the moment you wake up until the moment you close your eyes, you are making decisions. If you decided to get out of bed, that was one of the thousands of decisions you made that day.

Let's examine the example I just used through the lens of the pleasure principle: if you decided to get up and go to work rather than sleep in, you ultimately decided that the pain of getting out of bed was less severe than the pain of not having money in your wallet. Why? Because you need money in order to experience the pleasure of having a bed to sleep in and a roof over your head. On further inspection, this is really Freud's reality principle.

Of course, since you made this decision a long time ago when you started working, you didn't have to spend much mental energy weighing out the pains and pleasures involved in the decision to get out of bed in the morning. All of your subsequent thoughts and actions in regard to getting out of bed were based upon the principles of pleasure and pain.

Now that you understand how pain and pleasure are intertwined as dually opposing yet necessary forces, I want to show you the problem with giving in to immediate gratification. The problem with immediate gratification is that it's a dirty trick – it leads to long-term pain.

You will rarely experience the pain due to immediate gratification right away. Often times you won't see it tomorrow, a week from now, or even a month from now. But over time, the cumulative effect of giving in to immediate gratification will eventually lead to long-term pain. Why? Because in life, it's not the big things that make a difference. Rather, it's the hundreds, thousands, or millions of little things that separate the successful people from the failures. This is what mathematicians refer to as *"The Butterfly Effect."*

A meteorological aside:

Contrary to what sci-fi movies imply, The Butterfly Effect does not mean getting into a time machine and, because you stepped on a butterfly a million years ago, everyone in America is speaking German when you come back. The Butterfly Effect actually means that many small changes introduced into a larger system can result in large outcomes at a later time. It was described by Edward Lorenz, a meteorologist, to explain why weather predictions cannot be accurate more than five days out: the many flaps of butterfly wings, say in Brazil, causing a tornado in Texas weeks later.

Of course, it is much more than one butterfly, as it's the countless small perturbations on the planet that contribute to the big picture. And so, an entire branch of mathematics called *Chaos Theory* began. Similarly, all the small instant gratifications are cumulative on the karma odometer!

Let's say you eat a donut today because you gave in to the desire for the instant pleasure that you feel from putting it in your mouth. Mmm, yummy sugar! But what happens if you give in to that desire every day for the next month. Well, 30 (or more) donuts will eventually start showing up in your life in the form of weight gain.

Although there are many factors involved which can alter the math, generally it takes about 3,500 extra calories to gain a pound. That's about ten donuts. Thus, a donut a day means a weight gain of about three pounds a month, but that's not counting the extra calories from business lunches, ballgame junk food, or – say – the beers or the merlots. But let's just say a donut a day is your only guilty instant gratification: that adds up to 36 pounds a year!

Ten years? Well, now you see the problem. All of the small perturbations on your planet (each donut) contribute to the big picture in a "Butterfly Effect" fashion, all based on not delaying an instant sugar gratification. Your love handles won't be the only thing to worry about, because now you'll have a bucket full of health problems that likely include high cholesterol levels, diabetes, obesity, sleep apnea, atherosclerosis and heart disease, hypertension, low energy, and more. Not to mention that when you walk into a room, everyone will be saying, "Wow!" but not for the reasons you want.

SHORT-TERM SACRIFICES PRODUCE LONG-TERM HAPPINESS

"Sacrifice comes before success, even in the dictionary."

~VINCE LOMBARDI, American football player and coach, won five NFL championships

Let's see what happens when we choose to delay immediate pleasure and trade it for short-term pain. Instead of the donut, let's say that you go for an early morning run every day.

Initially, you suffer the pain of the run and you give up the pleasure of sleeping in. If you extrapolate this out as you did with the donut fantasy, eventually the short-term pain will turn into long-term pleasure. You will have a body worth showing off (people will say "Wow!" for the right reasons), you will feel mentally sharp, and your health will be at its prime. If you're overweight, hypertensive, and snoring the rafters down, you'll lose weight, your blood pressure will return to normal, and you won't get kicked out of bed anymore.

Let's look at another example of short-term sacrifices carried out over a long period of time. One of the most commonly recommended activities in the self-development industry is to read a chapter of a nonfiction book every day, or even ten pages. If you actually stick with that habit for a year, you will have read several books and gained a lot of invaluable insights.

Keep running with that habit for years, and you will become wise beyond words. You will learn strategies and discover new ideas from people who spent lifetimes condensing their best knowledge into the books you read. Over time, you will transform yourself into a completely different person. You won't even be able to recognize yourself, all because of what you *fed* your mind.

The key here is to remember that these daily practices are done over years, so don't think that you can try to speed-read ten books in a single day and shortcut the process. This would make as much sense as a 365-mile jog once a year.

TYPES OF IMMEDIATE GRATIFICATION

> "You are at the top when you are mature enough to delay gratification and shift your focus from your rights to your responsibilities."
>
> ~ZIG ZIGLAR

Gratification manifests itself in many ways throughout people's lives. Some people are able to handle one type of gratification while struggling with others. But in general, people tend to struggle with the following three forms:

1. Material Gratification
2. Emotional Gratification
3. Sexual Gratification

If you find someone who claims to be the ultimate master of handling every type of gratification in the world, they are either a monk, or they are lying (and probably a lying monk...who's also drunk!). Or, they could be someone who has read this book and taken action on the strategies I reveal.

Let's go through each form of gratification and see how we can identify the triggers, as well as how we can better prepare ourselves to avoid the problems they bring to our lives.

1. Material Gratification

> "Real happiness is never found outside of us; it's always found inside of us."
>
> ~UNKNOWN

We live in an age where material goods are available in overwhelming abundance. All the toys, gadgets, and devices that we could ever want are readily available by clicking a button on the Internet and having them delivered the following day (or the same day) to our home. With nothing but our finger, we can get virtually anything we want.

With all of this available 24/7, it's no surprise that millions of people all around the world are consumed by intense stress and worry. What's causing this stress and anxiety? The desire to accumulate as many material goods as possible. The more things there are, the more stress there is in trying to be the person who "has it all". No one said it better than Porgy, from the Gershwin musical:

Oh, I got plenty o' nuttin'
And nuttin's plenty for me
I got no car, got no mule
I got no misery
De folks wid plenty o' plenty
Got a lock on de door
'Fraid somebody's a-goin' to rob 'em
While dey's out a-makin' more
What for? ~Porgy, from Porgy and Bess

The storage business is a thriving industry ($50 billion in annual sales) because of people's wants (not needs) are fueled by the desire to over-accumulate. What we are physically able to keep around us is no longer the limit. These over-accumulators "stuff" has now spilled over onto other properties. The lesson we learn from storage facilities is that there is no limit to how much we can accumulate, and there is now no limit to how much we want. I submit that a superfluous lifestyle has no place on your climb up Maslow's pyramid.

I know people who have overextended themselves on credit to the point where they have a substantially negative net worth, and yet they will still go out, buy the hottest new Mercedes on the market, and proudly display their 88-inch high-definition television in the theater rooms of their interest-payments-only 100 percent financed homes.

If you are spending money that you do not have on the things you want yet don't really need, you are consciously choosing to give into immediate material gratification instead of pursuing the long-term benefits of delayed gratification. Without question, it's difficult to understand this rationale – the get now pay later – but why do so many people participate in this profitless (and pointless) game?

Do you know how many people I've run into that say they simply can't afford to pursue their dreams and refuse to quit their soul-killing day jobs? It's one of the worst excuses in the world for not chasing your dreams. Look, if you really want something bad enough, you will make the necessary sacrifices and overcome any obstacles to make it happen. Delaying gratification is one of the most important sacrifices that you can make if you want to pursue and achieve your dreams.

Ask yourself this simple question: *why do I want that new Mercedes when I know I don't have the money to buy it?*

You can probably think of many reasons, but a very common reason is the desire to increase your status and impress other people. Also, you want to live "*the sweet life*" right now, even if you have to borrow from your future to do it. A future which is uncertain – and which is especially tenuous given your choices in the present.

Technically, you're buying a car, but what you're really buying is the approval and admiration of other people in order to make yourself feel good. When you cruise down the streets, you feel validated. You feel like you matter. That is indeed the sweet life. But it's not your life – certainly not yet. And it's unlikely to be your life if you are unable to delay gratification.

If everyone on the planet magically vanished tomorrow and you were the only person left, the car would be a pointless purchase. With nobody around to admire your car or see it, what would be the point? You wouldn't feel any real pleasure from having that car, right?

In a way, living "the sweet life" (before its time) is intimately associated with impressing people. And impressing people is just a way to make you feel better by making others feel worse. It's your statement that while you are living it up, they are not; or at least, not as much as you can. That's your validation. But it's a lie: you are buying billboards for a product that does not exist – the *you* which you are putting forth as truth.

"People are insecure, and they need validation from others, and I think they use items to get validation from others."
~GARY VAYNERCHUK

Let's visit what would happen if you decided to chase your dreams first, then use the money you earned from pursuing your passion to purchase the car. Well, not only would you be able to afford it without going into debt (sweet!), but you are ultimately buying the car for yourself, not for others. Sure, you get the looks and the "oohs" and "aahs" from other people, but this will all pale in comparison to the pleasure and freedom that your dreams will have given you.

Can you see what the difference is, once you change your focus? The "oohs" and "aahs" you get from the lies you told when you could not delay instant gratification were just people believing the lies; the "oohs" and "aahs" you get when you've delayed instant gratification and earned them are people believing your truth. And that, my friend, is really the sweet life!

"Nothing you get will ever make you happy. Who you become will make you very happy or very sad."
~TONY ROBBINS

In the first self-serving, instant gratification scenario, wear-and-tear means that the car, and possibly your life, will be junk in a few years; however, you can't just trade in your used life for another one. There are no such trade-ins, only hard work, self-sacrifice, and prudent denial of mere wants. The wear-and-tear of immediate gratification is much worse than the wear-and-tear of delayed gratification. (Your mileage may vary!)

The car is just one example – another parable. In our world, there are limitless material options we can become obsessed with having. However, there's certainly room for discretion. I'm not saying you have to live in rags in a van down by the river. For example, there's nothing wrong with spending money on proper clothing and healthy meals, as these kinds of purchases should be seen as investments in your future dreams. After all, in pursuing them you're forced to play by the rules of propriety: you can't negotiate with a bank wearing pajamas; you can't "take a lunch" at the Sprout store.

Proper clothing creates a first-impression that helps you climb the ladder to success, and healthy meals will lead to a fit body and a sharp mind. When you see them as an investment, you'll make purchasing decisions based on how much return an item actually brings to your goals.

When it comes to any decision you make, you can either fulfill your short-term pleasures or your long-term pleasures. Your discretion, your call. It sounds simple in theory, but in practice, people face great difficulty when it comes to making decisions that are in their long-term best interest.

The talent of discretion is telling the difference between the clothes you need and a Mercedes you don't. Sure, that's an easy one. But what about getting the giganta-hertz computer with a 3D printer if all you need to do is a spreadsheet? In bookie jargon, the spread on your bet has narrowed, and as it narrows tighter, you have to draw a line somewhere. But know this: the line you draw divides the two possible futures you can have.

For example, let's say you have enough money to either purchase a designer purse or invest in an online training course that will help you master your craft. Ask anyone for advice on which choice you should make and they'll *tell* you to spend money on the course.

The decision that leads you toward prosperity and abundance seems like the logical, straightforward choice.

Unfortunately, what people *say* and what people *do* are two completely separate things. Many people will choose to spend money on a designer purse because it makes them feel good right now (even though they won't feel that great later). Why? Why would people actively self-sabotage their own best interests?

It all comes back to immediate material gratification, which high-performance coach Darren Hardy talks about in his book, *The Compound Effect*:

> *"We understand that Pop-Tarts won't slenderize our waistline. We realize that logging three hours at night watching Dancing with the Stars and NCIS leaves us with fewer hours to read a good book or listen to a terrific audiobook.*
>
> *"We 'get' that merely purchasing great running shoes doesn't make us marathon-ready. We are a rational species – at least that's what we tell ourselves. So why are we so irrationally enslaved by so many bad habits? It's because of our need for immediate gratification that can turn us into the most reactive, non-thinking animals around."*

Learning to sacrifice material possessions may be the best gift you could give your future self – even your future *material* self. Personally, I struggled with this early in life. But fortunately, I not only learned to delay my pursuit of immediate material gratification, I also realized that, as I mentioned previously: when we spend too much time polishing our image, we end up tarnishing our character.

> Don't be like the successful lawyer who parked his brand new Porsche in front of his office so he could show it off to his colleagues. Then, when the lawyer opened the door to his new car, a truck came flying by and tore off the driver's door of the Porsche.
>
> The lawyer immediately grabbed his cell phone and dialed

911. When a policeman arrived, the lawyer was still screaming hysterically. His Porsche, which he had just picked up from the dealership the day before, was now completely ruined and would never be the same. No amount of repairs from the body shop could make it new again.

After the lawyer finally calmed down from his ranting, the policeman shook his head in disgust. "I can't believe how materialistic you lawyers are," he said. "You are so focused on your possessions that you don't notice anything else."

"How can you say such a thing?" asked the lawyer.

The policeman replied, "Didn't you notice that your left arm is missing from the elbow down? It must have been severed when the truck hit you."

The lawyer looked down to his left side and screamed, "Oh my God! My Rolex!"

2. Emotional Gratification

"So convenient a thing it is to be a reasonable creature, since it enables one to find or make a reason for everything one has a mind to do."

~BENJAMIN FRANKLIN, Founding Father of the United States

As the snarky wisdom from Mr. Franklin implies, gratification can come from anything that pleases us, and thus, it comes in all shapes and sizes. Every bad habit that you engage in provides some form of gratification and takes you away from the things that you actually need to be doing. The snarky part: all of us can deceive ourselves into rationalizing excellent reasons to do such things.

One of the biggest challenges for many people in carving out their dreams is the desire for emotional gratification. As you already know by now, long-term gratification beats out immediate gratification when it comes to sustained success.

Unhealthy food choices is often linked to emotional gratification. Here's how it works: if we are honest, often what we eat is based on emotional gratification rather than physical gratification. You can easily eat a piece of delicious chocolate cake and get a sugar high immediately, but getting that lean and high-performing body means holding off the immediate emotional gratification of the cake for the long-term gratification you're going to get when you look and feel amazing.

The problem comes in when the instant payoff of immediate gratification overrules what's going on in your rational mind with regard to long-term consequences. In fact, when your rational mind is at odds with immediate gratification, Mr. Franklin reminds us of the "convenience" of being able to subvert our otherwise rational mind and recruit it to the immediate gratification cause!

It's not the actual cake and the sugar itself that keeps you hooked, but the emotions that you have associated with them. Because humans are often willing victims of, and slaves to, their own emotions, we give in to the emotions that lead to eating the cake.

When you learn to manage your emotions better, you control the desire for immediate gratification that often accompanies your misguided emotions. And in doing so, you are one step closer to your ultimate dream of having a lean, sexy body. You always have a choice over whether you're going to gratify your emotional self in the short-term or satisfy the mature person inside of you in the long-term.

David Laibson, an economist at Harvard and co-author of a paper titled, *The Monetary-Reward Experiment*, stated:

> *"Our emotional brain wants to max out the credit card, order dessert, and smoke a cigarette. When it sees something it wants, it has difficulty waiting to get it."*

It's not easy for our brain to choose long-term gains over short-term rewards.

A neurological aside:

Mr. Laibson, along with other co-authors of a study in *Science*, explored how instant gratification is fueled by our ancient limbic system – remember our caveman, our lizard brain? Guess what? This is where your emotions are processed. The neurotransmitter involved is primarily the reward neurohormone known as dopamine.

On the other hand, choosing to delay instant gratification involves the higher brain centers that keep the caveman in us all subdued. Thus, there are separate neural systems that operate in choosing between instant and delayed gratification. The one for delayed gratification is involved with our "executive" decisions.

Why isn't this "caveman-vs-modern man" (emotional-vs-rational) battle a surprise? Because any thinking (modern) person will instantly recognize the battle and what victory can mean to one's future. The dopamine we crave fraudulently says, "A short-term reward in the hand is worth two (or more) long-term gains in the bush." The decision to fight dopamine is a decision to oppose the caveman's natural tendencies toward repetitive rewards at the expense of everything else.

Fighting this primitive urge and doing the opposite of what we want weighs heavily on our emotions and takes extreme cognitive effort, which is why you must deliberately put yourself in a strong position when the temptation comes for seeking instant gratification. Throw the cake out (or any other unhealthy foods/drinks) if you know your ability to resist sugar will be difficult because there will definitely be a battle in your brain; so hedge your bets!

The *Catholic Catechism* warns children not to put themselves into the "*near occasion*" of sin. That is, once you're at a point at which you can't resist, giving in to the temptation is not *the* sin because you can't help it at that point; instead, *putting yourself into a position where you can't resist* is *the actual* sin. Regardless of what religious persuasion – if any – a person is, this is a brilliant distinction in the forensics of "giving in" to temptation.

If you fail in the "caveman-vs-modern man" battles regularly, then make the extra effort prior to temptations arriving. That is, identify your weak spots and pre-empt them. For instance, if you know getting up at a particular time is challenging, set an extra alarm away from your bed.

But is strong-arming our emotions bad? Does it go against our DNA? Our evolution? Does success eliminate emotions? Does it turn us into emotionless Vulcans? According to neuroscientist Benedetto de Martino, the answer is "no". Dr. de Martino believes that the people that we call "rational and successful" don't have fewer emotions or perceive them differently from anybody else. These are not cold, callous human beings who ignore the collateral damage on their way to the top. Rather, they understand these emotions very well, and in turn, are able to regulate them better. But "regulate" is too bureaucratic a term; rather, they are able to *police* them better.

In order to regulate your emotions, you need to understand why you make choices that lead to immediate gratification. These decisions that lead you off track may seem insignificant at the time you make them, but the long-term effects may be lethal. That, again, is why it is crucial to be aware of every decision you make, even (and especially) the tiniest ones. And if you remember that keeping yourself away from the "near occasion" of immediate gratification is just as important as denying yourself that gratification, you'll prevail with much less effort.

3. Sexual Gratification

"Sexuality is wonderful with the right person and damaging with the wrong person."

~THE NEW MESSAGE FROM GOD

One can argue that sexual gratification should be in the same category as emotional gratification. However, because it is such a strong force of nature, it is better to discuss it separately.

The impulse to seek sexual gratification is so potent that it has single-handedly destroyed the lives and families of millions of people. There are countless stories throughout history about people who will steal, lie, cry, beg, and even kill for a few short moments of sexual pleasure. It has literally changed history when you consider the political fallouts over time. The famous blue dress in the Oval Office caused an impeachment. Many senators and congressmen, cabinet heads, and other political figures have resigned from office because of an inability to police their drives, thus eliminating what might have come to pass in leadership circles. And then there's Hollywood.

The ability to delay the physical desire for sexual gratification, however, has the power to transform average people into powerful people with high degrees of self-control. The ability to channel sex into your goals and dreams is a powerful tool that shouldn't be taken for granted. Napoleon Hill touches on this in his book, *Think and Grow Rich*.

"When driven by this desire, men develop keenness of imagination, courage, will-power, persistence, and creative ability unknown to them at other times. So strong and impelling is the desire for sexual contact that men freely run the risk of life and reputation to indulge it.

"When harnessed and redirected along other lines, this motivating force maintains all of its attributes of keenness of imagination,

courage, etc., which may be used as powerful creative forces in literature, art, or in any other profession or calling, including, of course, the accumulation of riches."

According to Napoleon Hill, many successful people in the world use their sexual desires to empower themselves in other areas of their lives. Rather than lust after other people, that lust is channeled into the pursuit of their dreams.

The key is not to merely delay your sexual gratification, but rather to channel the energy from that gratification into other areas of your life. Don't misunderstand the point, though. This isn't a simple trade of one's energy for sex in exchange for energy in other areas. I would like to refine what Napoleon Hill says by adding that channeling your energy for sex is changing the way you *are* into a better version of yourself, but not just because you've avoided an ill-advised sexual encounter. It's because you've delayed instant gratification altogether. Your entire self is better at channeling *all* misapplied energy into other endeavors, whether it be energy for sex or any other temptations (i.e., material or emotional gratifications).

Some experts may argue that men have this primal need to spread their seed, which is conveniently linked to a high sex drive. This misses the point because any immediate gratification is all about trading away your energies wastefully. A man who gives into this need at every opportunity will have spent so much energy on this immediate gratification that his long-term needs can never be met. In order to control this unbelievably strong desire, a loving, and monogamous relationship is necessary. This type of relationship allows for sexual gratification, as well as structure and support.

Sexual gratification may be the most difficult to control out of the three gratifications we have explored. But when it's controlled, it has the ability to make incredibly powerful and positive changes in your life. If you can harness the desire you have for sexual gratification and channel that same desire into the achievement of your goals; you likewise can wield this weapon against the other gratifications that conspire to sabotage your dream. Then you will be unstoppable.

COGNITIVE BIAS AND THE FRAMING EFFECT

> "Humans all suffer from cognitive bias: unconscious and irrational brain processes that literally distort the way we see the world."
>
> ~CHRIS VOSS, Author of *Never Split the Difference* and former FBI hostage negotiator

As Ben Franklin said in the opening quote in the Emotional Gratification section, we use reason to rationalize what we want. This pertains to the pitfalls of the decisions we make which can lead us to give in to instant gratification. My other go-to expert in that section was neuroscientist Benedetto de Martino, who wrote:

> *"Human choices are remarkably susceptible to the manner in which options are presented."*

Dr. de Martino calls this the "*framing effect*," that is, how we frame what we're considering. The framing effect, he says, violates standard human rationality. Dr. de Martino also claims that this effect, which makes use of bias to frame things in a way that makes them seem reasonable, involves our old caveman friend, the limbic system of our brain.

In other words, we subjectively frame things that objectively are not good for us so that we will feel good about choosing these otherwise bad choices. These tricks we play on ourselves are collectively referred to as *cognitive biases*, and we use them to distort our contemplations by introducing influences that really shouldn't play a part in our decision-making process.

Some of the most common types (among literally hundreds) of cognitive biases are as follows:

1. **Confirmation Bias**: the mistake of only seeking out evidence that confirms our belief or makes a bad decision look good. It also means that often times we close the door on any thoughts that might refute us making a proper choice that will benefit us in the long run rather than a detrimental short-term gain.

   In Chapter Two, I spoke of the Confirmation Bias, which describes our brain's tendency to cherry-pick information that confirms (and conforms to) our existing beliefs. Our pre-programmed reticular activating system (RAS) interprets *what* we see and *how* we see it. It makes the definitions by which we live. And it makes us comfortable steering toward bad decisions, such as an instant gratification that comes at the expense of our future dreams and vision.
2. **Anchoring**: when we hold on to one single piece of information to justify a decision, even if all other "inconvenient" information argues against it.
3. **Halo Effect**: the tendency for a positive impression created in one area to influence and create a positive opinion in another or similar area.
4. **Overconfidence Bias**: when we overestimate the validity or reliability of our own judgments.
5. **Temporal Discounting:** People discount the future, which means they are disconnected from the consequences of their behavior. Even if you were to realize the consequences there is a good chance you would still discount them because, well, they are in the future. It's only when the consequences become manifested that many people suddenly take notice.

   This is one of the reasons why many people have

> underfunded their retirement. They don't think about it until it's almost upon them and then it's too late. Over half of the households in the United States approaching retirement have little to no retirement savings. Social security provides the majority of income for half of those who are 65 and older. Where there are some retirement savings, the average amount saved is only about $109,000.

These and other types of cognitive biases play pivotal roles in our bad decisions, in which we choose wants over needs, or instant gratification over delayed gratification. Previously in this chapter, I had said that the first requirement to start learning how to delay gratification is self-awareness. When it comes to cognitive biases, you are only fooling yourself.

THE BENEFITS OF TRADE-OFFS

"The chief cause of failure and unhappiness is trading what you want most for what you want right now."

~ZIG ZIGLAR

If a goal is worth having, you're not going to be able to achieve it overnight. Why? Because anything in life that comes easy and fast will leave you the exact same way. Yes! I am repeating the sentence above intentionally. But here's a twist on it: nothing important is ever easy. So what's so hard about it, exactly?

The trade-offs.

When you set out to achieve a goal, it's obvious that there are certain things you must do. For instance, if you are trying to lose weight, you likely know what it is you need to do. You need to get on a rigorous exercise program and follow it consistently. You need to pick a target weight you want to be at and select a specific date as to when you will reach it.

A neurological aside:

Following a consistent exercise program has proven to provide the additional cognition required to make the trade-offs that are necessary for achieving sustainable success.

In an investigation into the mind-body connection, a study in JAMA Internal Medicine revealed that consistent once or twice-weekly resistance training improved cognitive function. Also, a 2019 German study demonstrated that physical fitness improves memory, learning, and emotional stability. In an article titled, *Fitness literally boosts your brainpower, according to a new study* revealed:

> *"In a large study, German scientists have shown that physical fitness is associated with better brain structure and brain functioning in young adults. This opens the possibility that increasing fitness levels may lead to improved cognitive ability, such as memory and problem solving, as well as improved structural changes in the brain."*

Exercising regularly certainly has its benefits, especially since science suggests it boosts our brainpower. Each of us need all the assistance we can get when it comes to making the necessary sacrifices and trade-offs that will lead to lasting success. Keeping our mind (and body) in optimal condition is crucial because trading away instant gratification for a long-term result has to override our primitive brain using our cognitive brain. Therefore, this is more than muscular resistance training; this is resisting immediate gratification training.

Just as important as the things you must do are the things you must *not* do, which takes just as much cognitive effort. In the case of losing weight, you need to stop shoveling junk food into your mouth, which puts the extra pounds of fat on your body. Fast food is convenient in fast times, but don't let your pace of life determine what and how you eat. You need to stop lying down on the couch and missing your workouts. You need to say "no thanks" when your colleagues at work invite you for "Happy Hour Tuesday" with the $3 margaritas. In the long run, they're likely to be $3,000 margaritas! Or $300,000 margaritas.

> But it's worse than that because while you may have only spent $9 on three margaritas, think about how much of your valuable time you spent with your friends. And on a "school night," at that! That loss of two to three hours has a loss-of-opportunity cost, which is where your real expense is (this does not even include the lack of sleep which alcohol is prone to do to us or the lethargic behavior the following day because of the alcohol). Time is money, much more than money is money!

Even when you do all the right things with weight loss, the results will not come overnight. You will simply have to follow the program, consistently execute the plan, and stay committed to the process. Good things come to those who wait, and being able to wait requires the complete opposite of immediate gratification: steadfast patience.

It baffles me how many different weight loss and exercise programs are on the market. It is a multi-billion-dollar industry. But what these weight loss and exercise programs really need to focus on is teaching people how to strengthen their willpower and not give in to immediate gratification. Keeping the weight off means changing the way you live for the rest of your life; otherwise, you'll end up back at square one.

It's super simple (not necessarily easy, but simple) to lose weight. All you have to do is exercise regularly and eat properly. There is no secret. I understand there are exceptions for specific medical conditions, but seriously, don't use a cognitive bias to invent one because keeping yourself in shape allows you to perform at your best.

Earlier I told you about a school for children with no recess and how the students were happy because they were achieving within a predictable, regimental agenda. The same can be said of delaying gratification. Staying home to work on something you're passionate about instead of being passionate about going to a party may end up *not* being much of a sacrifice after you get into this pattern of thinking. In other words, you don't have to be miserable to sacrifice. All sacrifice means is engaging in a trade-off of long-term goals for short-term denials. It's foreplay for high achieving men and women!

ADDICTED TO DISTRACTIONS

> "Starve your distractions, feed your focus. Remember, what you focus on grows. If you want to achieve your goal, you have to stop giving attention to the things that are keeping you from it."
>
> ~CHARMAINE HAYDEN, Award-winning director of the modeling agency Face4Music

Let me tell you something about achieving a goal that you probably already know: once you've finally reached your destination after a lot of hard work and perseverance, you're going to feel incredibly proud of yourself and fulfilled. But getting to the endpoint is going to take work. And on the way to the goal, there are going to be a lot of distractions.

A very insidious form of instant gratification is living our days from one distraction to another. As technology has continued its exponential growth, it has become very easy to be distracted in the 21st century. People these days are addicted to distractions. Why? Because in essence, we walk around with a device in our pockets that champions distraction: our mobile phone (a.k.a. a party in our pocket). Although it's not really a mere phone. If you think about it, it's really an Internet computer that has a phone app among the other apps.

Sure, you need your phone for communication, but the capitalistic genius of the smartphone's allure is that it allows us to interweave active communication with inactive involvement in idle time-passing. Too many people spend too much time playing games and scrolling on social media with smartphones in between their calls. They scroll endlessly searching for the bottom of their newsfeeds. In fact, your mobile phone is the perfect way to demonstrate how immediate gratification is like a drug addiction. In truth, both immediate gratification and drug addiction involve a cheap pursuit of dopamine, and that's the problem.

A sociological aside:

We are designed to interact, reach out, and not to self-impose isolation on ourselves. We don't do well all by ourselves. People who voluntarily use sensory-deprivation tanks cite its effects of relaxation and anti-anxiety until too much becomes too much; that's when the panic and hallucinations make it very unpleasant.

Solitary confinement has been recognized as torture for millennia. University of Virginia social psychologist Timothy Wilson did research on isolation with subjects who were left alone with no distractions except a small device that could deliver small shocks. According to the study:

"27 percent of women and 67 percent of men found the experience of being alone with their thoughts so intolerable that they decided to shock themselves. One man reportedly shocked himself 190 times."

It seems that any interaction, even with a shocker, was preferable to being alone with just ourselves.

According to a case study reported by St. Paul's Collegiate School in their blog, "*Values Exchange*," babies were studied as to the effects of sensory deprivation. In this particularly unthinkable (and evil!) study, two sets of babies were separated: while both groups were tended to for comfort, hygiene, and feeding, one of the groups of babies received absolutely no social interaction. The result was that this *"experiment was halted after four months, by which time, at least half of the babies had died at that point."*

Such is the crucial need for interaction, affection, and not being left to just ourselves for long periods of time. To be happy, we must interact: socialize, engage, and stay busy. **And that means with people.**

Some will choose not to do this with people; they do it with "things," such as pixelated games on a smartphone screen. While these internal adventures can be entertaining and fun within limits, because they don't involve people, they only go so far and become self-limited, isolationist, and socially stagnating. This type of "happy" can be empty.

But isn't any type of "happy" a good thing? Perhaps not, as it pertains to our ultimate vision and goals. Let's explore this more.

When "happy" happens, it means the neurotransmitter dopamine. Once you engage the dopamine "reward" machinery, the feeling of the reward becomes more of a driving force than the actual thing you're doing. Said differently, you feel better from getting to the bottom of your newsfeed than from the actual news on the feed itself. When the waves of dopamine keep ebbing and flowing, you'll get caught in the undertow. You won't be able to think about anything else. You become a slave to your dopamine; you become a slave to your phone. In turn, your phone controls a large portion of your life. It's like the saying goes: people are prisoners of their phones, and that's why they call them *cell* phones.

A disturbing aside:

> In a study cited in the *Journal of the American Medical Association*, "In healthy participants and compared with no exposure, 50-minute cell phone exposure was associated with increased brain glucose metabolism in the [brain] region closest to the antenna."

In fact, when new habits like those that come from technology clash with our species, surprises happen. According to researchers in Australia, evidence of bone spur formation – our skeleton's reaction to stress – has been documented in the back of the skull due to the distorted posture perpetuated by cell phone use. Apparently, the constant looking down (pivoting the head down vertically on the neck) is an unnatural posture, against which our immune (inflammatory) processes step up to fight. These bone spurs have been referred to as "horns," which describes their outcropping shape, yet may sound melodramatic; nevertheless, bone spurs are abnormal (as are horns!) and fraught with orthopedic problems.

There is more to the "happy" I'm talking about than dopamine. True happiness which comes with interaction with people, includes bonding, which is hard to create from mere pixels.

Consider YouTube, another popular weapon of mass distraction. The few minutes you spend watching a YouTube video will likely lead you to another video, and another, and another. Perhaps you don't think you're gratuitously gratifying yourself, but you are. Anytime you mindlessly watch an online video, you're giving in to your desire for entertainment to avoid the problematic cognitive mental effort of actively thinking about and acting on your goals.

No one can argue that excessive habits which replace the usual activities of daily living are destructive to our quality of life. Does the habitual, profitless fluff of YouTube, inane texting, or social media count? Sit in the waiting room of any doctor's office, at the DMV, in a restaurant between courses, anywhere, and you will see the cellphones out and people's self-estrangement from each other. They are trading away engagement for Twitter or Tik Tok. If you were an alien visiting our planet and saw this, how would you report what life was like here?

What's driving this insatiable need to be numbed by time-wasting distractions? The culprit is dopamine. To the brain, dopamine is like candy. It's a neurochemical that is released whenever we experience some form of pleasure. Remember, from previously, that it isn't the actual experience, but the emotional payoff that comes from pleasure and makes it so addictive. We experience that "feel-good" emotion, which makes us happier, thereby motivating us to repeat certain behaviors that will lead to feeling even more enjoyment.

However, it also causes what researchers call "*seeking* behavior." A study published in 1998 titled, *What is the role of dopamine in reward: hedonic primacy, reward learning, or incentive salience?*, discovered that dopamine is what drives our arousal to seek something out. In practice, this sounds like a good idea. Why not feel better about positive behaviors that do us good, and at the same time feel even more motivated to repeat them? It's simply what humans have evolved to do.

A dopamine aside:

> The dopamine study above explained the complexities involved: it's not that we repeat actions because they feel good, but because they give us the emotional payoff. The study used the term "*incentive salience*" to describe a dopamine-related phenomenon that is separate from the actual pleasure of an action – the prominent ("salient") incentive – the "wanting" – that is then satisfied by the actual action.

If we want, we seek; and the seeking behavior of what we *want* sometimes gets to the point of ignoring the seeking out of what we *need*. This is dysfunctional behavior because seeking what we want instead of what we need runs contrary to strategies for our future which is based on the opposite (needs over wants).

Dopamine, however, turns out to be a bucking bronco. While it is beneficial in that it is an evolutionary ability of ours which has helped us survive and prosper, it can also become our most significant peril. It serves as a boobytrap in the system when we're pursuing our goals: dopamine is engaged in our brain within microseconds; feeling better about achieving our goals takes years.

Smartphones, social media platforms, and the Internet as a whole are specifically designed to reward behaviors fast – at megabits per second. Have you ever felt an insatiable itch to open up Facebook and check your notifications, even though you were just logged on five minutes ago? That's the power of dopamine in action, combined with some ingenious engineering from the people who designed the app. Unfortunately, these social media channels, in a quest to keep our undivided attention, is what sends people walking into traffic, driving into the opposite lane, or rudely glancing every other second at the phone while engaged in conversation.

> **"Facebook is the new cigarettes."**
> ~MARC BENIOFF

Don't think this hasn't been targeted as a problem, because when people become uncomfortable with the way society is changing, legislation tends to step in for our "protection." Such is the case when Senator Josh Hawley of Missouri introduced the SMART (**S**ocial **M**edia **A**ddiction **R**eduction **T**echnology) Act that would ban "addictive" social media features such as automatic YouTube reloads and unlimited scrolling without active refreshing. While the bill seems doomed to violate many aspects of the First Amendment, it underscores that the problem has been identified.

(Half of the problem is seeing the problem.)

Social media and similar platforms may be a problem for us, but an advantage for marketing. Such is how our devices are designed. And it is why they succeed because humans so easily give in to immediate gratification so they can feel good in the present.

Each minute you waste on immediate gratification, however, will take you further away from your goal. Your competitors are spending the same amount of time you are wasting: perfecting that product or service they're building and simply becoming better than you. While you're making meme's they're making millions. They don't require some government law to keep them on track with their lives.

RETURN ON INVESTMENT WAS INVENTED BY MODERN MAN

Immediate gratification robs you of your focus. Human beings are hardwired to focus on only one thing at a time. Your mind cannot focus fully on two things at once. Therefore, logic dictates that focusing on one thing automatically means you are not focused on another (i.e. your goals).

A neurological aside:

An everyday example of this is finding yourself in a different room, having forgotten what you were going there to get. This is normal – forgetting what you wanted while focusing on getting to the other room. This is part of our ancient brain wiring. Our past caveman selves moved from Point A to Point B, usually instigated by how life was happening to them.

Life happening to them is what usually was pushing them from Point A to Point B, that is, as much an escape as a decision to move on. Nevertheless, in the primitive brain the past was the past and was therefore forgettable so that one could be ready for whatever may be lurking in the future. Such as that mountain lion or that rival gang of cavemen.

But modern man is different. As I have mentioned previously, we have spent millennia building complex brain tissue around the ancient parts of our brain to evolve from life happening *to* us to our *making* our own lives happen.

When you are focused on immediate gratification, you are not focused on your long-term goals. You are devolving into your caveman. It is impossible for you to be in agreement with your modern-man goals and your short-term caveman pleasures at the same time. You can only be focused on one or the other, so you need to pick which one it's going to be. Who will be walking into that next room? Your caveman or your modern man?

Seeking short-term pleasures is so simple even a caveman can do it; seeking long-term goals is so complicated that only a modern man can do it.

All of this really comes down to our ability to make tradeoffs. Many of us want changes in our lives, but we don't want to make the sacrifices necessary to wait for the results. *We are the way we are because that's what we want – otherwise, we would be changing the way we are.* Unfortunately, when it comes to making the tradeoff of immediate pleasure for short-term pain, we often let our emotions get the best of us simply because we don't get to reap the benefits right away when we choose to delay gratification. We often let our caveman win because it may take days, weeks, months, or even years before we start to see the fruits of our labor. Vetoing the caveman requires cognitive effort. So does patience.

Do you have the patience to trust the process and wait for the results? Do you have the self-discipline to make the necessary tradeoffs in your life to achieve success? You can think of tradeoffs like playing a game of checkers: you surrender one piece of your own in order to take two from your opponent. You don't make two moves at once, but rather, you try to move up and avoid moving down, and eventually your checker piece will reach the top of the board. Only then will that piece have the freedom to move around the entire board.

EXCEPTIONS ARE THE MOST DANGEROUS THINGS WE DEAL WITH IN LIFE

> "The price must be paid and the process followed. You always reap what you sow; there is no shortcut."
>
> ~STEPHEN COVEY, American educator, author, businessman, and keynote speaker

Let's be honest: most people would admit they are not quite the way they want to be. They'd also admit that they're not in the process of making changes. So few people actually change because they suffer from the tyranny of now, and they think now trumps later. Thus, they become chess pieces instead of chess players.

Let's move now from checkers to chess, since we're exploring a more complicated strategy in life. If you think like a chess *player* instead of like a chess *piece* – that is, the "*mover*" and not merely the *"moved"*, you will orchestrate your own moves, instead of the moves against you forcing your game. Defense is prudent but only keeps you from losing; offense allows you to win. Again, as in tennis, don't just play "not to lose".

Playing not to lose can get you stuck in a blind rut. Many people are not the way they want to be because they have made so many exceptions in their lives that they can't see how far off course they've gotten. If rules have exceptions, then they're not rules anymore. If you are going to become the CEO of your life and achieve the goals you have set, you must burn in your mind this philosophy: **long-term happiness requires short-term discomfort.** And make it a rule!

What does that mean, exactly? It means there can be no exceptions. It means that you must commit to never doing certain things, even just once. (Think of monogamy. There are no exceptions there, or it's not monogamy.) Many people constantly make exceptions instead of doing the things they're supposed to do, but the problem is exceptions are rarely one-time events that exist in isolation. Invoking Benjamin Franklin once again, being able to reason ourselves into the self-indulgent path of least resistance becomes increasingly more "convenient".

When you make an exception once, you've made a precedent. You've broken the seal. You have set the groundwork for making another exception in the near future and made it easier for your conscious and subconscious mind to rationalize doing it. If you make enough exceptions over time, they eventually turn into bad habits that take control of your life. In fact, they *become* your life: they become you! And rationalizations become lies you make yourself believe – rational lies. Ben Franklin told you so!

Additionally, you must commit to following some form of structure in your life. To carve out the time needed to achieve your goals, you need to create a predictable structure that you can consistently follow over time. A structure, by its very nature, requires rules – a framework that defines how you live your life and pursue your goals. There cannot be any room for exceptions whatsoever to the rules and standards you have set for yourself.

If you'll recall again the school without recess, the students there were happy because they were achieving within a predictable, regimental agenda. Children are happiest when they are in a healthy structure. It's one of the things that are programmed into our subconscious during our infant and childhood learning periods, and I'll be talking about that in detail in Chapter Seven. However, with maturation comes an override of much of our infantile and childhood programming, simply because as adults they won't apply.

But some subconscious programming survives the maturation process which evolves from childhood to adulthood. The inner peace that comes from structure in our lives is one of them. If you've decided you are going to wake up at 6 a.m. every single day and go to bed at 11 p.m. every single night until you reach your goal, that's a structure you've created for yourself and it will please your inner child.

Now, if you decide to make an exception one day because you're just too tired – you will likely make that exception again. Probably even that very week! Night after night passes, and soon you are back to your old destructive habits, wondering how you failed yet again to stick to the structure that you set for yourself. That, my friend, is why exceptions are your enemy. Why no success? Who is your enemy? Look no further: your enemy is you when your life becomes your exceptions.

I'm reminded again of the game of *Jenga*. Think of your dream – your goal – as a Jenga game. A colossal structure. Jenga is a game in which a structure stands that consists of numerous stackable pieces of wood, extending vertically, some jutting out, some cantilevered, and others crisscrossing, all reinforcing each other and adding to the strength of the structure.

Players alternate turns suspensefully removing one piece at a time until the whole thing comes down. If this is your dream, think of each exception as pulling out a piece. At some point, you'll have nothing standing.

Exceptions are extremely dangerous to our future because they take us off the track that leads us to our goals. When you make an exception *once*, it makes it all that much easier to do it again and again. (Beware of the dopamine undertow!) And before you know it, the undesirable behavior that you made a one-time exception for will begin to appear perfectly normal – a new normal. Now we're talking habit, and that's a self-destructive booby-trap that is so fundamental to why we fail that it gets its own chapter, coming up next (Chapter Five).

Booby-traps are called that because they remain unseen to the unwary until it's too late. I've met a lot of people who are not satisfied with the person they've become, and more often than not, they aren't doing anything about it. That's because they don't realize how far off course the booby-traps/exceptions have taken them. If 40 is the new 30, it's amazing how fast 30 can become your new 40 when you've gotten off course. And you won't even see it. Why? Because of the exceptions you've made.

DISMANTLING YOUR LIFE ONE EXCEPTION AT A TIME

> "Exceptions are the exceptions, and finds are like ants; whenever you see one, you may be sure there are twenty."
>
> ~ANNE FORTIER, Canadian-Danish writer, author of *The Lost Sisterhood*

Getting "out of control," of course, is insidious. You won't notice it after you've been resetting your own thermostat slowly over a period of time. It is impossible to tell the difference between a room with a temperature of 90 degrees and one that is 91 degrees, but 91 degrees is noticeably different from 72 degrees.

The gruesome fable of the boiled frog cautions how gradual change can become imperceptible. The story tells how throwing a frog into boiling water will fail to boil it, simply because it jumps out; whereas putting the frog in tepid water and gradually increasing the temperature degree-by-degree will succeed because the frog will never notice the difference, and ends up dying by being boiled.

It's a pertinent metaphor for something called "creeping normality", and it teaches that change – for good or for bad – needs to be gradual to succeed or be accepted.

A nefarious example of the boiled frog phenomenon is the simple reality of weight gain, as we discussed in our donut fantasy. Over ten years, you are overweight enough to torpedo your heart health, blood pressure, sugar management, and everything else.

> A temporal discounting aside:
>
> One of the problems with envisioning the future is that most people are depressingly bad at compounding. They don't have the foresight to see the impact of small changes, be it good or bad, in the long-term. For example, if you gain just one pound a month, you can go from being normal weight to obese in a couple of years to being seriously obese in three more years and morbidly obese three years after that.
>
> Excessive weight gain is a crippling conundrum around the world and that's why I continue using it as an example. The "weight" is not the real issue though. However, the compounding future effects are: according to the Department of Psychology, the University of Gothenburg in Sweden, an unhealthy increase in BMI (body mass index) significantly increases risk for dementia.

Previously in this chapter, I had described playing "not to lose" and said it was like getting stuck in a blind rut. While this is intended to mean that you can't expect great things by playing it safe, it also means becoming blind to the way you have allowed your exceptions to become your life, up to the point where things sneak up on you and then one day clobber you. The amount of surprise over what blindsides you is directly proportional to how deep you were in your rut.

For example, if you are ten pounds overweight, you can handle it. But when you are one-hundred pounds overweight, the extra weight becomes painful enough that most people who are serious about surviving are willing to do whatever it takes to lose weight. Isn't it funny how we are always so indifferent to fixing problems until they become catastrophic? How many smokers have never been able to quit, until the day they get their cancer diagnosis?

That is why experts in human transformation say that success is measured in inches, not feet, or in the case of our overweight example, one less donut (down to zero) a day. It's all of the tiny decisions we make every day that either propel us toward our destiny or takes us further away from the life we desire. Remember the runner, Yamada, in Chapter Two, who measured his milestones bit by bit to the finish line? The finish line came to him, closer and closer, as each "bit" was achieved.

You may know someone who successfully made it through the Alcoholics Anonymous program after years of struggle, only to make that one exception that lands them back in the same place that drew them to AA initially: a slave to alcohol. Or, you know the person who lost a massive amount of weight through a program like Weight Watchers, only to gain all of it back because they chose to make exceptions to their diets.

We're talking about addiction, of course. But not an addiction to alcohol or unhealthy food, but to dopamine and the emotional payoff of getting what we want, not need. The problem with addiction is that in spite of even years of abstinence, just one exposure can jumpstart the entire craving-addiction again.

This pattern is sadly all too common in otherwise committed people. They put in all the hard work to change their habits and their lifestyle, stay on the righteous path for a while, and then throw it all away by making an exception. That *one exception* leads them spiraling back down to becoming their old selves again, and then they wonder how it all happened.

A behavioral aside:

Habit change and relapse is more about the process, rather than the specific habit. When behavioral change is not maintained, the slippery slope ensues. This is partially why the rates for permanently changing negative behaviors are dishearteningly bad. Even when people achieve success in the short-term, this is often lost over time as people fail to maintain new behaviors and slip back into old habits. It's also why most New Year's Resolutions rarely make it out of January.

One of the worst things in life any of us can ever experience is when we can no longer recognize what we've allowed ourselves to become, especially when we can't see what part of ourselves we've allowed to grow out of control. This can happen to anyone. And it's the primary reason why I found myself in a prison cell for nearly half a decade. When I traced back the root cause of my failure, it all hinged on the exceptions I made that led me slowly, but undoubtedly, down the wrong path in life. Unlike our overweight example, I had no scale that tallied the exceptions in my life into tangible measurements, which is part of the blindness that make exceptions so dangerous.

EXCEPTIONS CAN BE DEADLY

"Exceptions nearly ruined my life. Exceptions are the primary reason why I was not around for the first part of my son Thomas' life."

~JEREMY MCGILVREY

Believe it or not, exceptions can even kill. A heartbreaking example of the horrific consequences that come from making exceptions is the tragic story of the *Challenger*. The *Challenger* was the space shuttle that NASA launched into flight on January

28, 1986. Less than two minutes after liftoff, the shuttle exploded into a fiery ball and instantly killed all seven crew members.

How could something like that happen? The cause of the disaster was traced to the O-ring seals, which are circular gaskets designed to seal the fuel segments together within the rocket booster. While functional, they were not tested to see if they would work just as well in cooler temperatures.

This was NASA's first attempt to launch a shuttle in cold weather, as the previous launch was 20 degrees warmer (and considered to have been the coldest temperature ever for a launch at the time).

Despite not having enough data to determine if the O-ring seals would seal properly at temperatures below 53 degrees, the manufacturer of the rocket boosters (Morton Thiokol) was confident the O-ring seals would work just fine in cold temperatures.

But one man wasn't so sure. Allan McDonald, a director for Morton Thiokol at the time, explicitly refused to sign off the launch recommendations for the *Challenger* the night before launch. He was concerned that the cooler temperatures on launch day would make the O-rings fail, as the rubber would become stiff and not completely seal the fuel segments together. Should the O-rings not seal, McDonald believed, the rocket boosters would explode, blowing up the shuttle.

Sadly, Allan McDonalds's worst fears came true. All it took was one exception – an exception to not test the O-rings in colder temperatures – to cause a chain of events that led to multiple deaths.

Exceptions kill. And it's possible the exceptions you're making in your life are killing you. Certainly, they can kill your dreams. This is why it's always critical to be careful and conscious when it comes to making exceptions, even when it only involves the most trivial choices. If you get into the habit of making exceptions about one thing, you will make exceptions about other similar things. This leads to quickly and easily dismantling your life and derailing your success – merely by the exceptions you make. Your Jenga tower will come tumbling down!

SACRIFICE TODAY, SUCCEED TOMORROW

> "He who accomplishes little must sacrifice little, he who would accomplish much must sacrifice much, he who would attain highly must sacrifice greatly."
>
> ~JAMES ALLEN

Too many people fail to understand that if you're willing to live a few years of your life like most people wouldn't, you can live the remainder of your life like most people couldn't. That's why successful people know that you must sacrifice today in order to succeed tomorrow. Success will rarely come to people who fixate on instant results, but rather to those who work slowly and steadily at getting better and making progress over time. If you have a quick-fix mindset, then you need to shift it to one of continuous and repetitive improvements.

In life, all quick fixes are a mirage. And it's our ability to delay gratification and make smart decisions that will affect our long-term results. It's typically the tiniest decisions we make that end up shaping our lives. Little decisions made day in and day out will either take you to the life you desire or a life of disaster. As meteorologist Edward Lorenz discovered, a butterfly in Brazil can make a tornado in Texas. Or a rainbow in your future.

When you are on a long journey, similar to the journey to success, straying off course by just two millimeters will dramatically change your trajectory. What seemed like an insignificant, inconsequential decision eventually becomes a mammoth-sized miscalculation. From the foods you eat, to the place you work, as well as the people you choose to spend time with – every choice you make shapes not only how you live today, but more importantly, how you live the rest of your life.

One particularly doomed choice is the strategy of "get now and pay later." This foolish strategy has not worked, will not, nor will ever, work. You can pay the price now and play later, or you can play now and pay later. But don't fool yourself. Life will always demand payment. And the longer you wait to pay, the more it will cost because delayed payments are always paid with exorbitant interest.

If you want to go far in life and live in a way that others admire, you need to learn to give up some pleasures today for greater gains tomorrow. You need to learn how to refuse to play the instant gratification game that so many people fall victim to and in which you are actively encouraged to participate. As the saying goes: sacrifice a moment for a life.

GREED AND INSTANT GRATIFICATION

> "We want instant lunch, instant cure, instant miracles, instant salary, instant success – instant everything. This instant civilization we have obsessed with, has made us grow a tad too impatient in virtually everything about life. And, of course, that doesn't serve us so well."
>
> ~BONIFACE SAGINI, Author of *Thrills and Chills: Trudging Through Life*

Trusting in the process, realizing that there are some things in life you have to work for and other things you have to wait for – the chess player mentality – seems like a foreign concept to many people. A lot of people have become so addicted to instant gratification that they are blind to the negative impact it has on their lives. People seek instant everything. They want things now and they have been conditioned *not* to wait.

My reality (the same as yours) is that, as I stated previously, there are things I have to work for and things I have to wait for. Thus, I trust in the process. I have to work for things and wait for things consistently, trust that the process will pay off, and be patient for the time when the results eventually come. For me personally, all of success in life is nothing more than repeating a process over and over again, in intervals that are determined by "working for" and "waiting for" the results to blossom.

Failing to trust in, accept, or even recognize any process which requires persistence and patience reminds me of the fable about the goose that laid the golden egg. Let me share the story with you because I believe it illustrates perfectly the fatal implications when people pursue instant gratification.

> There was a poor village farmer who had a goose, and every morning the goose laid a few ordinary eggs. The farmer would take the eggs to the market and sell them, but the money he made was barely enough to support himself and his wife. However, one day, his circumstances completely changed.
>
> The farmer went to check on his goose, and to his surprise, he found a golden egg! After getting the egg appraised and confirming that the egg was made of pure gold, the farmer was overjoyed. He told his wife all about his good fortune, and she was equally pleased. They sold the golden egg on the market for a lot of money, and the couple was no longer poor.
>
> The very next day, the farmer and his wife were shocked to find that their precious goose had laid a second golden egg. It was just as real as the first one. What amazing luck! This miracle occurred every single day from there on out, and the couple began to acquire a fortune from all the golden eggs they were selling.
>
> But sadly, this story has a tragic ending. You see, immediate

gratification seduced the farmer and his wife in the form of greed. They wanted to become richer, and they wanted to do it faster. One golden egg a day was no longer enough – they wanted ten golden eggs right now.

> So what did the farmer decide to do? He decided to kill his precious goose by cutting it open. In his mind, killing the goose would allow him to get all of the golden eggs at once instead of having to wait. But to his disappointment, there were no golden eggs in the goose's dead body. And now there was no chance of the farmer getting his hands on another golden egg ever again.

Everything had been going great for the farmer and his wife. All they had to do was simply be patient and collect the daily golden eggs. Quite literally, the farmer didn't have to do anything and he would have amassed a massive fortune beyond his wildest dreams. No harvesting, no thinking, no hard work. He had everything he needed, but in the pursuit of instant gratification, he ruined it all in one second of poor judgment.

Didn't that story have the saddest ending ever?

The moral of this story – and how easily it applies in our own reality – is that often our desire for short-term results can ruin a good thing that is already in progress right in front of us. The final line in this story, as it was originally told, sums up the lesson perfectly:

"Those who have plenty want more and so lose all they have."

Remember: every time you delay gratification, you become stronger and move closer to your ultimate goals, and – most importantly...

A fortune – one golden egg at a time – is still a fortune.

CONCLUSION

"There are no shortcuts to any place worth going."

~BEVERLY SILLS, American opera singer

I fully understand why people want to seek out shortcuts in life. Given that we only have one life and one shot on Earth to make things count, it only makes sense that we seek out the fastest way to receive pleasure. However, taking shortcuts waves the red flag of impatience and shows a lack of self-discipline. If long-term results are what truly matter, we must learn to be patient and wait for them.

Don't call it an oxymoron, but personally, I've learned that the best shortcut is the long way. You might not like the long way, but it's the tried and true way that has existed for thousands of years. The long way, one sure step at a time, actually becomes the shortest way when it leads to sustainable success. If you try to skip the important steps needed to become successful, don't be surprised when you find yourself running in circles. Or blowing up when your O-rings fail!

Immediate gratification is the greatest saboteur of sustained growth and success. We can choose to please ourselves and hit a brick wall, or we can delay gratification and become more than we are right now. At the end of the day, it's ultimately up to us to decide in which direction we want our lives to go.

I began this chapter with the pitfalls of giving in to instant gratification instead of delaying gratification. Then:

- I expounded on the value of sacrifice as it applies to seeking instant rewards. From there,
- I demonstrated how this comes down to choice, rising above the mere "muscle memory" that has us sleepwalking through life and playing "not to lose."

- Part of this sleepwalking is being blind to the rut created from the exceptions that become our lives and
- these same exceptions are the enemy of commitment, causing us to trade away long-term goals for short-term immediate gains,
- seducing ourselves into bad decisions via cognitive bias and the framing effect.
- Along the way are saboteurs, such as distractors and our caveman limbic system, which results in our blindness until we have no idea what (or who) we've become.
- And the biggest distractor of all is the impatience that fuels seeking out instant gratification.

There's a beauty in how a lesson can unfold, even when it's scary as hell!

EXERCISE NO. 1: MAKE SWEET DECISIONS

The sugar, glucose, is what fuels your brain. In fact, while it also fuels the rest of your body, it is astounding that your brain, which comprises less than 2 percent of your entire body, uses 20 percent (or more) of all the available glucose. And effort raises this percentage, especially in the brain, where acts of self-control (i.e., delaying instant gratification), require more energy.

According to Dr. Carrie Wilkens at the Center for Motivation and Change:

> *"Studies have found that glucose level plays a significant role in decision-making and self-control, as it affects energy available to the entire system...Acts of self-control reduce blood glucose levels. Low levels of glucose predict poor performance on self-control tasks and tests. Replenishing glucose, even just with a glass of lemonade, improves self-control performance."*

This exercise is not so much an overt act to be repeated, but a lifelong commitment to a change in lifestyle – what is called good nutrition. Nothing except true drug addiction is more powerful of a temptation to resist than the instant gratification of impulsive eating that comes from craving.

When we eat healthy foods, as well as avoid putting ourselves in difficult situations when we lack proper food in our body we set ourselves up for success. Conversely, when we go long periods without eating (fueling our body/brain) we tend to behave (and think) at our worst. Consciously be aware of your glucose levels. Never negotiate important transactions when you're hungry (hangry).

Understand *low levels of glucose predict poor performance on self-control tasks and tests.* Therefore, don't put yourself in a situation where you need to perform at your best when you haven't first provided your brain and body with adequate nutrition.

Some healthy foods that provide glucose: grapes, dried apricots, honey, cured ham, sweet corn, plums, bananas, raisins, (my favorite) avocados. I've also found that M&M's do the trick. But like with many things – moderation is certainly key here.

EXERCISE NO. 2: IMPLEMENT THE POMODORO TECHNIQUE

A strategy I'd like to share with you is the *Pomodoro Technique.* Using a tomato-shaped timer, a student in the 1980s, Francesco Cirillo, developed his approach to time management ("*Pomodoro*" is Italian for "tomato"). A timer breaks down a task's duration into intervals, 25 minutes at a time, with short breaks in between. Each 25-minute segment is quaintly called a "Pomodoro." After a series of these Pomodoros, a larger break is allowed.

Here's how it works:

1. Choose a task you'd like to get done
2. Set your Pomodoro (timer in your phone) for 25 minutes
3. Work on the task until the Pomodoro rings
4. When the Pomodoro rings, put a checkmark on a paper

5. Take a short break (5 minutes)
6. Every 4 Pomodoros, take a longer break (15 minutes)

Each 25-minute work session equals one Pomodoro, where you work for 25 minutes undisturbed, then take a 5-minute break. After you have completed 4 Pomodoro's in a row, it's recommended you give yourself a 15 to 30-minute break. This technique proves to be the most effective when you plan out your Pomodoros in advance.

Using your phone, set the timer for 25 minutes, then begin working on your task. And do not, let me repeat, do not engage in any other activity other than the task you need to complete – the one you planned to spend your 25 minutes doing. Unless your home or office catches fire or an act of God takes place, force yourself to focus.

Do not check the time on the timer. Trust me, the timer will let you know when your 25 minutes is up. That's what it's for. No checking email. No checking text messages. No checking social media notifications. By the way, if you're serious about becoming the CEO of your life, you will turn off all social media notifications now on your phone and computer.

Get up when the timer goes off. Do not stay seated in the same place you were working. This is a good time to get a snack or coffee (glucose fuel), use the bathroom and check your messages. (Yes, I know you are dying to see what has taken place in the eternity of 25 minutes; after all, in Andy Warhol's world of everyone having 15 minutes of fame, it means during your 25-minute task someone famous is famous no longer, and someone who wasn't, now is.)

Do not take more than a 5-minute break between each of the first 4 Pomodoros. If you get distracted during a Pomodoro session, use the strategy the inventor of the Pomodoro suggests: inform, negotiate, call back.

1. Inform that you are in the middle of something
2. Negotiate a time when you can get back with them
3. Contact when you are finished

You may think this is all very elementary. After all, you're not a child. This really isn't the way you have to live your life; by the ticking of a metronome. But that isn't the point. The point of this, frankly, *over-bureaucratization* of your time is that you're re-learning how to focus and achieve according to a way that corrects the wrong way you have programmed yourself (i.e. becoming addicted to distractions). No, you're not a child, but the way you achieve – the way you manage your time in pursuing your goals – needs to have a framework in place to ensure you are not spending major time on minor things.

As you strengthen your willpower, focus, and self-discipline, increase your Pomodoro sessions gradually. Set a goal to work your way up to 50-minute Pomodoro sessions (but don't go much beyond that), followed by a 5-minute break.

Being able to focus without getting distracted on tasks that will have a high impact on your future is key to your success. Too many people spend major time on minor things then wonder why they're not successful. Think about it: when was the last time you turned off the world and turned on your laser-focused self to accomplishing your goals? When we allow ourselves to get distracted by something as simple as a text message, and take our focus off the task at hand to check it, we think to ourselves...*well, I'm already distracted so I might as well check my email now*. See the self-sabotaging cycle?

"Staying on message", staying focused on tasks that will yield the greatest dividends, and not getting addicted to distractions is the primary reason why I am able to achieve so much so quickly. A 10-hour work day for me is similar to a 40-hour work week for many people. Having the ability to put my head down and stay focused has allowed me to live an amazing life. And guess what? It will allow you to live an amazing life as well when you break the bad habit of gratifying yourself by continuously engaging in unproductive activities.

EXERCISE NO. 3: MINI-DELAYS IN GRATIFICATION

Start exercising the muscle in your brain that helps you delay gratification in all areas of your life. Begin by delaying little things. For example, if you're jogging, jog for an extra five minutes. If you're writing, write for an extra five minutes. If you're used to going to lunch at a certain time, test yourself by delaying the meal for 10 minutes and use that extra 10 minutes for work.

Delaying gratification for 10 minutes is a lot simpler than delaying gratification for a year, but eventually, your delayed gratification muscles will get stronger. When you win at the small exercises, you can ultimately win at larger ones.

For dieters, your body has a built-in challenge you can take advantage of:

> It takes about 10 minutes for a full stomach to invoke the "fed" signal in your brain. This means that if you keep eating a meal while you're still hungry, you're going to overeat by 10 minutes each time. The challenge is to: stop eating about 10 minutes before you think you'll be finished – before the time you think you'll be satiated.
>
> Leave food on your plate. The strange thing is that you'll probably no longer be hungry because in those 10 minutes your brain and metabolism will catch up with a "fed signal," which is a complicated process of stomach distention, rise in blood sugar, and release of insulin from your pancreas. This is an exercise with more benefits than just practicing delayed gratification, because an extra 10 minutes eating, per meal, per day, can add up.

Practice a lunch delay regularly or, alternatively, stop eating 10 minutes earlier than your hunger demands, and soon enough, you'll get used to such delays. You will eventually enjoy the delay because each time you successfully delay your gratification, you will feel your self-control getting stronger and stronger. And that's a great (self-rewarding) feeling.

EXERCISE NO. 4: CONTINUE TO EXERCISE YOUR "DELAYED GRATIFICATION" MUSCLE

If you are exercising and want to stop – keep going for an extra five minutes. If you are enjoying a dessert, eat only half and tell yourself you can have the other half tomorrow, especially since you're shamelessly violating your "10-minutes-till-full" policy. If you have been working on a project for several hours, push yourself to work an extra 30 minutes.

Whatever it is that you want to do or don't want to do, do the opposite for just a little bit longer. When you delay gratification and know that you did it purposefully, you will feel immense satisfaction with yourself. It is this kind of pleasure that you want to harness if you are serious about achieving your goals.

And I know you are.

EXERCISE NO. 5: GIVE YOURSELF MINI-REWARDS

Let's say you created a structure in your life to work on an important project for three hours each evening to achieve your goals, but you really want to skip a night to go hang out with friends. The instant gratifications are clear: you get to stop working and you get to go have some immediate fun.

By not completing those three hours of work, you are circumventing your own goals. As we discussed earlier, when you make one exception, it's highly likely you will continue to make more exceptions (greasing the slippery slope syndrome). Thus, it's likely that if you don't hit your goals for your project this week, you'll find it easier to slack off next week and the week after that. This is how people get derailed and it is one of the primary reasons why many people never become the CEO of their life.

So instead of putting off your work to go hang out with friends, choose a reward for yourself after the three hours of completed work. This reward can be anything beneficial that you really enjoy doing. Maybe you love checking out what's happening on social media, so you can promise yourself that you'll log onto Twitter or Tik Tok when you are done with your work.

> In the field of pediatric neuropsychiatry, this protocol is called the "*Token Economy System*," and it is used to help children with "maladaptive" (bad) behavior. And it almost always works.
>
> A limited number of bad behaviors are targeted for elimination. For example, they can be aggression, cursing, and non-compliance with chores. At the same time, engaging in behaviors that are desired, e.g., making the bed, an act of kindness, etc., will add tokens to the till. Thus, a child earns "tokens" for desired behaviors that take place, and he/she is penalized tokens for indulging in the bad behaviors. At the end of the day, the tokens added and deducted are counted up, and "privileges" things the child likes to do – watching TV, going for ice cream, video games, etc. – can be bought for the next day with the tokens that remain or have accumulated.
>
> In other words, privileges must be earned. Is this any different from giving yourself a mini-reward by earning it?

Maybe you can ask your friends to reschedule the meetup for another day. Perhaps you can treat yourself to a lunch or dinner at an upscale restaurant that you've wanted to try for a while after you complete your work. It is advantageous to spend a few extra dollars on a meal if it helps you achieve your goals.

Think of the reward as an investment in your goals. And when you promise to reward yourself, it is important that you actually give yourself that reward.

You have to train your brain to appreciate delaying gratification, so don't lie to yourself. Make a promise to yourself and then deliver on that promise. Don't indulge in the reward *before* you do the work! Like the "problem child," earn your privileges.

CHAPTER FIVE

Habits – Small Things that Make A Big Difference

"In truth, the only difference between those who have failed and those who have succeeded lies in the difference of their habits."

~OG MANDINO, Author of *The Greatest Salesman in the World*

Without a doubt, our habits and the impact they have on our lives is what dictates the quality of life we live. If we are enslaved with bad habits, our lives are not too pleasant. Conversely, if we are enslaved with good habits, our lives are pleasurable. But make no mistake about it, we are all slaves to our habits – the good ones as well as the bad ones. And for this reason, I'd like to begin this chapter by sharing a poem that was written by John Di Lemme. It's a perfect description of habits and the Herculean power they have on our lives:

I am your constant companion.

I am your greatest helper or heaviest burden.

I will push you onward or drag you down to failure.

I am completely at your command.

Half the things you do you might just as well turn over to me, and

I will be able to do them quickly, correctly.

I am easily managed – you must merely be firm with me. Show me exactly how you want something done, and after a few lessons I will do it automatically.

I am the servant of all great people; and alas, of all failures as well.

Those who are failures, I have made failures.

I am not a machine, though I work with all the precision of a machine plus the intelligence of a human being.

You may run me for a profit or turn me for ruin – it makes no difference to me.

Take me, train me, be firm with me, and I will place the world at your feet.

Be easy with me and I will destroy you.

Who am I?

I am a habit.

One of the biggest misconceptions I see floating around in the personal development space is the idea that we have the power to choose our destiny. That's partially true (as I fervently asserted in Chapter One). But in this chapter, I hope to put it more accurately: I believe we choose our habits, and then our habits ultimately decide our destiny. Stephen Covey described the power of our habits brilliantly in his book *The 7 Habits of Highly Effective People*:

> *"Habits are powerful factors in our lives. Because they're consistent, often unconscious patterns, they constantly, daily, express our character and produce our effectiveness...Or our ineffectiveness."*

ADDICTED TO HABITS?

> "Before you can break out of prison, you must realize you are locked up."
>
> ~DONNA CARDILLO, Fellow in the American Academy of Nursing, keynote speaker, columnist and author

As human beings, we are all creatures of routine. It's an important part of our survival. We live according to a circadian rhythm (day and night and wake and sleep), we have established a customary eating routine (breakfast, lunch, and dinner); there are daily routines, weekly routines, monthly routines, and even quarterly and annual routines. So we are open to establishing routines all the time. All a particular action needs to become part of any routine is repetition.

The reason routines are important to our survival is because we are complex beings who have a lot to do. Mentally, we are very busy. Routines that become automatic take very little mental exertion and allow us to automate the mundane activities of our daily lives without much thought – thought better used for the surprises and ambitions in each of our days.

Our automatic routines turn into our habits. Habits are self-perpetuating, which serves to keep the habit intact. Thus, you can see how bad habits can be just as active in our subconscious as good habits.

Our brains are wired for repetition such that, if done enough, an action will tie into our reward circuitry (via dopamine) and alter the brain areas that deal with stress. Once established, such repetition will be coupled with expectation, so that there will be a bit of anxiety if that habit isn't performed and its expectation realized; that is, if it goes unfulfilled. This anxiety may be subtle, but it is interesting that you will more easily notice a habit *not done* than you will notice a habit *done*. Think about those who suffer from obsessive-compulsive disorder. They are an extreme example of the anxiety that can occur, but their anxiety likely follows the same mechanism.

Expectation is built into our reward system, it's the way our brains are wired. However, it is the unfulfilled expectation that gets our attention because we miss out on the reward we get from doing a particular action. When an action goes unexpectedly missing, a warning bell goes off that can only be silenced by performing that action and collecting our reward (again, dopamine in action). For habits of survival, this is a good thing.

A musical aside:

Music uses the concept of expectation as a fundamental ingredient for manipulating our brain. A "home note" is established (the key the melody is in), and as the piece goes on, notes and musical phrases are used which distance themselves from this home note. There are many approaches toward it, but this tease is only meant to raise the tension in our musical brains.

Music creates anticipation in the listener's mind for the release of this tension. As the melody continues, the tension builds until there is the final resolution earned by the song returning again to its home note. Anticipation is answered, tension is released, and we are rewarded. Dopamine is released, and we have taken the ride the music meant for us to take – up and down, sideways, tangential, side trips, and the final resting place again at the home note. Along the way, we are emotional because of the tension that builds up from exploiting our expectations. From rock to rap to classical music, this feature is part of the musical hook that gets (and keeps) our attention.

The scourge of addiction and substance abuse involves the same reward system, except that, like obsessive-compulsive disorder, this is a faulty rewiring of the reward system. The anticipation of tension release consumes the addicted person. The definition of addiction is the craving for a substance that is so strong as to make the addicted person oblivious (at best) or uncaring (at worst) of dangers the substance-seeking creates. Although there is a physical side to addiction, which begins squawking at the cellular and biochemical level, the psychological addiction is based on expectation and the drive to fulfill that expectation at any cost.

A neurological aside:

The biology of addiction and its reward pathways in the brain explains the rushes of feeling good that a substance creates. Addiction occurs at the psychological level when the areas of the brain connected to stress become hypersensitive to any delay of the reward, while the areas of the brain used for self-control become inhibited - all of which makes for a perfect storm for addictive behavior.

According to Budygin et al., in a study from 2012:

"Pleasure produced from drugs of abuse occurs because most of these drugs target the brain's reward system by flooding the circuit with dopamine. When some drugs like cocaine are taken, they can release two to ten times the amount of dopamine; the resultant effects on the brain's pleasure circuit dwarfs those produced by natural rewards such as food and even sex."

In the 1950s, after the section of the brain for pleasure was identified in rats, rats who were allowed to pull a lever to stimulate that area of their brain nearly starved to death because they were too consumed with pulling the lever. Psychologists James Olds and Peter Milner found that "Rats would press the lever as many as 7,000 times per hour to stimulate their brains." Also, "A series of subsequent experiments revealed that rats preferred pleasure circuit stimulation to food (even when they were hungry) and water (even when they were thirsty)."

In the early 1970s, these experiments were extended – quite unethically – to human beings. The results, again identifying dopamine as the major player in the reward system, were just as dramatic, in spite of the study objective itself being ridiculous and irrelevant:

> A paper entitled, "*Septal stimulation for the initiation of heterosexual behavior in a homosexual male*" published in 1972, attempted to test the ability to change a "patient's" sexuality by allowing him to stimulate his brain's pleasure center when he looked at heterosexual images, as instructed by researchers. Surgically embedded electrodes in his brain allowed him to activate this area of his brain at will. However, while nothing was learned regarding sexuality, what was significant was that he:
>
> *"...stimulated himself to a point that, both behaviorally and introspectively, he was experiencing an almost overwhelming euphoria and elation and had to be disconnected despite his vigorous protests."*

Thus, while rewards are relative, there is always a potential for the fulfillment that a habit produces to generate so much pleasure that all other life-preserving actions are demoted in importance. This is inherent in the very definition of addiction.

The question, therefore, is this: is a person who has habits a person who is addicted to these habits? Where is the dividing line? Hopefully, on a subsequent edition of this book, I can have the neurological aside that identifies where that line is. Regardless, the transition of habit to addiction is a continuum, and most people know when they are crossing that line. (Sadly, this may have a genetic basis, as 15 percent of the population is genetically predisposed to addictive behavior, e.g., drugs, alcohol, nicotine, gambling, excessive exercise, dietary extremes, even religious fanaticism.)

The only thing that seems to make our routines are the habitual actions – strings of habits – for good or for bad. Addiction implies at-risk behavior for what is craved, so is it much of a stretch to say that bad habits that put your future and your success at risk are addictive in nature?

YOU ARE WHAT YOU REPEAT

It's not "You are what you eat," but "You are what you repeat". It's no secret we are what we repeatedly do, and what we repeatedly do are our habits. Habits are the things that people do without even thinking about why they are doing them. Charles Duhigg, author of *The Power of Habit* and perhaps one of the foremost experts on habits believes:

> *"Most of the choices we make every day may feel like the products of well considered decision-making, but," Duhigg says, "they're actually not. They're habits."*

The ingrained routines in our minds that make us, *us*, have an infrastructure of habits. Collectively, habits that make up our routines can fall victim to the lure of the expectations that hold them captive. Thus, creating chaos in our lives (and nervous systems) when we deviate from the structure we are accustomed to.

A while back I read about a zookeeper who was attacked by a tiger. No one could understand what happened because this person had been attending to this animal for years. After an intensive investigation, they reasoned that the attendant who ushered the tiger into the cage was holding a garden hose that one particular time and that was enough of a departure from the tiger's life "structure" to unsettle the animal. The tiger's world was its routine. When that changed, the tiger was not himself, and chaos and unpredictability came out.

We are not much different from animals, because we also want order and consistency. If your home or office is in disarray, more often than not – your mind is in disarray. Chaos and unpredictability can arise because we are subconsciously hardwired for structure in our lives. As stated previously, as human beings, we are creatures of routine. Anything less may indicate mental illness – a deviation from the routine in which we function best.

Think of hoarders. Hoarders often don't have space to even walk among the items and boxes they've collected. For them, the sheer enormity of the clutter mirrors the mental clutter that prevents them from organizing, stowing, and ultimately getting rid of the useless debris in their lives that pose as obstacles to their plans.

Similarly, our automated actions – our ingrained routines – done throughout the day can also get in our way. A research paper that was published in 2006 by Duke University stated, "More than 40 percent of the actions people performed each day weren't actual decisions, but habits." And several similar studies out of universities such as Yale, Michigan, and MIT have discovered that the vast majority of everything we think and do is a direct result of a learned habit.

Habits are like macros (i.e. keystroke shortcuts that run computer instructions, simplifying the user's actions). They are programmed to repeat – and very easily. They take the mental load off of our brains so we can concentrate on the more "executive" decisions, which are – numerically – the minority of our decisions. If they're bad automated actions, however, the metaphor of the hoarder comes to mind as such habits that represent the debris that creates obstacles.

Repetitive action turns into a habit. You engage in that habit without even thinking about it. Right now, you are the sum total of all your habits. Any action you frequently take, or any thought you frequently think, becomes *who* you are – so much so, in fact, that you cannot determine the difference between you and your habits.

So whether you realize it or not, the habits you currently have are dictating the quality of your life and they are determining the level of success (or failure) you will experience in the future. Your sequence of macros may be running a good program or a bad program. (Bad programs should motivate you to reboot!)

Installing a habit into your consciousness is like a tree trying to take root. At first, the roots are delicate and easily disturbed. But once those roots have taken their place deep in the ground, it is difficult to get rid of them. They have now become a part of you. That's precisely why you must choose your habits wisely.

In Chapter Two, I invoked the 1949 aphorism by neuropsychologist Donald Hebb: *neurons that fire together, wire together.* The more they fire together, the stronger their bonding with each other. The more neurons behind a habit fire, the more they remained wired. This means they're more likely to become automated, that is, "habit-forming".

THE STRENGTH OF HABITS

"Habits are like a cable. We weave a strand of it every day and soon it cannot be broken."

~HORACE MANN, American educational reformer and Whig politician

Are you beginning to see how incredibly powerful our habits are and how much control they have over our lives? For me, grasping the gravity of where my habits were taking me was a major turning point in my life. Discovering the negative patterns that ingrained themselves into the fabric of my behavior was an unsettling experience. However, it was a step I had to take if I was going to become – and remain – the CEO of my life. For you to become – and remain – the CEO of your life you're going to have to really assess your habitual behaviors (the ones that have unconsciously entrenched themselves into your life) and ruthlessly see where they are leading you.

There's a great story about a father and his young son who were taking a walk through the woods behind their home that extrapolates just how habits embed themselves in our lives.

> A father and his son were walking through the woods when the dad pointed at a tiny green sprout and told his son to pull it out. The young boy pulled it out with ease.
>
> They continued their walk, and this time he pointed at a sapling and asked his son to pull it out. The sapling was at the height of the boy's knee. The boy pulled at the sapling, and with a couple of tugs, the sapling was removed from its roots.
>
> The walk continued, and the father looked at a small tree that was roughly the height and size of his little boy. Not surprisingly, he asked him to pull that one out, too. With a lot of tugging and pulling, his son was eventually able to pull the tree out.
>
> Next, they approached a tall oak as high as the sky and sturdy enough to hold dozens of little boys on its branches. The father gestured to his son once again and asked him to pull it out. The boy looked at the tree, and without even making an attempt told his father that he couldn't do it. "It's impossible to pull the tree out," his son said.
>
> "My son, you have just demonstrated the power that habits will have over your life," the father replied. "The older they are, the bigger they get, the deeper the roots grow, and the harder they are to uproot. Some get so big, with roots so deep, you might hesitate to even try."

Right now, you have hundreds of habits, many of which you

probably are not even aware of. There are harmless habits, such as licking your lips when you are concentrating on something. There are also more insidious ones, such as drinking on a regular basis when the weekend comes. The foods you eat, the time you go to sleep – all of these things, and more, are habits.

Ultimately, every single thing that you think and do is connected to a habit. Most people operate from daily habits without thinking twice about them (unless they go a day without doing them). Consequently, many people spend the majority of their lives going through involuntary motions, muscle memory, and sleepwalking through their days.

In this tragic state, a lot of individuals never even recognize what is holding them back from the life they really want. They lack the awareness that allows them to see the bad habits they have built up over time.

Fortunately for all of us, awareness is a skill we can build. You don't necessarily need to have extreme intelligence, money, or any genetic gifts to become aware of what your good habits and bad habits are. But I've noticed that successful people tend to have a higher level of self-awareness than unsuccessful people do.

It's so critical to understand that successful people aren't necessarily smarter, more talented, or better connected than anyone else. Their higher level of awareness merely allows them to build better habits, ones that help them become well-informed, more knowledgeable, more competent, better skilled, and better prepared. Their awareness allows them to skillfully sidestep the reward system that reinforces habits they want to eliminate.

Think about this for a moment:

> **If it's true that you are your habits, but you don't like who you are right now, then one of the most important things you must do is to start changing your habits.**

In this chapter, I want to take a deep-dive and explore the importance of habits, discover how they're created, and show you how to replace bad habits with good habits. In this process, you're going to learn some of the strangest things about yourself as they relate to your habits.

WHO YOU REALLY ARE

> "Your net worth to the world is usually determined by what remains after your bad habits are subtracted from your good ones."
>
> ~BENJAMIN FRANKLIN

When we look at someone doing the same things over and over again, we think, *that's just how they are*, and automatically assume they're always going to be that way. We make this assumption, regardless of whether the things they are doing are productive or destructive. (Hence, the importance of first impressions.)

That's just how they are, however, is the same as saying that the things they do are "in their nature." Such a label is saying the things they do have always been what they do and are the result of a random arrangement of their genetics.

Question: Is the way their genetics "set" actually the way they were conceived, born, and what they eventually became? Answer: absolutely not.

No one was born with habits ingrained into their DNA – they were formed. This is great news because it means that any of us can change our habits. Some of us are "predisposed", but we aren't genetically *destined* to be a slave to our current habits. Our habits can be changed for the better. And when habits are reformed for the better, they can have a tremendously positive impact on our lives and the achievement of our goals.

Aristotle believed behaviors that occur without thinking about them are evidence of our truest selves and famously said, "We are what we repeatedly do. Excellence then, is not an act, but a habit."

Some of the most pressing philosophical questions of all time involve finding out more about who we are as people. Who is a person, really? *What* is a person? Is a person just eyes, nose, and mouth? The way he or she walks? Are people where they live or how they talk? These questions and many others have left philosophers scratching their heads for thousands of years.

If you really boil it down to the simplest elements, a person is composed of the habits they keep. In fact, the actual word is "*habitus*". A person's habits are their bricks, and each habit they pick up or create for themselves builds the house that we know as the person.

When you were born, you were an empty vessel that needed creating. As a child, you began forming habits because of the environment you found yourself in. The habits of your caregivers, your parents, your teachers, your schoolmates, and your friends have all played a role in the habits you embody now.

Not only were you filled with habits early on in life to help you navigate the world, but those same habits have designed you into the person that sits here today reading this book. There are millions of decisions you have made to reach the point you are at today, and each decision you have made is linked to a habit.

These decisions emerging from your habits will make you or break you every day, so it's in your best interest to build habits that take you toward positivity while eliminating the ones that guide you toward negativity. When you are able to do this, you won't have to "work hard" at building your character and being a good human being. Your habits will do the work for you.

U.S. Senator Dan Coats summed up the concept of habits perfectly by saying that habits are the daily battlefield of character:

"Character cannot be summoned at the moment of crisis if it has been squandered by the years of compromise and rationalization. The only testing ground for the heroic is the mundane. The only preparation for that one profound decision which can change a life, or even a nation, is those hundreds of half-conscious, self-defining, seemingly insignificant decisions made in private. Habit is the daily battlefield of character."

What Senator Coats is teaching us is that everything we do matters. That one microscopic action you take today is forming the foundation for one of two lives down the road: a life of success or a life of failure. And it's entirely up to you to decide which direction you want to go.

Very few people actually realize that each "automatic" habit is just the net result of a multitude of actions repeated over time. In fact, most of these habits are likely so ingrained in you that you don't think of them as entities that are separate from you. They feel like they *are* you.

As an example, let's look at walking on the right side of the sidewalk, especially when you see someone approaching from the opposite direction. You weren't born knowing that you should walk on the right side of the sidewalk when passing another person.

Somewhere along the way in life, you learned – through culture or another person – that this is an unspoken rule. You developed the habit. You might not even notice that this is a habit until you visit the United Kingdom and notice that people keep bumping into you as you stick to your habit of walking on the right side of the sidewalk.

Now, you might not think that there's anything wrong with this. After all, it's only a tiny habit that dictates how you walk on a sidewalk, right? Not necessarily. I only used this example to show you how you form a habit (without even realizing it). That's one half of it. What you really need to know about is the power contained within a habit.

The effect that a single habit can have on your life is similar to the domino effect. One bad habit cannot remain isolated from other habits and decisions. A bad habit results in bad decisions that have bad consequences, which then lead to other bad decisions that lead to even worse consequences.

The domino effect, when it comes to habits, can be both negative and positive. If you sleep in until noon each day, then when you wake up, eat leftover pizza, followed by watching a few hours of useless TV, more than likely your life is not all that great (it actually probably sucks). However, the opposite is also true. If you wake up early in the morning, eat a healthy breakfast, followed by spending hours focused on your most important tasks by implementing the Pomodoro technique (the exercise at the end of Chapter Four), then exercise before lunch, you will more than likely continue making positive choices throughout the day (and throughout your life).

It can be empowering to know that excellence or success is not one grand act, but rather a series of small actions combined that create the final outcome. This means that each choice and every step you take today, tonight, and tomorrow plays a role in your ultimate success. It also means that you can carve out your success one little bit at a time by changing one habit at a time.

THOUGHTS ARE HABITS, TOO

> "Your beliefs become your thoughts, your thoughts become your words, your words become your actions, your actions become your habits, your habits become your values, your values become your destiny."
>
> ~MAHATMA GANDHI, Indian lawyer, anti-colonial nationalist, and political ethicist who employed nonviolent resistance to lead the successful campaign for India's independence from British Rule

What you think and how you think are also habits too. If you take the time to carefully listen to yourself throughout the day, and I mean *really* listen to how you're responding to things in the external world and in your internal world, you will be surprised at how automatic and habitual your thoughts are.

Since our thoughts are also habits, you're going to have a habitual way of thinking. You might generally be positive about everything, or negative about everything. You can often see this habit of thought in other people, but most of us are blind to the habit of thought that takes place in our own minds.

That surly person you have to deal with every day might not have a clue that he has a habit of being cynical – he has probably never listened to his way of thinking or examined it carefully. He likely thinks that he is responding to his environment when, in fact, the environment is responding to his overall mood.

Beyond your overall thinking tone, the actual discrete things you think about on a daily basis are also habitual. What you think about is what you are, and so the kind of thinking habits that you have play a massive role in how you view the world around you. The way you think also has an enormous role in how you view your potential.

Successful people have developed the habit of picturing positive outcomes in their lives. They constantly and consistently think about being successful at whatever they set their mind to. And in turn, they typically succeed.

An Olympic athlete doesn't just think about her sport while at practice – she's constantly thinking about winning that gold medal. She's not thinking about the possibility that she could lose. She's only thinking about the possibility that she's going to win, and visualizing herself standing on the podium.

The soon-to-be-successful app developer is continuously testing, analyzing, and making adjustments to his game-changing app. And while doing so, he's not thinking about how this isn't going to work (if he does, he'll probably get what he asked for). He's only thinking about how this is definitely going to work – all he has to do is just figure it out.

There's a pattern here, and it has to do with the habit of success-oriented thinking. Similar to how Thomas Edison failed 10,000 times when trying to create the light bulb, any inventor or creator may try and fail hundreds of times before achieving success. But as long as they have the habit of success-oriented thinking, they will eventually succeed because they've hardwired themselves to do so.

A HABIT IS THE HUMAN BUILDING BLOCK

> "The chains of habit are too weak to be felt until they are too strong to be broken."
>
> ~SAMUEL JOHNSON, English writer, playwright, essayist, moralist, literary critic, biographer, and lexicographer

Your brain is incredibly busy because it's responsible for thousands of things that are continuously going on in your body. You can't blame it for trying to simplify the job. To make its job easier, your brain loves using habits. Habits allow your brain to automate certain actions so that it doesn't have to be involved in the process of actively doing them.

If your brain had to use up energy to consciously do all your daily activities, it would always be exhausted, and it would not survive very long. Brain activity is expensive from an energy point of view. In fact, the human brain uses more than 20 percent of the body's available glucose for the energy it needs to function. Thus, it is cost-effective – again, from an energy point of view – to automate certain actions.

You can train your brain to automate anything and everything, from a talent to an emotion. If you've been a negative person all your life and you want to change that, you can. All you need to do is actively be positive over a period of time before positivity turns into a habit, and your brain automates it. Again, quoting Dr. Hebb, "Neurons that fire together, wire together."

A military aside:

Many years ago I was in the U. S. Army. And during basic training one of the habits that was drilled into soldier's minds was how to clear a malfunctioning M16 rifle. The drill sergeants knew that if we were at war and under tremendous pressure and our rifles jammed we needed to know how to fix it without thinking. So what did they do? They ingrained into our minds how to fix our weapon when it malfunctioned. How did they do that? With an acronym (SPORTS) and an insane amount of repetition.

Even though it's been more than 20 years since I've held an M16 in my hands; I can still easily and quickly remember exactly how to fix it if it were to jam. The life-saving acronym: **S**lap. **P**ull. **O**bserve. **R**elease. **T**ap. **S**queeze.

Slap upward on the magazine to make sure it is properly seated.
Pull the charging handle all the way back.
Observe the ejection of a live round or expended cartridge.
Release the charging handle.
Tap the forward assist.
Squeeze the trigger and try to fire the rifle.

During basic training, we must have practiced SPORTS hundreds (if not thousands) of times. We could almost do it in our sleep. In fact, I bet some soldiers could. That's the power of repetition. The more you do something, the deeper it embeds itself into your brain. This gives you the capacity to execute without thinking. The U.S. military knows the power of habit and because they do I'm certain countless lives have been saved.

Scientists say that when we repeat a particular thought or action, it starts to carve out a permanent space in our brains called a *neuro-signature*. But it doesn't happen overnight. You have to form a routine and then repeat that routine regularly.

After a period of time where the habit has been repeated continuously, it becomes permanently embedded in our basal ganglia, which is the part of our brain responsible for remembering our habits. At that point, you automatically start doing the thing that you *used* to have to consciously think about doing before.

For example, you wake up in the morning and brush your teeth. It's not something you think about; it's just something you do. There is no question about whether or not you are going to brush your teeth; it's just part of your routine – a habit. It requires no energy or conscious thought whatsoever.

"All our life, so far as it has definite form, is but a mass of habits – practical, emotional, and intellectual – systematically organized for our weal or woe, and bearing us irresistibly toward our destiny, whatever the latter may be."

~WILLIAM JAMES

Another example would be the habit of turning off the lights when you leave a room. The first time that you did this, you would have consciously had to think about the fact that you should turn off the lights to conserve energy and save money in the process.

After repeating this action day in and day out, your brain catches on to this pattern: *leave room, turn off light*. In fact, it becomes *leave room "equals" turn off light*. Your brain has automated the action so that you don't have to think about it. It's the repetition of the action that hard-wires and then triggers the automated response in your brain. Your brain has realized that this is who you've become, and it is no longer just a thing that you do.

When you turn off the lights after leaving a room, even when there is someone sitting in the room, that's when you know you're in full automation mode. It is interesting that when turning off the lights becomes automated, and you try to purposely leave the lights on, you may begin to sense the subtle tension that failing your expectations creates.

Your brain is a beautiful and powerful organ, but it isn't there just helping you develop simple habits like turning off lights. In fact, your brain can automate anything you want. It will take some time and discipline, but your brain will get on board and automate any habit you want so that you don't even have to think about it any longer. That's the power your brain gives you.

Let's look at another example: if you decide you need to start running every day, at first it's going to require a lot of cognitive effort on your part to stick to the plan. However, once you make it a consistent habit, you will find your body actually craving the run and you'll feel odd when you don't go for a run. Habits unfulfilled are actually uncomfortable, while habits fulfilled stimulate your reward center (via dopamine).

Our brains are brilliant, but there is a massive downside to this automation process: the brain cannot tell whether you have a good habit or a bad habit – it can only do what you train it to do. This means that your bad habits are formed in the same way as your good habits.

If you're serious about success, then you must let your brain know this through your thoughts and actions. You must automate success into your life. But in order to do that, you must think about yourself as a successful person, imagine yourself as a successful person, talk about yourself as a successful person, and most importantly – do the things that the successful version of yourself would do: think, imagine, talk, do.

THINK. IMAGINE. TALK. DO.

> "I am the greatest. I said that even before I knew I was. I figured that if I said it enough, I would convince the world that I really was the greatest."
>
> ~MUHAMMAD ALI, Iconic American professional boxer, activist, and philanthropist

Speak into the future about how great you truly are, and just as night follows day, you will become great. (The Muhammad Ali technique.) When you think about what you want, imagine what you want, talk about what you want, and do what you want, you will find yourself becoming more conscious and aware of the habits that hold you back from being successful and consistently move to sidestep them. This aversion itself may become a good habit!

Each time you are able to focus your thoughts on positive future outcomes, you are beginning to manifest your dreams into reality. This enables you to start building the groundwork for habits that will guide you toward the direction of your goals. And it gets even better: since you already had the power to unconsciously create bad habits, you have the same power to create good habits in your subconscious that eventually will become automatic over time.

But in order to get there, you must first wake up to your unconscious bad habits and assess each one of them. This is the awareness I spoke about previously, and it is something that successful people nurture. There's a Chinese proverb that states, "If you don't change the direction that you are headed, you will end up where you're going." It's time to go in a new direction, and the only thing that can take you there is your new habits. That is, the *you* that the new habits become.

WHY PATTERNS ARE POWERFUL

> "Systems permit ordinary people to achieve extraordinary results predictably."
>
> ~MICHAEL GERBER, Author of *The E Myth*

In the 1990s, neurologists at MIT created a neurological loop for rats which contained a cue, a routine, and a reward. The rats were placed in a maze (cue), and they had to find their way out of the maze (routine). When they made it out of the maze, they were given a piece of chocolate (reward).

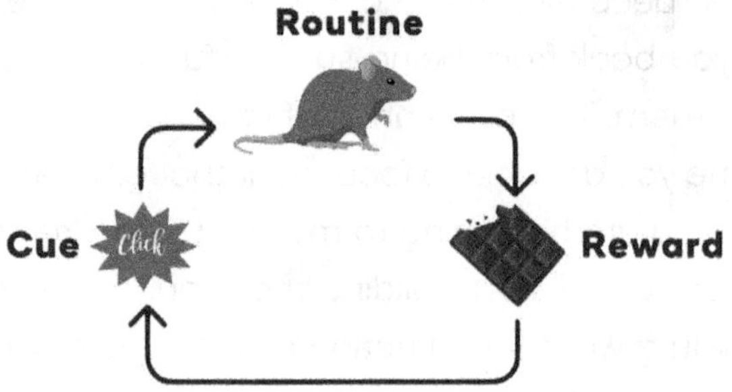

The Habit Loop

The rats were forced to navigate the maze repeatedly as neurologists measured their brain activity. What the neurologists discovered was that each time the rats repeated the neurological loop (each time the rats went through the maze), their brains worked less and less overall with each repetition.

Such "working less and less" means less energy consumption, and energy better spent on the noteworthy actions above and beyond mere survival. For both rats and humans, this is good for energy conservation, both for the rat's brain and your own brain, but it also has a downside: routines and habits are mesmerizing. Think about your own mazes.

For example, you may put your dry-cleaning in your car (cue) and tell yourself you're going to drop it off on your way to work. You pass one stoplight after another on your way to the office (maze). You sit there at a stoplight with your dry-cleaning right next to you, the dry-cleaners right across from the stoplight you're stopped at; yet, you drive right by and continue to the office (routine). You arrive at work and later in the day remember that you forgot to drop off your dry-cleaning. You think to yourself, *son of a*...then tell yourself, emphatically, that you'll do it on the way home without fail. But on the way home (reward), going through your maze, you forget again.

> The tragic side story to this is the parent who forgets the child in the hot car because they were in full automation mode. Society prosecutes these individuals, which may or may not be appropriate; but this mistake can be easily accepted by anyone who understands the power our habits have over us.

If it is not lost on you how your own mazes are mesmerizing and hypnotic – that is, how all this relates to humans and their habits – you're getting it. Most people have a routine for their work days. They wake up at a particular time, shower, dress, eat breakfast, and head toward their job. After eight hours at work, the routine may involve returning home and maintaining a couch potato position in front of the television until it's time to go to bed. And then the routine starts over the next day to be repeated all over again.

Awareness begins when you recognize this routine of good and bad habits as it relates to your present and, subsequently, your future. If you think about it, a routine is simply a series of habitual actions repeated again and again over time. It's a system, a framework you've created for your life. And as leadership expert John Maxwell says, "The secret to success is found in your daily routine."

The catalyst to success in life begins when we focus first on changing our daily routines before we change anything else. Our daily routine is the fundamental foundation upon which everything else in our life is built. Remember when I said there are daily routines, weekly routines, monthly routines, etc.? They all start with daily routines, so not only is it essential to have a routine but what you do within that routine is of the most significant importance.

Think about your typical day and the things you do regularly without exception. These things you do every day are the very things that have developed you into the person you currently are. And your daily person becomes your weekly person, then your monthly person, and so on.

If you exercise regularly, this is who you are, and it will be reflected in your overall physical and mental health. The fact that you exercise regularly will also affect other areas of your life that don't seem to be directly related. This happens because exercise is known as one of the keystone habits. (We'll talk more about keystone habits and why they are crucial to your success later in this chapter.)

When people exercise regularly, it affects the type of friends they choose to hang out with. It also dictates the kinds of foods and drinks they decide to put into their bodies. Science has proven that people who exercise regularly change their brain chemistry and create an overall positive effect where they naturally seek out health-positive people, behaviors and attitudes.

> **The "*mind-body connection*" has been well documented: physical fitness portends well for excellent mental fitness. As I've mentioned before, the synergistic benefits are much more than the mere addition of their benefits.**

Here's another example: let's say you're someone who wants to boost your career development. This will require new knowledge, so you commit to reading a book about your chosen field for 30 minutes every day. Reading routinely will change your perception of the world, open your mind to new possibilities, and lead you to take actions that help you get higher-paying jobs with more responsibility.

It's no surprise that:

1. changing your perception of the world and
2. opening your mind to possibilities

...leads to an improved ability to handle more responsibility – the higher pay is just a bonus!

I hate to break it to you, but sometimes career success is really that simple. It's why for many people, twenty years of experience is nothing more than one year of experience repeated twenty times. The simple act of taking on better habits that contribute toward your personal development and growth will help you avoid the sinister trap of going nowhere fast in your career (and your life).

Let's go back to the "exercising" example and say that instead of exercising every day, your habit is watching four hours of television each night. If that's the case, your lifestyle will likely reflect that.

For the most part, a person who has a habit of watching four hours of TV every night after work will eat particular kinds of food, hang out with particular kinds of people, and will live a certain kind of lifestyle. That certain kind of lifestyle probably won't lend itself to the likelihood of converting to a lifestyle of exercising or exerting much physical activity.

One of the main things this lifestyle is lacking is: structure. Sure, there's technically a structure in eating junk food and being lazy, but there's no real plan. It's your inner reptile brain – your caveman, and actual "plans" are over its head. On the other hand, exercising regularly forces you to create a game plan for your daily schedule that allows you to get it done. There's no choice – you won't exercise regularly unless you have a set time and place for doing it. (That sounds like a habit to me – a good one.)

A health behavior aside:

A study from 2003, followed more than 50,000 middle-aged women for six years. It showed that for every two hours spent watching television per day, the subjects had a 23 percent higher chance of becoming obese.

Research also shows that children who have televisions in their bedrooms have a higher probability of being overweight than those who don't. Studies that followed children for years showed a strong association between the amount of TV watched and the risk of obesity in adolescence and adulthood.

A 2011 study from the Harvard School of Public Health (HSPH) indicated that watching more than two hours of TV per day was associated with an increased risk of type 2 diabetes and heart disease. More than three hours of daily television viewing increased the risk of premature death.

Continuing with the exercise example, in order to get your workouts in, you'll eventually find yourself reverse-engineering your days:

"So, if I want to work out from 5:30 p.m.-6:30 p.m., I need to leave work by 5 p.m. sharp, meaning all of my important tasks have to be done by then. If I get home by 7 p.m. and I go to bed at 10 p.m., that means I only have 3 hours left to do other things.

"Family dinner (cooking, eating, cleaning up) will take an hour, so it'll be 8 p.m. I'll also need an hour for doing chores and getting the kids ready for school tomorrow, which brings us to 9 p.m. I usually spend an hour with my wife after the kids are asleep, which puts me right at 10 p.m.

"Wow, I won't have time to do the usual things I do at night, such as watching TV or playing video games. I guess those things

aren't as important as my daily exercise routine or the time I spend with my family."

Suddenly priorities, like habits, become intuitive.

Do you think you would use this same thought process if you approached exercising in a randomized and sporadic way? Of course not. Through reverse-engineering, you realize that having a set routine, a structure for how your day will unfold - coupled with doing certain tasks at specific times of the day - is the only guaranteed way you will be able to exercise regularly.

Routines and habits provide structure to our daily lives, which in turn, helps us do more things and do them faster. As I explained earlier in this chapter, routines and habits are more cost-efficient for the brain.

Personally, I love structure. But I know many people don't. More accurately, they don't love the efforts necessary to design structure into their lives. However, if you're going to engage in the systematic processes that produce long-term results, you must train yourself to embrace structure. Why is this key? Because structure is a script you follow. It is a manifesto. It has a beginning (structure), a middle (adhering to that structure), and an end (the reward that comes from structure). Structure makes for a good script. It makes for an excellent life script, and you're the main character, so you want it to all end well.

Does structure the way I've described sound familiar? Remember the habit loop of cue-routine-reward? Can we use this similarity to make structure a habit? Is there really any difference between cue-routine-reward and beginning (structure), middle (adhering to that structure) and end (reward)?

Good habits and routines - including those that your structure has become, also help remove mental clutter so that our brains are able to pay attention to the things that are truly important. Habits and routines help prioritize the plot elements in your life script.

HABITS AND HOMEOSTASIS

"A nail is driven out by another nail; habit is overcome by habit."

~DESIDERIUS ERASMUS, Dutch philosopher

In the first stage of changing a habit, it can feel excruciating (or at least extremely uncomfortable); the expectation in your subconscious is being challenged. But just as our body has the ability to adjust to a changing environment through a process called homeostasis, we have a similar (*mental*, if you will) homeostatic ability to adjust to a new habit. It takes our bodies some time to adjust to a new environmental factor, and likewise, it also takes time for our brains to adjust when we attempt to remove a bad habit and replace it with a positive one.

If you live in a place that experiences cold weather or have visited such a place, you know what it feels like when you first step outside on a particularly chilly day in the mid-winter season. At first, you're so cold you can't think of anything else but turning around and going back into a warm place. But you have responsibilities, which means you have places to go and things to do; and you have a brain that can allow you to navigate the mere environmental obstacles.

We are warm-blooded creatures, so when we go outside on that cold day, there's a part of our brains that adjusts our metabolism to generate more heat and keep our internal "working" temperature constant at 98.6 degrees. In even colder circumstances, we begin to shiver, and this adds heat to our system. Circulation adjusts to shift flow for the sake of heat retention.

Therefore, we are really designed – actually, well-designed – to continue out into the cold. In a few minutes, you feel less of the chill as your body adjusts to the weather. Furthermore, if you continue in the cold weather, you'll discover that in about twenty minutes or so, you don't feel nearly as cold as you did when you first went outside.

Your brain adjusts to new habits in a similar fashion. At first, there is resistance, but eventually, it goes with the flow. All you need to do is give it time to adjust. The new habit is going to make you uncomfortable. Your brain – and, apparently, tigers too – live most comfortably with structure, which is nothing more than the status quo in your life. Like the hoarder, your brain will initially see new habits like clutter and attempt to sidestep or even discard it.

If you go out into the cold and immediately jump into a heated car, your body won't adjust to the cold, and when you get out again, you'll go back into freeze mode. In order to change your habits or pick up new ones, you will have to go through the period of fighting your own *habitual* (i.e. "habit") homeostasis. Transitions are always temporarily uncomfortable, but if you have faith in your mind and body, you'll discover the resilience I talked about in Chapter Three.

Ultimately, it's smooth sailing after you make it through the initial discomfort because the new habit will eventually change from being a mere one-time thing to an integral part of who you are. Neurons fired together...remember? This happens because, thankfully, your newly wired-together habits are what creates the new structure for your days, and in turn, your weeks, months, years and...your life.

Robert Ringer, the author of *Million Dollar Habits*, talks about the millions of people who spend their lives working hard, long hours, only to die broke. Ringer says the way to avoid falling into this trap is to develop the right habits and practice them regularly:

> *"Remember, a successful life is nothing more than the sum total of many successful years, a successful year is nothing more than the sum total of many successful months, a successful month is nothing more than the sum total of many successful weeks, a successful week is nothing more than the sum total of many successful days."*

Therefore, to reverse engineer a successful life, you have to strategize back through the years, months, weeks, and days to come, of which a new one is tomorrow! Understand that success in any area of life rarely comes from one act, one decision, one thought – or a single day. More often than not, success comes from our habits that have been developed over time – years. And these habits inevitably and consistently push us toward either success or failure.

Right now, at this very moment, if things are going great for you in life, it's because of the choices you made in your past. These choices have developed into habits. And these habits are producing your current results. On the contrary, if things are not going so great for you, it's because of the poor choices you have made in your past that have developed into bad habits, which are producing your current poor results.

Are you beginning to see how the habits you have developed throughout your life can single-handedly decide (or destroy) your destiny and control how the remainder of your life is going to play out? I hope so. Take a second now and really put some serious thought into why you do the things you do.

Paying close attention to why you think the way you think – and act the way you act – is paramount to your success, but close attention is often neglected. This is because the nature of your habits is that they are automatic, performed in the background of your mind – the things you don't normally pay attention to. Yet, such attention must be rekindled, which is crucial if you're going to notice the habits that are supporting your quests or, alternatively, sabotaging your dreams.

Studying yourself, and learning why you do the things you do is key to making the necessary changes that need to be made. You'll take a giant leap forward once you begin to understand why you behave the way you do. Figuring out what makes you tick and realizing the current patterns in your life are crucial to being aware of the changes that need to be made.

Why is it important to study ourselves? Because our habits can be tricky. Habits hide themselves in the tiniest, most hidden recesses of our lives and then, without us even noticing, become deeply ingrained in our brains. Habits become extremely powerful forces in our lives. They are so incredibly powerful that without us even realizing it, we desperately hold on to them, even when they defy all common sense, logic, and reason.

"Half the problem is seeing the problem."
~LAURIE ANDERSON

Worse, a comfortable status quo, the path of least resistance, can be an addiction. In drug lingo, the difference between dependence and addiction is that dependence only pertains to your physical or psychological need for a drug; yet addiction takes this a step further in that it means you will seek the drug in spite of risks to your health, relationships, employment, and even freedom. Therefore, I submit that an "addiction" to bad habits poses just as much of a destructive risk, but to your future instead of to your present.

While research has proven that such an addiction consists of unconscious/subconscious life-destroying cravings that cement in as habits, the opposite is feasible; that is, the unconscious/subconscious can be used to make success-producing habits automatic. For that reason alone, consciously practicing positive and productive habits – day in and day out – is the best way to win in life and achieve any long-term goal.

HOW TO ERASE BAD HABITS AND INSTILL GOOD HABITS – THE BOTTOM LINE

"We should focus on the early signs of bad habits and do our best to cut them down in their budding stage before they reach full bloom.

Because unfortunately, bad habits never go away on their own."

~ZIG ZIGLAR

Your habits dictate the direction your life is headed, one habit at a time. Whether that direction is one that takes you toward your goals or away from your goals will be entirely up to you. It is up to you to be consciously aware of the habits that stop you from achieving your dreams, as well as the ones that are currently helping you get closer to them. It takes courage to wake up and assess yourself. It also takes a tremendous amount of self-honesty. Both of which require significant cognitive effort.

The combination of your habits will ultimately decide whether you will achieve your goals or not. In other words, if you have ten bad habits that sabotage your chances of achieving your goals and three good habits that help you achieve your goals, then your habits are generally taking you toward the direction you don't want to go. In fact, any step backward now will take you one more step to get you to your goals. Think of this as your "*habit bottom-line*". Are you in the red or in the black?

Ask yourself this: when you took some time a few paragraphs ago to reflect on your current habits, did you see them helping you, hindering you, or doing nothing at all toward the achievement of your goals? If you are serious about success, then you must seriously think about getting rid of those habits that are not contributing to the realization of your goals. How is a *habit bottom-line* mentality different from the business mindset of profiting by improving the bottom line? It isn't.

It bears repeating: *"Your net worth to the world is usually determined by what remains after your bad habits are subtracted from your good ones." ~Benjamin Franklin*

Since the culmination of your habits is what created the person you are today, it might be time to delete your old habits, the ones that are not producing the results you desire and create some new ones that will. Think of it like your very own do-it-yourself project where you are building a new "you" from scratch. But how exactly do you do that? How do you demolish old habits and develop new ones? Let's turn to the Massachusetts Institute of Technology for some assistance.

Ann Greybiel, a scientist at MIT who oversees basal ganglia experiments (the part of our brain responsible for remembering our habits) offers some guidance about habits and how they are embedded in our brains:

> *"Habits never really disappear. They're encoded in the structures of our brains, and that's a huge advantage for us, because it would be awful if we had to relearn how to tie our shoes every day or how to drive a car after every vacation. The problem is, our brains can't tell the difference between good and bad habits, so if you have a bad habit, it's always lurking there, waiting for the right cues and rewards."*

Cues and rewards? Remember the habit loop we discussed earlier in this chapter? The habit loop is simply a formula our brain follows when we engage in a habit: *when I see a cue, I do a routine in order to receive a reward*. What habit reversal experts have discovered as the best way to change a habit is to keep the cue and reward the same, but change the routine. Once you identify the cue and reward of the habit, you want to intentionally and strategically plan a way to change the routine.

Let me share a personal example with you: while I was going back through this book and making edits, every time I'd get stuck on something, I'd revert to a bad habit of checking my email, text messages, or Skype for any new messages.

What was my habit loop? The cue was my mind struggling with how I wanted to reword or restructure some of the content. This cue provoked a profitless routine of engaging in these distractions, i.e., returning emails, Skype messages, and text messages. The reward was that neurotransmitters (messengers such as dopamine) would activate the "reward" centers in my brain, aka, pleasure when I engaged in these distractions. And pleasure via dopamine is a powerful and addictive positive reinforcement that entices us to repeat (routines/habits) actions.

How did I fix my bad habit of engaging in distractions when I got stuck? First, I recognized the habit loop that was throwing me off course. Second, I broke the habit loop down:

1. What was the cue?
2. What was the routine? (i.e. the habit I needed to target and change)
3. What was the reward?

Since I knew I had to keep the cue and reward the same, the moment the cue reared its ugly head (e.g., coming across a challenging part of this book), I ate a few M&M's and took a drink of coffffee (my new routine), and this provided my brain a reward in the form of dopamine from the chocolate and caffeine.

Thankfully, I was able to carefully dissect the behaviors that were steering me off course, instill a new habit, and get myself back on track. Maybe I gained a few extra pounds from the chocolate, and maybe I put a few extra *f*s in the word *coffee* in the last paragraph from all the caffeine, but had I not been able to identify the problem – it's unlikely you would be reading these words now.

Trust me, my urge and propensity to check my email, text, and Skype is still there, just like scientist Greybiel stated: "If you have a bad habit, it's always lurking there, waiting for the right cues and rewards." But now I have a plan. I've trained my brain to follow a new formula. And that has made all the difference in my ability to stay on track.

Think about a particular bad habit you have. Mentally walk through your habit loop: *cue, routine, and reward*. Now, begin thinking about ways you can replace the routine, which will help you replace the bad habit. Understand, it's up to you to install good habits in your brain and eliminate the bad ones, since the part of your brain that holds them (basal ganglia) literally cannot discern the difference between good habits and bad habits. Only your conscious brain can address your subconscious' *habit bottom-line.*

If you are a doer (not a dabbler), if you are genuinely committed to developing the best possible version of yourself, you need to intentionally install and practice habits that will take you toward your desired destination. If you want to know where your current habits are taking you, assess your habit bottom-line by taking an honest look at yourself in the mirror and asking if your habits are in true alignment with your goals. If the answer is "*no*", then you need to do one of two things: change your habits or change your goals.

My hope is that you will keep your goals and change your habits. Because when you make the decision to change your habits, without even realizing it, you're making the decision to change your routine. And when you change a routine, you change your day, your month, your year, and your life. Before you know it, you've created a brand new *you* – and a brand new future.

HOW TO FIND THE SOURCE OF YOUR HABITS

> "Some rules are nothing but old habits that people are afraid to change."
>
> ~THERESE ANNE FOWLER, Author of *Z: A Novel of Zelda Fitzgerald*

The longer a habit has been with us, the more likely it's turned into an unconscious expression of who we are. That "person" you are expressing might not be the person you want to be. If this is the case, then you need to really dissect your habits.

Perhaps some of the habits you've picked up aren't just a result of what you've learned, but rather a result of the way you've been treated. For instance, when you were in grade school kids may have made fun of you or laughed at you if you ever answered a question wrong in front of the class. As a result, it's likely you stopped answering questions in class altogether.

Perhaps you became one of the shy and quiet kids who never stood up for themselves or had an opinion about anything. If that was you, it's quite likely that this carried over into your adult life. You could be an adult who won't speak out at meetings or demand what you deserve, and as a result, life is controlling you instead of the other way around. You've become the chess piece – a pawn – instead of the chess player.

Even something like your self-esteem is a crafted habit. The way you feel about yourself is a result of years of viewing yourself in a certain light. This perception of yourself may be true or untrue, but since you've always thought that way about yourself, you've probably never really examined it. Furthermore, you may have felt as if you never fully had the power to change yourself.

The way you act – or don't act – is a result of one or more habits that you have encoded into your brain. It is not simply something you were born with. If you have a habit of never chasing after your dreams, this can be changed. If you have a habit of staying quiet in situations where you should be speaking up, this habit can be changed as well. Alternatively, whereas staying quiet may reflect on your self-esteem, the equally bad habit of speaking too much, interrupting, and not listening can reflect on your self-esteem as imbued into you by others. Let's face it: bad habits are bad habits, and you should know when you have one with just a little self-reflection. (*"Half the problem is seeing the problem."*)

All habits can be changed, no matter how long you have been doing them. Some might be more difficult to change than others, but make no mistake about it: you can change them. And when you set out to change them, make sure other people's habits don't influence you to return to your bad habits.

What do I mean? Often times our habits come from the people we spend the most time with. An egregious example of this can be found within families. I'm sure we all have that one acquaintance or family member that constantly complains of aches and pains. Sure, there could be some legitimate aches and pains, but what eventually happens is that the complaining itself becomes the problem and not the actual pains. In other words, the behavior of complaining becomes a habit that is inseparable from that which is complained about.

It gets even worse: if you happen to know the complainer's child, you will likely find that the child complains in a similar fashion, and it will have nothing to do with the child having aches and pains. Children can (and often do) pick up habits from their parents and have them molded into part of who they are. In some cases, actually, in most cases, these habits even define who they become when they mature into adults.

It's both amusing and sad at the same time when you see an entire family in a doctor's office, each waiting their turn to be called in. One by one – mother, father, and even each child – they all grunt or groan as they lift themselves out of their chairs. This pattern of behavior has become the "family" way one rises from a chair.

You may have habits that you picked up from your parents, yet those habits have nothing to do with who you are today. If you take time to think about some of the habits you've had since childhood, you may realize that those habits aren't a representation of who you are now, but rather something that was ingrained in you while you were growing up.

To put it another way, even though you "are" your habits, I hope I've proven to you that your habits are only a temporary state of being; a blueprint in your brain that can be redrawn to eliminate your unfavorable habits. Yes, they may be very difficult to get rid of. Yes, the addiction to the expectation, fulfilled by a habit, will fight you. And yes, they may feel like they are part of you as they've been around your whole life, but they can be changed. You can completely eliminate your bad habits, install good habits, and transform into an entirely different "you". You will still be your habits but in a new and improved way. You've traded up!

Now that you know the truth about habits, it's time for you to seriously think about the following question as it pertains to your life:

> **If you are your habits, and if one (or more) of those habits are directly responsible for robbing you of your ultimate potential, then you need to decide what you value more: do you value that habit more, or do you place a higher value on becoming the best possible version of yourself?**

You can't have both, because having a bad habit and being the best person you can be cannot coexist. It's time to start making this kind of hard decision about every bad habit in your life. You will have to make sacrifices in breaking the bad habits that seductively give you relief and comfort. At the same time, you'll also have to make sacrifices in creating the good habits that break you out of your comfort zone.

J Paul Getty, the founder of Getty Oil, said that anyone who wants to succeed in life must first understand the importance of their habits in reaching success:

> *"He must be quick to break those habits that can break him – and hasten to adapt those practices that will become the habits that will help him achieve the success he desires."*

So what do you do about bad habits that you've identified and want to eliminate because you know that they will only continue to wreak havoc on your life? You need to thoroughly understand your habit loop and then replace the routines which will, in turn, replace the habit.

New habits will not find their groove in your life overnight. It takes patience to develop a new habit. However, with time, self-discipline, persistence, and effort, you will gradually remove the bad habits and replace them with new positive ones.

CHANGE YOUR HABITS, CHANGE YOUR LIFE

"The first step toward change is awareness."

~NATHANIEL BRANDON, Canadian-American psychotherapist

If you want to take your life in a different direction, the very first thing you must do is have stark conscious awareness. You need to wake up and say, "Wow! I am actually doing this bad habit every day and it's ruining my life. I need to catch myself and change my habit loop before it happens again and take a different, more constructive action in its place."

Being conscious of your habits will take work, and at times, it will be difficult to be aware of every single decision you make. But you ultimately have two choices: you can either exert the extra effort needed to be aware of your bad habits and change them, or you can continue with the same routine that has steered you away from becoming the person you want to become. I promise you that being aware of each decision you make and the direction it's taking you is more difficult, but it will put you on the right path toward the life you truly desire.

You may find that it takes a lot of effort just to fix a single bad habit. That's perfectly okay, especially if this is your first time actively working to eliminate a bad habit. Each time you succeed, you'll have more energy to eliminate the next bad habit.

That's called momentum, and it will be on your side. Once that second bad habit is gone, you'll have the energy to eliminate a third bad habit, a fourth bad habit, and so on. Within no time, you'll find that it feels "effortless" to drop multiple bad habits at once without having to exert much mental energy. When momentum shifts in your favor, you'll be able to create a massive transformational shift in your life that accelerates the speed at which you achieve success.

And contrary to popular belief, changing your habits – and therefore changing the direction you're headed in life – is not nearly as complicated as you may think. In fact, it's actually quite easy. Nathan Azrin, a neuroscientist who specializes in habit-reversal training, said the following about habits and awareness:

> *"It seems ridiculously simple, but once you're aware of how your habit works, once you recognize the cues and rewards, you're halfway to changing it. It seems like it should be more complex, but the truth is, the brain can be reprogrammed. You just have to be deliberate about it."*

The first step to forming new habits that will create a new and successful "you" is to become aware of your habits, both the good and the bad ones you currently have. Go through your entire daily routine and figure out what you do every day and why you do it. Each habitual action that you perform is either moving you toward your goals or further away from them. There is no middle ground – it's one or the other.

When you do this self-examination, you will be addressing habits that influence every part of your life. Yes, every single thing matters when it comes to achieving the level of success you want. Even something as seemingly innocent as what you do in your spare time will have a significant effect on the level of success you will achieve in life.

When you're examining your habits, you need to decide if the successful people you aspire to be like would participate in them.

Seriously ask yourself: is this a habit that SpaceX CEO Elon Musk would have? If you find yourself answering Musk would certainly not have a habit like that in his life, then you need to reconsider that habit in your life. However, keep in mind that even after you succeed at replacing unproductive habits, don't think that you can rest easy and never worry about it surfacing again. It's a part of your life, but just make it a part of your "past" life.

If there's anything to always stay on alert for when removing destructive habits, it's this: habits rarely go away permanently. Instead, they just sit somewhere in the background and will pop up in your life again if so much as the slightest opportunity appears for them to do so. That's the reason why the saying, "Old habits die hard" exists. Therefore, never underestimate the power of a habit to escape from your conscious awareness and find its way back into your life through the subconscious backdoor.

A behavioral change aside:

Psychologists James Prochaska and Carlo DiClemente made a valuable contribution to habit change literature by identifying five stages of change. Their work helped clinicians and others recognize that you need to identify where someone is in the behavior change process to effectively communicate and influence them.

The original Transtheoretical Model of Change (TTM) had five stages:

1. Precontemplation: In this stage the person has no awareness of the need to change.
2. Contemplation: Here the person recognizes the need to change but is not yet taking any action.
3. Preparation: In this stage, preparations and plans are made about how to change.

4. Action: The person now takes action to change.
5. Maintenance: The all-important phase during which the person continues the new behavior.

More recently, a sixth stage has been added called "termination" in which an old habit has been so dismantled that efforts to counteract it are no longer necessary.

LIFE ON COMPLETE AUTOPILOT

"Bad habits are easy to develop but difficult to live with. Good habits are difficult to develop, but easy to live with. If you are willing to be uncomfortable for a little while so you can press past the initial pain of change, in the long run your life will be much better."

~JOEL OSTEEN, American pastor, televangelist, and author

Repeated thoughts and actions have an amazing ability to lodge into our subconscious and automate patterns of behavior. Repeated expectations that are satisfied by habits create an addiction to the things we repeat. The more we repeat any pattern, destructive or constructive thought, or action, the more our brain will become addicted to this pattern.

The reason why we (unknowingly) become so addicted to our habits is that our brains adapt to repeated behaviors, creating neuro-pathways. These are networks of the same synapses of the brain cells involved for each occurrence. The rewards from habits become just as much a part of these neuro-pathways, which combines the cue, routine, and reward into a blurred but strong association.

Several times in this book I have cited Dr. Hebb's, "Neurons that fire together, wire together." This is more than just a clever phrase, however. It is a whole neuroanatomy lecture crammed into one sentence.

A neurological aside:

Neurons stimulate other neurons by "neuronal firing". That is, a biochemical called a neurotransmitter is released by a neuron's dendrites (neurotransmitter-laden branches at the end of a neuron), and it is received by the axon of the adjacent neuron. In this way, the adjacent neuron is recruited into the process, stimulated to produce and release its own dendritic neurotransmitter for the next neuron.

A simple thought, action, or feeling involves thousands of neurons that make up a "neuronal (neural) network" which gets activated whenever the same thought, action, or feeling is repeated. These neuronal networks strengthen each time they are repeatedly invoked. That is, they bond stronger and are more easily engaged into action. You are forming new neuronal networks all of the time, even by reading this sentence. And it seems that the brain's neuronal networking capacity is unlimited.

In fact, there are as many possible connections among the brain's neurons as there are particles in the universe! Do the math. I can't, but neurophysiologists have.

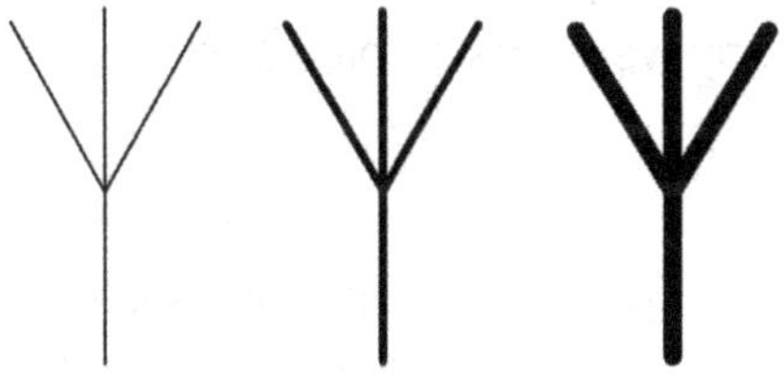

The three figures above are schematic representations of neuronal networks (although simplified for the purpose of illustration). The one on the left symbolizes a single neuronal network of a thought, action, or feeling, that is, an impulse traveling and spreading along a connected path through brain tissue.

With repetition, however, it's almost as if the solidity of the relationships among these neurons increases, and the "bandwidth" for increased speed and efficiency increases as well. Thus, the middle figure, schematically represented as heavier, symbolizes the strengthening of the first figure on the left, and with repetition, the bonds along the neuronal network become stronger and are apt to fire more readily. The bonding within the network has become optimized – automated and instant, as symbolized by the boldest figure on the right.

Therefore, each time you go through the "habit loop" for a particular habit, not only are the neural pathways strengthened, but the threshold for their firing is lowered, thereby programming your brain to engage in this activity or thought without you thinking nearly as much about doing it. When the neural pathways become incredibly strong (via repetition) the result is that you will cling to your habits, even though they could possibly be negative habits that are producing poor results in your life.

The opposite – "use it or lose it" – is also true. Neuronal networks are probably never completely dismantled, but over time, their thresholds for engaging can climb back up to levels requiring more cognitive effort. Consequently, the less you engage in a given activity or thought, the weaker your habit loop becomes. Such synaptic decay weakens habits, and this can be used to your advantage when eliminating bad habits.

Besides the reinforcement of a habit or its use-it-or-lose-it property, the neurology involved in habits is one of expectations, the payoff when an expectation is fulfilled by doing the habit, and the craving for the next installment of expectation-payoff-craving. (Translated: cue-routine-reward.)

When craving the payoff becomes part of the habit itself, it is highly similar to an addiction. Like any addiction, in which a person is driven to their addiction regardless of the consequences, such cravings will cause people to neglect some of the most important things in their lives. But because it doesn't involve opioids, cocaine, or other illicit substances, this similarity is often overlooked. Research from the University of Michigan stated:

> *"Particularly strong habits produce addiction-like reactions so that wanting evolves into obsessive craving that can force our brains into autopilot even in the face of strong disincentive, including loss of reputation, job, home and family."*

With habits' similarity to addiction, this is all very sobering; and one of the scariest things about the habits you have today is that even after examining your life, you still may not even realize that many of your former habits still exist. In fact, bestselling author and neurologist Dr. David Eagleman has said that 95 percent of everything we think, feel, do, and achieve is subconsciously decided. This means that often times you don't have the awareness of what you are doing when you are doing it. As stated a few paragraphs ago, it's the engagement of a neural network with a minimum amount of mental effort that's easier for your brain, but not necessarily so good for your future. Awareness, on the other hand, requires tremendous cognitive and mental effort.

The reason you're missing out on this awareness is because these subconscious thoughts, feelings, and actions have become deeply ingrained in your brain, and this rewired brain of yours has evolved into "*you-as-your-learned-habits*". These habits are programs that dictate what you are going to do in life, and in turn, put your actions and thoughts on complete autopilot. Even more complicated (and remarkable) is that neuronal networks can make "*mega-neuronal* networks" with other neuronal networks, which is why it can be so challenging to end a group or sequence of habits once they've been soldered together through repetition.

What does "*you-as-your-learned-habits*" mean for you? It means that your habits dictate nearly everything you do. Without even being aware of it, your habits and routines control almost every aspect of your life. They *are* your life. Therefore, it's likely that you have spent an exorbitant amount of time throughout your life sleepwalking through the choices and decisions you've been making on a daily basis. You have been unconsciously programmed with habits and routines, whether you realize it or not. You are going through the motions of your life, primarily with muscle memory. Today, you *are* these habits on autopilot without needing a single thought or even a tiny drop of mental energy.

So if it's true that our habits unconsciously control the majority of our behaviors, how do we regain full control of ourselves? More importantly, how do we reverse our habits so that desirable, more productive behaviors become automatic to us?

The same way you get to Carnegie Hall: practice, practice, practice. The very first step is to practice being *consciously* aware of all of the things you think, say, and do on a daily basis. That includes the important decisions you make throughout the day, as well as the ones that appear to be insignificant. Be mindful, because your unconscious brain needs supervision, not a rubber stamp. Whether it's the way you habitually think when a challenge appears in your life, or your decision to drive home and lie down on the couch instead of going to the gym, it's crucial that you become completely aware of what you're doing and – just as important, if not more so – what you are thinking. Awareness is the first step toward loosening the mysterious yet deadly grip our habits have on us. Think of it as "auditing the books" on a secret organization that runs its business under the table.

Once you are consciously aware of what you are doing and thinking about, you start to understand exactly where it is that your habits, both good and bad, are coming from. With awareness, you can trace your steps and discover how your habits became a part of your life. You'll realize that your habits did not appear overnight, but rather as the result of daily actions and routines repeated consistently over time.

Darren Hardy, the former publisher of *Success Magazine*, says it best:

> *"Picture where you are in any area, right now. Now picture where you want to be: richer, thinner, happier, you name it. The first step toward change is awareness. If you want to get from where you are to where you want to be, you have to start by becoming aware of the choices that lead you away from your desired destination. Become very conscious of every choice you make so you can begin to make smarter choices moving forward."*

When you come to the realization about the power your habits have over your life, you will be in a position where you can actively choose to change the unproductive habits that have made their way into (and poisoned) your daily routines. With stark awareness, you'll finally have the internal power needed to take back control over your habitual thought processes and the behaviors (and results) these thoughts are producing in your life. Once you reach that pivotal point, you can begin to eliminate the bad habits while replacing them with positive habits that will take you closer to achieving your interval goals, and in turn, your vision.

While I've laid out some great strategies to help you replace unhealthy habits in the exercise section of this chapter, let me warn you that being consciously aware of every single thing you think and do is no easy task. It requires a tremendous amount of cognitive energy to objectively assess yourself. However, the only way to become the CEO of your life is by being brutally honest about the habits you currently have and the direction they are taking you. You will have to be honest enough to admit that you don't like the direction you're headed. When you get to this point, you will also find that you need courage to take the first step in a new direction. This will initially feel uncomfortable, but there is no other way around it.

KEYSTONE HABITS

> "Keystone habits start a process that, over time, transforms everything. Keystone habits say that success doesn't depend on getting every single thing right, but instead relies on identifying a few key priorities and fashioning them into powerful levers."
>
> ~CHARLES DUHIGG

There are thousands of habits to choose from, so you might be wondering where the best place is to start. Are there certain habits to develop that are better than others? It turns out that there are, and they are known as "*keystone habits*".

As I mentioned at the onset of this chapter, Charles Duhigg is one of the foremost experts on habits, and he defines keystone habits as the vital few habits that make it much easier to successfully take on other productive habits.

> A keystone is a central stone in the middle of an arch, upon which the other stones depend to remain in place. Securing the keystone will affect the other associated stones, so think of building keystone habits as a "chain reaction" in which you find yourself automatically incorporating other productive behaviors into your life.

You don't need to take on every single keystone habit, because mastering one or two of them will already be a good enough start to instill consistency, routine, and structure in your life. Here are some keystone habits extremely successful people have adopted:

- **Physical exercise**
  When you choose to work out regularly this positive activity tends to spill over into many other aspects of your life. Most prominently, your self-confidence. An *Inc.* article titled, *If You've Got This 1 Character Trait, You'll Probably Be Successful, According to Neuroscience* stated:

> *"It's a scientifically-proven fact that successful entrepreneurs are supremely self-confident even to the point of being overconfident."*

Without a doubt, confidence is key to success (in business and in life). When you look good...you feel good. When you feel good, you perform at your best. (More on this when we discuss the *confidence-competence loop* in Chapter Seven.)

- Meditation
  Calming and clearing your mind through the power of meditation enables you to engage your "higher mind" which promotes executive-level thinking. When you think more clearly, you function more effectively. There's a reason why I've incorporated meditation into two separate sections in the exercise portions of this book. Uncluttering and detangling our minds is crucial to achieving the ultimate level of success which I believe can be defined as: peace of mind.

- Going to bed at a reasonable hour and getting 8 hours of sleep
  This is referred to as "sleep hygiene". Having evolved as "circadian" creatures, it is important for humans to respect our nighttime physiology as much as our daytime physiology. Sleep is an important time for clearing out brain toxins from the day's mentation and consolidating memory. A study out of Boston University revealed:

> "Sleep physically washes toxins, including those that can lead to Alzheimers, from your brain."

The adage *you can sleep when you die* is not only remarkably harmful – it's also laced with lunacies. Sleep is essential for success. And a good night's sleep is crucial for a good day after.

- **Tracking what you eat**
  Food is fuel. And unhealthy food is unhealthy fuel. Quickly and thoughtlessly devouring your meals can lead to harmful toxins in your body. Many of us consume breakfast, lunch, and dinner without much thought. When you track (and monitor) what you eat you consciously choose better eating options.

  Healthy eating habits certainly play a vital role in how productive (or unproductive) you are throughout the day. Another important takeaway is this: oftentimes we eat out of habit. When we track what we eat we are better able to stop senseless consumption of food.

- **Cutting alcohol out of your life**
  People who have alcohol dependencies tend to plan their lives/routines around drinking. When they go on vacation, they seek out the best bars. When they meet up with their friends, they order drinks. The moment you cut alcohol out of your life, it opens up a new routine, as well as a lot more room for productive activities. Let's face it – there's a reason why "hangover pill" sales have exploded, and that's to help people recover the following day from the poisonous effects alcohol has on our bodies.

  Often success in life is nothing more than an accumulation of hours, days, weeks, and months of productive activities/routines. Being bogged down by the after-effects of alcohol parlays into many adverse areas of life – not to mention cirrhosis of the liver.

- **Gratitude Journal – write down three things you are thankful for every day**
  Repeatedly writing down what you are grateful for allows your reticular activating system (RAS) to be on the lookout for

more things that will bring happiness into your life. This is a process that done regularly overtime will produce exponential rewards.

Combine scribbling down what you're thankful for with some random acts of kindness (i.e. paying for the person's order who's behind you in line at the coffee shop, giving an unexpected compliment to someone you love, sending a hand-written thank you note to someone who's had a positive impact on your life) and watch the list of things in your life you have to be thankful for explode.

- Planning your schedule the night before
  In Chapter Two, I discussed the benefits of writing down the tasks you want to complete the following day the night prior. When you do this it allows your subconscious (more powerful mind) to work on executing your plans while you sleep. I challenge you to repeat this process (writing down your tasks/goals for the following day before you go to sleep) for 30 days in a row and see how it changes your level of productivity.
- Going to church
  Whether you are part of an organized religion, consider yourself merely spiritual, or are even agnostic or atheist, "going to church" need not be actually going to church, but any keystone habit that has the magic of many people, together achieving a communion of spirit that is considered outside of – beyond – the body bolsters positive enrichment. It can be joining a reading group, attending a sports event, volunteering in a community project with others for what you privately consider an important cause, or even being part of a support group. At the very least, it is a meditative exercise that you experience privately while simultaneously sharing it publicly.

- **Families regularly eating dinner together**
  This isn't just good for you, but for every member of the family. Sadly, it is almost extinct. There is a very traditional – and very human – need that centers on "the hearth" and the dinner table. It is the one place all family members can connect together, recollect together, and revisit each other. It is the glue that holds families together, going back to ancient times when the hunter-gatherer men and the child-rearing women and their offspring came together each day to consolidate the profits of their days (things hunted, children raised, and eating to live – instead of living to eat).

Simple to do, but simple not to do may come to mind when you review the keystone habits I just listed. But let me warn you, don't fall into the trap that many short-sighted foolish people do when it comes to these pivotal habits. Do not think that these habits are too boring or too corny to incorporate into your daily routines. Because the simplicity of these habits is what makes them so effective (complexity is the enemy of execution). Select one or two keystone habits, make them automatic behaviors, and then move on to the next one (or two).

Undoubtedly, keystone habits are not sexy. They're not entertaining nor thrilling. But review the list of keystone habits again, and you will realize that each one pertains to function – as an individual, as a community, and most importantly, as a human being in a community of other human beings. Function is life; dysfunction is pathology, and loss of function is death. I assure you that if you'll simply focus your efforts on mastering a few of the keystone habits, you will be shocked to see the dramatic impact they have on your life, as well as how well you function on a day-to-day basis.

CONCLUSION

> "Everything you are used to, once done long enough, starts to seem natural, even though it might not be."
>
> ~JULIEN SMITH, Author of *The Flinch*

One of the lessons I've had to learn the hard way is that habits can be tricksters. Why? Because they disguise themselves as little everyday decisions that seem insignificant at the time, but over the long haul, make a world of difference. That's why my personal definition of habits is: *small things that make a big difference*. (The "butterfly effect".) You see, the problem with habits is that they tend to have a cumulative effect on us, but unfortunately, the results don't show up until much later in life. Therefore, if our habits are bad, by the time the damage is evident, it's often too late to alter the results and undo the irreparable harm that has been done. The process of destructive habits in our life is similar to a sinking building – albeit splendidly built – sinking into a bad foundation.

How our brains become so addicted to our habits and why we cling to them, regardless of how good or bad they are, have puzzled the best and brightest brain scientists in the world. Even after decades of research in the field of neurobiology, commissioned with virtually unlimited budgets, researchers are still learning how biological mechanisms in our brains play such a shockingly important role in controlling our thoughts and actions. Such mechanisms instigate our habits from the insignificant to those in some individuals who suffer from an extreme dysfunction of habit-clinging called obsessive-compulsive behavior. Thus, there is no doubting the role that biochemicals and neurophysiology play in the full range of habits, from living a life of bad habits to actual psychosis.

In spite of all the scientific evidence that proves just how powerful our habits truly are, the bad ones that have woven their way into the fabric of our daily routines are not impossible to expunge from our lives. Having bad habits is not a permanent state of being, and change is far from impossible. Neuroscientist do not dispute that what we regularly think, say, and do becomes firmly wired into our brains. These patterns of thought and action do indeed exert a strong influence over us, but it's equally true that they can be interrupted.

You can eliminate bad habits from your life, and in turn, reprogram your neurons so that new productive patterns embed themselves into your brain. In other words, you can **re**wire yourself to become more than you currently are, and you can do this with gradually less effort over time.

If while reading through this chapter you came across some thought-provoking moments that helped you see some of the negative habits you've developed, ones that are not contributing to you becoming the best possible version of yourself – understand that just like those habits have been conditioned in – they can be conditioned out.

Now it's time for some deliberate thinking as to how you're going to change the habits that are not contributing toward your success. You need to shine a bright light on your negative unconscious habits and expose them to your conscious awareness. When you do this, when you focus on your current habitual patterns, make sure you don't make the mistake of viewing yourself as to how you behaved in the past, or how you want to "get around to behaving" in the future. Instead, look at yourself as you are **right now** in the present moment. Be brutally honest about where your habits have taken you up to this point and make the commitment toward building a better future – one new habit at a time.

Forcing yourself to focus on the negative aspects of your life is not enjoyable. However, once you become starkly aware of the thinking-patterns and routines you regularly engage in that are not propelling you forward, then you will be in an incredibly powerful position to make the changes that you now know are necessary.

After you think long and hard about your current habits, and practice radical honesty, you'll know two things without needing anybody else to guide you: you'll know exactly which habits need to be eliminated in order to reach your goals, and you'll also know the habits you need to install to put yourself on the path to achieve your goals.

Then...practice, practice, and practice. This is nothing more than repetition – the repeated firing of the brain cells that are required to strengthen the neuronal networks associated with embedding new and improved habits. I had said earlier that you must practice constantly if you want the change from bad habits – to good ones – to permanently take root, and the exercises that are coming up next can be part of the retraining "reprogramming/rewiring" process that interrupts old habits and ingrains new ones.

EXERCISE NO. 1: HABIT STACKING

One of the easiest ways to develop a new habit is to identify a positive habit you already have and stack your new desired habit on top of it. Let me share some examples with you:

- After you pour your morning coffee, sit down in a chair and read one page (or more) of a book.
- After you brush your teeth, meditate for three minutes.
- After you get in bed, close your eyes and vividly visualize your dreams coming true. (When you visualize your dreams before you go to bed, it puts your subconscious to work while you're sleeping to discover every possible way to bring them into reality.)
- After you take your work clothes off, immediately put your workout clothes on.

These are just some simple examples, the important thing is that building on established habits is an easy way to write a "script" for your new way of living your life, replete with all of the good habits and their stackings that become the new you. The script you write for the stacking strategy is as varied as your creativity.

Habit stacking is a proven strategy that allows you to build new habits into your life without experiencing the unanchored, unnerving feeling of having to start from scratch (or not knowing where to begin). This technique plays off of an ingrained behavior you have already become "addicted to", making the new habit much easier to create.

EXERCISE NO. 2: DEVELOP THE AUTOMOBILE UNIVERSITY HABIT

One of my secret weapons to success is adopting this acronym: NET. What does NET stand for? No. Extra. Time.

Too many people have a bad habit of turning their cars on and turning their brains off. I bet you've driven for miles and not remembered a thing you passed, or how you arrived at your location, again, all muscle memory.

For many of us, the cue is getting into our cars, the routine is passively listening to the radio while we drive, and the reward is arriving safely at our destination. For this exercise, all I want you to do is to slightly change the routine. I want you to plug in an uplifting or educational audio message after you start your car. This can even be looked at as a form of habit stacking, but I've listed it here as separate because of the unique environment your car offers. It's a place where, if decreed by you, no one can get to you. It's as quiet as you want and it is that extra time – previously disputed by you as even existing – that comes in vast – depending on your commute, really vast – volumes.

Learning new things and exercising your mind while you drive is a great opportunity to fill previously wasted time and maximize every minute. Wherever you go, the new *you* should arrive more educated because your education "sets the curve" in life.

EXERCISE NO. 3: IDENTIFY YOUR HABIT LOOP(S)

Think about one of your bad habits. It could be getting up to get an unhealthy snack when a commercial comes on TV, or it could be grabbing an alcoholic drink when you get home from work.

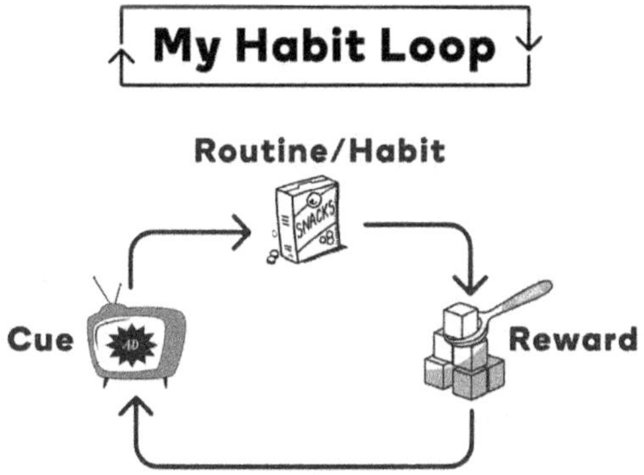

What I want you to do is identify the habit loop. For instance, the cue for the unhealthy snack is the commercial break, the routine is eating the snack, and the reward is the sugar high (or other unhealthy ingredients) and fulfillment of the snack. For the alcoholic drink, the cue is arriving home, the routine is getting (and drinking) the drink, and the reward is the sensation or feeling the alcohol provides.

The key is to replace the routine because the cues and rewards almost always remain the same. For the unhealthy snack, when a commercial comes on, get up and do ten push-ups (or get a healthy snack) instead of going to the refrigerator or the pantry. For the alcoholic drink, simply pour yourself a glass of ginger ale or something equivalent that does not have any alcohol.

Altering the routine/habit sounds simple in nature, but I know it's not. The more we repeat any pattern, the more our brains become addicted and want to repeat the process. Therefore, each time you go through the habit loop, each time you do the habit, the stronger the behavior becomes. Conversely, each time you refrain from engaging in the habit, the weaker your habit loop becomes.

Do you want to take this to the next level? Turn to pages 554 and 555 and write down all the unfavorable habits you can currently think of. Then, consciously engineer a new habit loop for each bad habit. Use habit stacking, use mental rehearsal (that's the next exercise) – do whatever it takes to rewire and reprogram your brain with positive, success-oriented habits. Rinse (your brain) and repeat. Repetition will sooner or later rewire and reprogram your mind as it revises your neural networks.

EXERCISE NO. 4: MENTALLY REHEARSE

Mentally view yourself changing the routine when the cue/trigger arrives. In Chapter One, I touched on scientific research that revealed *thinking* about an action uses the same neurons as *doing* the action. Just like the athletes who imagined their routines improved the physical execution of their actions, you can emulate this strategy because the same neurons are involved in thinking about your habits as doing them (or not doing them).

Continuously see yourself engaging in an alternate routine when the cue rears its ugly head, mentally rehearsing it throughout the day. Drill confidence into your mind with constant positive self-talk, reminding yourself how proud you are of yourself for removing that bad habit from your life.

EXERCISE NO. 5: INTENTIONALLY INTERRUPT YOURSELF

Set a time to wire the new pattern/habit into your brain (basal ganglia). Set a timer on your phone. When the alarm goes off, there's your cue. This acts as a way to break you free from the subconscious activities you're probably engaging in. Now, use your conscious mind paired with self-discipline to form a new habit. The reward will present itself in the form of self-fulfillment upon completing the task with a shot of dopamine, which is kind of like candy for our brains. Repeating this process day-in and day-out is key for programming new habits into your daily routines.

An example would be if you want to expand your knowledge in a certain field, you could purchase a book on the subject (print, or audio), then set a timer to go off in your phone at 12:25 p.m. each day to alert you it's time to begin reading. More than likely you're eating lunch at this time so this is a great way to feed your mind as well.

EXERCISE NO. 6: REMOVE THE CUE – OUT OF SIGHT OUT OF MIND

Although I've recommended that only the routine needs to be changed and that the cue and reward remain the same, there is still a "rogue's gallery" of particularly problematic cues that would serve you well to modify in addition to the associated routines. And forcing yourself to jump through hoops to engage in bad habits is extremely beneficial (i.e. making yourself drive to the store for that unhealthy snack or alcoholic drink because you consciously chose not to have it in your home).

There are countless cues that entice us to engage in bad habits. But undeniably, our mobile phones are one of the worst cues for encouraging us to head down a destructive path of unproductivity. Our phone is unquestionably a weapon of mass distraction. We get distracting notifications all day long. Personally, my cell phone is turned off for the majority of the day. While I'm working i.e. engaging in productive activities – you cannot reach me. I'd like to encourage you to adopt a similar strategy. Turn off all notifications on your phone (or at least only allow important notifications, i.e. calls from close family members). Keeping your notifications constantly on means that the "notifiers" are determining how and when you are notified; instead, shouldn't it be you who determines this?

A clarification aside:

When my editor was editing this section she asked: "How do people get a hold of you." To which I replied, "They don't. I get a hold of them." I'm not trying to sound brash or callous, I'm not instructing you to shut the outside world out (although I certainly have a tendency to do), I'm trying to encourage you to *"stay on message"* and not take your eye off the ball so to speak.

Try this: right this very moment, go to the notifications section of your phone and turn them off. If you will not do this, at least do it during the time you set aside for automobile education. Make your car time sacred. From there, it'll be easy to "re-legislate" your good habit (by extending it). Set a timer for a certain amount of time beyond when you have arrived somewhere, as an extension of the sacred timeframe.

Whether it's a Facebook notification or seeing a liquor bottle sitting on the shelf when you get home from work, removing the cues will allow you to successfully interrupt the bad habit's routine. It's like putting the safety on a gun; the trigger won't work. This is key because as you've learned our habits are incredibly powerful. And we need to do everything we can to set ourselves up for success.

If you've ever discussed quitting smoking with an ex-smoker, you will find that he or she most likely had to remove the cue to succeed. This meant leaving a party at which he/she knew would end up with a lit cigarette in his or her hand, or substituting coffee for that after-dinner cigarette. What the ex-smoker is referring to is removing him or herself from the "near occasion" (see Chapter Four) of the cue, when the routine after a cue cannot be avoided.

EXERCISE NO. 7: BUILD YOURSELF UP – POSITIVE SELF-TALK ONLY

The likelihood of you immediately eliminating a bad habit is not realistic. A mistake I used to make was mentally beating myself up with horrible, negative self-talk when I found myself doing a habit I knew I wanted to remove from my life. When you find yourself engaging in a habit that you know is unhealthy, do not give yourself a verbal spanking.

Instead, tell yourself this:

> *Sure, I messed up. But this failure in my behavior is feedback. Now I have this new awareness; I am better equipt to be certain this transgression does not happen again. People aren't perfect. I'm not perfect. And next time I will do better because my dreams and desires are stronger than any bad habit I have developed. What has been conditioned in, I will condition out. Nothing is going to stop me from becoming the CEO of my life.*

CHAPTER SIX

Friends – They Will Make You Or Break You

"If you've never outgrown friends, you aren't growing."

~GRANT CARDONE, Author, sales trainer, public speaker, social media influencer and real estate mogul

Up to this point, I have equipped you with the best self-improvement strategies (along with the science to support them) I've come across after spending more than 20 years endlessly studying everything I could find on the subject of self-mastery:

- Vision
- Goal Setting
- Resilience
- Instant Gratification
- Habits

You can consistently implement every lesson in the previous chapters day after day, and yet still fail. How, you may ask?

The answer lies in your external world. Everything and anything outside of you can be a key factor that literally makes or breaks your chances of achieving anything significant in life. Your external world is both powerful and influential, so much so that even the most dedicated person will never be able to fully become the CEO of their life until they conquer these external elements.

When I talk about your external world, I'm not just talking about the city or neighborhood you live in. What I'm talking about are the following three elements:

1. Inputs: Influences that feed your mind (TV, books, movies, music, podcasts, blogs, etc.)
2. Environment: Your immediate surroundings (home, city, community, etc.)
3. Associations: People who you spend your time with (family, friends, co-workers, business partners, etc.)

INPUTS

"Garbage in, garbage out."

~GEORGE FUECHSEL, former IBM programmer

The most blatant example of false input is the "breaking news" of news networks such as CNN, FOX, CSPAN, etc. Everything is touted as breaking news. All lawmakers on both sides of an issue are described as outraged. And everything is designated *what you need to know* but can wait until after the commercial break.

"Enemy missiles launched minutes ago! Are you the target? Find out, right after this..." To invoke Shakespeare's Macbeth, it is breaking news – not life – that is a "tale told by an idiot, full of sound and fury, but signifying nothing."

The real problem with what news marketers label as breaking news is that there is no perspective. Enemy missiles are given the same weight as a Kardashian's behind. And for you to navigate life, you need perspective, because without it you cannot prioritize your days or your life.

Besides fake news, the Internet wields the double-edged sword that is both freedom of speech and freedom to lie. The irony is that the more truthful a source is, the more vanilla it is in being informative. Mayoclinic.com's content is going to be very carefully written not to mislead patients medically, yet an irate anti-vaccination zealot will cite "studies" that prove immunizations cause bunions. Again, no perspective.

The attraction to fake news and the Internet is that it's so easy. Simply watching TV or treading the waters of the Internet invites engagement appropriate for the attention span sponsors want to create. Cat videos or *War and Peace*? Your choice.

Such a choice is really easy because changing your input is simple – all you have to do is change the channel and make a conscious decision to watch and listen to positive, educational content instead of rotting your brain with depressing and unproductive garbage.

In the exercise section of the previous chapter, I recommended you, "plug in an uplifting or educational audio message after you start your car." This is an excellent way to feed your mind with positive input that will promote lifelong learning – which is a key tenet to sustained success.

ENVIRONMENT

> "You just get the vibes of your surroundings and it rubs off on you."
>
> ~GORDON LIGHTFOOT, Canadian singer-songwriter

If you're surrounded by dirt, you can still become a beautiful flower. However, sometimes it is what else that surrounds you that can make you what you are. Being in a financially depressed neighborhood or a family home or intimate relationship of dysfunctional emotions and abuse will victimize you into a type of impotent imprisonment. Sometimes, you just have to leave.

In *A Confederacy of Dunces*, the Pulitzer Prize-winning first novel by the late Southern writer John Kennedy Toole, protagonist Ignatius Reilly claims to be "writing a lengthy indictment against our century." He curses his outlet of relief – the movies as:

> *"technicolored horrors, filmed abortions that were offenses against any criteria of taste and decency, reels and reels of perversion and blasphemy that stunned my disbelieving eyes, shocked my virginal mind, and sealed my valve."*

Thereafter, while continually exposed to the indignities he perceives, Ignatius suffered severe gastric disturbances which had the unfortunate consequence of "sealing his valve" for the rest of the novel.

This metaphor of toxicity from one's environment, being equated to gastritis, is an excellent one. For Ignatius, his solution was to (spoiler alert) leave the area and remove himself from the indignities he suffers, resulting in his valve finally reopening and giving him relief.

Although changing your environment is a bit trickier than changing a channel, sometimes you just have to do it to re-open "your valve," as Ignatius O'Reilly did. It is simple in principle: if you don't like where you live or work, you can move or change jobs.

ASSOCIATIONS

> "Show me your friends and I'll show you your future."
>
> ~MARK AMBROSE, American singer-songwriter

The media you consume along with your location or job are a few of the things you could change to improve your probability of success, but what about changing your associations? That seems to be an uncomfortable decision which proves to be emotionally painful for many of us. Science has proven that humans are hardwired to seek and form connections with others. However, these connections differ from that of mere members of a flock, gaggle, pride, or pack. The connections I speak of are relationships. They are, in fact, one of the things that make us human. Unfortunately, many people find themselves connecting with the wrong individuals. They find themselves entwined in unhealthy associations with people who neither inspire nor empower them.

Breaking free from the death grip that deep-rooted friendships have on our lives can be extremely difficult. It can be so challenging that many people choose to hold on to toxic and negative connections because they're unaware (oblivious to the obvious) of the poisonous effect they have on their future. **Such loyalty to others is actually a disloyalty to themselves.**

Don't underestimate your own role in these relationships. You probably wouldn't be in any of them if you weren't getting something out of them yourself. When assessing the toxicity of your associations, some trade-offs are acceptable, but is the co-dependency positive or negative?

Ending friendships can be emotionally painful. But choosing your future over your friends is a decision you must make if you are genuinely committed to becoming the CEO of your life. Whether you realize it or not, the people you allow into your life have a profound impact on the habits you develop, along with the intentions and ideas you choose to act on – or not act on.

In fact, studies have shown that we allow people who we don't even know to make choices for us without even realizing it. Before I dive in and show you how much the people closest to you impact the quality of your life, let me show you how people you don't even know influence the choices you make.

BE INFORMED, NOT INFLUENCED

> "It's much better to walk alone in the right direction, than follow the herd in the wrong direction."
>
> ~UNKNOWN

Making decisions solely based on the choices of the people around us can derail us in ways we can't even imagine. How does this happen? It happens because of something called the *Herd Mentality Bias*. This is a common term found in the financial industry, but not so much in the personal development industry. Along with the confirmation, anchoring, halo effect, and overconfidence biases I listed in Chapter Four, the Herd Mentality Bias is yet another worth paying attention to.

What is Herd Mentality Bias? In behavioral finance, Herd Mentality Bias refers to an investor's tendency to follow or copy what other investors are doing. When it comes to buying and selling stocks, investors are largely influenced by emotion and instinct, rather than by their own independent analysis. You've probably seen this in action: a stock's price going up wildly beyond its true worth, or investors getting into a selling frenzy based on fear. As such, the Herd Mentality Bias is a great way to describe how other people can easily guide you in the wrong direction if you allow them to.

There was a fascinating article I read on a corporate finance website that describes how the Herd Mentality Bias activates our natural inclination to follow others. Specifically, they used restaurants as an analogy to describe investors who have a bad mental habit of following and copying what other people do.

Here's the analogy that was used: let's say you're going out to eat and you want to try a new place. You see two restaurants right beside each other, and you know absolutely nothing about either one. Which restaurant would you pick?

In the article, the study revealed that the overwhelming majority of people would go to the restaurant that appears to be more crowded and full of people, rather than the one that appears to have more open tables. Why? Because many people base their decisions on the choices that other people have made. Research has revealed that people are firmly wired to herd, and will use emotion and instinct to drive their decision-making instead of thinking for themselves. And it really doesn't matter if the bias is based on how many people are being seen to "vouch" for a particular person, place or thing.

A "herd of one" can just as easily fuel the bias. To use a dating analogy, if an average-looking person goes into a bar "scene" looking to meet people, specifically of the opposite sex, the likelihood of generating any interest is small. That, as many will tell you, is very challenging. That person is a complete stranger: there are no others to vouch for him or her. However, if he or she enters the same bar with a very attractive person as a date, suddenly the ice melts, and there are inviting looks (if not overt come-ons). Now, this person is no longer a stranger, but someone who has been evaluated and accepted – even championed – by another person who looks normal (even attractive) enough to have no trouble "connecting." This is still herd mentality, and it shows just how even one person can affect how we make decisions.

Whether it's a "crowd of one" or a sizeable "herd", people find it psychologically painful to go against the crowd. So instead, they often make their choices based on other people's preferences. This usually leads to the *Bandwagon Effect* (the momentum that accrues from the herd mentality), which is a psychological phenomenon in which people do something primarily because other people are

> **"Be careful when you follow the masses. Sometimes the M is silent."**
>
> ~UNKNOWN

doing it, regardless of their own beliefs, which they may ignore or override.

Whether it's the Herd Mentality Bias initially, or the Bandwagon Effect that results, too many people allow their plans to be sabotaged by going with the flow of others. And too many people follow the footsteps and behaviors of others, even when they are headed in the wrong direction.

ARE YOU FOLLOWING THE WRONG PEOPLE?

> "Be careful who you call your friends. I'd rather have four quarters than one hundred pennies."
>
> ~AL CAPONE, American gangster and businessman

A famous experiment conducted in 1896 involved processionary caterpillars. What makes these caterpillars interesting and unique and gives them their name is the fact they instinctively lockstep with the caterpillar directly in front of them, forming a miniature train.

French naturalist Jean Henri Fabre demonstrated these caterpillars' unusual behavior with a simple experiment. He took a flowerpot and placed a number of these caterpillars in single file until they formed a never-ending circle around the circumference of the flowerpot's rim. He made certain that each caterpillar's head touched the caterpillar directly in front of it.

Fabre then placed the caterpillar's favorite food, which is pine needles, in the middle of the flowerpot. Then, he gave them a little nudge. Each caterpillar followed the next, thinking they were heading for the food. Round and round the caterpillars went. Twenty-four hours, then 48, then 72, and so on. They just kept going around the flower pot rim, thinking they would eventually make it to their destination, which just so happened to be their favorite meal. Fabre estimated these caterpillars traveled the equivalent of a human walking about 90 miles – or completing three and a half marathons – without any food, water or rest.

These crazy creatures went around the rim of the flowerpot for seven full days and seven full nights, following one another nonstop. Finally, after a week of this mindless circling, the caterpillars started to drop dead from exhaustion and starvation.

With an abundance of their favorite food less than six inches away, they failed to reach the food because of the drive to follow the caterpillar ahead. All they had to do was stop senselessly following each other around the rim of the flowerpot, and head toward their food that was only inches away. Unfortunately, like these caterpillars, many human beings who are following the wrong crowd confuse motion with meaning and activity with accomplishment.

Stop and reflect on that phrase a moment: *confusing motion with meaning and activity with accomplishment.*

Sadly, many people get locked into their lifestyles and are not able to change their direction. They continue to do the exact same thing, follow the exact same peers, and yet expect a different result. I'm pretty sure this correlates with the definition of insanity attributed to Albert Einstein:

"The definition of insanity is doing the same thing over and over again, but expecting different results."

The influence our peers have on us is insanely powerful, and I use the phrase "insanely powerful" in homage to Einstein's definition. So powerful, in fact, that we follow our friends' footsteps without even realizing they're leading us severely off course. We think like our friends. We act like our friends. And we follow the example our friends set for us. Napoleon Hill recognized and shared how we become like the people we spend time with:

"Men take on the nature and the habits and the power of thought of those with whom they associate in a spirit of sympathy and harmony."

Everyone likes to "belong", so taking it one step further than what Napoleon Hill said, I feel that we take on the nature, and habits and thoughts of our associates for inclusion, which is a natural human tendency for stability and security. In other words, it is based on fear, the very thing that thwarts the resilience I discussed in Chapter Three: fear of being left out and fear of missing out. This also includes the fear of failure, which is less humiliating when being part of a group that fails rather than doing so all by yourself. The protection and benefits, however, are only as stable and secure as the associates we choose.

YOUR REFERENCE GROUP

"We know that we are often judged by the company we keep. We know how influential classmates, friends, and other peer groups can be. If any of our companions are prone to be unrighteous in their living, we are better off seeking new associations immediately."

~JOSEPH B. WIRTHLIN, American businessman and religious leader

Harvard psychologist Dr. David McClelland's research into social behavior shows that the people with whom we associate are known as our "reference group". Dr. McClelland says that this reference group determines as much as 95 percent of our successes and failures in life.

What does that mean for you? It means you need to raise the standards for yourself. You have to feel worthy of being around people of a higher caliber and start setting the bar – higher than ever – for the person you see yourself becoming in the future. Your standards should serve as your compass for choosing the people you associate with. Ideally, those people will expect more of you and force you to level up.

Ultimately, your life will organize itself around the standards you set. And who you spend time with is who you become. If you spend time with people who have low standards for themselves and expect less of you or nothing more than what you're already putting out right now, then that is all that they – or you – are going to get. These types of people will not be able to help you up, and sometimes they'll even pull you down. When you are going through a struggle and you are not able to see greatness in yourself, the wrong people will not speak the confidence into you that will help you keep going.

> **"Surround yourself with the dreamers and doers, the believers and the thinkers, but most of all, surround yourself with those who see greatness within you, even when you don't see it yourself."**
>
> ~EDMUND LEE

Life is far too short to waste valuable time with the wrong people. You should always be in constant pursuit of raising the standards of people you allow into your life. Inevitably, you are going to outgrow some of your friends on your journey toward your dreams. The mistake many people make, however, is holding onto their friends for the rest of their lives in a way that stops them from associating with others. The higher you go, the tighter your inner circle has to become, i.e., the more selective you have to be about who comprises this circle.

At times, it might feel good to compare yourself to people on the low-end of the success spectrum, but this is a fool's game as you will never truly get better at the game of life. You are choosing to belong to a mutual admiration society of wannabes, and therefore choosing the wrong circle as your inner circle will become your spiral down the drain. In the words of King Solomon of Israel: "Walk with the wise and become wise, for a companion of fools suffers harm."

You can only reach beyond your present self and continue to grow when you are constantly raising the standards and increasing the level you want to play at. Don't think you can't "jump" circles.

> A chemistry aside:
>
> The number of electrons is one way different atoms (elements) differ from each other. An atom can lose or gain electrons and fundamentally change, and in the process, energy is either gained or lost. This corresponds as a colorful metaphor for changing your circles. You will either lose or gain a type of energy (drive, ambition, vision, and goal-seeking) depending on which circle you move to. The answer is to jump to the right circle so you gain the energy you need. In the chemistry world, that is the difference between sodium and potassium being poisons but becoming harmless table salt with electron shifts; in the business world, that is the difference between losing and winning.

This is not to mean that you should desert the people who you care about, abandon those in need, or "ghost" loved ones by summarily dismissing them from your life. This is not about a selfish disregard for those who can no longer do you any good. It's about re-centering your life, goals, and dreams toward those who *can* help your goals and dreams.

You can still *care*; you just can't be *careless*. You can have several "circles". There's plenty of room in the human heart for many of them, but the inner circle toward your goals should be the most selective – the tightest – according to the rationale I proposed.

When your inner circle has higher standards than you, only then will you recognize where you're failing and strive to do better. When you spend time with people who expect more of you than what you are currently doing, you will rise to their expectations. More importantly, you'll be able to tap into their support when you need an extra push to climb out of a funk. So create an inner circle that delivers the goods...not the *bads*.

The path to success is not linear, and it's extremely easy to get stuck in a place where you feel like no escape exists. Therefore, having healthy associations and friendships will help you overcome setbacks faster and reach your goals with greater ease.

THE BIG 5

> "There's an economic theory out there that if you take the incomes of your five closest friends and average them, the resulting number will be pretty close to your own income. I think the same thing is true of ideal incomes. You're only going to be as good as the stuff you surround yourself with."
>
> ~AUSTIN KLEON, *New York Times* bestselling author of three books: *Steal Like an Artist, Show Your Work!*, and *Newspaper Blackout*

Legendary personal development expert Jim Rohn believed that we become like the combined average of the five people we spend the most time with. Rohn stated:

> *"You can determine a person's attitude towards life, overall health, and their income simply by meeting the top five people that they closely surround themselves with."*

How your inner circle, more specifically, your top-five friends directly affects you is profound. If the members of your top-five friends are religious about working out, it's unlikely that you're going to be obese. If you're closely associating with happy and positive people, the chances of you being a grump are almost zero. If your friends are all millionaires, it's unlikely you're broke.

Could making more money really be that simple? Could improving our attitude be so easy? Could having better health be as straightforward as hanging out with healthier people? The short answer is: "Yes".

An interesting experiment conducted at Dartmouth College discovered when students with low grades became roommates with students who had higher grades, the lower-scoring students' grades went up. So now all we need to do is figure out how to become roommates with millionaires, right? That way, we'll all become rich. Not so fast!

Successful people know and live by Jim Rohn's advice of being the average of the five people they most closely associate with. They know that if they bring someone into their circle who is not like them, it has the potential to affect their level of financial success drastically. When someone is attempting to become their friend, they do the mental math very quickly: if four of us are making $1,000,000 a year, and we bring someone in who's only making $50,000 a year – this could potentially drive my annual revenue all the way down to $810,000. They subconsciously think to themselves, "losing nearly a million dollars in the next five years by allowing this new person into my circle is a very bad idea."

Person 1: $1,000,000	Person 1: $1,000,000
Person 2: $1,000,000	Person 2: $1,000,000
Person 3: $1,000,000	Person 3: $1,000,000
Person 4: $1,000,000	Person 4: $1,000,000
Person 5: $1,000,000	Person 5: $50,000
Average: $1,000,000	Average: $810,000

A loss of $190,000 for becoming friends with someone who makes $50,000 per year? For most people, that is just unacceptable. That's why it's so hard to form friendships with people who are substantially ahead of you on the income totem pole. This is also in part why the rich get richer and the poor get poorer. Breaking into these types of circles can be difficult. Trust me, I know, because early in my life (before I learned how) I tried. Looking back, I can see how foolish I was, because when you're the one bringing down the average, the others will protect their interests by taking corrective measures. Such measures may simply be barring your entry into their circle.

An economic aside:

It used to be that the title millionaire symbolized success on nearly every level. However, besides the relentless devaluation of money from inflation, the sheer overhead of living has outpaced whatever increases in income are offered based on the cost of living. And necessities, in the wrong hands, don't come cheap.

For example, Peter Thiel, an initial co-founder of PayPal and early Facebook investor, stepped forward to finance ex-pro-wrestler Hulk Hogan's legal battle with Gawker.com, which published sensitive pictures of him without permission. But Hogan (real name Terry Bollea), because he was a mere single-digit millionaire was unable to afford fair legal representation even with his millionaire title. This all underscores the value of money. While Sonny and Cher sang about how "I got you, babe" being enough, although it may have been romantic, it was also juvenile and flies in the face of reality. The rich get richer because of decisions they make in their lives, but the poor get poorer, not only from poor decisions but because they have been economically pre-declined instead of pre-approved.

If you're in the pre-declined group of people, this is a call to arms. This is a wake-up call. You need to see where your circle's average has you, and if it's not what you want, it's time to change circles.

Unfortunately, life rarely gives us the opportunity to become "roommates" with millionaires. And the critical mistake many people make is that they forge their way and attempt to establish new friendships by brute force before they are ready. This has the potential to burn bridges they could have formed had they learned the skill sets necessary to be accepted by these prominent individuals and likely kills the chances of becoming friends with the people who they seek to have in their inner circle.

Think about it like this: let's say you want to hang out with successful entrepreneurs who have built multimillion-dollar businesses. That's going to be difficult if you're broke because you will not be able to afford to engage in the same activities as they do. The same goes if you're trying to hang out with people who are in great shape when you're not; it's going to be very difficult for you to have the commonalities necessary to maintain a win-win friendship. If you're someone who currently has a bad attitude, people who are positive about life will find you unpleasant to be around and will distance themselves from you at all costs.

> **"The less you associate with some people, the more your life will improve. Any time you tolerate mediocrity in others, it increases your mediocrity. An important attribute in successful people is their impatience with negative thinking and negative acting people. As you grow, your associates will change. Some of your friends will not want you to go on. They will want you to stay where they are. Friends that don't help you climb will want you to crawl. Your friends will stretch your vision or choke your dream. Those that don't increase you will eventually decrease you."**
>
> ~COLIN POWELL

So what do you do? Before I show you how to break into these elite circles, I want to warn you about what you should *not* do. An egregious mistake I see too many people make is that they keep an inner circle full of people who are lowering their grade point average, so to speak, in life. Just because you have some work to do when it comes to improving yourself, developing your skills, and strengthening your will to succeed does not give you a pass to continue surrounding yourself with people who also have work to do and skills to develop

– yet lack the will and self-discipline to do so.

In fact, you are better off being alone in an isolated inner circle of one while you're searching for the right five people, rather than being surrounded by the wrong five people. Why? Because like attracts like. And as the Apostle Paul so eloquently stated in the Bible: "Bad company corrupts good character."

Think of your circles as lenses. The worse your circles are in regard to the people who define them, the cloudier your vision becomes:

- The lowest circles have no "vision" at all, and vision is fundamental to setting proper goals (see Chapter One).

> In fact, the worst circle is "eyes-closed", and you're sleep-walking through your life with the muscle memory I discussed earlier.

- The better your circle, the clearer your lens and the better clarity you have to set your goals (see Chapter Two).
- When you can improve your perspective along your journey, this allows you to engage your resilience (see Chapter Three), as well as
- clearly see the long-term gain in delaying short-term gratification (see Chapter Four), and also
- make sense of eliminating bad habits while developing good habits (see Chapter Five).

At the beginning of this chapter, I stated that you can consistently implement every lesson in the previous chapters day after day and still fail; and I asked, "How?" I answered by blaming your external world. I explored the pitfalls of your external world as faulty inputs, environments, and associations. To risk over-using the "circle" metaphor, the irrefutable proof that associations are crucial in either avoiding or succumbing to all of these pitfalls has now come full circle.

Me? I vote *avoiding* these pitfalls. You should, too. If you truly respect yourself and care about your reputation, from this point forward you will only navigate toward your goals with people of high-caliber and quality. That may mean you will have to learn to be okay with being by yourself for the period of time it takes you to find your tribe. Sadly, not many people are willing to go it alone until finding their right inner circle. Tap into your resilience, because you must summon the inner strength to be by yourself on your journey while you're searching. Because if the right people see you trying to achieve your goals with the wrong people, then the probability of the right people allowing you to enter their circle is highly unlikely. After all, they're not dumb. That's how they became the "right people" you want.

"Friends are as companions on a journey, who ought to aid each other to persevere in the road to a happier life."
~PYTHAGORAS OF SAMOS

Mel Robbins, the author of *The 5 Second Rule,* suggests you do something she calls a *friends cleanse*. Robbins describes a friends cleanse as:

> *"You get intentional about cleansing out and detoxing toxic behavior from your life; you put your friendships through a filter and make sure they are really empowering you."*

Now is the time to do some serious thinking about the people you associate with and how they affect your ability to succeed. Incorporate a "friends cleanse" into your life because if you're hanging out with four losers, you'll soon become the fifth. Or, according to Jim Rohn's law of averages, you will become the "average" loser in the group.

Too many people fail to change their associations, and it destroys their dreams.

Sacrificing your dreams for your friends is certainly a decision you will look back on and regret. You must find the courage to walk away and change your inner circle if the one you currently have is not fully supporting your ambitions and encouraging you to grow. Trust me, I know walking alone is not easy. But if you lean on your resilience muscles, continue to stay strong and keep going, you'll realize that success in life is more of a direction than a destination. And it's unlikely you will be able to go in the direction you need to succeed if you're carrying dead weight in the form of friends who are not inspiring and empowering you.

HOW DO YOU ATTRACT BETTER FRIENDS?

> "You can make more friends in two months by becoming interested in other people than you can in two years by trying to get other people interested in you."
>
> ~DALE CARNEGIE, American writer and lecturer, author of *How To Win Friends and Influence People*

Whether you want to admit it or not, each relationship you have in your life will affect who you are – as well as who you become. If you are going to be successful, you need to be surrounded by people who constantly and consistently encourage you to grow. This is not debatable.

But the million-dollar question is this: how do you find people to join your inner circle who will force you to level up? How do you associate with winners, with people who are already doing the things with their life that you want to do with yours? The answer isn't easy, but it's simple: work on *you*.

Probably the quote that has had the most significant impact on my life is, "Success is not something you pursue; success is something you attract." The more attractive you make yourself, the more you will attract top-level people into your life. I'm not talking about high-end designer makeup and purses or Swiss-made watches and suits; I'm talking about making yourself attractive by becoming obsessed with creating the very best version of *you* possible. One of the ways you can do this is by immersing yourself with knowledge.

> **"My name is Brian Rose and my job is to listen, the oldest method of learning known to man."**
> ~BRIAN ROSE

Knowledge can be consumed in many ways. But learning new information from individuals who have first-hand experience in subjects you're passionate about should be a top priority for two reasons: one, it gets you in the presence of high-caliber people. Two, it adds tried and true wisdom to your knowledge bank.

A mimicry aside:

Dutch psychologist Rick van Baaren uncovered, "Mimicry creates bonds between people – it induces a sense of 'we-ness', you know that what you're doing is ok, and you become more generous." This was discovered in a study van Baaren's team conducted in an American-style restaurant in Holland. In half of the experiments, the psychologists instructed waitresses to repeat customers' orders back to them. In the other half, the waitresses were instructed to say something positive, such as "Coming right up!"

The results revealed that the waitresses nearly doubled their tips when they repeated the customers' own words back to them – "mimicry for money". The customers thought they shared a connection with the "mimickers/waitresses." Similar results were discovered with other outward signs of camaraderie, such as touching a customer's shoulder or crouching to be at eye level when taking the order.

The waitresses in the van Baaren study made themselves attractive by "joining the club," so to speak, with their customers. It's really symbolic for what happens when you make yourself attractive for the people you would like to attract. Everyone wants a win-win, and the best way to do that is to put yourself into the "we-ness" the waitresses created.

Before the waitresses could mimic their customers, however, they had to listen actively.

Active listening isn't just hearing, but receiving. One of the most crucial skills to not only learning new information but attracting new friends to join your inner circle is shutting up and listening. **Listen, listen again, and then listen some more should be your motto when you're engaged in a conversation.** Yes, listening is actually a skill; it requires patience and restraint.

Listening to someone, especially someone who has knowledge to bestow, is not just a passive response; it's an interaction. What someone says to you is an invitation, and listening is accepting that invitation. It is giving the person your undivided attention, which is a gift that often is returned in kind. It makes the person feel good and feel respected. Asking a question and then answering it is biting the hand that feeds you and deprives you of the response you really needed to hear; that is not a win-win, but a win-lose and the loser will be you.

> **"I've learned that people will forget what you said, people will forget what you did, but people will never forget how you made them feel."**
>
> ~MAYA ANGELOU

Listening to listen – not listening to reply will make the speaker feel good, which is the greatest first impression you can make. If you value what he or she has to say, listening is the best way to ensure more is to come. If the speaker feels important when they are talking to you because of the undivided attention you are displaying, and if you're exercising some subtle forms of mimicry throughout the conversation, then you're likely on your way to forming a new friendship – and in turn, adding a prominent member to your inner circle.

Don't call it a Jedi mind trick, call it active listening with a purpose.

The economic phenomenon called the *Pareto Principle* (also known as the *80/20 rule*, the *law of the vital few*, or the *principle of factor sparsity*) is often a truism in everything you do toward your goals. In fact, it is named after an Italian economist, and it refers to the relationship of distribution. There seems to be an 80/20 relationship which infers that, for instance, 20 percent of the people own 80 percent of the wealth.

When I apply the Pareto Principle to finding better friends by making yourself more attractive; I believe there should be 80 percent listening and only 20 percent talking when you're engaged in a conversation with someone you're trying to recruit into your inner circle. Active listening makes you attractive, which thereby attracts more of the people you want to attract. A cycle then begins: the more people with knowledge you attract, the more you increase your capacity to learn and increasing your capacity to learn will consequently attract more of the right people into your life. The cliché "vicious cycle" comes to mind, but this is more like a "vital cycle" for attracting the right people to join your inner circle.

FISHING FOR FRIENDS

"Surround yourself with people who lift you up. Part of self-love is having a higher standard for your inner circle."

~UNKNOWN

Increasing your capacity and hunger to learn will assist you in attracting the right people into your life. Learning new information about things you are passionate about will open up new communities and opportunities you never knew existed. The more you learn, the more you'll discover communities of people you can reach out to and network with. But you can't do this unless you have something to offer. That's where knowledge comes in.

You see, there's a saying: *The person who needs nothing attracts everything.* When you approach these communities (Facebook groups, online forums, networking functions, Meetup events, etc.) with the intention of offering value instead of extracting it, and when you employ your new "active listening with a purpose" skills, you'll quickly attract the right people.

When you give people your undivided attention while they're talking, by listening to listen (instead of listening to reply) you will easily win new friends and begin forming an elite inner circle.

So the real question here needs to be: who do I need to become to get better friends? When you become that person, when your self-image improves because you became more than you currently are, you'll have the confidence to approach people you feel worthy of being around. Because chances are if you're not currently a person who feels comfortable being around high-caliber people, more than likely they are not going to feel comfortable being around you (no matter how much you listen).

Hell on Earth is meeting the man or woman you could have been. And do you know what's keeping you from becoming that person? You guessed it: the people you associate with. Your peer group plays a vital role in shaping your self-image. You subconsciously tell yourself (that is, think it without even realizing), "Well, if my friends aren't authors, I can't be, either." Or, "If my friends aren't millionaires, I can't be, either." And so, your subconscious behaviors and beliefs follow suit. This type of thinking acts as a governor in your life that trumps any opportunity to accomplish the things you really want to achieve.

Personally, I've always believed you should pay any price to be in the presence of great people who will raise the bar and encourage you to reach your full potential. You want your closest relationships to inspire you and push you. If your inner circle is not inspiring you to improve regularly, then it's time to start making some serious changes. You are maintaining the status quo at best, and at worst being held back.

Like it or not, you become just like the people you surround yourself with because they will ultimately shape who you are, as well as the person you develop into. It won't be instantaneous – it happens subtly and slowly over time. The more time you spend with them, the more they will influence you. This means that the fastest way in existence to change into the person that you want to become is to spend time with the people who are already the way you want to be. Because at the very least, you will be the average of your exemplary "gang of five".

PEARL DIVING

> "Every time you dive, you hope you'll see something new – some new species. Sometimes the ocean gives you a gift, sometimes it doesn't."
>
> ~JAMES CAMERON, Award-winning Canadian filmmaker and environmentalist

A friend of mine who's a surgeon explained how, over several years, he came to perform procedures a certain way:

> *"When I finished residency and began doing surgeries unsupervised, I had a variety of other surgeons as assistants, as well as assisted a variety of them myself. Coming out of school, you bring a skill set*

that is a bit nepotistic. It comes from professors who simply said, 'This is the way we do it here.' Then, when you operate with people trained at other programs, you see that there are many ways to do a certain procedure. Over the years, some techniques you "steal" and make your own, others you try but dismiss as less effective. Over time, you have built up a way of doing surgery based on the best steps and techniques you've assimilated into your own individual style. It's the e pluribus unum *education."*

Then I asked, "What if all you did was operate with bad surgeons?" His reply:

"Then I'd be a bad surgeon myself. And probably out of business. Those surgeons fall out of the system eventually, but even good surgeons are hard-headed about keeping some ineffective techniques. Your ultimate worth is based on how well you can distinguish the pearls from the garbage and on the 'pearls-only' surgeon you've become. Your best chance for that is working with the ones who have the most pearls."

The pearls are certainly out there. Since it's natural for us to follow the people we spend the most time with, why not spend the most time with the people you want to follow? That is, the ones with all the pearls. Follow (and become friends with) those people who represent who you want to become in the future. If you have a desire to run a marathon, obviously you can't just Google "running groups" in your city and show up where they meet and run 26 miles. This is not the way to follow. But you can begin running on your own, then in a few months – after you've gotten enough of your own pearls to be ready – you can meet up with people who are practicing and preparing to run a marathon.

If you truly want to build a multimillion-dollar business, you can't just look in the Yellow Pages for successful entrepreneurs and call them up. Again, not the way to go about doing it. But what you *can* do is search for places where successful business owners give back by speaking at startup events and giving talks in community settings. At these events, the pearls just pour out! You can attend them, network with other growing people who are trying to achieve what you are seeking and work your way up the ladder by implementing the new ideas you discover. Invoking my surgeon friend's term, it's called "pearl diving". Furthermore, if you run on your own, or network at startup events and – in other words – gather pearls that you yourself can offer, then you become more attractive because everyone wants to be a part of a win-win scenario.

While you're attending networking events or other community gatherings don't throw your hands up and get discouraged if the people you are trying to befriend are making it difficult to associate with them. Always remember that you simply cannot make people do what they don't want to do. But don't give up on your quest for finding high-caliber people and go back to hanging out with low-quality people, simply because you're finding it difficult to make friends with the people who you seek to have in your inner circle.

Initially, it can be emotionally painful to go it alone while you're searching for the right friends. Continue working on yourself, mining for pearls and attending community events and I assure you the right people will begin to form your new and improved circle. But whatever you do – do not go back and conform to the familiar. Do not go back to your old ways of life by going back to old friends – friends that will not assist you in your pursuit of reaching your full potential.

If I had chosen to hang out with people who lowered my grade point average in life, instead of working on myself alone, it's highly unlikely I would have the quality of friends I do now. Today, professional athletes, powerful politicians, and ultra-high net worth individuals make up my inner circle. That would not be possible if I didn't have the strength and discipline to develop myself so that I had something to offer or associated with people who my current friends would not approve of.

With apologies to Harry Nilsson, one is not the loneliest number, and working *on* yourself, alone, need not be lonely. Let's reverse-engineer this:

> You have a vision of your goals and dreams, and you need to become the person you need to be to achieve them. This implies that you are confident in your ability to get there, which further implies self-esteem. Translated: you like the person you want to be when you like the person you need to become. Further translated, you like yourself. And as Dr. Wayne Dyer said, "You cannot be lonely if you like the person you're alone with."
>
> **Reverse engineering:**
>
> **Your vision ← your goals ← confidence ← self-esteem ← liking the person you need to be ← liking the person you want to be ← your vision...**

In Chapter Five, I talked about creating good habits. Liking yourself can be a very good habit, and just as I discussed how you can develop good habits with reverse engineering, the above strategy applies. Notice this strategy does not include anyone (or anything) other than you. You are the primary (really the only) ingredient that determines if you will live a life of abundance or one of abuse. Each toxic friend you allow in your life will sabotage your success. That's why until you find the right associations – working on yourself by your self is key.

It is impossible for you to develop yourself if you are surrounded by people who are not improving themselves. No matter how much you may want success, if the people around you have bad habits, you will subconsciously pick up on those habits, and this will make it extremely difficult for you to grow. *Bad surgeons make for more bad surgeons, and bad surgeons make for unsuccessful surgeries.* Similarly, the wrong people in your circle make for unsuccessful futures.

One of the primary reasons why you should work on yourself is so you can develop an inner circle of people who are currently doing with their life what you want to do with yours. These people can provide the direction you need to get to the next level. Their habits will rub off on you, and soon enough, you'll be modeling the behaviors that will help you live the lifestyle you desire. But you must remain a growing person if you want to stay in the presence of high-caliber and quality people. *Good surgeons make for more good surgeons, and good surgeons make for successful surgeries.* Similarly, the right people in your circle make for successful visions and futures.

You may not even realize it, but successful people are always monitoring who wins access to their life, and therefore who are awarded access to their inner circle. That's why it's so crucial to develop the best possible version of yourself so that you will have something to bring to the table. This is the "attractiveness" I spoke about earlier.

If I would have continued hanging out with people who were not growing as individuals and allowed their negative habits to impact the way I behaved, it's unlikely Russell Brunson, co-founder of ClickFunnels, would have reached out and asked me to write a chapter in one of his books. That's the power of attracting the right people by making yourself attractive. And remember: being attractive has nothing to do with materialistic items. Russell did not reach out to me because I drive a fancy foreign car or have a watch that doesn't tick. He reached out to me because I spent a tremendous amount of time developing the best possible version of myself. And because of that, I had something of value to offer.

For me, the better I develop my skill and will, the better I take care of myself, the more I display a great attitude – the better the chances of the right people showing up in my life. *Skilled surgeons make for better surgeons, and better surgeons make for the best surgeries.* Similarly, the right circle of skilled people makes your best future.

With each new level of success you achieve, it's essential to continuously evaluate your circle. Are your friends growing with you? Or are you outgrowing your friends? Understand that the higher you climb the ladder to success, the tighter your circle must become. Jay Z (Shawn Carter) said it best, "Circle got smaller, castle got bigger."

EXAMINING YOUR INNER CIRCLE

> "Evaluate the people in your life; then promote, demote, or terminate. You're the CEO of your life."
>
> ~TONY GASKINS, Motivational speaker, author and life coach

Nobody understood the power of having the right associations better than Napoleon Hill's mentor, Andrew Carnegie. He not only knew that your inner circle determines who you are and who you become in life – he lived it! Carnegie surrounded himself with fifty like-minded people, and he regularly met with them in his mastermind group sessions.

In Carnegie's book, *The Gospel of Wealth*, he attributes his entire fortune to the knowledge and support he gained through his mastermind. Carnegie was able to prove that when two or more minds come together, it creates a third mind (or *mastermind).* Stephen Covey also expanded on this concept in his book, *The 7 Habits of Highly Effective People*. Covey believed that the whole is greater than the sum of its parts. This means that one plus one does not equal two: it actually equals three (or more). Simply put, two heads are better than one and are actually more than two. This also reflects the meaning of *gestalt*: an organized whole seen as more than the mere sum of its parts.

Having a tight circle of friends that come together to talk about ideas and strategies is incredibly powerful. Whether you refer to it as a mastermind or just a get-together really doesn't matter. But what does matter is the quality of people you brainstorm ideas with.

> **"A mastermind group is a space where people believe for each other things which each alone find difficult to conceive or believe for him or herself."**
>
> ~UNKNOWN

It's said that Thomas Edison, Henry Ford, and Harvey Firestone all had vacation homes by each other in Florida. These brilliant individuals who left their mark on this world understood the importance of associating with high-caliber people. Call it *haute gestalt* if you will.

In fact, Henry Ford was first introduced to Thomas Edison as "the man trying to build a car that ran on gasoline." When Edison heard this, his face lit up. He slammed his fist on the table and said, "You've got it. A car that has its own power plant; that's a brilliant idea."

At the time, Ford was struggling with getting his idea of "a car that has its own power plant" off the ground. He was struggling with self-sabotaging thoughts. Ford would later reveal, "I had a good idea, but I started to doubt myself. Then along came one of the greatest minds that ever lived and gave me complete approval."

Not only do the people we surround ourselves with determine the level of confidence we have in ourselves and how we see our true self-image, but they also determine how we see our self-worth. Who you associate with will impact the way you think about who you believe you are, and the way you think will impact the way you behave as well as the ideas you choose to act on or to not act on.

I know it may be tempting to hang out with friends that like to joke around, play, and party, but these friendships are more than likely not encouraging you to grow.

All work and no play makes Jack a dull boy, but all play and no work makes a boy who doesn't have jack.

For your dreams, work trumps play, so dull trumps fun; and this comparison underscores the whole concept of delaying instant gratification. What's trumping what in your circle? You really need to start thinking about your inner circle in the present moment as you read through the remainder of this chapter. Take some time to reflect on who you're spending the most time with.

Understand, I'm not stating 100 percent of your time needs to be focused on work, but it bears repeating: *short-term sacrifice produces long-term happiness*. Make the sacrifices now, so you can play later.

Carefully examine whether your friends are going somewhere or merely running around in circles, as it will impact the outcome of your life significantly. You don't need to elaborate on your answers now. I just want to get you thinking so that you can carry out the exercises at the end of this chapter. The questions I'd like you to seriously consider regarding your current inner circle are as follows:

- What kind of lifestyle do you all enjoy?
- What sort of activities do you do together?
- How is the moral compass of your friends?
- Do you ever talk about goals and the future?
- Do you talk about ideas, people, sports, or daily happenings?
- Do you encourage one another to pursue possible business opportunities?

When you answer these questions regarding your current inner circle, ask yourself: what do you see? Who do you see? Do you see success, hope, and happiness in the people you are spending your time with? Or do you see failure, negativity, and despair? Do you feel energized after you spend time with your inner circle, and ready to take on the world, or do you feel drained of your energy and ready for a nap?

Whatever you currently see and feel in your inner circle is a direct reflection of who you are at the present moment. Don't like what you see? Then it's time to start changing the people you're spending your time with.

You might dislike the fact that you live in a tiny beat-up apartment, but if the majority of the people in your inner circle also live in tiny beat-up apartments, there's a slim-to-none chance that you'll be moving to a multimillion-dollar mansion any time soon (if ever). You might dislike your 9-to-5 Monday-through-Friday job, but if the people around you are in the same proverbial boat, you're going to be stuck there for a very long time, never leaving port. The point I'm attempting to make is that your inner circle sets the bar for how well you are going to do in life, or how poor you are going to be in life.

As the old saying goes, birds of a feather flock together. Have you ever thought about what your flock says about you or how they influence you? If not, now is the time to start thinking. Don't turn a blind eye to the people in your life who are not contributing to your growth (physically, spiritually, emotionally, financially). Don't go through life without objectively thinking about your flock. Don't allow your friends to subconsciously lead you astray.

Have the inner strength to pull away from the people in your life who don't inspire you. Because if you don't, they will impair your ability to attract the right people and opportunities that will help you leave your mark on this world. And that's a terrible travesty as well as a slap in the face to the people who are counting on you. Time to get the *flock* out of there.

THE EMOTIONAL CONNECTION

> "You can love them, forgive them, want good things for them...but still move on without them."
>
> ~MANDY HALE, Author of *The Single Woman: Life, Love, and a Dash of Sass*

Without question, the hardest thing about terminating a friendship is severing the emotional connection that holds people together. Friendships are built on emotional bonds that encourage us to maintain the security and acceptance we seek for survival.

As an adult, you might have childhood friends who no longer share your beliefs, and yet you still care deeply about them. You might have people who randomly showed up in your life because they happened to be co-workers, neighbors, or partners during extracurricular activities that you were a part of.

It's relatively easy to make objective decisions about people who are merely casual acquaintances in our lives. It's pretty simple for most of us to regulate the amount of time we spend with these types of individuals. Each friendship may be a bit harder to govern depending on the context and depth of the emotional ties, but changing, or even terminating casual relationships that show up in our lives and are no longer beneficial is doable for most people.

However, without question, the hardest relationships to make an objective decision about are the ones that include our family, especially when we have family members who have limited beliefs and cannot (or will not) go where we are going in life.

Family members are often one of the primary reasons why people don't succeed. It's not that the people we are related to are inherently bad individuals, but they simply do not have the capacity to understand what we are trying to accomplish in life. I love how Joel Osteen says it:

"Just because somebody is related to you doesn't mean they're connected to you. They may have your blood, but they don't have your spirit."

My take on it – You can get the same blood from a transfusion, but spirit comes from within. Friends can easily turn into *family* when they are "all in" for your success.

An awful lot of people maintain strong ties with family members who they know are destructive to their potential. They hold on to these relationships because they're too scared to hurt their family members' feelings or make them upset by distancing themselves. So what do many of us typically do? We put off ending the relationships that we know we should let go of, and hold them until the very last day we have on this Earth.

True strength is not holding on; it's letting go.

Why is it that people choose to endure and deal with ridiculous amounts of conflict and heartache from negative family members? We do it out of feelings of obligation and the deep-rooted emotional connection we have with them simply because they are related to us, even though they have been creating drama in our lives for a long time. In spite of knowing that these people are not good for us or our health, we still continue to spend time with them.

The painful irony is the longer you maintain these unhealthy relationships, the more difficult it becomes to walk away and leave them. As weeds grow, their roots go deeper. Each time you're with this negative family member, the bond between each of you continues to grow. Eventually, you'll have to break the bond – or at least learn to stop giving it your energy – if you want to experience the level of success you desire.

Too many people become prisoners of poisonous relationships with their relatives because they have not clearly set the boundaries for their relationship, or because they have allowed the boundaries to be broken too many times by family members. Others maintain ties despite having to endure emotional abuse because they have this false idea: family always comes first, no matter what. Unfortunately, it's easy to see this happening from the outside, but it's hard to see this on the inside when you are the one going through the experience with people you love.

One of the most difficult decisions many of us have to make is choosing our future over our family. It's not easy to do, but you must find the courage to do it if you want to live a peaceful and prosperous life.

It does not matter how or why a particular person is a part of your life. The only thing that matters is how he or she affects your ability to function as your best self. As long as you accept and allow other people to project their negative behaviors on you, you're not loving yourself. And it's impossible for you to succeed in life without loving yourself. Self-love is one of the first steps to making the decision to cut unhealthy people out of your life, (regardless of who they may be).

> **Family second? Or a distant third? What exactly am I saying here? I don't want you to misunderstand: I do believe in family first, but only if it's a true family. If there are people in your family holding you back or sabotaging your goals (either purposely or accidentally), that is not a family because they are not being true family *members*. It takes more than a blood type or a roof (or a reunion) to make a family.**

Family is a spirit – a soul; it implies unity. You owe the members of your *unified* family the family-first ethic. But what do you owe the dysfunctional members of a dysfunctional family that allows their dysfunction to bring you down with them? Nothing! A unified family may not have to do the same work you do toward your dreams, but they have to appreciate the work you have to do. So what's the test of a unified family? It is this: if they support your goals and vision. If not, then your family is just a blood type, a roof, or a reunion...and made of saboteurs.

TOXIC RELATIONSHIPS

> "Bad relationships are like a bad investment. No matter how much you put into it you'll never get anything out of it. Find someone that's worth investing in."
>
> ~SONYA PARKER, Author of *Letting Go of Mr. Wrong: A Woman's Guide to Realizing Her Self-worth*

One of the most common denominators among people who never reach their full potential is the existence of a toxic relationship in their life. Almost all of us have experienced a toxic relationship at some point.

These types of relationships aren't just limited to our co-workers, friends, and family members. When it comes to romantic relationships, the deep emotional connection shared by two people can keep them connected for a very long time, even when the effect on one person's life is overwhelmingly negative. Worse, toxic relationships become entangled, thereby creating toxic codependency.

Too often, we make the mistake of holding on to a relationship that we know is damaging to our mental health and overall well-being. Rather than having the courage to walk away when a relationship becomes toxic, we allow ourselves to stay, and in turn, we feel exhausted and drained of energy. Thus, toxic relationships are insidious in that they exhaust us and drain us of the very energy we need to leave them.

When we're completely drained, we burn out. We become oblivious. Worse, we become oblivious to the obvious or unaware of where we are and where we're headed. The self-awareness and alertness I discussed earlier are dead. Instead, we become defined by the very impossibility of leaving. No doubt there are valid reasons to leave, but they just can't get any traction with such a lethargic mindset. We are living within the cliché, *"It is what it is"*. And that's a lie.

Don't believe it. That's the oblivious rationale in full bloom. Nothing is, simply, *what it is*. *What is* = [your dreams + goals + vision] when you make them a top priority in your life. And if your dreams, goals, and vision are absent in your life because you are oblivious, then you – the real you – are incomplete and unfulfilled.

Unfortunately, you cannot (and will never be able to) achieve your dreams when they are sabotaged by entanglements, one of which can become money. Since intimate relationships often involve living together, so many couples commingle their finances, too, as part of the package. That may result in your partner demanding a say (or a veto) in an investment you feel is important to one of your goals to your vision. This raises your frustration to even higher levels. Eventually, you may choose to give up.

"A husband and wife may sleep in the same bed, but they have different dreams."

~CHINESE SAYING

Our goals get pushed to the back burner and our self-esteem drops to all-time lows when we are in these soul-sucking toxic relationships. Similar to toxic family relationships, the more time you spend in a toxic intimate relationship, the more difficult it becomes to leave. You become entangled with emotions that make it extraordinarily challenging to walk away. It won't be lost on anyone that the bonding through expressing affection physically (i.e. sex) adds different entanglements altogether. This only adds to the difficulty in extricating oneself.

When you're in a toxic romantic relationship, it doesn't matter if you're at work, at the gym, or simply walking your dog; wherever you are, the negative emotions and feelings that toxic relationships disgorge occupy all the space available in your brain and force you to feel drained, demotivated, and depressed from the emotional toll these relationships possess. They can – and usually do – make you physically ill.

Your heart hurts, the core of your body hurts; everything hurts from the outrageous amounts of stress that toxic relationships cause. Earlier I had alluded to family first; in toxic relationships, the toxicity puts itself first, no matter what (work, gym, or the dog). How can you do anything else but navigate the toxicity? Forget inner circles. This is a black hole.

Toxic relationships prohibit you from focusing on the tasks that you need to complete to achieve your goals. They keep you from giving your best self to your children. You are constantly on an emotional roller coaster, but it often feels like there are substantially more downs than ups, and – like a roller coaster – the downs are fast while the ups are slow.

You can easily find yourself sucked into a downward spiral fueled by heartache and hurt when you're involved in a toxic romantic relationship. It feels like the weight of the world is always on your shoulders. You don't have enough energy to fight. As a result, you stay and allow a perpetual cycle of endless low self-esteem, despair, and depression to consume you. It's like making minimum payments on a high-interest credit card debt: you'll never climb out.

You don't know when or what the next fight will be; all you know is that it's around the corner because this is the pattern that persists. It's easy for your friends to advise you to walk away. It's so simple in theory. You're not happy, so move on, right? Instead, though, you attempt to convince yourself that this time – this apology, this explanation, this overture – will be different. But you know it won't. And because you don't leave, you unknowingly send your partner the instructions to continue treating you disrespectfully, and so what continues is just that: making your life miserable and disrespecting you.

And if fear of losing money, due the losses inherent in a collapsed financial arrangement, is also holding you back, you're being penny-wise but dollar-foolish.

Dang! Does this sound like someone talking to you who has been involved in a toxic romantic relationship? I hope so because I understand exactly what you're going through. And I know how difficult it can be to walk away, especially if children are involved. I am writing these words to you from my heart. I need you to know that it is not impossible to break free, to stop being a punching bag. It is not impossible to recover from all the damage that has been done. And it's not impossible to find real, lasting, and unconditional love after you heal. It takes a strong person to remain single. But you have to find the strength to do so if you ever want to experience the happiness you know you deserve. You deserve a true family, a unified family.

"The more chances you give someone, the less respect they'll start to have for you. They'll begin to ignore the standards that you've set because they'll know another chance will be given. They're not afraid to lose you because they know you won't walk away. They get comfortable depending on your forgiveness. Never let a person get comfortable disrespecting you."

~UNKNOWN

Let me share a poem with you that may expose my non-masculine side, but I believe it is extremely impactful and relevant to the topic of toxic romantic relationships. It was written by the poet John Mark Green and is geared toward women. However, I believe there are some great takeaways for both genders.

Unstoppable

You tried to cage and contain her, drain her of her worth.

Beat her down to nothing, with relentless fists of words.

Control and de-soul her, but she is too resilient.

Bamboo to your storm, bending but not breaking, now taking back her true form.

Courage building like a tsunami, ready to lay waste to your city of empty promises,

She will rise above your shallow ruins, like the moon in all her fullness; free and beautiful, luminous.

Your hungry night tried to devour her, but she made her own light that darkness could not swallow.

You are hollow and aimless, she has carried life, hidden within; a seedling, growing skyward toward the sun of better things.

Your heart is salty earth; your body is a walking mausoleum.

You fear freedom and love control, mistaking intimidation for true power and captivity for devotion.

Devoid of emotion, you're dead inside.

Wanted to bury her with you, in a graveyard of lies.

But she will rise, she will shine, she will.

She is so much more powerful than you.

Unstoppable.

CONTROL GOVERNS TOXIC RELATIONSHIPS

"Letting go doesn't mean that you don't care about someone anymore. It's just realizing that the only person you really have control over is yourself."

~DEBORAH REBER, *New York Times* bestselling author

You cannot know what a toxic relationship is unless you know what a healthy one is. In a healthy romantic relationship, each person is "all in" for each other; in a toxic relationship, he or she is all in for him or herself. The pathology of the toxic relationship is that one or both people have not learned how to submit fully to their relationship. By that, I don't mean giving up individuality or discarding goals that aren't the other's; I mean being "all in" for the combined entity that makes up the committed couple.

A relationship has its own maturity learning curve, and some of them never mature adequately to sustain the bond. Previously I explained how a family is not really a family unless it is unified in love, spirit, and soul; likewise, an intimate relationship parallels the family, and the mutual assimilation is just as crucial.

Whether mutual assimilation fails in a couple or within an entire family, people who remain unable to detach themselves from toxic relationships constantly feel tired and stressed out, with no energy left for themselves. They have this twisted sense of responsibility as if they have to take on the role of a martyr by burdening the heavy load of trying to please their partner. Another holdback is that as bad as the relationship is, it's a "known" and they are hesitant to jump into the unknown.

Until toxic relationships are eliminated, you will never have the stamina you need to achieve your goals because you will always feel emotionally drained. You'll be too emotionally busy to strive for your goals. And you'll always be making minimum payments as your emotional debt accumulates until you are emotionally bankrupt.

If you spend enough time in a toxic relationship, you will find yourself taking on the same characteristics and habits of the person you are with. Wow. Two martyrs! That can never end well. For that reason, it's critically important for you to choose healthy romantic relationships because your partner's traits will eventually rub off on you. (The trap, of course, is that entanglement often happens before the person's true nature is revealed.)

I've learned that when you spend time with a romantic partner who is negative and cynical, there's a good chance you'll eventually become the same way. Alternatively, if your significant other has a positive, success-oriented mindset, the likelihood of you having the same mindset dramatically increases. Although there's more to it than this, still, you could literally do nothing else but choose a partner who is highly ambitious and motivated, and your odds of success and happiness increase tenfold.

In spite of having full awareness of all the negative consequences, however, many people find themselves continuously stuck in toxic relationships and are seemingly unable to escape. Why? It's because the primary factor that drives toxic relationships is control. It could be the control of money, children, or numerous other things. If one is "all in" only for himself or herself, there will be no giving up control to the other.

The one in control likes things just the way they are and will not see them altered. Even if you can't see it or admit to it, the control factor is definitely there. You are controlled by the other person unknowingly (or even to some extent, knowingly) and so you stay. If control were not a part of it, you would never choose to be involved in a relationship that results in nothing but negativity. Being controlled is a powerful set of bars, regardless of who is holding the key to the lock.

The emotional ties you have developed over time make it exceedingly difficult to end the toxic relationship. Even if you are left drained after dealing with the person, the emotional bond gives them control over you, and you persist with maintaining the relationship out of guilt. You know that the relationship does not benefit you in any way, yet you choose to stick around.

The person on the other end might appear to be helpless and

needy, but they are consciously (or unconsciously) controlling you by using your desire to be a good, helpful human being. That is how you always end up finding yourself at their every beck and call and entering on stage to take part in their drama.

If you're going to escape the clutches of a toxic relationship, you need to be willing to do two things: one, realize that you are currently in a toxic relationship ("*half the problem is seeing the problem*") and two, make the conscious choice to end it despite how difficult it may be. In fact, you can make ending it a goal, which makes sense, since I went to great lengths in Chapter Two to explain how interval goals are needed to get you to your vision. A toxic relationship is a bad habit, and therefore an obstacle to your vision.

If you are always giving, yet receiving next to nothing, that is the key sign of a toxic relationship. If that is you, then you need to gradually start making some changes. Don't let poisonous people continue to control you or make you feel guilty. Guilt is both a weapon for the other person and a profitless emotion for you. Until you put your foot down, your partner will continue to walk all over you, use you, put demands on you, and keep your self-worth at all-time lows. This kind of partner will make you miserable and unproductive for the rest of your life if you allow them to.

"Happiness, we have learned, changes everything, even if you have to lose everything first...It's a kind of happiness that isn't the hard work that people claim relationships should be and isn't made up of thrills or highs and lows. It's a quiet kind of contentment that arises out of a relationship whose participants are at peace with one another."

~RUBY MCCONNELL

Understand that you are in no way, shape, or form responsible for the happiness of other people (other than your children). You are only responsible for your own happiness. You must understand that not everyone in the world wants to be happy, and some people like the attention that unhappiness brings them.

Get to the point where you do not need other people to make you happy. Learn to find happiness by yourself – completely alone with your thoughts – because the person who is not able to make themselves happy will never find true happiness with someone else.

Eliminating a toxic relationship requires tremendous willpower and courage. Above all else, getting out of a toxic relationship requires action. You might be reading this right now and nodding your head in agreement. You might believe that cutting the wrong people out of your life is important, but your accepting that as a given is simply not good enough. You need to commit yourself to the process fully and actually take some concrete action in terminating any toxic relationships you have. **If either of you can't be *all in* to the relationship, you should get yourself *all out*.**

Let me ask you: how committed are you to following through? Is your commitment to becoming the CEO of your life strong enough that you are willing to take action and cut out any (and all) toxic relationships in your life? Don't simply nod your head and say "yes" – let your actions do the talking.

KNOW WHAT YOU WANT AND KNOW WHAT YOU DON'T WANT, BUT ALWAYS KNOW WHAT YOU HAVE

> "As many conventionally unhappy parents did in the 1950s, my parents stayed together for the sake of the children – they divorced after my youngest brother left home for college. I only wish they had known that modeling their dysfunctional relationship was far more damaging to their children than their separation would have been."
>
> ~DR. BRUCE H. LIPTON, *The Honeymoon Effect: The Science of Creating Heaven on Earth*

You need to start acting like a day trader when it comes to the negative and toxic relationships in your life; learn to cut your losses early and sever the emotional investment before you lose your sanity. And if you ever have the opportunity to end a toxic relationship early in the budding stage, do not hesitate to do so.

There is no force greater than love and connection, but be careful if you're the type of person who cannot live without being in a relationship. Self-esteem either makes us or breaks us in life. And if we are unable to break free from a toxic relationship, it will be next to impossible to feel good about ourselves and maintain a positive self-image. Romantic relationships either build self-esteem or destroy it. They either lift us up or tear us down.

Think about yourself five years from now: what advice would the future "you" give yourself about the current relationship you are in? You probably know that now. In five years, one of two future versions of yourself will be looking back: the grateful one who had the strength to walk away from the toxic relationship, or the person still in this toxic relationship and living in a self-imposed cycle of unhappiness.

Your romantic relationship should inspire you. Your significant other should inspire you to develop the best version of yourself so that you can give it to them and your children. If the person you're in a relationship with is not inspiring you, encouraging you, and making you happy, it's possible (and likely) you're in the wrong relationship.

Now is as good a time as any to throw in *Corinthians* 13:4-7:

> [4]*Love is patient, love is kind. It does not envy, it does not boast, it is not proud.*
>
> [5]*It does not dishonor others, it is not self-seeking, it is not easily angered, it keeps no record of wrongs.* [6]*Love does not delight in evil but rejoices with the truth.* [7]*It always protects, always trusts, always hopes, always perseveres.*

And to throw in *McGilvrey* 6:

Love is unity, love is "all in". Love shares the vision, it is the support of the others' goals and dreams. It does not obstruct or hinder, it is not easily discouraged, and it perseveres with resilience. Love delays immediate gratification. Love is a good habit.

Cutting toxic relationships out of your life is vital to your success. And just as important to getting rid of the wrong people is holding on to the right ones. If you are lucky enough to find yourself in a great relationship, make certain you do not take the person for granted. Because I've discovered what we take for granted ends up getting taken.

I love the following saying:

If you treat him/her like you did in the beginning, there won't be an end.

Nurture the positive relationships in your life. And be intentional about taking care of yourself. Always be improving and growing. Never let yourself go. Because if you do, there's a chance your significant other will let you go as well.

The final point I would like to make when it comes to romantic relationships is something I refer to as: *The Social Media Effect*. Facebook, Instagram, Tik Tok, Snapchat, and many other social media platforms have made it increasingly easy to find a false sense of hope, appreciation, and security when our relationships inevitably get hard.

We now have thousands of people at our fingertips we can turn to when our relationships hit the rocks. So after an argument, we pick up our smartphones, swipe through hundreds of flawless faces and check our notifications. Each "like," comment and enamoring inbox message caresses our ego, which allows the natural "feel-good" hormone dopamine to flood our brain. But remember: what you see on a screen is 2-dimensional, and a relationship is

3-dimensional. (Actually 4-dimensional if you consider time.)

When you find the person who loves the "unretouched" you – when there is no filter on your face – and you begin to feel that this person becomes an expendable option, you make the mistake of making the people in your social media feed become your priority. Do not allow the false illusion of a fictional "fairy tale" relationship to cloud your judgment. The reality is: all relationships are hard. That's why I believe fairy tales are the enemy of true love. Don't lose what is real chasing something that is fake.

HOW FRIENDS INFLUENCE THE WAY WE BEHAVE

> "You will never gain anyone's approval by begging for it. When you stand confident in your own worth, respect follows."
>
> ~MANDY HALE

Seeking acceptance from others can (and usually does) have lethal implications. When your desire to fit in is so strong that you're willing to sacrifice your morals – this is the moment when you head in a direction that you will eventually regret. I understand we all have a need to belong. It's human nature to want to connect with others. However, this "need" sabotages us (and our success) when we associate with the wrong people and unconsciously allow their bad habits to rub off on us.

There's no better way to show what happens when you seek acceptance from the wrong people than to look at what happens when you associate with people who use drugs. It's important to see how this chain of events takes place from beginning to end, so I'm going to show you exactly how this kind of transformation unfolds over time. It is insidious, but it happens much faster than you think, and it's also far more likely to occur than you may imagine.

Let's say you have some friends who use drugs, but you refuse to engage in the same behavior they do. At first, you have a strong will and you're able to decide that you will not be like them; after all, they're just friends that you hang out with occasionally. This is the phase where you are objective and level-headed, and find the behavior of using drugs to be completely unacceptable.

The standards for yourself are high; you are a rational-thinking person who will not use drugs simply because your friends are using them. You may think this right now, but I can assure you that the behaviors of the drug users are already rubbing off unconsciously on you.

If you continue to hang out with people who use drugs, over time, you'll gradually begin to tolerate their behavior. Maybe you're not doing what they're doing, but your attitude about their choices and actions begins to subconsciously and subtly change. This is the phase where getting comfortable with – and tolerating – the poor decisions of the drug users takes root in your mind.

Continue hanging out with them even longer, and you will transition from a state of tolerance to acceptance. This phase of acceptance is the tipping point because it's your very last chance to escape before it's too late. After this, if you still choose to continue associating with people who use drugs, you will eventually find yourself participating in the destructive behavior of your friends; you will begin using drugs.

Let me break this concept of *Tolerate, Accept, Participate* down further: when you hang around with people who use drugs, you start out being objective about – and unaccepting of – their behavior. If you keep hanging around them long enough, you begin to subconsciously convince yourself, "Maybe this isn't so bad." You start to become tolerant of the poor behavior. Then, after being around it long enough, you begin to accept their behavior. And with acceptance comes your inevitable participation.

Statistics show that 57 percent of young adults ages 18 to 25 have participated in illegal drug use. And I can almost guarantee the participation of using drugs came from the influence of their friends. Drug dependency is a serious problem in the world. Lives (and families) are ruined every day because of someone's inability to break free from their addiction to drugs.

You think it can't happen to you. You believe you have some form of special protection. (Even though drugs have killed people way smarter than us, much more talented than us, and more careful than us.) You believe you're in complete control. But you're not. And that's why the worst thing in life any of us can ever experience is when we can't recognize what we've allowed ourselves to become, or rather, we can't recognize what part of ourselves we've allowed to grow out of control. It can happen to anyone.

And it happened to me.

Let me share a very uncomfortable story about myself with you. Know that my heart is racing and I'm beginning to tremble from the mere thought of writing these words.

For the first 30 years of my life, I had the belief that drugs were only for losers. I grew up watching my mother and her loser friends use drugs. Almost all of these people were on welfare and were leeches to society. As a result, I had the belief that people who used drugs were failures.

But later in life, when I first became a millionaire, I was blindsided by the wealth coming faster than the wisdom. I started hanging out with extremely successful people (so I thought). Unfortunately, several of these people used drugs. For years, I watched my wealthy friends use drugs but never engaged in the activity. However, my beliefs began to shift. My ability to tolerate this bad behavior slowly allowed the voice in my head to go to work on me. That voice began convincing me to accept that maybe drugs weren't just for losers. Maybe successful people use drugs as well. Maybe they have that special protection, whereas losers don't.

Still, I abstained from using drugs even though many of my friends were regularly using them, especially on the vacations we took together. But eventually, my tolerance, which led to acceptance, evolved into participation.

I'll never forget that one evening in a Miami nightclub where everything changed. The insanely popular and stunning Latin woman I was dating flew to Florida with me on our way to the West Indies. She came back from the bathroom, sat next to me, and said a girl gave her some cocaine in the restroom. She asked if I wanted to do it with her. And at that very moment, I made an *exception* to a rule, and to the way I lived my life for decades. I crossed a line that I could not cross back. This was a very slippery slope because once participation in the *tolerance-acceptance-participation* sequence took over, I continued using cocaine for nearly a year after that.

I even used this disgusting drug during a live TV interview where I was promoting my financial planning firm. The night prior, I had a party at my house, and people were staying up all night using this drug. I tried to go to bed around midnight but could hear how much fun everyone was having in my home, and that made it incredibly difficult to go to sleep. Eventually, I gave in. I stayed up all night partying with everyone. That morning, I had my driver take me to the television station since I had not slept in nearly 35 hours and was in no condition to drive. During the commercial breaks, I would go to the television set's restroom and continue using the drug so I could stay awake.

On my way home from the TV interview, I started rethinking the choices I was making in my life. I became sick to my stomach thinking about the person I had become and began to slip into depression. I could not believe what I had allowed to become the new "normal" in my life. When I arrived home, people were still at my house using the drug. I told everyone to find a ride home and leave as soon as possible. I sat my girlfriend down and told her the truth. I told her that I never used an illegal drug before I started dating her. I also told her I knew the story about someone, "giving her cocaine in the bathroom" was a lie. She said she found it hard to believe that I had never used drugs prior to the time I did with her because she saw so many of my friends using drugs, and that led her to assume I did as well.

Sharing this was not easy, especially since my sons Thomas and Tristan will know their father used drugs. But this may be the greatest gift I could give them, as they will hopefully be able to learn the lesson without paying the price. I am willing to expose a personal story that leaves me naked and extremely vulnerable so I can paint a picture of how this unfolds:

Tolerance, acceptance, and participation.

I am deeply ashamed of this past behavior. For so many years, I was hell-bent on living a drug-free life. But all it took was a mindset shift that set in when I began associating with the wrong crowd.

You might think you have an iron will like I did. You may think you will never cross the line and participate. But know that the odds are stacked against you. If there are people in your life right now who you are tolerating their drug use, you'll eventually find yourself accepting it. And the probability of your participation increases with each passing day.

Let my story be a cautionary tale that warns you of the danger your friends pose in your life. Let this massive mistake I made save you from all the hell and heartache I have endured. Because I honestly believe that the root cause of my failure (a 40-year prison term) stemmed from my inability to think clearly. And my inability to think clearly came from using drugs.

THE SCIENCE BEHIND THE INFLUENCE OF OUR PARENTS AND PEERS

> "I believe in environment more than hereditary in determining your traits."
>
> ~STEVE JOBS (Jobs was adopted at birth)

Famed neurologist and psychologist Sigmund Freud was known for making the determination that who we are as adults is directly linked to our parents and our upbringing. When this school of thought became accepted, a lot of popular psychology placed the blame of our successes or failures as adults on how we were raised as children; therefore, if you had the wrong parents, you were just out of luck.

However, several studies that have taken place after Freud's findings have questioned his theory. One study I found particularly interesting that began in the 1970s was the *Colorado Adoption Project*. Two hundred forty-five women who were about to give their children up for adoption were recruited, along with another 245 women who kept their biological children. Both the children adopted out, and the ones who weren't were followed over time and provided with intelligence and behavioral tests at regular intervals.

The biological children were similar to their parents with respect to behavior and intelligence, which was expected. The researchers expected the adopted children to be similar to their adoptive parents, due to Sigmund Freud's hypothesis that parental influence shapes who we become.

The Colorado Adoption Project attempted to question whether the environment (nurture) has any influence on us compared to our genetics (nature). The parameters of the study, broken down into numerous strata and categories, makes the data difficult to wade through. But the general consensus regarding cognitive ability, however, was this: before age five, the adopted children were indeed similar to their adoptive parents. However, the extraordinary finding was that the adopted children had little in common with their adoptive parents after age five and onward. Their cognitive abilities were about as similar as two random strangers on the street.

In 1995, Dr. Judith Harris released her groundbreaking book, *The Nurture Assumption*, and turned decades of research on its head. When discussing the Colorado Adoption Project, she brought up the conventional wisdom that 50 percent of what determines who we are is based on genetics, and the other 50 percent is determined by our environment. Her breakthrough, however, was that peers were an important and influential part of one's environment and that this environment is far more influenced by one's peers than even one's parents. Therefore, this represented another environmental factor in action. Using a number of studies, Dr. Harris demonstrated that who we are has much more to do with the peers surrounding us and how well we relate to them.

According to Dr. Harris, peer influence was far more influential in shaping a child's personality than their home environment. In a sense, this ushered in a new model: nature vs. nurture vs. *neighbor* (my take on it!).

It makes sense when you think about it: when we're young, we want to be like our moms or dads. But as we grow older, we want to be like our friends. We want to be part of the "cool" group. So we dress just like our peers and seek acceptance from them, rather than dress like our parents and seek acceptance from our parents.

"You're not going out like that, are you?" ~any parent

As children, our peers influence the type of clothes we wear, the hairstyles we choose, the language we use, and ultimately they begin to shape what type of person we become. As we move from childhood to adulthood, the power of peer influence does not decrease. Our peers continue to play a major role in who we become or don't become in life.

If members of your peer group drive Lamborghini's, vacation in the Hamptons, and run multimillion-dollar businesses, it is unlikely that you're driving a decade-old Toyota Camry.

Are you beginning to see just how powerful your friends and their influence on your life truly is? I really hope you are having some thought-provoking moments as you're reading these words because choosing the right people to share your life with will be a significant factor in determining the choices you make. These choices will either bring stress and setbacks, or success and security. It all comes down to who you allow into your life to influence your decisions.

HUMAN SEE, HUMAN DO

> "A mirror reflects a person's face. But what they really are is shown by the kind of friends they choose."
>
> ~COLIN POWELL, Former United States National Security Advisor, and retired four-star general in the United States Army

Have you ever noticed yourself picking up a trait from someone you spend a lot of time with? For example, perhaps a person says a particular word in a certain way or tilts his or her head in a certain direction, and one day, you find yourself doing the exact same thing.

Everyone is aware of the contagious yawn. When we see someone else yawning, we yawn. In fact, you may feel like yawning just from reading the word "yawn". What you might not know is that this phenomenon goes far deeper than the casual yawn. It happens all the time within us, and we aren't even consciously aware of it. When we see people act a certain way, we automatically and subconsciously tend to copy them without even realizing it.

Let me explain some of the science behind us uncontrollably modeling other people's behaviors. In the 1990s, Italian psychobiology professor Vittorio Gallese conducted a study on neurological processes and behaviors using monkeys. In this study, he discovered the existence of "mirror" neurons in the brain.

These neurons fired when monkeys performed an action, but they also fired when the monkeys *heard* or *saw* someone performing that very same action. Later studies confirmed that this behavior also happens in humans. The mirror neurons are ultimately what allows us to understand and mimic the actions of others. They actively fire in a way that makes us sense and imitate others. They are also important in empathy, i.e., the ability to understand and – more importantly – share feelings with others. In fact, one of the theories of autism is that there is a defect in the afflicted person's ability to have empathy, possibly involving the dysfunction of their mirror neurons. They don't "get" the interactions with others that are intuitive in everyone else. Thus, they are often unfairly judged as not having feelings.

What does all of this scientific talk mean? It means our brains see no difference in when we actually perform a habit or an action, versus when we watch someone else engaging in the same habit or doing the same action. This is not unlike the phenomenon of the same neurons firing when thinking about an action and doing an action (as discussed in Chapter One).

The fact that subtle mirroring happens all the time without us realizing it is both fascinating and a bit scary: while mirror neurons create such human interactions as empathy, comfort, and support, their dark side is evident in the herd mentality I discussed previously, and even the mob mentality whose actions are more extreme than those of any individual in that mob.

This begs certain questions. Can mirror neurons be what incites mobs, religions, and even entire nations to act a certain way (e.g. genocide, as in the Hutus and the Tutsis massacre in Africa, the Crusades, or the ethnic cleansing in World War II and thereafter)?

In Harper Lee's book, *To Kill a Mockingbird*, there is a memorable scene in which a mob is bent on a lynching. The main character, Scout Finch, a young girl says hello to one of the mob ringleaders, reminding him that his son is in her grade at school. In doing so, the would-be lyncher's individuality is re-established, and the frenzied mob is fractured, ultimately preventing the lynching from happening. Scout Finch's father, the attorney for the targeted prisoner, says:

"So it took an eight-year-old child to bring 'em to their senses."

This is incorrect. It took re-establishing each mob member's individuality to bring them to their senses.

The psychology of any mob may very well be shared among its members by mirror neurons. Because of our mirror neurons, we think and feel what we see in others. The most insidious example of mirror neurons in action can be seen through a phenomenon called "*emotional contagion*", where one person's emotions can trigger similar or identical emotions in other people. Quite literally, you can "catch" emotions from the people that you spend time with. This is certainly in play in the mob scene I just cited. It is also the principle at work in patriotic speeches, motivational events, and even pep rallies.

Our mirror neurons cause an emotional response within us that makes us mirror what we see other people doing. In fact, numerous studies have shown that if a person has a strong attraction to you, he or she is far more likely to mirror more of your actions. Likewise, if you have a strong attraction to someone else, the likelihood of you modeling him or her is significantly higher.

If we unintentionally mirror the actions of people whom we observe only infrequently, can you imagine how much we mirror the people we spend the most time with? We observe the people closest to us on a repeated basis, and therefore, our chances of mirroring them multiply.

The neurons in our brains will fire regardless of whether we are doing the action, thinking about the action, or simply *watching someone else do the action*. As far as our brain is concerned, in all cases we are *acting*. This should greatly concern you because without even realizing it, you are modeling the behaviors and habits of the people around you. The more neural firings that take place, meaning the more you see someone behave a certain way, the more the associated neural pathways in your brain are strengthened. (*"Neurons that fire together, wire together."*)

You might think you can improve yourself while being surrounded by negative people who engage in negative habits; you can try to choose to act (or not act) on the firing of your mirror neurons. But science suggests that this is far more difficult to do when all of our immediate surroundings are populated with negative people with whom we engage – seeing them and mirroring them in our minds. In other words, you cannot just turn off your mirror neurons; they're on autopilot. It takes mental exertion to disregard them, and that can be difficult. Why?

The reason is the mob forming in your brain, made up of your mirror neurons that reflect the actions of the negative people who are sending them malicious data. You're the only voice that can rise up against this mob, which is hard to do when the reference point is the herd mentality that is present. There won't be a Scout Finch there to pick your mob apart in your mind, so you're on your own.

Continuously seeing others behaving in a negative manner, your brain is likely to have you mimic that behavior as part of the norm of what you yourself should be doing. How does all of this affect the level of success you achieve? If you're watching someone be unproductive or engage in bad behavior, your brain is led to believe that you are participating in the behavior. To make things worse, your brain is telling you it's normal, maybe even a good idea, especially in the *tolerance-acceptance-participation* trap. If you are spending time with people who you don't want to be like, you are also spending that time mentally programming yourself to be just like them. That's the bad news.

The good news is that you can just as easily spend time with positive people who you want to be like and pick up their good habits. This is why it's important that you do some brainstorming, and figure out who the right people are and get them into your life as soon as possible. If science has proven that we unconsciously mirror the behaviors of the people we spend the most time around, then why not actively be around successful people who you want to be like?

Advanced research in the area of mirror neurons has now proven that not only do we unconsciously model people's actions, we also unconsciously model their thoughts. A study in a journal called *PLOS One* that caught my attention was *Mind Messaging: Thoughts Transmitted by Brain-to-Brain Link*. **Mind messaging is an extraordinary breakthrough because it reveals people we spend time with that have limiting beliefs about themselves, can cause us to have limiting beliefs about ourselves (without us even realizing it).** This breakthrough begs you to consider the opposite potential: think of the level you could go to – the heights you would soar to – simply by surrounding yourself with people who have limitless mindsets.

There are so many reasons why it is better to be alone than to be with the wrong people. Mirror neurons are just one of them. Albeit an extremely important one. It's just not worth it to sabotage your success by hanging out with the wrong people. Therefore, if this book convinces you of nothing else other than to change the people you spend your time with, then I will deem it successful – assuming you trade up, that is!

ONLY QUALITY PEOPLE

> "Pay any price to stay in the presence of extraordinary people."
>
> ~MIKE MURDOCK, American Contemporary Christian singer-songwriter, televangelist and pastor

Motivational speaker Les Brown says that you should aim to associate with OQP: *Only Quality People*. What are quality people? Quality people are those who enrich your life. Understand, however, that these people don't have to be the wealthiest, the best-looking, or have extreme intelligence. However, they should be able to add value to you and your life in a measurable way.

This is what the "*O*" means in OQP. It simply adds the absolute that there are to be no negative people allowed! Make yourself an exclusive club. But don't take the OQP principle too far to the point where you become unfairly dismissive. Just to be clear, the primary purpose of the OQP principle is to create mutually beneficial win-win relationships. Protecting yourself from negative relationships happens to be an additional bonus.

If you do not feel enriched by a particular relationship, there's a good chance the other person feels the same way. This does not mean either of you are bad people, but it simply means that right now, the two of you do not have anything of real benefit to offer each other at this stage of life. It's nothing to take personal, nor is it anything for either person to feel bad about. Relationships like this are what I call "stagnant relationships".

Stagnant relationships are those in which you and the other person see each other and do the same thing that you've done together for years, but neither of you is bringing anything new (or something of value) to the table.

These relationships will not only keep you in your present situation, but will also pull you back when you try to grow and move forward. They violate the very premise of OQP, which is – besides searching for and including people who will help you achieve your goals – keeping people out who will hold you back. The falsely comforting familiarity of the person and the things you do together may convince you that they are needed in your life, when in fact it's not a need, but rather something you have just become accustomed to. This is a serious pitfall: your life has become only the things you do together because you have come to see that what is a part of your life equates with what is needed in your life.

These relationships are a bit more challenging to identify when they are neither improving nor degrading your life, so you'll need to pay close attention when identifying any stagnant relationships that may exist in your life. The promise of OQP may not even occur to you because life can be very comfortable when a relationship doesn't change. That's a trap, however, because even though you may be comfortable within a static relationship in which you don't have to deal with any relationship changes, you are ignoring the fact that many things *around* the relationship can change. This will indeed happen, so your peace and tranquility can change when you're least able to deal with it.

You might have that one friend with whom you party hard. Then, you might have that other friend with whom you binge-eat. You might even have another friend where you do nothing but gossip about other people. In every situation, you find yourself behaving in a way that you don't want to behave: in a "low-quality" way. However, you do so out of habit (and clinging to the *known*) because that is what your relationship is dependent upon. And if your relationship is based upon low-quality behavior, then you are supporting this behavior and are not a high-quality person yourself. That is a tough truth to acknowledge.

This truth can be elusive, though. Just like someone can become addicted to drugs or alcohol, a person can also become addicted to someone's company. There is a sense of comfort and camaraderie we feel when we're around old friends, but success does not grow out of comfort. Success grows from feeling uncomfortable and pushing past your comfort zone. The metaphors that come to mind for shattering the comfort bubble are many: the butterfly out of the chrysalis, the baby from the womb, the chick from the egg. These metaphors may be clichéd, but they make my point: it's a bit of a struggle to go beyond the humdrum of knowns into the mayhem of the unknown. However, when you are able to do this, you put yourself in an incredibly powerful position to reach your full potential – and become the CEO of your life.

DREAM STEALERS

> "Life's full of lots of dream-stealers always telling you that you need to do something more sensible. I think it doesn't matter what your dream is, just fight the dream-stealers and hold onto it."
>
> ~BEAR GRYLLS, British former SAS serviceman, and survival instructor

There's an old tale that talks about how people will intentionally (or unintentionally) try to drag you down to their lower level when you aspire to live up to a higher standard. Many people have different names for it, but it's commonly known as the "*crabs in a bucket" syndrome*.

Let me share a short story with you and see if you can identify who the crabs are in your life:

A man was walking on a beach and he noticed a fisherman down the shoreline with a bucket next to him. The man walked up to the fisherman and discovered that the bucket was full of crabs, but he was surprised to see that the fisherman forgot to put a lid on the bucket.

He turned to the fisherman and said, "Why aren't you covering your bucket? Your crabs are going to escape!" The fisherman smiled and said, "Not at all. Crabs are unlike any other creature you'll catch. If a crab is by itself, it would definitely escape. But when other crabs surround it, it has no chance of getting out."

Perplexed, the man asked why having more crabs in the bucket made a difference. "If a crab tries to crawl out of the bucket and escape, the other crabs will latch onto the lone crab and drag it down to the bottom so that it shares the same fate as the rest of them," replied the fisherman.

In life, you're going to meet many crabs, and they will sabotage you in ways you can't even imagine. Some will call you nasty names, say awful things about you to other people, and make you doubt yourself. But the worst ones are those who attempt to stop you from achieving your goals. I have a special name for those people, courtesy of Bear Grylls: *Dream Stealers*.

Dream stealers are people who will not support you or your goals, and instead, will ridicule the vision you have for your life. These people have decided they cannot succeed, therefore they do not want you to succeed either. Dream stealers are always telling you why you can't achieve your dreams, and they will point out all the reasons why your plans won't work. Worse, the more you listen to them, the more these reasons will begin to make sense.

Dream stealers love to complain. They get their energy from bringing your mood down. They will try to find the "bad" in every situation, and every conversation you have with them will leave you feeling hopeless and drained, even if you are having the best day in the world.

You can have an iron will paired with an unshakeable commitment toward your goals, yet if you surround yourself with dream stealers, they can (and will) wear away your resolve until you don't believe in yourself or your dreams anymore.

You might have some resolve leftover, but it won't compare to what you had before you encountered a dream stealer. If someone is constantly telling you that something is impossible or silly, you will eventually start believing them and you will act accordingly.

It's one thing to randomly encounter this type of person in the form of a hater or a critic, but the real danger is having dream stealers in your inner circle. Their negativity will rub off on you. You will start believing all the reasons why you can't succeed and forget about all the reasons why you can.

When you need support during your challenging moments on the journey to success, the dream stealers won't help you and may even work to keep you stuck at the bottom (of the proverbial crab bucket). If you want to rise to the top, you must be aware of the powerful influence that dream stealers have and make every effort to stay as far away from them as possible.

Surround yourself with people who build you up, support you, and support your dreams. With this kind of encouragement from your inner circle, you will always remain in forward motion, and ultimately, you will achieve the success you seek.

You will rarely read about this kind of thing in self-help books, but if you genuinely want to be successful, it's imperative that you associate exclusively with what I call *Dream Supporters*. These are highly motivated, success-oriented people who will see greatness in you (even when you don't see it in yourself). OQP!

You must surround yourself with like-minded people who believe in you and build you up because like-minded people who support you and believe in you are like fertilizer to your dreams. They are a key ingredient to your success and a mandatory requirement if you want to succeed in any area of life.

CONCLUSION: AND NOW, YOUR NEW CIRCLE OF FRIENDS

> "I've had to do a clearing in my life of some people whose energy I realize was not supportive of who I wanted to be in the world. And I recognize the people who are not going to take responsibility for their energy so I have to take responsibility for the energy I allow to be brought into my space."
>
> ~OPRAH WINFREY

In the universe, everything comes in waves, rising and falling, circling, or repeating a dance of serial creation or destruction. Even our brains engage our nerve tracts in waves, which means that there is energy exchanged with everything around us. This is why Professor Moran Cerf from Northwestern University in Illinois believes that we mimic the brainwaves of people we spend the most time with. He likens these brainwaves to the "vibes" we get from others:

> *"The more we study engagement, we see time and again that just being next to certain people actually aligns your brain with them."*

Scientists are beginning to explore how people, constantly emitting and exchanging energy, are interacting with the energies of others. Have you ever heard someone say, "I'm getting good vibes from that person," and understood precisely what they meant? If so, then you've experienced and felt the energy (or aura) being transmitted by someone, whether you consciously knew it or not. The National Institutes of Health calls this our "*Biofield*," which is explained as:

"...an organizing principle for the dynamic information flow that regulates biological function and homeostasis (to) organize biological processes...from the subatomic, atomic, molecular, cellular, organismic, to the interpersonal and cosmic levels."

Translated, in quantum physics, the waves of energy from everything (and everyone) can interact with the waves of energy from everything (and everyone) else. Therefore, "vibes" are real and you are absolutely affected by them. This is one of the primary reasons why you need to make sure that the people you associate with – and certainly, the person with whom you are in a romantic relationship with – are emitting positive vibes and positive energy. If you allow yourself to be around people who transmit negative vibes and negative energy, you'll find yourself in a perpetual cycle of anxiety and adversity.

In the words of Mark Hanna (Matthew McConaughey) in a famous scene from *The Wolf of Wall Street*:

"This is not a tip, my friend. This is a prescription."

Rx: positive people (vibes) medically necessary. Relationships aren't just a "nice-to-have" part of our lives. They are fundamental to our happiness and success. Take a look at any successful person's timeline and you will almost always see a key relationship or two that allowed him or her to live a life of prosperity.

There has been an overwhelming number of published studies validating the benefits positive relationships provide, but in my opinion, none says it better than one of the longest-running studies in history. Researchers from Harvard spent the past century trying to unearth the secret to lifelong happiness in an 81-year-old study known as *The Harvard Study of Adult Development*. Harvard researchers tracked the lives of 724 men and their children since 1931, and what they definitively concluded was that the secret to lifelong happiness and health was: productive and positive relationships.

Having productive and positive relationships comes with a multitude of benefits. In addition to lower stress levels and a greater overall feeling of satisfaction with your life, you will find that it's much easier to maintain a clear and focused mind as you grow older when you have positive people (and vibes) around you. The right relationships have the power to change your perspective on the world, connect you with the resources necessary to reach your full potential, and crush any obstacles that may come your way. Also, productive and positive relationships are fun and they energize your soul!

It's time for you to begin evaluating the current relationships you have in your life. Figure out who empowers you and who encourages you – if there are people who don't do either of these things then remove them from your life or at least distance yourself from them as soon as possible. Once you've decided who gets to stay in your circle and who must go, you're going to need to find replacements to maintain the circle's size and momentum. In order to find new people to spend time with, you're going to have to get yourself out there. The following are just some of the ways you can meet new people and possibly add them to your new inner circle of friends:

- Join online and offline industry-specific groups, both locally and nationally
- Update your LinkedIn profile and connect with new people
- Join a new sports club
- Take up a hobby that is in line with who your future self is going to be
- Contact someone who is living the life you want and invite them to lunch
- Attend trade shows and other business events where you know like-minded people are going to be
- Take a public speaking class
- Take a class related to your goal

- Join Facebook groups
- Join a gym
- Get involved in church activities
- Email authors of books or popular blogs on topics that inspire you and interview them

This list is somewhat generalized, therefore I'd like to encourage you to create your own list of niche-specific or industry-specific forums or gatherings. Get creative and uncover as many ways as possible to add quality people to your inner circle. But please remember that you will not be able to form new associations by staying put in your home. John Adams, in a 1795 letter to his son, wrote, "Move or die, is the language of our maker in the constitution of our bodies." And even though this was advice on general health, it applies figuratively to exercising social opportunities that align with your goals.

While you can certainly reach out to people on the Internet, you will achieve far more success if you are able to meet people face-to-face and establish a genuine human connection. Remember what I stated previously in this chapter: reaching out to people via social media and the Internet is 2-dimensional; meeting face-to-face is 3-dimensional. And we are all 3-D creatures.

Your primary goal, once you develop these new relationships, should be to provide value to others instead of selfishly thinking about what you can gain from the relationship. Implied here is making yourself attractive by applying the Pareto Principle discussed earlier (80 percent listening and only 20 percent talking). A win-win scenario makes for gestalt (more than the sum of its parts, explained previously), and gestalt breeds gestalt. Once you connect with the right people, they will help you connect with other like-minded people.

When you finally have the right connections solidified, make sure you hold on tightly to them. Never forget that the people you spend time with will reflect your beliefs and your expectations. If your beliefs and expectations are changing, and you are working to improve the type of person that you are becoming, inevitably you will need to change the people you surround yourself with. This is a necessary shift that will inevitably have to take place, no matter how hard you try to avoid it. Wherever your associations are headed, you will find yourself going in the same direction.

How do you get the momentum going in your favor before your desired associations show up? How can you increase your chances of connecting with the right people before you've even started looking for them? The secret is to grow yourself, and in the next (and final) chapter of this book, I'm going to show you exactly how to do just that.

EXERCISE NO. 1: TOP FIVE PEOPLE

On the second chart (the first is an example) write down the names of the five people you spend the most time with (look at the call log in your phone if the names don't quickly come to mind). After you do that, I would like you to evaluate how each of these people are doing in terms of their individual success. Rate each person on a scale of 1 to 10 (1 = awful, 10 = exceptional) across the following areas: Income, health, and attitude. That should leave you with three rankings for each person.

NAME	**INCOME**	**HEALTH**	**ATTITUDE**
Jackie	5	6	8
Chris	7	2	5
Juan	3	9	5
Tom	8	7	9
Becky	4	7	3
YOU	**5.4**	**6.2**	**6**

The example above would show that you need to do some work on associating with higher quality people.

Fill This Out Now

NAME	**INCOME**	**HEALTH**	**ATTITUDE**
YOU			

Regularly studying and evaluating ourselves is crucial to ensure we don't get derailed in life. And this exercise which uses Jim Rohn's law of averages is a great way to perform a self-assessment.

Since you are the average of the five people you spend the

most time with, add up the numbers in each column and divide by five. This will tell you where you are (according to Jim Rohn's law of averages). It should leave you with an average ranking for your income, health, and attitude – three final numbers in total.

Let me ask you: do these numbers reflect how you see yourself? Did this just become a mind-bending experience where seeing is believing? It's funny (or sad) that so many people go through life pretending everything is okay even when it's not.

Don't make the mistake of following the wrong people off the track – because that's a surefire way to get derailed. Remember the advice of Tony Gaskins:

> *"Evaluate the people in your life; then promote, demote, or terminate. You're the CEO of your life."*

The truism: *the only way your life is going to get better is if you get better* is an indisputable principle to self-development. And the best (and fastest) way to get better is by changing the people you surround yourself with. Of course, if any of these individuals are family, you might not want to eliminate them from your life completely. Remember, there are circles and...there are *circles*, so you may need to spend less time with them and more time with people who are going to help you reach your full potential.

Furthermore, don't feel bad about making different choices regarding who you're going to spend time with. When you create a better life for yourself, then you can also help your friends and family create better lives for themselves as well.

EXERCISE NO. 2: OQP CHECKLIST

If you meet someone new, but you are unsure if they fit the profile of OQP, ask yourself the following questions to evaluate them:

- How do I feel when I am with this person?
- How do I feel after spending time with this person?

- Is this person living the kind of life I want to live?
- Is this person a negative or a positive force in my life?
- Can I learn from this person?
- Do we engage in positive activities together?
- Does this person encourage or discourage me?

If all the answers are positive, you've got an OQP person in your life. However, if just one of the answers is negative, re-evaluate your relationship with this person. Sometimes you can work things out through honest communication, other times you'll have to choose between your friends and your future. My goal is that you will always choose your future.

In addition to performing this exercise when you meet someone new, it's wise to routinely review this checklist with the people who make up your inner circle. Each year on your birthday is a great time to assess yourself and the direction you're headed. During this self-assessment mentally walk through this list with your current inner circle and then make adjustments if necessary.

Do you want to take this exercise to the next level? Then, right now, this very moment, pull out your cell phone and place a note in your calendar on your birthdate to review your top 5 friends annually. When the notification alerts you (at your convenience since you have all notifications turned off) review the people you communicate with most and grade them on the above scale of 1 to 10. Then, have the discipline to make the necessary adjustments.

EXERCISE NO. 3: JOIN/FORM A MASTERMIND GROUP

All of us need accountability. All of us need to be pushed. And all of us need to understand that asking for help is not a sign of weakness – but rather a sign of wisdom. For these reasons, I'd like to recommend that you join/form a mastermind group.

Mastermind groups are vitally important to your success

because they offer a combination of brainstorming, education, peer accountability, and support in a group setting to strengthen your business and personal skills. Like the Edison-Ford-Firestone *haute gestalt* at their Florida vacation houses in their day, keep in mind that gestalt breeds gestalt.

To join a mastermind group, you can either search for one on the Internet, or you can form your own. The first mastermind I was a part of I formed myself. The way I did it was by writing down the most successful people I knew. I put all their names on a list. Then I contacted them and gave a short explanation for what I was trying to do. More than half of the people I contacted told me no. But eight or nine said yes.

My first mastermind group met once a quarter (now I recommend more than that). We kept it simple. We discussed three things:

1. What was currently working in our business
2. What was not working in our business
3. What resources we found helpful

That's it. Just those three things. For each business owner that had a challenge (what was not working), all the other business owners offered guidance and resources.

At the completion of our meetings, each of us would state a big hairy audacious goal (BHAG) that we would achieve before the next time we met. Then when we met next, we'd tell the members if we achieved our goal or not. The level of peer-pressure and accountability was priceless.

These mastermind meetings encompassed a form of "going back to school" so to speak. However, when you finish this book, going back to school is not going to be alien to you, because I will introduce you to the concept of becoming a lifelong learner in the final chapter. The reason for (and value of) additional schooling is that when most of us left school – a time when work was assigned and these assignments due by a certain date – we took a break;

we relaxed. Our own assignment due dates became determined on our own schedules. This is a setback of sorts because we forgot how to set assignment due dates for our own priorities (if we set them at all).

Without accountability to a third party, accomplishing things in a timely manner becomes sloppy, less efficient – and slower. A mastermind group and its accountability can help you remember the one thing in your schooling that was just as important as your algebra, composition, or history class: the accountability of due dates and deadlines.

Take action now. Start thinking about the most successful people you know. Or if you're struggling to find the kind of people you would like to get advice from, look on the Internet for mastermind groups that have already been formed. Do your due diligence to confirm they're legit – then join a group that best fits your needs.

Another excellent reason for being a part of a mastermind group is the vast amount of networks you can tap into. Believe it or not, the majority of the referrals I receive come from my mastermind groups. And I'll be the first to tell you that you are really fooling yourself if you think you're so good at life that you can achieve success all by yourself. Joining a mastermind group is a key element to your sustained and continuously increasing success.

CHAPTER SEVEN

Lifelong Learning – Constant And Never-Ending Improvement

"I do not think much of a man who is not wiser today than he was yesterday."

~ABRAHAM LINCOLN, 16th president of the United States

"Money only spends once, knowledge can be monetized forever."

~TOM BILYEU, American entrepreneur, co-founder and CEO of Impact Theory

Your internal programming began the moment you were born. You learned gestures and sounds, which eventually became words. You learned that you had to cry sometimes to get attention. You learned that some things you put in your mouth taste good while other things taste awful. You also learned how to crawl, walk, talk, develop ideas, feel emotions, and experience feelings as you grew up.

Each new nugget of knowledge you ingested became part of your internal programming. As you grew older, you learned more about how to behave and what to expect in response to certain events and happenings. If you went to high school and college, you were programmed with specific knowledge about specific subjects, which also helped to fill out the identity you formulated about yourself as you aged.

Unfortunately, for many people, once their formal education was completed, they stopped learning and the repetition of previously learned behaviors took over. These types of people begin to live the same day over and over again, never developing much beyond their initial schooling years. You can see the dullness in the eyes of those who have stopped learning. Those are the eyes of people who have died inside and are only functioning so that they can merely get by in life. For them, the zombie apocalypse came early!

But why have they stopped learning? It's because they have stopped challenging themselves to grow and experience new things. In their mind, they believe they have acquired all the knowledge they need to succeed from their formal education. Also, many feel that doing the minimum is all that is needed in their lives and careers. But sadly, those who *do* the minimum...*get* the minimum.

> **"The person who stops studying merely because he has finished school is forever hopelessly doomed to mediocrity."**
>
> ~NAPOLEON HILL

In the final exercise of the previous chapter, I talked about another obstacle is that when school ends, so do the assignments with deadlines, leaving you to police your own responsibilities. This is a dangerous transition period, fraught with laxity.

It's shocking that millions of adults in today's society have not picked up a book since high school, and yet still wonder why they can't get ahead in life. At the same time, they haven't turned in a mandatory assignment since then, and don't challenge themselves with any form of real accountability. These people fail to realize that they are responsible for their continued education once their formal education is completed, and ultimately hold themselves back from achieving their full potential. Having no deadlines is having no pressure; this is similar to a vacation that never ends, or taking a gap year that spills over into decades.

Why should such a break or gap occur? If you remember from Chapter Four, I told you of a school for children with no recess or field trips, just learning. I explained how the children were happy because they were achieving; and that needing a "break" from it all with recess, otherwise, would imply that learning was drudgery. The point of this school was that if the children see learning as a joy, no break is needed.

The reason so many people take a break from school after their formal years end is because they seem to need it. What does that tell you about our school system? If learning were a joy, there would be no need for a break, and this would foster the attitude of the joys of lifelong learning. Otherwise, their education is over – a wrap.

"The school system is actually fundamentally corrupt. It's anti-education."
~ROBERT KIYOSAKI

When formal education ends, many people believe that it's their employer's responsibility to give them whatever additional guidance, workshops, deadlines, and coaching needed to succeed. In other words, they come out of the formal system thinking any further efforts on their part are no longer required (or expected), and any continuing education would have to come *to* them – if it came at all.

However, if you are serious about prospering in life, you must take charge and make your continued self-education a top priority. Putting your education into your own hands is the only way you can expect to continually develop, change, learn, evolve, and grow as a person.

Whether you like it or not, you are constantly being molded by the hands of education, your environment, and the passage of time. You arrived here with the physical parts of a human, but the "you" (that is you) was programmed right here on Earth. And it's up to you to decide if you're the one molding yourself, or if someone else is going to mold you. I can promise if you let someone else do it, you won't be happy with the end result.

Take a good look in the mirror and seriously ask yourself: am I happy with the person I've grown into? Am I happy with what I've programmed myself to become? Am I in the process of getting better each day?

If you're not the kind of person you want to be yet, don't lose hope! You have been programmed over time to be the way you currently are, but you also have the power to reprogram yourself with new information and become the kind of person you want to become. That's where education comes in. People often equate learning and education to the formal kind you receive through your school years, but that kind of education provides you with just a tiny blip of basic knowledge. It cannot provide you with all of the education you need to become the best possible version of yourself because the school years give you nothing more than conventional wisdom.

Furthermore, the best possible version of yourself comes from new acquisitions of knowledge and clever implementation in new ways that are creative. Creativity is what builds the new you – the best version of yourself you can be. In fact, many successful leaders will tell you that formal education doesn't even scratch the surface of the real knowledge you need to succeed in life.

"Formal education will make you a living; self-education will make you a fortune."

~JIM ROHN

Your education after formal schooling has to have the dynamism that comes from tangential thinking, wandering outside the box, and experimenting by cooking up innovative concepts that turn into something new and unique. These new insights will not happen on their own, but through educational breakthroughs, you can bring them to life.

If you desire to become the CEO of your life and leave your mark on this world, it is a requirement that you make a commitment to become a lifelong student. The book-knowledge part of your life is over; now you must enter the "took" knowledge: **knowledge that has been seized and inserted into your plans.**

You must force yourself to go beyond formal education and find new ways to learn what is necessary for making constant and consistent measurable progress. It is entirely up to you how far you go in life, and that means you can become your own greatest asset or liability.

A neurological aside:

When you watch a baby learning to grasp an object of interest or crawl toward a colorful new toy, what do you see? These are, of course, learning activities that add to their fine motor skills and their cognitive awareness of the environment. But it goes deeper than that. What you are witnessing is *wonder*. You are seeing a sentient being who is confronting a new experience in existence - something that has never been felt, seen, heard, or experienced before. The baby's brain is wide open and all "walk-ins" are welcome. No one (or thing) is turned away.

Neurons are firing and neurons are wiring. Memories are being made. But the driving force is wonder. Wonder is thrilling; wonder is fun. Wonder is mind-blowing. Wonder makes dopamine. Because of this, learning should never be a chore. It is a joy depending on how you look at it.

The take-home message here is: keep wonder in your life, and that means keeping education in your life. For those who don't, it's no wonder why they don't succeed. No wonder (pun intended).

We all know that we can't keep doing the same things over and over, and expect different results. We know this is the Einsteinian definition of insanity. But many of us fail to understand that we are hopelessly doomed to keep doing the exact same things over and over unless we learn new ways to do them. Until this happens, we can't change. If we can't change, we can't create anything new, and ultimately we cannot change our life. It is simply impossible. This is a static condition with no dynamism.

Lifelong growth and personal improvement is the only surefire way to learn the strategies that are necessary to sharpen our skills and achieve success. Previously I called this a dynamism; you need to keep your lifelong self-education dynamic instead of settling for a static knowledge base that never changes (because neither you nor your life will change).

DON'T LET GO OF THE STEERING WHEEL

For too many people, dynamism is dead. They are stuck in dead-end jobs. They're utterly and completely fed up with the results they have in their life. But if you ask them when was the last time they took an intentional step to learn a new skill set that would help them break free from a life they hate, many would scratch their heads and trip over their words. More than likely, they would spend more time making excuses rather than revealing their plans. For such people, there is the additional obstacle of blamelessness. It is never their fault; it is always someone else's fault and their destiny is out of their control.

> *"No point in steering now."* ~Dave Thomas, as Doug McKenzie in the movie, True Brew, when he realized his car going downhill had *faulty brakes.*

Living a life you love is not easy. I'm certain you already know that. But I need you to really grasp that until you make the deliberate decision to learn new things, you will be stuck doing things you probably don't want to do. And more likely than not, you'll be stuck working at a place where you don't want to work and possibly working for someone for whom you don't want to work.

Our work is going to take up a large portion of our lives, and we all have to do what we have to do until we get to do what we *want* to do. Unfortunately, a lot of people never get the opportunity to do what they *want* to do because they are so busy doing what they *have* to do. They are on a self-imposed, never-changing, and static path; a path without any strategy; a path set in acceptance of the status quo. Such people are living paycheck-to-paycheck, and I'm not talking income but meaning, in their lives. They're not even steering; they don't see the point.

For those with a vision, goals, and a strategy to achieve them, when they're living to work instead of working to live, it allows them to have a totally different perspective on life – one of joy and achievement.

If you're in need of changing so you can have a new life – one that you will love living – you're going to need to make the changes that will allow you to create a new "you". And these changes can only be made by learning about new ideas and strategies, and then implementing these techniques so that you can eventually live the life you desire. It all starts with your hunger for knowledge and a thirst for being a lifelong student, but the important thing is that you start...somewhere. You need to start steering the wheel by taking control of your self-education. This is the only way to permanently break free from a life of drudgery and create a life of delight.

THE CONFIDENCE-COMPETENCE LOOP

"Do!"

~ARISTOTLE, Greek philosopher

"Be!"

~FRIEDRICH NIETZSCHE, German philosopher

"Do-be-do-be-do..."

~FRANK SINATRA, Legendary singer

The *confidence-competence loop* is a concept in which competency fuels confidence, which itself fuels further competency. That is, when you feel competent in doing something, you feel confident doing it; competence erodes fear so much that it can be thought of as the opposite of fear. Once engaged, it is like a chicken-and-egg sequence.

But the confidence-competence loop is more like an upward spiral than an actual loop. This implies that it must begin somewhere, at some initial point. It's a beginning for you in that it is something you've never done before, attempted with neither competence nor confidence. So, besides the aforementioned hunger for knowledge and thirsting to be a lifelong student, such a beginning requires something else: courage.

Thus, the confidence-competence loop (more correctly, the confidence-competence *upward spiral*) begins by doing what you fear, and courage is the set of bootstraps by which you lift yourself initially. Rest assured, however, that once it begins, the sky's the limit on where it ends.

Competence begins with *doing* and continues with confidence:

Doing confronts fear →
→ Competence eliminates fear →
→ The elimination of fear boosts confidence →
→ Confidence creates competence → etc.

The more confidence you have, the more competent you become, and on and on the cycle continues...You're doing, being, and doing again. (Cue up Sinatra!)

In psychology, there are four stages of learning which involve psychological states that relate directly to incompetence, competence, consciousness, and unconsciousness. They are depicted as the "*Hierarchy of Competence*" (adapted from Noel Burch):

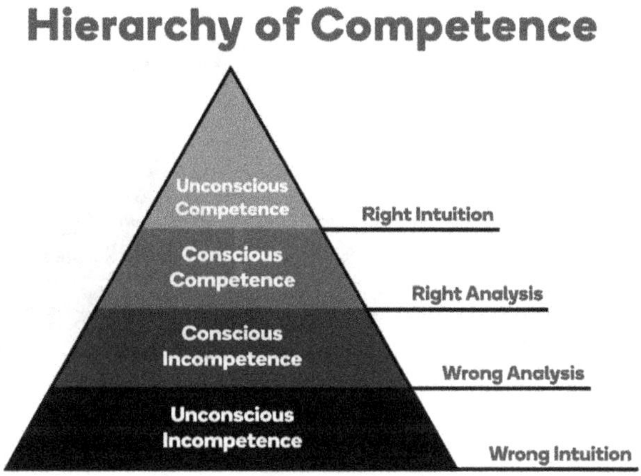

1. Unconscious incompetence
   This is your "clueless" stage: you either don't understand how to do something or you don't even know that you don't know. How long the clueless stage lasts is relative to one's desire to learn, and relies on one's courage to begin by doing – that is, confronting one's fear.

2. Conscious incompetence
   You realize you don't know about something or how to do it, but also realize that a new skill learned toward filling this gap is valuable. Here, mistakes become part of the learning process.
3. Conscious competence
   Now you know about something (or how to do it), you must concentrate and stay focused to pull it off, whether it can be done in steps or in one fell swoop.
4. Unconscious competence
   Here, your conscious has reprogrammed your subconscious to the point where knowledge or a skill becomes intuitive, and can be done without focus and even while multitasking; at this point, you are able to teach what you've learned.

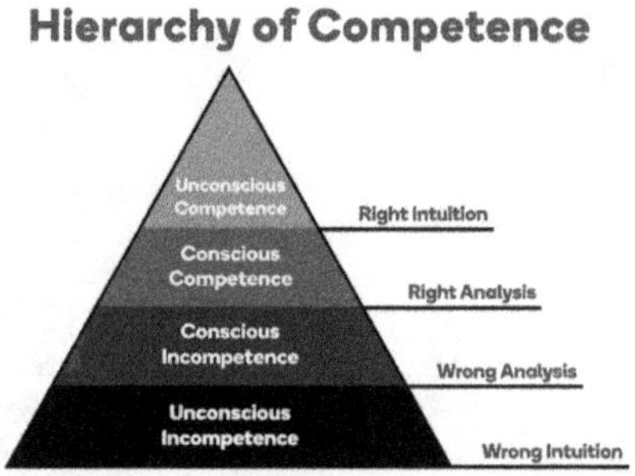

If you think this is reminiscent of Maslow's Hierarchy of Needs I discussed in Chapter One, you're clever but mistaken. Maslow's pyramid involves you as an individual, providing needs in sequence: body and physiology, safety, belonging, self-esteem, and self-actualization. Burch's Hierarchy of Competence pyramid, on the other hand, begins fairly high on Maslow's pyramid, with all four stages located in the two highest tiers – self-esteem and self-actualization. The similarity, while not geometrically relative, are functionally relative once you get to the top. Unconscious competence is self-actualization by achieving one's full potential, be it in skills you have or life in general.

THE LAW OF USE

> "Knowledge, properly applied and acted upon, is the key to lifting the veil and opening your eyes to the opportunity that is in front of you. The more knowledge you have about a subject, the better equipped you become to link your daily experiences to new opportunity."
>
> ~ZIG ZIGLAR

One particular insight that shows how lifelong learning is essential to being successful is the *Law of Use*. The Law of Use fuels the confidence-competence loop and it states that if you possess something, you must use it or you will lose it. If you do not use the gifts you have been given, it's the same as not having them at all, and eventually, you will lose them as time passes.

One of the best ways to show the Law of Use in action is through an ancient parable that was told in the Bible about a master and his three servants (*Matthew* 25:14-30):

> A master was leaving on a long journey and left his servants with some very simple instructions: *"I have these talents that I would like the three of you to take care of while I'm gone. When I return, we will review your work and see how well each of you did."*

Back in those days, a *talent* was a specific measure of silver equivalent to about fifteen years' worth of daily wages. So it was a considerable amount of money. While this parable is about faithfulness, to see how faithful each servant was as a dutiful steward of his given responsibilities, it is also a wonderful example of how inaction out of fear is never profitable.

The master gave five talents to the first servant, two to the second servant, and just one to the third servant.

When the master returned, he met with his three servants and asked each of them how well they fared with the talents they were given.

The first servant said, *"I was able to double my five talents, giving me a total of ten talents."* The master was pleased to hear this.

The second servant said, *"Likewise, I was able to double my two talents, and now there are four."* The master was also happy to hear this.

The similar results from both servants indicate that they were able to put what had been given to work, and over time their talents gradually grew. Thus, the first two servants were faithful to their responsibilities to their master, acting as prudent stewards.

The third servant said, *"I did something different. I took my one talent and was very careful with it because you are a harsh man and I was afraid of what would happen if I lost it. So I wrapped it up and buried it in a hole where nobody would be able to see it or steal it. And since you came back today, I dug it up, and now it's here, safe and sound."* Although this third servant felt pleased with himself, the master became furious when he heard his report.

The third servant was driven by fear, the same thing that stops many of us from venturing forward (doing something for the first time, building competence, and thereby building confidence). As I discussed in Chapter Three, fear of failure prevents us from taking the necessary risks that are crucial for our personal growth. In this case, the servant's fear of displeasing his master and incurring his wrath was not worth risking the talent he was given. On the surface, he might have been doing the safest thing, but it was the safest thing for himself; deeper down was a failure in not doing what was best for his given responsibilities. He was entrusted as a stand-in for his master but failed.

It was naïve for the third servant to think that keeping his talent hidden was the best way to preserve it and assure his master that he was trustworthy. However, his master, outraged, didn't see the servant's strategy as cautious, but instead saw it as wasteful; it wasted an opportunity the master himself entrusted to his servant to capitalize on during his absence. After discovering the third servant did not put his talent to work, the master took it away and immediately gave it to the first servant.

The third servant's waste of his talent, out of fear, resulted in accomplishing nothing. The first servant, on the other hand, was wise enough to put his talents to work. He used them diligently and allowed his talents to grow in number. He proved his ability to put his talents to good use, and for that reason, he was given the extra talent. Likewise, the second servant put his talents to use and profited from his wise choice.

The takeaway from this parable correlates with the Law of Use: what you have and use will multiply, and what you don't use will disappear. The person who uses his or her talents and resources to the fullest will end up having more, and the person who doesn't will end up having less or none at all. Remember the John Adams quote, *"Move or die..."* in Chapter Six, I used it in the context of making the best use of opportunities, but here it also serves as an indictment against doing nothing with your resources.

The word "talent" as a Biblical monetary unit of value, and the modern definition – meaning one's abilities – is an ironic coincidence, because one's abilities and the monetary rewards that come from them figure prominently in the Law of Use: it's one of the primary reasons why the rich get richer and the poor get poorer.

While this story is a parable that teaches about faithful verses unfaithful service in getting one's final reward (Heaven), for our purpose we can seize a different moral by the way it makes unmistakable character assessments of those who use their resources and those who don't.

We are all gifted with "talents"; they can range from the ability to sing to the ability to teach. They can also range from the ability to understand numbers to the ability to write beautiful poems. You have many gifts, but you must discover them, and you absolutely must use them. If you don't discover your gifts and use them, you will lose them. It's that simple. Whether it's your ability to paint a picture, craft a poem, or lead a business, the Law of Use is a parable in and of itself (just like the bonds of neurons which weaken over time when not reinforced). Heed it, or it becomes the *Law of Disuse*.

All of us are given a remarkable amount of skills that we can use to thrive in the game of life. If you are not succeeding, it is simply because you have not uncovered and/or put to use the skills you have been blessed with. You are not practicing the Law of Use.

The more knowledge you gain, the better you will understand your gifts and the more you can offer the world. However, you must continually recall and apply this knowledge. Because as the saying goes, *"If you don't use it, you lose it."*

In that sense, the Law of Use certainly applies to your brain. You must constantly challenge your brain and force it to grow, or it will atrophy like any other unused body part or muscle. While neurons that fire together, wire together, those synapses are only reinforced by re-synapsing; otherwise, those bonds can loosen and even separate, resulting in loss.

At any time, you are either gaining knowledge or losing knowledge; there is never a middle ground. If you're not creating, you're disintegrating, and it can be argued that something even uglier is happening: you're rotting. Thus, you're either growing or dying. ("*Move or die!*") This is how your brain differs from a computer. On a computer, if there are no changes at all – neither gains nor losses of data – it can continue to execute its designated tasks successfully.

Your brain, however, is a breeder reactor, and the more it "flexes," the more it "lifts" or, alternatively, the less it works, the less it's able to work. That's why one of the greatest dangers you face in life is your mind growing soft. Your mind works just like a muscle and must be exercised daily if you want it to continually grow and remain strong.

How many times have you witnessed a person who retires from a job he or she loved, develops an accelerated loss of cognition and even suffers a premature death? This is a familiar tragedy that is bursting with caution. The idea of retirement has changed over time. For your father, it meant a well-earned period of rest; today, it all too often serves as an excuse for someone to become idle at the mercy of the Law of Use.

Idleness (balking in the face of Newton's first law: *the law of inertia*) is a poor investment because – in a sense – you're the thing being poorly invested. Benjamin Franklin, one of America's first millionaires whose face is on the hundred-dollar bill, was known for saying, "An investment in yourself pays the best interest." It's crucial that you make it a priority to invest in yourself. Why? Because you are your most appreciable asset. Don't bury yourself in the ground; no one can rob you but yourself.

THE SCIENCE OF LEARNING

> "You take the blue pill – the story ends, you wake up in your bed and believe whatever you want to believe. You take the red pill – you stay in Wonderland, and I show you how deep the rabbit hole goes. Remember: all I'm offering is the truth. Nothing more."
>
> ~LAURENCE FISHBURNE as Morpheus, *The Matrix*

The Law of Use may be the simplest concept to understand in this book. It is also the most frequently used concept, so it's fitting that I feature it in some detail in this final chapter. In fact, the Law of Use is an undercurrent in all of the chapters:

- in Chapter One to start your chain reaction that culminates into a vision for your future;
- in Chapter Two to explain how achieving each goal adds fuel toward conquering the next goal;
- in Chapter Three to get you to take action and overcome your fears;
- in Chapter Four to get you use to gaining momentum by delaying gratification;
- in Chapter Five to warn you of the insidious nature of accumulating bad habits and the feasibility of instilling good habits; and
- in Chapter Six to explain the power of using the right associations to get more instead of staying put and getting less.

These are all nuances of the same thing:

Do more to get more; do less to get less.

The loop of do, be, do, be, do...continues and builds upon itself, because what we don't use becomes weak; what we do use, however, grows strong. Therefore, logic would lead us to believe that if we read the books, attend the classes, and watch or listen to the educational programs, we're strengthening our brains and developing our skills – correct?

It takes more than a book or a seminar to obtain [and retain] knowledge.

More than likely this is not the first personal development book you've read. So, why are you not living the life of your dreams?

You've probably read the books. You've more than likely recited the affirmations. You've consumed the content. Or have you?

What if I told you we've been lied to about *how* we learn. What if learning new things and gaining new knowledge has little to do with taking a class or reading a book to acquire the skills we seek? Did I just lose you? Are you thinking I've watched too many science fiction movies like *The Matrix*? Well, what if I told you that *The Matrix* was not a sci-fi movie, but a real-life documentary?

Okay, now either I've definitely got your attention, or I've totally lost you. Either way, seriously consider the idea I am proposing. You've consumed a multitude of personal development content, yet you're still searching for the "missing link," correct?

Remember the definition of insanity? Doing the same thing over and expecting different results, right? Ask yourself: is reading (or listening to) yet another self-help book really going to do the trick when the last five, ten, or twenty-five didn't? Before I reveal why you aren't living your dream life (even though you've consumed the content), let me take a step back. Let's look at the science behind how we learn.

Reported in the journal *Neuron*, MIT researchers have demonstrated that different types of learning correspond with different brainwave frequencies. And according to Earl K. Miller, a Picower Professor of Neuroscience at the Picower Institute for Learning and Memory and the Department of Brain and Cognitive Sciences:

> *"When neurons fire, they produce electrical signals that combine to form brain waves that oscillate at different frequencies."*

Through special equipment such as an electroencephalogram (EEG), brain waves can be detected and recorded. These sophisticated machines show that different parts of our brains create different types of waves, they also show that our brainwaves change over time, from birth to maturity:

In the initial part of our lives, our brain is operating at a very low frequency (3 to 7 Hz, or cycles per second) and downloading everything it sees into our subconscious mind. The scientific terms for these early-learning frequencies are the *Delta* (first two years) and *Theta* (years two through six) waves. These names are given to the two predominant types of brain waves produced in implicit learning; that is, learning that is subconscious, like the "muscle memory" I've mentioned several times throughout this book. Thus, for these initial years, our subconscious is basically a sponge, a receiver of sort and during this time we do not yet have the appropriate consciousness to create new things. We only have the capacity to absorb information.

On the other hand, explicit learning (conscious learning) resonates waves at different frequencies (*alpha-2/beta* waves, at 10 to 30 Hz), which Dr. Miller said:

> *"...showed us that there are different mechanisms at play during explicit versus implicit learning."*

Even more remarkable is that as explicit learning succeeds, the alpha-2/beta waves decrease and the delta-theta waves (implicit learning wave signatures) increase. This means that as we repeat learned tasks and they become automatic ("muscle memory"), they are reinforced as implicit learning.

The first six years of our lives is an extraordinary time of super-learning (subconscious learning). Remember, if you will, my take on the phenomenon of wonder, which is the incentive that seems to kindle this period of learning. Studies have shown that children can learn three languages between the ages of two and six. In our early years, we are like a sponge soaking up every ounce of information around us. We are learning everything possible, from how to cry when we're hungry to how to tie our shoes.

Much of this learning, or rather I should say programming since everything is being immediately downloaded into our subconscious comes from our parents during the first six to seven years of our lives. (There is an innate sense of "the way things are" that we get from immersion in "the things that are".) The way our parents respond to us, they tell us if something is good or bad, acceptable or unacceptable, praiseworthy or disappointing – and in turn, we *learn* what is acceptable and what is not.

Most of the time, we read this by looking at our parents' eyes, but it can just as easily be the raising of an eyebrow or the turn of a lip. Studies have shown that babies can recognize their parents' faces within a few days of being born. So if our parents cringe when we're about to put our hand in the dog food bowl, we know that is bad. The same goes for when we get too close to the street. Our parents give us this look, and that's all it takes for us to turn around. If we are a toddler playing in the backyard and a snake slithers up next to us, more than likely our mother screams, "Snake!" and rushes us away with a terrified look on her face. We instantly download the program that "snakes are bad", thereby installing a subconscious fear of snakes into our adult lives.

Unless you're a herpetologist, having a fear of snakes could certainly have its benefits. But what happens when our parents or caregivers program us with the wrong information during these first few crucial years of our lives? Think about this: children are not born afraid of the dark. They spend the first nine months of their lives in the dark. Babies are born with the ability to swim, so why is it when you try to take a three-year-old into the pool, he clings to you for dear life? This all comes down to programming. If your parents always told you to eat all your food – it's possible you were being programmed with a mindset of lack (or scarcity) of resources.

We now know both scientifically and biologically that the first six years of our lives are the programming stages. It is *implicit* learning (as opposed to *explicit* learning). We know that these years shape much of how our lives unfold. But what's fascinating is that philosophers knew this over 400 years ago. That's why Aristotle said, "Give me a child until he is seven, and I will show you the man." And John Watson, one of the founding fathers of the school of psychology called *behaviorism*, stated:

> *"Give me a child at birth from any background and let me control the total environment in which he is raised, and I will turn him into anything I wish him to be, whether doctor or lawyer, beggar or thief."*

Scientifically speaking, this is all much more complicated than simply the debate on nature (genetics) versus nurture (upbringing). It brings into question many factors that debunk and overturned previous scholarly research.

A genetic aside:

Traditionally, it was assumed that a child inherited the total of his/her nature from the relative balance between maternal and paternal DNA contributions at conception, and the mix thereof – and that was that!

Enter *epigenetics*.

It turns out that with inheritance, it's true the DNA contributions are not altered – just portioned from the allotted maternal and paternal "donations" to the brand new fertilized egg. But it has also come to our attention that this unaltered DNA is not all that unaltered. It's unsettling for scientists to think that anything in the human body is worthless, so geneticists were delighted when what was originally thought of as "junk" DNA – extra pieces that seemed to serve no function – turned out to be, definitely, *non*-junk, and quite functional indeed.

These "epigenes" have been identified as the switches that turn genes on and off; "toggle-switches" (switched on or off) genes that are then delivered to the new life and the lifetime that lies ahead for the fertilized egg. This explains how, in simpler animals (so far, anyway), parents can learn a behavior, and that learned behavior can be inherited to their offspring. Of course, we're talking about non-complex organisms here, but the point is made. Scientists can sigh a breath of relief, knowing that it still is a valid truism that nothing in biology should be considered worthless or wasted.

At human scales, then, the DNA that makes us up is inherited with certain genes switched off or on, which may leave the gene structure unaltered, but leaves the gene function variable. Like HTML (hypertext markup language) can determine how a word processor formats text when it's displayed on a screen, all in the background, it appears as if there is a *hyper-gene markup language* that determines many of our little quirks. Sure, they're fine-tuned by the inherited master genetic plan, but how they're expressed begins at conception (nature) as our inherited epigenetics, which are then manipulated (to varying degrees) by our environment (nurture).

This ultimately ends up as an automatic decision-making process in a flowsheet similar to computer language, along the *IF* and *IF NOT, THEN*...lines, just like in programming code itself.

So the million-dollar question you need to ask is: what are those programs you were given prior to age seven (that first impact from the "school of hard knocks," albeit attenuated by genetics and epigenetics) that produced the person you are today? Whether your programming arrived into your fertilized egg unaltered, epigenetically altered, or was nature-driven or nurture-driven, they're still programs that make you, *you*. You are a walking, talking, loving, and living set of instructions, following those instructions within your programming.

Do you remember what programs you received when you were two years old? Obviously, you don't, because science proves you weren't consciously there. You were merely viewing the world like someone who is looking through a window in observation mode only – and not actually participating. This is why discovering the unhealthy programs that have been downloaded into your subconscious mind is the area that needs to be addressed before you can ever experience real, lasting, success.

Subconscious is below our conscious. This means that we behave in a certain way without even realizing it. And leading psychologists believe 70 percent (or more) of our subconscious minds are filled with limiting, self-sabotaging, and disempowering programs. This is the reason why you can read all the self-help books you want, or attend all the self-improvement seminars in the world, and yet still be unsuccessful.

How do you uncover what disempowering programs were downloaded during the Delta and Theta stages of your life, during your time of immersive, and implicit super-learning? It's actually quite simple. Fortunately, you don't have to travel in your mind back in time and try to figure out what those programs were. Because even if you took that approach, all you would do is reinforce them. So trying to go back and figure out what unhealthy programs were downloaded is counterintuitive.

The simplest way to discover what programs were downloaded into your subconscious is to closely examine your *current* life (this should be somewhat reminiscent of the habits evaluation I had you do in Chapter Five – yes there's a method to my madness). What are the things that come easy to you? For anything and everything in your life that currently comes easy, there is a program in your subconscious mind that is bringing those things to you.

Conversely, all the things in your life that you're struggling with, anything that you put a lot of effort into but just aren't able to get the results you want – these are things associated with programs embedded in your subconscious that do not support the outcome your conscious mind desires. You then struggle by trying to unwire the heavily soldered wiring from your implicit learning (your delta/theta days) with the explicit learning that came after.

The implicit learning is the 800-pound gorilla; the explicit learning is Bambi. You're trying to overpower the gorilla with a little deer; you're trying to override that implicit program with the wee percentage of your brain that is your explicit programming. And frankly, you haven't got a chance.

Let me share a story with you to help drive home this important point I'm trying to make. Many years ago, I bought a record for a turntable that had a scratch on it. It made the needle jump back one groove such that when it hit that spot, the same few seconds of the song repeated over and over. Unfortunately, this happened enough to burn this loop into my brain as an "earworm", sometimes known as a "brain worm" or "*stuck music syndrome*". Since then, I have moved on from records to cassettes, to CDs, to streaming, and even today, when that one spot comes on in that song; I hear the repeated sequence – or at least it comes to mind. It's like I'll never be able to *unhear* it.

Like the skipping record weaving a sound bite into our implicit learning, when a conscious event interweaves into your subconscious, explicit learning becomes implicit learning. Unless explicit learning – like the dozens of self-help books you may have read in the past – becomes implicit, the content and strategies revealed just won't stick as strongly. This is why you can go read Dr. Gary Chapman's book, *The 5 Love Languages,* and still be miserable in your relationship. You can read Robert Kiyosaki's book, *Rich Dad Poor Dad,* and still be broke. You can watch one YouTube video after another on how to get chiseled rock-solid abs, but still be overweight.

> *"I don't care how much knowledge is in your head. If that knowledge doesn't go into your subconscious, your life will stay exactly the same as it was,"* says research scientist Dr. Bruce Lipton.
>
> *"You could be the brightest, smartest academic, and I say fine, but did you change your life, and the answer is no. You have to take the knowledge that you were walking within your conscious mind and put that knowledge into your subconscious programming."*

Many self-help books produce limited or temporary results because they communicate only with the conscious mind. These unsuccessful techniques and principles rely purely on insights, reason, willpower, positive thinking, and motivation. Conscious insight-based training teaches us what to do to be more effective in our lives. But it does not give us the necessary mind management tools to accomplish that goal. The missing piece is the ability to align our subconscious beliefs with our conscious goals in order to create effective, sustainable change. We need to learn how to *unhear* the scratched record.

For too long, there's been the belief that the subconscious mind and the conscious mind are one and the same. The people who falsely believe this think that if they educate their conscious mind, the subconscious mind will follow suit. But that's just not the case. This has been one of the largest problems in learning. We educate our conscious mind and become very intelligent, but our life doesn't change. Why? Because we were not able to change or alter the main part of our brain that makes us tick, the subconscious.

U.S. News & World Report published an article titled, *The Secret Mind: How Your Unconscious Really Shapes Your Decisions*. From their article:

"According to cognitive neuroscientists, we are conscious of only about 5% of our cognitive activities, so most of our decisions, actions, emotions, and behavior depends on the 95% of brain activity that goes beyond our conscious awareness."

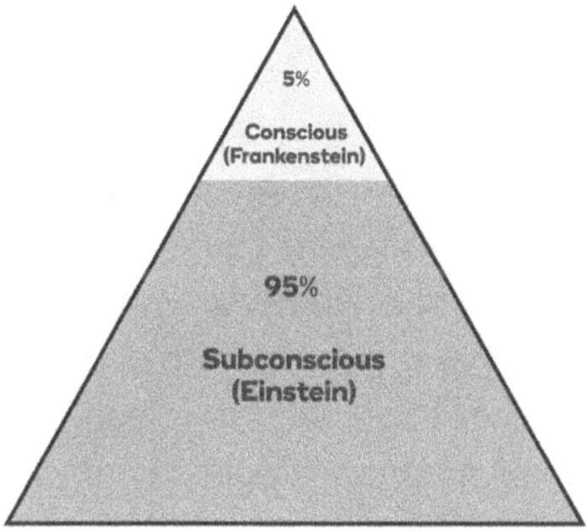

If we ever expect to create sustainable and permanent change in our lives, we must shift our focus from training the Frankenstein part of our brain (the proverbial 5 percent sewn together from the bits and pieces of our explicit learning) and focus on the Einstein part (the proverbial 95 percent that is our innate, subconscious mind.) Otherwise, all we're doing is wearing ourselves out and getting nowhere.

Further scientific research proves that our subconscious mind (the proverbial 95 percent) is one million times more powerful than our conscious mind (the proverbial 5 percent). Our conscious mind processes at 40 bits per second and our subconscious mind processes at 40,000,000 bits per second. Although computers and brains are apples and oranges, these estimates are based on measurements involving processing by the human retina, in which information strikes the back of the eye with data, that is then organized for transmission through the optic nerve. As such, actual numerical quantitative measurements of the conscious and subconscious brain are not completely possible, but they are able to be qualitatively compared. And what we know at this point is that our subconscious is significantly more powerful, faster, more efficient – and able to run circles around – our conscious mind.

Thus, in our formal learning, we've been trained to use our

conscious mind instead of our more robust subconscious mind. Consequently, when you are unable to achieve your goals, it's because you've been "training" the wrong part of your brain – the clumsier, slower, less voluminous, and superficial part of your mind to achieve them. However, the foundation of your subconscious mind continues unaltered.

A marketing aside:

To illustrate how false conditioning is so tenacious, consider an infamous mind trick from marketers who figured out the importance of the subconscious mind a long time ago. When watching a commercial that's selling shampoo, what do these savvy marketers show you? Do they show you how clean your hair will get, or how quickly their shampoo will wash out of your hair? Not a chance. Instead, they show you an attractive man singing in the shower while he washes his full head of hair. Then, his beautiful wife walks into the bathroom singing as well. Next, their perfect child is sitting down having breakfast after he got himself out of bed and dressed himself. Lastly, this beautiful family walks out of the house together, hand-in-hand. Then at the very end, they flash the bottle of shampoo on the screen.

They were not selling to your conscious mind how effective their shampoo is. Rather, they were romancing your subconscious mind and telling you this: if you do not feel like singing in the shower in the morning, if your spouse does not come in singing in the bathroom or you don't have a spouse, if you have to drag your kid out of bed in the morning and force him to eat breakfast or you don't have a child, then the real problem is that you're using the wrong brand of shampoo. Who knew, right?

While the percentages may be questioned by scientists as not being quantitatively exact, this simplification still makes the point: you are for the most part running on autopilot, living life on your muscle memory – sleepwalking through your implicit-learning programming. Are you beginning to see the problem? The 5 percent part of our brain cited a few paragraphs ago – that is, the conscious part – is what we are spending our time attempting to train. We are trying to train our minds so that our alpha-2/beta waves (explicit learning) can be recalled at will when what we really should be doing is trying to train our minds such that our delta/theta waves (implicit learning waves) are changed. This is kind of like a bodybuilder only using light weights that don't stimulate muscle or expand size, then getting on stage and expecting to win a gold medal and become Mr. Olympia. Or, the gorilla versus Bambi.

As this chapter continues, I will frequently refer to the 5 percent of conscious brain activity complementing the 95 percent of subconscious brain activity. I realize these numbers are presented as if they are empirical, verified values, and whether that's accurate or not is unimportant; what's important is that when I'm talking about our subconscious (as I will refer to it as "95 percent") and our conscious (as I will refer to it as "5 percent"), you understand it's a relative expression in which your subconscious brain dwarfs your conscious brain in both its neuronal networks and sheer processing power.

Such a dominance makes perfect sense because if you think about the moment we encounter a threat, the conscious part of our brain shuts off and the subconscious takes over. Immediately, our subconscious mind rushes blood to our arms and legs, diverting it from other organs so we can go into "flight or fight" mode when we encounter danger. And we have been doing this since the beginning of time.

It's crucial you understand the vast difference between your conscious and subconscious mind because if you continue training the less effective part of your brain, you'll never get the results you want. This is why I believe we have been lied to when we were told that if we read the books and get the information we'll be successful. Nothing could be further from the truth. And the evidence is in the results – or rather, lack thereof – that we end up with after we consume the content.

What you are reading right now is not theory. It's fact. This is all scientifically proven by many, many neuroscientists. And as you can tell, I'm insanely passionate about shining a bright light on this dark area of education. They say necessity is the mother of invention. And I believe it's time we invent a new way to learn. Agree?

Let me circle back around and state that I do not believe *The Matrix* is a documentary. (Yes, Elvis is really dead and we actually did land on the Moon. There is a chance, according to Elon Musk however, the *simulation hypothesis* is true.) I was just using that as a pattern interrupt because I was trying to get you thinking. But I do believe an injustice is being done in the way we are taught to learn. The proof is all around us. All you have to do is take a close look at anyone, and you'll notice they are running on programs all day long. They are not consciously aware of their choices. Instead, their subconscious – their faster and more efficient brain – is governing their emotions, thoughts, decisions, and actions.

Okay, enough about the education problem. Let's shift our attention and focus on the solution. Let's see how we can reprogram our subconscious so we can set ourselves up for continued and sustainable success.

STRONG EMOTIONS HELP REPROGRAM OUR SUBCONSCIOUS

> "Whatever we plant in our subconscious mind and nourish with repetition and emotion will one day become a reality."
>
> ~EARL NIGHTINGALE, Author of *The Strangest Secret: How To Achieve Greater Success & Happiness*

What did you eat for dinner three nights ago? You probably don't remember. And if you do, you had to think about it. Let me ask you another question: where were you on 9-11 when the airplanes hit the Twin Towers in New York City? More than likely, without giving it much thought, you know exactly where you were and what you were doing. (Or Pearl Harbor the generation before, or the sinking of the Lusitania the generation before that.) Why? Because of the emotional connection. March 9th and May 27th are dates deeply ingrained in my mind. Did something happen in my life prior to age seven that burned those dates into my subconscious? Nope. March 9th is my son Tom's birthday, and May 27th is my son Tristan's birthday. I have deep emotional ties to those dates.

Strong emotions help shape our subconscious. They quickly and easily move into the 95 percent part of our mind. The stronger the emotion, the more it buries itself in our brain. These emotions can be both positive (our children's birthdays) or negative (9-11). When something we deem important happens in our lives, we file it in a place where we can quickly access it at any time we choose. Sometimes this works to our advantage, and other times to our disadvantage.

A neurological aside:

> Memory and emotion are intimately tied together, and at night when you sleep is when the daily housekeeping is done. During sleep, the day's short-term memories are organized, sorted, and assigned importance – the important ones assigned to long-term memory. This is done by the hippocampus of the limbic system. Also, in the limbic system is the amygdala, which is an important area for addressing emotions. This is why sleep is important, and the concept of "sleep hygiene", or a healthy sleep routine, is crucial to be at our mental best.

If you step over a bug to spare it, but when you look up someone runs up to you and slugs you in your jaw, twenty years later the bug is long forgotten, but not the jerk who hit you. If you see him on the street, you'll react. Why? The reason is that there was not only pain (and probably a doctor's bill) associated with the attack, but anger as well. Emotions run memories deeper into our mind.

FALL IN LOVE WITH YOUR NEW LIFE

"Pay attention, don't let life go by you. Fall in love with the back of your cereal box."

~JERRY SEINFELD, American comedian, actor, writer, producer, and director

"Life moves pretty fast. If you don't stop and look around once in a while, you could miss it."

~MATTHEW BRODERICK, as Ferris Bueller, in *Ferris Bueller's Day Off*

One of the best ways our emotions can work in our favor is when we fall in love. Falling in love is such a powerful emotion that it assists us in breaking free from the automatic programs we unconsciously run on all day long, (that 95 percent purported to run our lives). If you were to record your life the day *before* falling in love, you would see it only took you five minutes to get dressed (your subconscious programming and muscle memory dressed you). You'd see yourself finishing your dinner in ten minutes (you used your subconscious programming to eat), then watch yourself wipe your chin with your sleeve.

But the day you fall in love, everything changes. Everything. If you record yourself that day, you will notice it took nearly an hour for you to decide what you're going to wear (your conscious mind is now dressing you). When you met that special someone for dinner, you took in every moment (you used your conscious mind at dinner) and certainly used perfect etiquette, napkin included.

The recording would show you dabbing your chin with your napkin, not your sleeve. And even without the recording, you are able to remember everything about that evening, including what you both ate many years after it happened.

What changed? The answer is your awareness. We become hyper-aware of everything in our lives when we fall in love. The tiniest things matter. In this new state of awareness, we are better able to loosen the grip our subconscious has on us and live in the moment. This allows us to become starkly aware of our thoughts and behaviors.

Reflect back on implicit (subconscious) learning versus explicit (conscious) learning. Besides one using programming and the other using conscious decisions, what else is different? Yes, the brain waves are different, but what is the qualitative difference between short-term memory events and long-term memory events? The answer is...importance.

When you experience something you recognize as important, this adds an emotional attachment to it. Not only is this reinforcement enough to override your subconscious programming, but it's strong enough to stay in your long-term memory. The crux of all of this is that important things make you pay attention.

> *"Coach Smith called me in one day and showed me two films. One was from the beginning of my sophomore season, the other from the beginning of my junior year," Michael Jordan said. "They were totally the opposite."*

What Coach Smith was showing one of the greatest athletes of all-time was that his automatic programming had taken over and Jordan needed to wake up and get back on track. In Michael Jordan's sophomore year at the University of North Carolina he was constantly hustling down the court and playing defense, but in his junior year (after Jordan achieved some level of success) he was always looking for the fastbreak instead of playing defense.

Unfortunately, we don't have a Coach Smith to show us a recording of ourselves performing poorly. However, we do have the ability to become hyper-conscious of our thoughts and actions. We can break free from the death grip our subconscious has on us and on our behavior when we raise our awareness, and when we pay attention.

A clarification:

> I don't want you to misinterpret the point I'm trying to make. This whole time, I've gone on and on about how superior the subconscious is, even referring to your conscious as a "Frankenstein" of random parts of your conscious learning. Now, it appears as if I'm saying the conscious is a superior form of learning because that is where awareness arises.
>
> What I'm actually saying is that when you take in what you learn from the awareness that your consciousness allows, and then move it into your subconscious as automatic, you have the best of both worlds. Also, the subconscious and conscious work together, regardless of the percentages cited. They don't work one-at-a-time or one-instead-of-the-other.
>
> This chapter isn't a shift back from emphasizing the subconscious to emphasizing the conscious, but an explanation of how you can use them together, (a concept known as hemi-sync, which researchers have said we can do simply by crossing our legs or arms, and in doing so engages both parts of our brain which encourages them to work together) and recognize what each brings to the table.
>
> You can repeat in your conscious mind bits of knowledge over and over until it enters your subconscious, but that has to start with awareness, which arises out of your conscious.

Personally, I'm insanely conscious of all of my choices. Let's say I'm walking somewhere and I see I can cut across someplace to get there quicker. I will intentionally make myself take the long way because I do not want to accidentally "program" myself to look for shortcuts. Taking the longer way seems unpredictable and not automatic, but it raises my conscious awareness. This is brain science in action.

By now it shouldn't be lost on you that I have used a multitude of science-based studies and research throughout this book. Mirror neurons, Maslow's Hierarchy of Needs, reticular activating system, the habit loop, the Bio-Dome experiment, the confidence-competence loop, the Colorado Adoption Project. The reason why I did that was to make you aware of what's really going on in your mind. This book would be useless (like many other self-help books that only focus on training the conscious mind) if you were unaware of how things actually work. You don't need another self-help book to realize that hanging out with nine losers will make you the tenth. You already know if you don't have anything to aim for, you will miss every time when it comes to achieving your goals. And it's no secret that we are what we repeatedly do with regard to our habitual behavior.

How I wanted to make this book different (and stand out) was to illustrate concepts that can be scientifically proven. I didn't want you to just take my word like you are called upon to do in other books. I wanted to provide airtight evidence that my strategies produce real, and lasting results through valid scientific research. I wanted to show you the science behind how things actually work. Why is it so important to truly understand how things work (i.e., setting goals, achieving your vision, forming good habits)?

> **"The good thing about science is that it's true whether or not you believe in it."**
>
> ~NEIL DEGRASSE TYSON

When you understand how things work, you are engaging in your sense of wonder, and that is a new and special awareness that enables you to wake up and make the changes necessary to embark on a new path.

Awareness is the solution for helping us break free from the unconscious patterns we routinely engage in throughout each day. Developing stark awareness is crucial because until we wake up, it's unlikely we'll be able to get out of our own way because we cannot even see we are in our own way. So up until this point, it really isn't your fault why you're not currently producing the results your conscious mind desires. But as the American poet and civil rights activist Maya Angelou reminds us:

> *"Do the best you can until you know better. Then when you know better, do better."*

This book provides you with the information to do better. However, it's completely up to you if you're going to make the conscious choice to implement what you're learning.

Moving forward, you must take ownership and complete responsibility for altering the path you're currently on. Understand falling in love does not necessarily need to be with a person. It can be with your calling. It can be with a passion to develop the best version of yourself. It can be with maintaining the mindset of becoming the CEO of your life. You can fall in love with the pursuit of giving the best version of you to your children. My point is: you just gotta fall in love with something because that's the easiest (and perhaps the only) way for you to break free from the death-grip your subconscious thoughts and behaviors currently have on you.

OUR BELIEFS PROGRAM OUR SUBCONSCIOUS

> "Beliefs have no boundaries and know no limits. Our beliefs are what we become in life."
>
> ~UNKNOWN

A key component to reprogramming our subconscious mind is taking control of our beliefs. This is important because all behavior is belief-driven. Tony Robbins writes in *Awaken The Giant Within*:

> *"Once accepted, our beliefs become unquestioned commands to our nervous system, and they have the power to expand or destroy the possibilities of our present and future."*

If you were programmed early in life with the belief that you were not good enough, that program is continuously playing in the part of your brain that dictates 95 percent of how you think and act. If you grew up with the unconscious belief of money being scarce, continuously reinforced in your mind, it should come as no surprise that when you get a little bit of money you hold on to it for dear life instead of investing it in ways to make it or yourself grow. (Think of the third servant burying his one talent.) If you grew up in an environment that displayed a toxic relationship between your parents, this is likely an area in which you will struggle throughout your adult life because of the programming that was downloaded and unconsciously reinforced in your beliefs.

Our beliefs are so incredibly powerful that statistics show one-third of all medical healings, including surgery, are the result of the placebo effect. This means it's not the sugar pill that heals us, but our beliefs.

In one particularly fascinating piece of research titled, *Study Finds Common Knee Surgery No Better Than Placebo*, the patients who underwent arthroscopic knee surgery were no better off than patients who *believed* they underwent arthroscopic knee surgery. Wait! What? So doctors cut people open, removed part of their body, yet this procedure is no more effective than simply taking a sugar pill? That's correct.

The study took place in the United States. To paraphrase precisely what happened:

> *180 patients with knee pain were randomized into three groups. One group received debridement, in which worn, torn, or loose cartilage is cut away and removed with the aid of a pencil-thin viewing tube called an arthroscope. The second group underwent arthroscopic lavage, in which the bad cartilage is flushed out. The third group underwent simulated arthroscopic surgery: small incisions were made, but no instruments were inserted and no cartilage removed.*

"We have shown that the entire driving force behind this billion-dollar industry is the placebo effect," said lead investigator Dr. Nelda P. Wray, a health services researcher at the Houston VA Medical Center and Baylor College of Medicine. Dr. Wray continued, "The healthcare industry should rethink how to test whether surgical procedures, done purely for the relief of subjective symptoms, are more efficacious than a placebo."

What we believe can heal us. And there's a tremendous amount of evidence that proves it. But guess what? What we believe can also kill us. There's something called the *nocebo* effect. The nocebo effect is when we believe in negative outcomes. The very belief we have is what we bring about. It's what we draw into our lives.

So what does the *placebo* and *nocebo* have to do with becoming a lifelong learner? It really boils down to what you actually believe because, in reality, none of us act in accordance with what we know we can do; instead, we act in accordance with what we believe we can do. Our actual beliefs, the ones deep down in our subconscious mind, govern how we operate. This is the 95 percent part (the Einstein part of our brain) that controls virtually everything in our lives, including our physical health.

You could read the books, watch the YouTube videos, and attend the workshops, but if your subconscious beliefs don't support what you are learning, you'll never be able to live the life of your dreams. Until you're able to interrupt and permanently change your patterns of beliefs, you'll be stuck in a never-ending cycle of frustration. You must create new imprints/beliefs in your subconscious that can override the old imprints/beliefs that are not producing the results you want in your life.

When I was released from prison, I was speaking to a group of business owners at an event, and one of the questions from the audience was, "How did you do it? How'd you make it in all of those maximum security prisons?" Without hesitation, I found myself saying:

"The days I doubted never outweighed the days I believed."

My beliefs literally saved my life. My beliefs are the primary reason why I'm back on top. Let me share a personal story with you.

When I was released from prison, I had nothing. On one of the initial dates with my son Tristan's mother Nerissa, long before he was born, we went downtown to meet some of my friends. It was raining that day. And if you know anything about downtown Houston, finding parking is outrageously difficult. There was valet parking at the place where we were meeting my friends, but I did not have the ten dollars to pay for valet. So the story I was telling myself was: *This is not my life! It's not supposed to be like this!* I was so angry and my son's destined mother knew it. Probably because I could not keep that voice to myself. I was saying out loud, "This is not my life!"

Not having a measly ten dollars to pay for valet parking was kind of like being told the world was out of oxygen. It was not registering with me. When I finally found a place to park, nearly half a mile from where we were meeting my friends; I was furious. Rage was pouring through my veins. My beliefs did not support this life. I was in crisis mode. And the beautiful thing about the word "crisis" is its Late Middle English meaning of a "turning point," usually attributed to a disease, which poverty is!

We got out of the car and walked the half-mile to meet my

friends. When we arrived, both of us were drenched. The emotions I felt that day, looking at Tristan's future mother, getting soaked (she was an award-winning international fitness model at the time), and knowing this was not my life, were insurmountable. Before I went to prison, the imprint in my brain was one of wealth. I was one of the top financial advisors in the world. And even though I had just spent nearly half a decade in a prison cell, it was not enough to remove the imprint of being rich. It just was not registering. In my mind, there was a glitch in *The Matrix*. Two plus two was not equaling four. So these dire circumstances just didn't add up to me.

Because of my internal self-image and the beliefs that had been ingrained in my mind; I went to extraordinary measures to educate myself, to reinvent myself. The unwavering belief that I deserved more out of life governed the amount of energy I exerted to learning everything I could to get back to the lifestyle I believed I deserved (and was previously accustomed to). This belief regulated the type of jobs I took, and how I used them to achieve my ultimate vision: getting back to where I knew I belonged.

One job I took shortly after I was released from prison was selling cars. Even though I was the top salesman every month at that car dealership; I knew that career was not for me. I needed much more. I deserved much more. And I was going to make the necessary sacrifices, and learn everything I needed so I could get to where I am now.

A reference point aside:

Several years ago, Nerissa (my son Tristan's mother) and I went to couples counseling. The primary reason was that I spent all my time at work. And when I was home I was working. From the moment my eyes opened to when they closed – I worked. And I didn't just do this for days on end, or months, but I did it for years. Why? The counselor we saw put it perfectly when she was attempting to explain my behavior:

> *"Jeremy has a reference point of being a millionaire. And until he gets back there, not you nor anyone else is going to stop him."*

During several of my speaking engagements, I've shown a text message Nerissa sent me many years ago. It read: *"You do nothing around here...you work from morning until night, yet I hardly see any money."* A lot of people did not believe in me, my own family did not believe in me, but I believed in my reference point – and that made all the difference.

> **"What lies behind you and what lies in front of you, pales in comparison to what lies inside of you."**
> ~RALPH WALDO EMERSON

If there were only one characteristic I could program into your mind, it would be to ingrain the belief that you deserve better. You deserve more than you currently believe you are receiving. The moment your subconscious downloads the program that states you deserve more, you immediately break free from the routines and habits that are preventing you from achieving your goals.

The instant the new program is downloaded: you get angry; you go into crisis mode; you begin to fight; you begin to match your actions and thoughts with the new beliefs (no more spending major time on minor stuff).

It's important to realize that just like false beliefs have been conditioned in you, they can be conditioned out of you. I grew up with a mother who constantly pointed at other little boys in my grade and would say she wished they were her son instead of me. That certainly had an adverse short-term effect on my self-confidence, but in my early teens, I overrode that program and developed supreme self-confidence.

You have the power to rewire your mind. You can take back control of your life when you override the false beliefs that are sabotaging your success. Take ownership of your results. Let today be your rock bottom.

A NEW WAY TO LEARN

> "Create the intention with your conscious mind, but then through repetition is how you move it to the subconscious mind which is the 95 percent part that runs your life."
>
> ~DR. BRUCE LIPTON

Doctor Lipton's quote succinctly summarizes several chapters in this book: learn with your conscious mind through awareness, then saturate your subconscious with what you've learned through the power of repetition.

However, for centuries, psychologists believed that consciously changing our subconscious wasn't possible; they believed that if we did not get the knowledge early in the subconscious programming period (from age 2 to 6) of our lives, we were just out of luck as adults. They believed that once we reached adulthood our subconscious was set and closed to new influences. Today's scientific reality is that nothing could be further from the truth.

It's almost a commonality these days to hear of someone who grew up in the most impoverished conditions, yet became über-successful. Heard of Jennifer Lopez? She grew up in the Bronx in a tiny apartment. What about Tom Cruise? He grew up in poverty with an abusive father. Leonardo DiCaprio was raised by a single mother who worked several jobs to support them living in Los Angeles.

So how did they do it? Was it the affirmations? Perhaps a secret formula only the exceedingly lucky stumble upon? Did the "haves" whisper in Jennifer's, Tom's, and Leonardo's ear something the "have-nots" will never discover? Of course not. Each of them achieved extraordinary success and became household names with the exact same strategy. Would you like to know this priceless technique?

Malcolm Gladwell revealed a clue of what the formula entailed in his phenomenal book, *Blink*:

> *"Ten thousand hours is the magic number of greatness." Gladwell continued, "an extraordinarily consistent answer in an incredible number of fields...you need to have practiced, to have apprenticed, for 10,000 hours before you get good."*

Gladwell should be pleased that by the time we turn six we've spent over 25,000 waking hours of learning and an equal time sleeping to consolidate what we've learned. And the way we have learned? Through repetition, i.e., "*practiced*" and "*apprenticed*" way over the "*10,000 hours before you get good*."

Think about it. How did you learn your ABCs? What about tying your shoes? How did you learn that? The answer is through repetition. You had to repeat it over and over again and then finally you got it. It became second nature to you when it became a subconscious habit.

When you first learned how to drive a car, the same thing happened. You had to practice over and over again, and now you can drive down the road for miles having a conversation with someone and not even remember how you made it to your destination. How is that possible? Through repetition, you programmed your subconscious to drive the car.

> **"It's the repetition of the right information that will really alter what's going on inside."**
> ~BOB PROCTOR

Jennifer Lopez, Tom Cruise, and Leonardo DiCaprio used repetition to program their brains and imprint powerful patterns to become icons. This is the exact same technique every person on this planet has used to succeed.

Successful people don't practice until they get it right. Successful people practice until they can't get it wrong. They understand that our brain becomes addicted to anything we repeat. Repetition causes subconscious expectation, and expectation – fulfilled – releases the reward neurohormone dopamine. Dopamine is positive reinforcement for more repetition, and more repetition makes for good (or bad) habits.

Successful people do the same thing day in and day out. It's not exciting. It's not fun. It's actually quite boring. But it's extremely effective. And it's the reason why I was able to write this book.

If I had attempted to use the 5 percent part of my brain – my Frankenstein mind – to write a 150,000-plus word book, it would have never happened. Instead, I had to channel the 95 percent part – my Einstein mind – to help me write *CEO*. How did I do that? I programmed my brain's subconscious mind so that my life would go in a pattern each day, researching and writing the words you are reading now. The words came from the 5 percent (my conscious mind), but the *process* came from the 95 percent (my subconscious mind). Think about it, a kid who failed kindergarten (true story) could never write a book like this...or could he?

Another crucial component was my *belief* that I could write a book. This was partially due to the fact that I have already written a bestseller. But as I mentioned in the first chapter, I consciously created a new imprint in my mind by printing out the cover of this book and taping it to the cover of another book before I wrote a single word. This had a dramatic effect on my subconscious and helped me *see* this book as real (long before it was). It became emotional, and emotions give things importance. It also provided my mind's eye with additional resources and extra motivation that helped me *"stay on message"* and complete this massive project.

It assigned an image that represented my belief.

Since science suggests that 95 percent of our activities come from our subconscious mind, it would have been short-sighted and foolish of me to think I could use the 5 percent (conscious mind) part to write a book of this caliber. Are you beginning to see why you haven't been successful up to this point (or at least scratched the surface of your full potential)? You were approaching it wrong. You were trying to override the system. You were trying to get the 5 percent part of your brain to overpower the 95 percent part, which just isn't possible. It would be like Pee-wee Herman (Paul Reubens) trying to arm wrestle The Rock (Dwayne Johnson). Who would you put your money on? Exactly. So why do people keep betting on a 5 percent chance at success?

Every day, smart people read the right books, attend the right classes, and say the right affirmations, yet never live the life of their dreams. This is because they wake up every morning and consciously go after their goals using only 5 percent (their conscious mind) of their brain to achieve them.

As hard as we may try to advance every day, what has been programmed into our minds overrides the 5 percent (our conscious efforts) every time. A dictionary is just the words; the plot, characterizations, and setting, however, motivates the process. Trying to get a 95 percent result out of 5 percent is pure alchemy: you're more likely to force lead to lose three protons and turn into gold. Or throw all the words of a dictionary into the air and expect them to land as a well-written and bestselling book.

This underscores what I said previously, that you have to use both parts of your brain, the 95 percent and 5 percent. But the 800-pound gorilla, your subconscious – the juggernaut of your whole mind – has to be led by your conscious mind. Therefore, a new way of learning, I believe, is understanding how to train your subconscious mind, rather than your conscious mind. This is key because your conscious mind is rather limited in scope. Try as you may, your more powerful mind, your subconscious, will overrule it nine out of ten times (or in keeping with the figures, nine and a half times out of ten). Why? Because your conscious mind can only focus on one thing at a time. This was demonstrated in a very popular study that won Christopher Chabris and Daniel Simons the satirical "*Ig Noble Prize*".

This study centered on the now-famous experiment referred to as *The Invisible Gorilla*. The researchers had participants watch a video of people passing a ball to each other. The participants who watched the video were asked to count how many times the ball was passed. Simons and Chabris discovered that nearly half the people who viewed the video failed to notice when a person in a gorilla suit walked in the middle of the people tossing the ball, looked directly at the camera, pounded on his chest and then walked off. The gorilla was in plain view for almost nine seconds. But somehow, half the people who watched the video completely missed the gorilla.

> **"Anywhere from 95 percent and perhaps more closely 99 percent of the day we operate from the subconscious mind, the more powerful mind of the two; 5 percent or less – probably just 1 percent of the day – we're actually controlling our lives with our own intentions, desires and beliefs we actually entertain in our conscious mind."**
>
> ~DR. BRUCE LIPTON

No, it's not the 800-pound gorilla I used to symbolize your subconscious. This was a man in an actual gorilla suit. Before, I used the gorilla to represent the strength of your subconscious, but this is an experiment that emphasizes – unless you are primed to expect the unexpected – you're likely to miss the unexpected. It is an experiment about the awareness I've been talking about, and how *"inattentional blindness"* will have us missing the "gorillas" in our lives that are attempting to reveal information that may be important to our decision-making process. When we live our lives blind to the unexpected, we are operating from our subconscious, our 95 percent brain.

A common mistake people make is believing they are operating from their conscious mind all the time, but unfortunately, that is not possible, as the world-renowned psychologists Simons and Chabris proved in their *Invisible Gorilla experiment.*

> *"Most of what we do every minute of every day is unconscious,"* says University of Wisconsin neuroscientist Paul Whelan. *"Life would be chaos if everything were on the forefront of our consciousness."*

For the conscious mind, "business as usual" is trying to pay attention to life's moment-by-moment obstacles – an otherwise good thing; but this blinds us to the unexpected things that are cordoned off by our subconscious minds (sometimes a bad thing).

While the intention to educate yourself and become financially free may come from your conscious mind, if your subconscious mind does not support the intention (via belief), then you're actually in conflict with yourself. Since 95 percent of your behaviors and thoughts are coming from the subconscious, which is the dominant program running in your mind, the 5 percent part, your conscious, may be saying, "Hey! I want to learn this stuff so I can become the CEO of my life," but the 95 percent is running the program that overrides and overrules your conscious intention every time. The major portion of your mind is stubbornly set in its ways and is very resistant to change; and being the 95 percent gorilla in the room (and not invisible!), it makes for a very effective bully.

"I do not understand what I do. For what I want to do, I do not do. But what I hate, I do," the apostle Paul writes in the New Testament. This is akin to when we set New Year's Resolutions that don't make it past February or when we tell ourselves to go for a run but, instead, find ourselves sitting on the couch and watching TV or looking for the bottom of our social media feeds. What's happening here is that the 95 percent (subconscious mind) part of our brain is running the show.

How do you begin to reprogram your more powerful mind, your subconscious mind, so you can do the things you know you should be doing? Reprogramming involves re-firing your neurons and the more you strengthen the neuro-pathways using a variety of inputs – visual, verbal, and video – the more you align your conscious mind with your subconscious mind. If you can inject emotion into these inputs, the alignment becomes even stronger. This substantially increases your chances of achieving your goals because now you have the "Einstein" part of your brain working in your favor.

Utilizing a strategy of rational and purposeful repetition focused on your vision and goals is why the exercises in this book have been tightly engineered to strengthen your neuro-pathways toward them, which helps reprogram your brain. When you did your vision board (hopefully you did that exercise), the images you used to make your collage were creating new neurological connections in your mind. When you wrote out your perfect day, the neural connections were taking note. When you mapped out a plan on your battle board to achieve your interval goals, new signals were being formed to bring awareness to your reticular activating system (RAS). When you got excited about making your vision board, describing your perfect day, and creating a plan to accomplish your goals, you were adding emotion to turbo-charge the process.

A neurological aside:

Let's talk about using visual, auditory, verbal, and video inputs. A schematic diagram of how the universe presents itself to you is this: data in the form of electromagnetic waves (vision) and undulations of your eardrums (hearing) – and even temperature and pressure – is just that: data. The organs struck, or vibrated or pressed by the data send signals to your brain through the optic nerve, acoustic nerve, and other sensory nerves, where they are redistributed to the respective areas of your brain that interpret what they are. These are called the "associative" areas of the brain. For vision, it's in the occipital lobe; for hearing, it's in the temporal lobes, and for the others, they're in other specialized areas.

To make matters more complex, there is *cross-talk* among the associative areas. This cross-talk makes it possible for your senses, for example, to respond instantaneously (and simultaneously) to a speeding, honking car about to run you over. They even affect your motor nerves, initiating a reflex to get you to turn your head toward the commotion, simultaneously and without thinking.

The point here is that your associative areas are subconscious. Therefore, when you strengthen the neural-pathways for vision, hearing, and the other inputs by paying attention, you're inputting (reprogramming) into your subconscious through the awareness of your conscious. You are no longer "inattentively blind"; no man in a gorilla suit will get past you. Does that mean you can alter your subconscious background programming with foreground conscious intentions? You bet! And that's the whole point.

The universe can (and will) give you anything you want in life. But in order to get what you want you must first synchronize the programs – you must learn with your conscious and then through repetition move what you learned to the subconscious. Unfortunately, there is no shortcut to this process. You have to roll up your sleeves and discipline yourself to pound new programming into your subconscious through repetition. Additionally, if you want these new programs to stick, you have to constantly force yourself to consciously maintain steadfast awareness of your habitual behaviors – ensuring your new programming "sets". And the best way to verify that your conscious intentions have moved into your subconscious routines is to track your daily activities (see timesheets on page 552).

Again, there's a method to my madness, and that method is to do anything and everything possible to break you out of the hypnotic slumber you find yourself in – going through life running faulty programs – programs that were embedded in your subconscious early in life that are not producing the results your conscious mind currently desires.

THE WORLD IS CHANGING, THEREFORE YOU MUST CHANGE

> "One of the most important global beliefs that you and I can adapt is a belief that in order to succeed and be happy, we have got to be consistently improving the quality of our lives, constantly growing and expanding."
>
> ~TONY ROBBINS, American author, philanthropist, and life coach

Now that you know repetition truly is the mother of all skill (it's not just a clever saying, but the basis of Gladwell's "10,000 hours"), it's important to understand how quickly this world is moving and changing. Therefore, the kind of person who isn't constantly learning new information – then using repetition to move the new information into their subconscious will simply be left behind in the blink of an eye.

Today, things are moving faster than ever before, and this pace of change and innovation is not slowing down anytime soon. According to Tim Sandel's 2018 op-ed in the *Digital Journal*, up until about 1900, it took nearly a century for the total amount of human knowledge to double. By the mid-twentieth century, it was doubling every generation – about every 25 years. By 2000, it began doubling every year. Now, human knowledge is doubling nearly every day, thanks to "the Internet of things" and the connectivity that has enhanced communication, collaboration, and data-sharing.

If you desire to become – and remain – the CEO of your life, you must keep pace with the speed at which things change. As the world changes, you must change, and in order to change, you must constantly be learning or you will find yourself in what Alvin Toffler called *"Future Shock"*, defined as the confusion and inability to function due to failure to relate to evolving knowledge and technology:

> *"Future shock is the shattering stress and disorientation that we induce in individuals by subjecting them to too much change in too short a time."*

Future shock is what author, Gerard DiLeo, refers to as "*technopause*", when even "smart" TV remote controls prove daunting. We've all met that one person who thinks that their lack of knowledge regarding technology – or even simple operation of a computer – is charming, quirky, or eccentrically cute. This person will also tell you that they preferred the simpler times when things weren't moving so fast. A mindset like this may be amusing to people who are afraid to adapt to technological advancements, but I can tell you that they aren't going to be very successful in the modern world. Why? Because the present-day doesn't care what you prefer; the present-day simply says, "Hello, I'm here. Deal with it or get out of the way."

If you want to be a successful person in today's ever-changing world, you need to be able to adapt quickly to new innovations, and you need to keep up with modern technology. You must match your talents to what the world is asking for today, and not what it was asking for a decade ago. John Maxwell stated it perfectly:

> *"The person who insists on using yesterday's methods in today's world won't be in tomorrow's business."*

Think about the business world today. Do you think a business degree from 1980 has any relevance in today's world of search engine optimization (SEO), Instagram, Snapchat, or YouTube? The successful people today who were educated in 1980 have never stopped educating themselves.

If you truly value yourself and believe in the contribution you are capable of making to the world, then you will devote yourself to becoming a lifelong learner.

Let's put this in perspective: you can learn something new today and every day for the rest of your life, and you will still not have even scratched the surface of all the knowledge the world has to offer you. Just think, then, if you wait until tomorrow to learn something brand new. For every day you wait, you're going to be one day behind in achieving your goals, vision, and the life you want. The possibilities of our world are limitless, and you are a part of this world; therefore, your capabilities are limitless as well. But it must be a parallel course, not a catch-up.

Becoming a lifelong learner requires a lot of energy and a heck of a lot of awareness. You're not competing with your competitors; you're competing with the world to stay on top of all the new things it is offering every day. You lose energy (here, used synonymously with motivation) when your life becomes dull and routine because of "inattentional blindness," that is, when the programs in your subconscious fully take over. That is why you must get interested in something. Throw yourself into it. *Be* somebody. *Do* something. Cue up Sinatra again and don't sit around moaning about things. The more you immerse yourself in something bigger than yourself, the more energy you will have.

> **"Success isn't owned. It's leased. And rent is due every day."**
>
> ~J.J. WATT

At the same time, it's important that you don't overload yourself in the beginning and suffer mental burnout prematurely. I've often heard that one of the primary reasons people who want to begin an exercise routine can't stick to it is because they try to take on too many new habits at once (going to the gym, starting a new diet, waking up earlier in the morning, etc.). This typically leads to discouragement at best, and sets one up for failure at worst.

When you attempt too much too quickly, you're almost guaranteed to fall short of your desired result. The secret of building motivational momentum is to start small (achieve small wins) with the simple stuff and work your way up from there. ("Momentum" is the operative word here.) Take on one thing at a time, grow it, and then move on to the next thing. Don't bite off more than you can chew. Like the goals I discussed in Chapter Two, and the habits I talked about in Chapter Five, achieving one thing will make it easier to conquer the next thing.

The road to developing a new and improved "you" is a thousand-step journey, and you can only succeed if you commit to taking one step at a time. Marathon runner Yamada, whom I discussed in Chapter Two, understood this well, but because it goes against your previous programming and your previous subconscious beliefs, the little-bit-at-a-time approach may be uncomfortable for you at first. That's why the Latin root of education is *educere*, which means "to lead out from darkness to light, from ignorance to knowledge," makes perfect sense in this stepwise approach. You are leading yourself out of darkness (previous patterns and routines) and into the light (new patterns and routines).

Start small. Stay focused. Understand that personal development is similar to walking into an operating room while a physician is performing surgery. If you walk into the room at the beginning or the middle of the operation, you'd think the doctor was killing his patient. But if you walk into the room at the end, you'll see that a miracle took place.

WHAT ARE YOU TRADING AT TODAY?

"If you're not getting better – you're getting worse."

~PAT RILEY, NBA basketball coach, won five championships

Millions of people invest in the stock market in anticipation of great returns, and yet very few people invest in themselves, which is where the greatest returns of all exist. The value of what you produce in this world is directly connected to how much you invest in yourself. Likewise, much of your lasting value is directly related to what you can contribute to the world.

So how do you become more valuable? You must learn more. You must educate yourself to be better than the person you were yesterday. Learning will help you hone in on your skillset. Learning will help you figure out the one thing that you can do better than anyone else in the world.

If you can produce something that no one else can, then you are extremely valuable. You need to figure out what it is that you can do for the world that only you can do, and/or that you can do better than anyone else on the planet.

The higher the number of people capable of producing a particular thing or providing a particular service, the less those people are valued and paid. For example, most grocery store clerks are paid minimum wage. The reason for that is because there are a large number of people who have the abilities needed for a grocery store clerk position, as there are few specialized skills required.

Looking at this from the other end of the spectrum, a neuroscientist is paid exceptionally well because the knowledge he has can only be found in very few people. He has spent years developing a very complex and specialized skill that cannot be easily duplicated or bought. Thus, he is many times more valuable than a grocery store clerk.

What does this mean for you? It means that you need to spend more time developing yourself with specialized skills so you can improve your worth and set yourself apart from everyone else. Find a way to become uniquely valuable to the world, and you will never have to worry about your personal value ever again. When you develop your intelligence in areas that you can dominate, then your pride, your income, and your confidence will explode. Remember the confidence-competence loop?

If you really want to see the power of self-development in action, look no further than people who are in sales. Anyone in sales is lucky enough to see the direct correlation between what you produce and your monthly income. The sales job tells you in dollar figures exactly how much value you brought to your customers that month. The numbers don't lie, so you have no choice but to improve beyond – or fall behind – the other salespeople.

Going along with the sales analogy, the single best way for salespeople to bring more value to their customers (and therefore bring in more sales) is to educate themselves on how they can do their job better. When they can do their job better, they end up being better. Again, the confidence-competence loop. And when they end up being better, they contribute substantially more value to their customers and, in turn, more revenue for their company.

Top salespeople invest in themselves because they perceive themselves as a stock; a valuable commodity whose price has the ability to rise each day. Why does the price rise? It's because there are a greater number of buyers than sellers. In other words, buyers are buying the stock because they recognize its value, and sellers are selling the stock because they do not believe the stock

> **"Invest as much in yourself as you can. You're your own biggest asset by far."**
> ~WARREN BUFFETT

has value. If the price lowers, then you know there are more sellers and buyers. Put simply, if the knowledge you hold is only held by a few people, then you are extremely valuable. This plays right into the classic supply-and-demand scheme of capitalism.

Ask yourself: what are you trading at today? You should seriously consider this question because **the value you place on yourself is the same value others will place on you as well.** This is why it's critical for you to have a high level of confidence in your abilities. All IPOs (initial public offerings) begin with a pricing strategy based on an evaluation formula. Your self-evaluation of worth is essential in determining your sense of self-value and, with it, your confidence. You develop your confidence when you put in the work to master your craft. That's why investing in yourself is the most secure, low-risk, high-return decision you could ever make in your life.

Tony Robbins captured this beautifully in his book, *Awaken The Giant Within*:

> *"Most people never feel secure because they are always worried that they will lose their job, lose the money they already have, lose their spouse, lose their health, and so on. The only true security in life comes from knowing that every day you are improving yourself in some way, that you are increasing the caliber of who you are and that you are valuable to your company, your friends, and your family."*

YOU MUST RECOGNIZE YOUR VALUE

> "It is the capacity to develop and improve themselves that distinguishes leaders from followers."
>
> ~WARREN BENNIS, American scholar, organizational consultant, and author

The kind of person who continuously learns new things and develops their skills throughout life is the kind of person who expects the best life has to offer. A truism I wrote earlier applies well: *Those who do the minimum...get the minimum*. The person who learns continuously goes far beyond the minimum, of course. This type of person has a deep desire and a hunger to get better every day and realizes that in order to increase their self-value, they can never allow themselves to become complacent. I could just as easily say, *those who do the maximum, get the maximum*.

But there's a catch: people typically won't add value to themselves in the form of personal growth and self-mastery until they see value in themselves. This is why so many people get caught in dead-end jobs, or in lifestyles they don't like. And it's also why people who are living the life of their dreams continue to prosper. It's a never-ending cycle when it comes to personal self-worth. This cycle either leads you down a path you love or down a path you hate. So here's your epiphany: the choice is entirely up to you. *You* choose if you want to grow. Alternatively, you and you alone choose if you're going to continue running the old faulty programs in your subconscious mind and not grow.

But you need to make a decision. Do you feel worthy enough to invest the time, money, energy, and effort that is required to grow yourself? Do you truly and honestly believe that you can become an in-demand person and raise the value that you can bring to the world?

People who truly value themselves want to keep adding more value to themselves. Why? Because they know that the value other people place on them is directly proportionate to the value that they place on themselves. This means that if you place a small value on yourself, you can rest assured that the world will not raise your "trading price".

If you bring enough value to this world, your legacy continues to live on, long after you're gone. And your legacy is determined by what you accomplish during the short time you get in this world. What you accomplish depends on what you contribute, and contributions rely on what you learn. As I wrote earlier, your brain is a breeder reactor, and the more it "flexes", the more it "lifts". Educating yourself, of course, is flexing it. Therefore, smarts breed more smarts.

Lifelong learning is a continuous bonus of smarts breeding more smarts. And it begins, like all things, with a first step. The first step toward becoming a lifelong learner is recognizing why you deserve to give yourself this precious gift. None of us will take the steps necessary to add value to ourselves unless we first believe that we are somebody who is worth becoming immensely valuable.

As we see the positive changes that come from the results of growing ourselves, it builds momentum and accelerates our inner desire for increased improvement. Eventually, we become successful people who naturally want to improve all aspects of our lives.

For each of us, since our external world is a reflection of our inner world, we must accept that our external world will not improve until our inner world improves. Therefore, if you want to improve your current external world, you must first focus on improving yourself. You must first focus on replacing the false beliefs in your mind that subconsciously tell you that you're not good enough and that you don't deserve to live the life of your dreams. You must override the previous programming and condition new beliefs into your mind. Is it going to be easy? Nope. But as I like to remind people, the Stone Age did not end because we ran out of stones. It ended because people learned how to condition out the wrong habits and condition in the right habits.

Personally, getting better has been an obsession of mine for many years. There's rarely a day that goes by where I'm not reading, learning, and trying to improve myself. That said, I don't claim to have a perfect life. Like everybody, I have ups and downs in my day-to-day life. But no matter what happens; I invest in my personal growth regularly. Why? Because I believe I'm worth the investment. And do you know what else I believe? I believe you're worth the investment, too – that's why you're reading this book and have made it to the final chapter.

One of the best ways to look at the concept of adding value to yourself is to step outside of yourself for a moment and see yourself as an object. This object has no limit to how valuable it can become. This object is more valuable than gold, platinum, and diamonds because it has the ability to make itself so valuable that any number would not do it justice. Just like the story I shared with you in Chapter Four, this object is the goose that lays the golden eggs.

You are that valuable object, and you can become as valuable as you want to be by simply adding knowledge to your mind *bank*. The best part about this bank is that it is virtually infinite in how much it can hold. There is no limit as to the knowledge, wisdom, and skills you can acquire. Successful people are fully aware of this, and you will very rarely find a well-accomplished person who isn't a student for life – it hasn't happened, and it's unlikely it ever will.

A tangent aside:

In Chapter Two, I told you of a client – a new father – who said that when he goes to the mall, he sees baby strollers everywhere. These baby strollers did not suddenly appear. They were there all along.

When you learn something new and learn it well, it never fails that in the not too distant future you will find yourself contributing to a conversation with this very information, your contribution being pertinent and learned – seemingly in the nick of time – for just this conversation. But such conversations, like baby strollers, are everywhere. You will notice this when you know something others

don't and you can contribute. This moment presents itself as an increase in your value.

When you become a student of subjects you're interested in, your confidence and competence will improve. With this newfound confidence, you will believe in your abilities far more than you used to. When you believe in your abilities with a greater sense of conviction, you will find yourself thinking thoughts of a more positive nature. And with the right thoughts entering your mind, you will perform in a way that is consistent with your new self-perceived value.

As your value grows, so does your self-confidence (confidence-competence loop). It's a perpetual cycle of positive personal development that continues to repeat itself over time, as long as you continue to invest in yourself on a regular basis.

So how can you get started? Look at your calendar and see if you have any time blocked off for investing in yourself. Your calendar and time management are a reflection of both your priorities and what is truly important to you, (remember exercise number seven from Chapter Two: Tracking Your Time). You don't have to have fancy-schmancy time-management software, micromanagement programs, or multi-device alerts enabled; all you need is a simple calendar, which turns out to be incredibly powerful at managing your time.

Do you know what you're going to do *today* to invest in yourself? If not, you need to schedule some time to make that investment happen. You can start by blocking off an hour in the morning or evening to invest in yourself. But that hour has to be there and you have to stick to your commitment. Make it a habit (see Chapter Five).

Merely saying that you're going to invest in yourself and actually taking the time out of your day to do it are two different things. Just saying it is merely penciling it into your schedule – actually doing it – i.e., taking time right now to set it in stone is the level of commitment you need to show yourself (and the world) you are serious about reaching your full potential.

STAY TEACHABLE

> "An open mind is the beginning of self-discovery and growth. We can't learn anything new until we can admit we don't already know everything."
>
> ~ERWIN G. HALL

Zen master Shunryu Suzuki wrote in the book, *Zen Mind, Beginner's Mind: Informal Talks on Zen Meditation and Practice:*

> *"In the beginner's mind there are many possibilities, but in the expert's mind there are few."*

Maintaining a teachable (that is, receptive) mindset becomes more difficult as you start to achieve some degree of success. However, if you can admit that you don't know something, you've already taken the first step toward improving. Therefore, honesty with yourself is essential for turning what you don't know into what you can learn.

Self-honesty makes you open to learning, developing, exploring, and accepting new ideas. You become fueled with the desire to learn, and it is in these "student moments" that you discover unexpected nuggets of knowledge. Don't discount the importance of a single nugget of knowledge, as it can become the catalyst for revealing a solution to an unforeseen problem.

The difference between people who maintain a teachable mindset (a receptive mindset) and those who are stuck in their ways and unwilling to be open to new possibilities is summarized by political theorist Benjamin Barber:

"I divided the world into learners and non-learners. There are people who learn, who are open to what happens around them, who listen, who hear the lessons. When they do something stupid, they don't do it again. And when they do something that works a little, they do it even better and harder the next time. The question to ask is not whether you are a success or a failure, but whether you are a learner or a non-learner."

Barber's division between learners and non-learners is that while making mistakes helps reveal the nuggets, not repeating them reveals we learned the lesson – we obtained wisdom.

With each day you're building yourself as a learner, you're feeding the "you" that you want to become. Not learning something new regularly is similar to not feeding yourself something healthy and nutritious. Can you get away with eating junk food for a day or two? Sure! But if that day or two becomes a week, a month, or even a year, your bad habits will come back to haunt you in the form of obesity and many other diseases. More accurately, can you get away with not eating at all for a day or two? Again, sure. But when starving yourself continues long enough, you die. Do not become a mental anorexic! The prognosis is not good.

Even more poignant is the moral imperative here. You are blessed with an amazing organ: your brain. The more we learn about it, the more amazing it seems. And the more you put into it, the more that everything about you – body and mind – improves. Therefore, to starve it may just be a cardinal sin, and not learning is the same as starving your brain. With the gift of such a miraculous organ bestowed upon you, your moral obligation is to seek its highest potential. In other words, it's yours to lose, but staying teachable will make it yours to win and allow you to fulfill your deepest desires.

Furthermore, staying teachable means even the slightest degree of success won't tempt you to pause (take a break from it all), because if you do, it can become difficult to return to and maintain a "student mode" mindset (Isaac Newton's First Law will haunt you). The wealth of knowledge that is out there for us to harness and use is beyond our understanding, so if you want to be world-class at your craft, you first must be willing to admit that you don't know it all, even when it seems you do.

The more we learn, the more we often are tempted to be in denial of what we don't know. This is why knowing more than before can mislead us into thinking we've "finished the course"; this is where many people stop learning, which is a trap. The terrifying part of this trap, not learning regularly, is that you won't even realize the moment when you've become an empty robot. If you don't learn new things, you will just repeat the same old things you've always known as life whizzes right by you. What may have worked for you in the past becomes irrelevant when the world continues to change (and learn) all around you. Before you know it, you'll end up being that ninety-year-old who talks about the good old days because their present days are unbearable. Staying teachable is, therefore, a lifelong process, so all your future days stay the good ol' days.

THERE IS POWER IN KNOWING WHAT YOU DON'T KNOW

> "To know is to be ignorant. Not to know is the beginning of wisdom."
>
> ~JIDDU KRISHNAMURTI, Indian philosopher, speaker and writer

If you want to put up a light fixture and you don't know how to do it, but put it up – or try – anyway, the results may be shocking – literally. It is ironic that in this case, the smarter person knows that they do not know how to do it and goes about learning how, but the stupid person does not know that they don't know. (The one who thinks he or she is smarter is actually dumber.)

Based on this rationale, if you're feeling insecure about the realization that you know less than you think (or should), you may be smarter than you think (or know). Certainly the Greek philosopher Socrates knew this:

> **The Oracle of Delphi declared the ancient philosopher, Socrates, to be the wisest man in the world. In response, Socrates went out and looked for other people who were more intelligent instead of accepting such a generous title. Which only proved that the Oracle was right.**

In this very act of looking for others who knew more, Socrates showed that his mind was open to learning, instead of forming opinions about experiences he had never possessed.

This is precisely why the Oracle said Socrates was so wise: Socrates was fully secure and at peace in admitting what it was that he did not know. Socrates was perfectly okay with looking at someone straight in the eye and saying the words, "I don't know," with full conviction. Socrates understood that admitting to not knowing is the first step toward knowing. Wise indeed!

If you initially find yourself lacking the information you need to succeed, that's perfectly fine. Nobody starts off knowing everything they need to know. Not even Socrates. But never forget to wake up each morning and ask yourself how you can get better today. Because what you do today is more important than what you do tomorrow, so focus on today, today. And the key to getting better today – and every day thereafter – is unrelenting persistence.

Think about persistent learning like breaking a rock: the first hit to a piece of rock is not the one that breaks it, nor is the second. It is the power of all of the hits combined – done consistently over time – that eventually breaks the rock into pieces.

The same thing happens with personal development: it's not the first or second day that leads to your breakthrough. But if you stick with it over time and never give up, the combined efforts will add up and transform you into a completely unrecognizable person from when you initially began.

There won't be a single day of learning or development that's going to change you, but rather a collection of knowledge (and implementation of the knowledge you gain) that you gather each day will make a profound difference. What you do each day to craft yourself will eventually culminate into an extraordinarily successful new you.

MISTAKES ARE AN ESSENTIAL PART OF THE LEARNING PROCESS

"Mistakes are the portals of discovery."

~JAMES JOYCE, Irish novelist, poet, and literary critic

Stanford psychologist Carol Dweck has spent several years researching the critical foundation of successful education, and the one variable that always appears in bright light is the ability to learn from one's mistakes. For this reason, I'd like to encourage you to not dismiss your mistakes because you will want to learn from them as often as possible when it comes to your lifelong learning quest.

Mistakes become special lessons in the learning process. So rather than avoid mistakes and fear them, do the opposite and focus on the mistakes you have made. Investigate them to learn their lessons.

Right now you are enrolled in a never-ending school that people like to call "life". In this school, mistakes do not exist as "life-errors", but only as opportunities for learning. And these lessons are repeated until you pass the test. Even better, if you have an open mind, you have the advantage of it always being an open-book test.

Every step of the way, there is something to learn. Each step you take gets you closer to your goals. If one of those steps has you landing face-first down in the dirt, that's fine. You're not walking along a commonly treaded path; you're walking where few others have had the courage to go.

Regardless of how rough the terrain becomes, you are still one step closer to success because you are learning and growing along the way. That's why it's crucial for you to understand that growth is nothing more than a process of constant trial and error, experimentation and adaptation, feedback and improvement. However, this process also allows you to experience the joy of wonder, which is the payoff of anything learned.

You cannot expect to realize your goals and improve yourself without learning the lessons from your mistakes. If goals were so easy to achieve, everyone would be living their dream life. So remember, put one foot in front of the other and make sure you keep moving forward. This simple instruction translates well to Chapter Two's one-goal-at-a-time philosophy. If you fall, get back up and continue putting one foot in front of the other. That's resilience, as you saw in Chapter Three. Keep going, and success will be waiting for you at the other end. That's this chapter!

You might feel fearful about the possibility of making mistakes, but the mistakes you make are equally as important as the things you do right when it comes to the process of learning and personal growth. When you understand precisely what you did wrong and why it was wrong, you significantly increase your chances of getting it right the next time. But it is only through making mistakes that you can figure out what you don't know and discover where you went wrong.

In medicine, arriving at a diagnosis involves the consideration of signs and symptoms. But the present ones are just as important as the ones that are *not* present. For example, if there is no right lower abdominal pain and nausea, then it's unlikely to be appendicitis; yet, having this exact pain and nausea is enough to prep the patient for the operating room. In this instance, having the traditional right lower quadrant pain of appendicitis is called a "pertinent positive" symptom, whereas *not* having it is called a "pertinent negative".

Missing either the pertinent positives or pertinent negatives in life can certainly be perceived as mistakes, and a lot of people falsely believe that mistakes automatically equal failure. However, the word "fail" is a misnomer because there is no such thing as failure when it is seen as a lesson. It's a failure only when you don't learn from it. Instead, what you might be tempted to call failure is a golden opportunity for you to step back from the situation and dissect the key lessons you need to learn so that you can move forward.

What you perceive as a mistake leading to failure is really just a pertinent negative, equally as important in your continuing education as the things that go right (pertinent positives). Thus, a mistake is really a blessing in disguise that is designed to help you learn something new. It's hard to arrive at a correct medical diagnosis with only pertinent positives, and it's impossible to conquer something new without knowledge of the pertinent negatives on your road of discovery.

The so-called setbacks you encounter on your path to success are simply indications that you need to tweak your plan. The challenges give you a chance to regroup and figure out how to get through the roadblocks by learning the solutions. Consider them turning a pertinent negative into a pertinent positive. Most successful people will tell you that a roadblock is what forced them to change their plan, and it ended up being the best thing that could have happened. I love the quote by General Oliver P. Smith, "Retreat, hell! We're not retreating, we're just advancing in a different direction."

WAKE UP TO THE IMPORTANCE OF SLEEP

> "*Sleep*: when we are kids it's a punishment – when we are adults it's a privilege."
>
> ~ANY MOTHER

The next section (Accelerated Learning) would be premature without a word on the importance of sleep to memory, learning, brain health, and physiology in general. Before I discuss the two fundamental accelerated learning methods, up next, I feel now is the best place to teach you about laying the most basic foundation for any learning at all (as well as overall health) – sleep.

According to a University of Colorado Boulder study published in the *Journal of the American College of Cardiology (JACC)*, 6 to 9 hours of sleep a night was optimum in preventing heart attacks. People who slept less than 6 hours were 20 percent more likely to have a heart attack, and people who slept longer than 9 hours were 34 percent more likely to suffer from a heart attack. It seems, then, that there is a sweet spot on the amount of sleep we need for optimum health – not too little; not too much; but 6 to 9 hours, which is *"just right"*:

> *"You can ride lots, eat well, avoid cigarettes, be built like a World Tour pro, and have no genetic predisposition for heart disease, but if you skimp on your sleep – or get excessive amounts of it – your heart may still be at risk."* ~Selene Yeager, *Bicycling.com News, based on a study by* Iyas Daghlas, Jacqueline Lane, et al. from the September 19, 2019 *JACC*

Professor Matt Walker of the University of Berkeley calls sleep the "sweet elixir of life, the Swiss army knife of health":

> *"Sleep, unfortunately, is not an optional lifestyle luxury; it is a non-negotiable biological necessity. It's your life support system, and it is Mother Nature's best effort yet at immortality."*

Studies have demonstrated that even a one-hour difference in sleep has staggering effects on our immunity, learning ability, memory retention, and even psyche. Evidence points to a significant rise in heart attacks (up 25 percent), car accidents, and even suicides when an hour is lost with Daylight Saving Time. Likewise, a similar drop in these events is observed with the extra hour of sleep awarded on the night of converting back to standard time.

Some people see sleep as a waste of time, but we have evolved on a planet with night and day, and there are important functions that go with it. Besides cognitive and cardiac health, sleep is a way for your brain to press the "save" button for everything you learn. If you choose to commit yourself to become a lifelong learner, sleep needs to be a crucial part of your strategy.

In Chapter Two, I had discussed how short-term memory is converted into long-term memory by sleep. To the point, this assumes the sleep is normal and adequate (no sleeping pills, no sleep apnea, and – most importantly – enough hours straight through, at least 7 to 8). The best way to accomplish this is with the concept of "sleep hygiene", that is, going to bed at the same time every night and waking up at the same time every day. The crucial secret to good sleep hygiene, therefore, is consistent regularity.

A neurological aside:

And then there are your glia cells. *Glia*?

I have spoken frequently about neurons, their synapses, and their networking. But around the synapses of neurons are another type of brain cell called glia. These cells are originally derived from our immune system, and their purpose is to attack foreigners in the brain. But they also do many other important things, one of which is to provoke what is called the "*sickness response*" in our bodies when we get sick. The sickness response is produced by inflammatory substances from the glial cells that do many things to make us heal faster:

- Raises your temperature (any freshman chemistry student will tell you that heat catalyzes reactions to take place faster, so a fever speeds up the reactions that heal you
- Makes you less hungry, so you can metabolize your energy more efficiently for healing instead of digesting
- Makes you sleepy, so that you'll conserve your energy and thereby have more for recovering
- Reorganizes the physiology's priorities to cope with the battle against infections

Another important thing that glial cells do at the synapse points of neurons is modulate the actual synapse. Thus, a synapse is not "bipartite" (two components – a pair of neurons), but is *tripartite*, with the third wheel being the glial cell. Glial cells act as governors or enhancers, depending on what is needed in the body. Therefore, they fine-tune all the synapses among your neurons and are indispensable in the normal processes scientists once thought only neurons orchestrated.

The newest headlines about glia are that they accumulate the debris around them that builds up during the brain's function, and it is during sleep that this debris enters lymphatic-like channels to be collected and dumped into the circulation for clearance. This explains why sleep deprivation can make you discombobulated at best, and crazy at worst. Toxic build-up affects every aspect of the brain's activity and prowess, and not in a good way.

This might also explain why excessive abuse of amphetamines results in psychosis since sleep cannot happen normally (or at all) with such stimulants.

When you reduce your recommended seven to eight hours of sleep a night, even by an hour, you are mucking with your brain's activity and detoxification, memory consolidation, learning potential, cardiac health, psychological state, and even your sex hormones. But having inadequate sex hormones are the least of your problems compared to having half your brain tied behind your back, which happens when your sleep hygiene is inconsistent.

On the other hand, when your sleep hygiene is optimal, you are embracing the circadian rhythm of the rotating planet we have evolved to live on, thereby keeping your immune system within normal performance parameters and completing the handshake that is a very powerful mind-body connection. In essence, you are building a very nice brain for yourself, and the world needs all the good brains it can get.

ACCELERATED LEARNING METHODS: COACHING AND MENTORING

Learning each day is important, but traveling down the road of self-learning can be difficult. How so? Being your own teacher and student is a challenge that many people find frustrating. That's why I believe: it is difficult, if not impossible, to improve yourself – by yourself. However, I'll never present you with a problem without providing a solution, so here we go!

Coaching

> "You will never maximize your potential in any area without coaching. It is impossible. You may be good. You may even be better than everyone else. But without outside input, you will never be as good as you could be. We all do better when someone is watching and evaluating...Self-evaluation is helpful, but evaluation from someone else is essential."
>
> ~ANDY STANLEY, *The Next Generation Leader*

You may have gotten to where you are today because you did certain things that worked out well. But know this: what got you to where you are won't necessarily keep you there, and it likely won't take you to the next level. And even if you are already aware of this fact, you might not know what your next steps of action should be. At this point in your personal growth, just having a great mind and heart for learning are not enough. You must be deliberate about improving and learning from those who are further down the road to success than you are.

Looking down that road will allow you to realize that your willingness to make changes in your life is what helps you transition from where you are now to where you want to be in the future, i.e., down that road to success. When you want something you have never had before, you must be willing to make the changes and do something you've never done before to get it.

The best way to describe how easy it is to get caught up in doing the same things over and over again is by using the jar analogy:

> **A cartoon I saw in a newspaper said something along the lines of,** *"You cannot read the label when you are inside the jar. You need help from the outside to be able to read it."* **It showed a picture of a person stuck in a jar with a label on the outside of the jar. Another person was sitting outside of a jar, holding a mirror in his hands so that the person inside the jar could read the label properly.**

How does that relate to doing the same things over and over again? When we can't see our own labels, it's easy to get trapped inside our own viewpoints and habits. Sometimes our own expertise can blind us from seeing what is obvious to somebody who is not in our heads and does not share the same biases as we do (back to the *oblivious to the obvious* syndrome I talked about in the previous chapter). We become convinced that we have "tried everything out there." We are 100 percent certain we know what works and what doesn't.

Warning bells should sound anytime you feel you are 100 percent certain about anything because sadly, this form of unintentional self-sabotage stops us from identifying valuable opportunities for growth or discovering new things worth trying. And this is what causes us to do the same things over and over again – even though they don't work. We continue to do these things because we don't know any better – *you don't know what you don't know until you know*, as Dr. Seuss might say. And like I mentioned earlier, knowing what you don't know is what makes Socrates (and you) wise.

Helping you uncover the negative patterns you're unconsciously engaging in and identifying blind spots is where a coach can come in handy. But what is a "coach", exactly? Kevin Hall's book, *Aspire: Discovering Your Purpose Through the Power of Words,* states that the word "coach" is derived from the horse-drawn coaches that were developed in a town called Kocs during the 15th century. At first, the vehicles were exclusively used to carry royalty from one place to another.

As time passed, coaches also carried mail, valuables, and passengers who were not royalty. But its origin is what makes a coach so great: they are there to get you to your desired destination.

> **"A coach remains something, or someone, who carries a valuable person from where they are to where they want to be."**
>
> ~KEVIN HALL

A coach can look at your situation from an unbiased and objective perspective, an "outside-the-jar" view point. A coach can see things that you cannot see. Your knowledge and skill set are limited to what you've learned in the past, and perhaps what you may need is new knowledge. A coach can provide that new knowledge to you to help spark the flame that provides the light source needed to assist you on your own knowledge-seeking journey.

Sometimes we need that extra push, that outside point of view, to kick us out of the zone that we've settled in (and settled *for*). The only way you can see your way out of the zone is to get a perspective from someone that can see your situation from an objective, third-person point of view.

In Chapter Six, I spoke about dimensions when lambasting how a 2-D relationship on a social media screen is no replacement for a 3-D relationship with a real person in the flesh. As removed from the 2-D of a screen that the 3-D of a live person is, think of coaching like you're jumping yet another dimension.

A geometry aside:

In geometry, a 3-D representation of a 4-D shape is called a *tesseract*. For example, a cube is a tesseract of its 4-D analog, just like a 2-D square is a tesseract for its 3-D analog (cube). Of course, being 3-D creatures, we cannot perceive at the 4-D level, which is why the tesseract was invented. It's all the stuff of mathematical esoterica over which theorists thrill.

The metaphor here is that seeking a coach to get you along on your journey is like taking out of you only what your "tesseract" is showing; it's like learning from someone who can see beyond the mere length, width, and depth of any current knowledge barriers. A coach is important because when you're in the picture and can't see the frame (that is, a 2-D creature trying to see the 3-D world), they can look at you from an outside-in perspective and help you catch the blind spots that are invisible from your frame of reference.

> *"Let us imagine a wheel with multi-coloured spokes rotating through the plane on which lives a two-dimensional being. The movement of the spokes will appear to a two-dimensional being as changes in the colour of a line lying on the surface."*
> ~Pyotr Demianovich Ouspensky, from *Tertium Organum*

Ouspensky was a Russian philosopher of the early Twentieth Century. I cited him above to make a point: our perception is always limited.

Outside of your bubble – your jar – is a whole world of perspective that supersedes your own. Like a magician leading you to believe what you expect to see while launching the illusion you don't expect – and then explaining the trick – a coach can explain the illusion and help you see a bigger picture of your goals, your mistakes, and your likely next moves. Your future is like a magician's trick: it will be an illusion until you understand the perspective.

Perspective is what matters, so no matter who you are, what you have accomplished, or how low (or how high) your life has taken you, you can benefit from working with a coach. If you've never had one, you have no idea how much a coach can improve your life. It can make the difference between success and failure. It can make or break you. And it can steer you away from one of the most significant problems people incur who struggle to make sustainable progress in their lives: having 20 years of experience, but that experience really only being one year of experience repeated 20 times.

Coaching, therefore, helps you discover your weaknesses – and identify what changes need to be made – from worlds outside of your own. A coach can help you see the blind spots and the unproductive patterns in your life that have become unconscious to you. They can help you see in other dimensions, and will allow you to expand your perspective in ways you could never have imagined.

> **"Don't look at the teacher...look at their students."**
>
> ~UNKNOWN

The key is to find the right coach who is dedicated to helping you and who can see your vision. The right coach knows that helping you is a part of his or her success as well because your subsequent accomplishments prove that what your coach teaches and practices actually work.

If you can find a coach who is already the type of person who you want to be, you are already halfway there. Like the Chinese proverb says, "To know the road ahead, ask those coming back."

A coach will fulfill three primary objectives:

1. They will make you engage in conversations that you are uncomfortable having, yet are mandatory for your growth.
2. They will force you to do some things that you normally avoid doing, but are necessary to help you escape your comfort zone.
3. They will help you become something you did not think you could become.

Sometimes you need a voice separate from your own to tell you what needs to be done. You need the help that can provide you with that extra push to get you over the hump you couldn't see (your tesseract) and into the next stage – and next dimension – of your life. That voice can also provide you with a real way to assess your progress accurately so you can see if you are getting better or worse. You're unable to do that from within the frame, bubble, or jar.

Such outside observations are more than just passively witnessing a process; they actually contribute to the process. In the 1950s, Henry Landsberger of the Western Electric Hawthorne Works electric company described the results of studies to determine the relationship between productivity and work environment. *The Hawthorne Effect* was the name given to the alteration of behavior by the subjects of a study, due to their awareness of being observed.

The Hawthorne Effect fits beautifully with how coaches can help you measure your growth, as measurement is key to improvement. In fact, measurement itself can even create improvement. Researchers who conducted experiments in productivity at the Hawthorne Work Plant discovered that when people knew their work was being measured, their productivity increased. If you know that your coach is measuring your work, just imagine how much further you will get in achieving your goals.

A quantum mechanics aside:

In the ultramicroscopic quantum world, a particle is neither in one position or another, but exists in both positions simultaneously (or in many) as a cloud of probability. Weird, I know. I don't feel bad for not understanding this, because even the quantum physicists don't fully understand it. When a particle is minding its own business, it is somewhat omnipresent, its cloud of probability (of all possible positions) giving it its omnipresence characteristic.

Now here's the mysterious part that the physicists (and therefore, I, too) find even more puzzling: when a particle that is minding its own omnipresent business is observed and measured (presumably by that physicist), it's probability cloud collapses, and it assumes only one position (the observed position). I love this stuff, and I indulge myself in trying to find ways to relate science to the lessons in this book. As such:

> You don't know where you stand until you are observed and measured from outside; hence why you need a coach. Until that time, all you can be are possibilities. A coach will help you collapse your probability cloud and become the one thing you were meant to be.

MILLION DOLLAR COACHING FOR FREE

"The advice that is readily available all over the Internet for free is worth way more than $1,000,000 if you apply it."

~UNKNOWN

Good coaching may cost you good money. For some people, the coach you would like to work with may not be available, or you may not have the budget to hire them. But that should not stop you. I have been able to learn so many valuable lessons from some of the most brilliant minds in the world that have coached me on sales, personal development, marketing, and countless other subjects... for *free*. How would I possibly learn from the smartest people on the planet without paying a single cent? The answer is the Internet.

The Internet has leveled the playing field. It allowed people who do not have the money to pay for the best education – or the best coaches – to learn from the experts for **free**. It is highly likely that whatever subject you want to master, all you have to do is go to YouTube and search for that subject. More than likely, countless experts are teaching exactly what you want to know for free.

Want to learn how to master personal development from perhaps the foremost expert on the topic? Simply go to YouTube and search "Tony Robbins" and watch endless hours of his content for free. Want to learn how to master one of the most important skills needed for virtually every business venture: sales? Go to YouTube and search "Grant Cardone" and watch countless hours of videos – again, for free. Want to learn how to develop unshakable self-confidence? Go to YouTube and search "Garrett J. White." Yet again...all this invaluable information is completely and 100 percent free.

These über-elite experts in their field get paid exorbitant amounts of money to speak at high-profile venues. Often times they take their own film crews to video their talks, then post their talks on their YouTube channels. Translation: you get it free.

The problem this presents: Typically people who don't pay – don't pay attention.

Consistently, I say on my podcast, "I'll provide the 'how-to', but you must provide the 'want-to'." That's why it's crucial you develop a burning desire to seek out the experts that will teach you how to master your craft. We are living in unprecedented times where we can be coached by geniuses for free. We just have to have the discipline to spend our time feeding our minds with content from these coaches, instead of feeding our minds with content that will not produce real results.

Mentoring

> "I like to think of mentoring as a responsibility and a privilege on the road to life. No matter what mile marker you are walking past at this point in life, there are thousands of people behind you who would love to learn how you made it so far so fast."
>
> ~BRENDON BURCHARD, 3-time *New York Times* bestselling author

There is a fine distinction between coaching and mentoring. Many see it as the same thing, but for our purposes, I have divided it into two separate things, based on the directional flow of knowledge.

> **"All of us, at some time or other, need help. Whether we're giving or receiving help, each one of us has something valuable to bring to this world. That's one of the things that connects us as neighbors--in our own way, each one of us is a giver and a receiver."**
>
> ~FRED ROGERS

A coach teaches you, so it's an *education* for you; but the coach – from his/her point of view – sees it as "mentoring," a *service* that also reinforces key lessons for himself/herself. In other words, a student from the opposite direction.

Remember the discussion on how repetition creates subconscious learning? Mentoring creates similar reinforcement. In addition to having a coach on your success team, you will want to give back by *becoming* a mentor. You get as much as you give because there is no better way to learn than to teach.

While it's important to understand that asking for help (in the form of a coach) is not a sign of weakness, but – on the contrary – is a sign of wisdom, it is also important to take Brendon Burchard's quote to heart: offer any new, improved insights you may gain to someone else.

1. Have a coach; then
2. be a coach (mentor), too.

Is that being too giving? Absolutely not. Mentoring teaches two people at the same time. There's a saying in the surgical industry that states, *"See one, do one, teach one."* This clever little phrase says it all, while succinctly covering the entire educational cycle that sends knowledge from a coach to you and then to someone else.

Handing down wisdom by teaching someone reinforces what you have learned. Even more potently, it makes you step up your own game. And even more importantly, it gives back to the world in an effort to make a better place for those who come after us. I'm not talking about giving away trade secrets; I'm talking about helping someone else get up to speed, someone who will be a great – and a forever-grateful – member in your network. It's a win-win for all involved.

THE ROAD TO HELL IS PAVED WITH INATTENTION

> "Pure hell forces action, but anything else can be endured with enough clever rationalization."
>
> ~TIM FERRISS, American entrepreneur, author and podcaster

Sometimes people are tempted to wait before getting the help (i.e., coaching) they need. You shouldn't wait, though, because if you do, that is, doing nothing, your bad situation can grow into an *insurmountably* bad situation. Then, when you can't stand it any longer, you act because you have to, but the uphill climb can be prohibitively steeper than it would have been had you gotten yourself moving earlier. You shouldn't wait to take action when you know something must be done, especially when it comes to your personal development. Hire a coach or get free coaching via other resources, such as YouTube.

But don't wait! So many of us are incredibly clever at rationalizing why we should put things off. However, if you look at the word, "rationalize", we're really just telling ourselves *rational* lies to justify our procrastination. It really is a variation of the sarcastic quote from Ben Franklin in Chapter Four, which can be re-written as:

> *So convenient a thing it is to be a reasonable creature, since it enables one to find or make a reason for putting off the things we know we need to do.*

For some people, putting things off only becomes an ingrained and automatic part of who they are – a bad habit, and you know how I feel about those. It's almost as if they're stuck in some hypnotic pattern they can't snap themselves out of, and actually, they are because they are operating on their subconscious programming and muscle memory. People who are conscious of the bad situation they find themselves in but do nothing to change merely sleepwalk through their daily decisions. Their minds wander from one thing to another and this causes them to shoot in different directions (chase one shiny object after another) and make no progress toward their goals.

> A Harvard study that gathered real-time data using an iPhone app in 2,350 subjects clocked a whopping 30 percent to 46.9 percent of mind-wandering during all activities except sex. Thus, as the study concluded, "Our mental lives are pervaded, to a remarkable degree, by the non-present." This means our minds are wandering for up to nearly half of our waking hours, unfocused on what we need to be doing. Furthermore, the Harvard study

discovered that wandering of the mind correlated directly with a feeling of unhappiness, supporting the notion that living in the here and now – that is, mindfulness – is the key to happiness.

The trick to snapping out of this unconscious trance is to train and sustain your focus. You have to continually pay attention and redirect your attention toward your goals in order to become the CEO of your life. All the world's greatest teachers and learning materials are useless without the sustained concentration needed to absorb what you are learning and consistently put it into action.

The very first step toward becoming more focused is to "grow up and get serious" in the words of goal-setting expert Gary Ryan Blair. Famously known as the "Goals Guy", Gary has helped over a half-million people achieve seemingly impossible goals in 100 days or less with his time-tested rapid execution system, *"The 100 Day Challenge."* In Blair's system, the very first lesson taught before setting any goals is that you must get serious.

What does that mean, exactly? It means that you must become fully committed to achieving whatever you set your mind to. In Blair's own words, *"behavior never lies,"* and every single action you take tells the world whether you're serious or just screwing around. It also determines if you are taking one step closer to or farther away from becoming – and remaining – the CEO of your life.

You may already be at a point in life where it's clear that you are serious about your success. You've decided that enough is enough, that you will no longer sit on the sidelines and watch other people achieve the kind of results you want and know you deserve. However, perhaps you're still not quite sure what to do. You know that you don't like where you are, but you don't have the motivation to change your present situation.

Without question, such motivation doesn't come easy. It's far easier to accept being average than it is to aspire for greatness. Disagree all you want, but the universe does not reward people who stand by and merely wait for results to come to them without an equivalent amount of effort put forth.

Unfortunately, for many people, the only thing that will pull them out of a mental state of passive acceptance is hell. Hell can mean different things to different people, based upon the lifestyle that they're accustomed to. For one person, hell could be driving a Honda, for another person it could be not vacationing in the Hamptons; and somebody else might experience hell because they don't have enough money to feed their children.

The varieties of hell can differ from person to person, but ultimately, it is one's personal hell that forces change. It is this hell that forces people to wake up and understand that they are doing something very wrong in their lives. It is this hellish kick in the pants that most people need to jolt themselves out of the automatic routines that have been mindlessly running their lives. Is that you? Are you running on autopilot? Are you stuck in a rut and unable to find the strength to pull yourself out? Do you need hell to kick you in the pants to make changes, or are you going to do something about changing your life before falling into the eternal, fiery pit?

> **"At some point denial is no longer an option."**
> ~BILL CLINTON

Many people stay in their own self-created hell. They don't do what is required to "resurrect". This is why C.S. Lewis wrote in *The Problem of Pain*, "The gates of Hell are locked from the inside." I would suggest that you don't wait for hell to change you or even to change *for* you, because it won't. Hell certainly won't freeze over, so stop waiting. Things will remain the same until you change.

Get the necessary knowledge before you fall into that pit of despair because falling down there will mean that you have to spend a lot more time getting back up. In order to change your life before you fall into the pit, you must become a different person.

This new person requires new knowledge. Every day offers an opportunity for this new knowledge, giving you an unlimited amount of chances to become the person that you want to be. All you need to do is educate yourself, continue educating yourself so you can condition out the faulty programs that were conditioned in, and never stop approaching endeavors as a novice – which will keep wonder in your life. Remember, you came to this world with no assets but you. It is how you leave this world that will define you. Microsoft co-founder Bill Gates said it best:

> *"If you are born poor it's not your mistake, but if you die poor it's your mistake."*

At the end of the day, it's not about money – it's about memories. And when you look back on your life you will see one of two things:

1. Someone who complained about the hand they were dealt;
2. Or someone who played the hand they were dealt like it was the one they wanted.

You are obligated to make a difference. And leaving this world better than before you arrived is the price of admission. To do that, you have to matter. To matter, you have to create the best version of yourself possible. That means becoming (and remaining) a lifelong learner. When your hunger for knowledge persists throughout your lifetime, you will leave the world with your legacy. A legacy may be a posthumous honor, but it means that those who depend on you now will continue to benefit from your contributions for generations to come.

CONCLUSION

> "The only way to remain great is to keep applying the fundamental principles that made you great."
>
> ~JIM COLLINS, American author, consultant and lecturer on the subject of business management and company sustainability and growth

Siedah Garrett's lyrics, made famous by Michael Jackson's mega-hit song *Man in the Mirror*, are a perfect way to end this final chapter:

I'm starting with the man in the mirror
I'm asking him to change his ways
And no message could have been any clearer
If you want to make the world a better place
Take a look at yourself, and then make a change

What do you see when you look at the man or woman in the mirror? Do you see someone who is giving it their all? Or do you see someone who has given up? Be honest. What do you see? More than likely, you've got some work to do. But that's okay, as long as you realize it.

My goal for my two boys is to always be able to look at them and ask: Is that the best you can do? Regardless if it's a grade they receive on a physics exam or a performance on an athletic field. If Tom or Tristan reply, "Yes dad," that will please me. But if they reply, "No dad, I could have done better," that will not make me very happy.

All I want from you (same as from my children and myself) is for you to do your best. That's it. Understand that progress is a process. Always maintain a chess player mentality. And never stop giving it your all. If you're in a bad situation – change it. If you're in a good situation – make it better. That's what I did. In 2014 I started applying to Harvard. And in 2019 I finally began taking classes. Going back to school at 41-years-old may not make sense to a lot of people. But how can I give my boys (and you) the advice of always seeking constant and never-ending improvement (CANI) if I don't live it myself? Answer: I can't.

This world will chew you up and spit you out if you let it. You probably already know that. And the only way I believe you can win is by educating yourself. Education is by far the most powerful weapon you have in your arsenal. Understand, you don't need Harvard; you just need to never lose your hunger for knowledge. There's enough free education on the Internet (including Harvard lectures) to provide intelligence on virtually any subject that interests you. You just need to foster the fortitude to seek it out.

Fall in love with learning. Because an uneducated life is an unfulfilled life. And don't make the mistake of thinking it's too late. Too many people think their time to learn has passed after graduate school, college, or even high school. But nothing could be further from the truth! Today's world has rendered this woefully out-of-date. Consider how the notion of retirement has changed in just one generation, simply by increasing life expectancy.

The whole concept of retirement was instituted on a false expectation because the original age of 65 was first established by Otto von Bismarck as a deception. While he offered what appeared to be populist compassion, Bismarck, the "Iron Chancellor", knew that the life expectancy in Germany in 1880 was well below 65. (Translated: it looked like his government was being generous, gaining him brownie points with the people, but the statistical reality is that there would be little capital outlay from the government.) When the United States followed suit and instituted its own retirement age as 65 in 1935, the life expectancy at that time was still under 62. Now that the average life expectancy is approaching 80, the joke's on the government. But watch out! The government can't take a joke.

> **"I tell everyone not to retire, but to rewire."**
> ~DR. RUTH WESTHEIMER

Why am I sharing these troubling facts? Only to reiterate that the world is changing. Knowledge is doubling at an ever-accelerating rate, and we need to keep learning way past the time we would have been dead in the 1880s or even 1930s; if not, we might as well be dead in this new millennium.

Is 50 the new 40? Is 70 the new 50? The truth is that if you're alive, you owe it to yourself to keep learning. That's the way any older year becomes the new younger year.

It's said that when world-famous cellist Pablo Casals was 95-years-old (the new 65?), a young reporter asked him, "You are ninety-five and the greatest cellist that ever lived. Why do you still practice for six hours a day?" Mr. Casals answered, "Because I think I'm making progress."

At the end of the day, there is no weapon more powerful than the obsessive drive to constantly seek new ways to improve. Nothing provides more sustainable results than the relentless pursuit of working to become the best possible version of yourself.

When you prioritize building the inside first, the outside ends up building itself. When you prioritize reprogramming your subconscious, your conscious reaps the rewards. And when you eventually achieve your goals, you'll discover that what you learned along the way to reaching them was significantly more valuable than the goals themselves.

Never lose your hunger for personal growth because the only thing that will change who you are today and who you will be a year from now is the people you know and the knowledge you retain. If you don't end up better tomorrow than you are today, then what's the point of living today? Or tomorrow? Or the rest of your tomorrows? Face it, you might as well retire!

Instead, one year from today, you should be able to look back and be overjoyed with all the changes you have made and the exponential growth you have experienced. 365 days of learning something new; 365 days of opening your mind to new possibilities. 365 days of new programming; and 365 days of new, enriching experiences. And if it's a leap year, you can even add one more!

Successful learning, to be clear, requires that you condition some of the junk out that was conditioned in. Conditioning the negative beliefs out of your mind requires patience, consistent effort, and reinforcement. That's because your subconscious, while at first gullible in the delta/theta implicit learning years, ends up being insistent on what it has learned – whether true or false – in the later alpha-2/beta explicit learning.

If you desire to become the CEO of your life, you must motivate yourself to learn more, do more, and become more than everyone else around you. You have to open your mind, maintain a beginner's mindset, and invest the time, effort, and money that's required to develop superior skills. And when you do, you'll be able to look into that proverbial mirror and see someone winking back at you.

EXERCISE NO. 1: UNDERSTAND YOUR SUBCONSCIOUS PROGRAMMING

Throughout the day, ask yourself: what program am I currently running?

Since science has proven that nearly 95 percent of everything we think and do is an unconscious program we're running – it's important to intentionally install pattern interrupts into your life so you can break free from the hypnotic trance so many of us find ourselves regularly in. This is vital to your success because we all know that what we repeatedly do is who we are (thanks Aristotle).

When you discover what program you're running on, ask yourself: if I repeat this day in and day out, will it get me closer to my goals or further away from them? If the answer is closer to your goals, this is a good program, keep doing what you're doing. However, if the answer is further away from your goals, make a conscious effort to stop what you're doing and refocus. Do a Control-Alt-Delete on the faulty program, then reboot!

Tracking your time is a great way to study yourself. And as I've mentioned several times throughout this book, you are the most important subject that you should be studying. When you track your time it allows you to see the truth, it allows you to step outside of yourself and *really* see what programs you're actually running. Behavior doesn't lie.

Make copies of the timesheets I provided on page 552 and routinely (at least once a quarter) as well as randomly pull out your timesheets and document your time. While you're documenting (and examining the results) employ unadulterated self-honesty. Never forget success in life is nothing more than compounding one productive day on top of another. Therefore, when you regularly run the right programs – day in and day out – you will not have to go looking for success because success will come looking for you... that's just the way the universe works.

EXERCISE NO. 2: TAKE SEVEN AND SYNCHRONIZE YOUR BRAIN

If you find yourself engaging in activities that are not healthy or productive – take seven rhythmic breaths to help reset your mind. After that, take a short break (3 minutes). It's the pause that relaxes and refreshes your brain.

Once you find yourself refocusing, slowly cross your legs and/or arms. This encourages both of your brain's hemispheres (left and right) to work together (hemi-sync), thereby, reducing tension in your body. Some scientists believe that we have the ability to use our full brains capacity (not the proverbial 10 percent so many of us have been led to believe – see glial cells discussed previously in this chapter). And one of the ways we can do this i.e., use our entire brain is by simply intersecting our brain's hemispheres.

According to research scientist Dr. Bruce Lipton:

> *"Crossing your arms and legs actually engages both hemispheres – which calms the system down, but engages the whole brain process."*

When our right hand, (which is controlled by our left brain) crosses the midline of our body, it simultaneously gets picked up by the opposite hemisphere. When you cross your arms or legs what you're doing is causing the right and left parts of your brain to synchronize.

This is one of the exercises that certainly falls into the category: simple to do but simple not to do. However, don't fall victim to the simplicities of success.

Staying on track all day long requires a tremendous amount of cognitive strength. Do the best you can to reset, refocus and synchronize your "brains" because regularly course-correcting throughout the day is the only surefire way to achieve sustainable success.

EXERCISE NO. 3: DISCOVER YOUR PASSION

Get on YouTube and search for topics that interest you. Look for credible experts talking about these subjects. Take notes. Be open-minded. Test/implement the strategies that these experts reveal. If they work, attempt to teach them (see next exercise) so that you can have a better understanding of the strategies, as well as some feedback on the results you get (or don't get).

EXERCISE NO. 4: TEACH SOMETHING

> "Knowledge will not attract money, unless it is organized, and intelligently directed, through practical plans of action."
>
> ~NAPOLEON HILL

Stephen Covey (author of *The 7 Habits of Highly Effective People,* which I have cited several times throughout this book) has said that to truly learn something, you need to teach it. When we teach, we become genuinely motivated to learn the material because we're not just doing it for ourselves, but for others.

Teaching also forces us to look at a concept with a beginner's mindset, which can provide greater clarity and insight. The missing link to personal development is teaching people how to organize and use knowledge after they acquire it. And when a question is asked which you cannot – as the student's mentor – answer, there's a new opportunity for you (as a student) to learn.

This week, teach one of your skills to someone. You can find a community organization such as a youth group or perhaps an entrepreneurial MeetUp that may be interested in the knowledge you have to offer. Donate your time in a quest to help others – expecting nothing in return. You'll sleep better for it, and as you know by now, sleep is crucial to success.

If you can maintain a beginner's mindset to the very end, your thinking will keep changing and you will continue growing and learning. Be careful to never allow your learning to turn into nothing more than just knowledge because, without action, knowledge is just useless data; and without sharing, knowledge is just useless vanity.

EXERCISE NO. 5: WRITE A BOOK

Okay, stay with me here. This is not nearly as difficult as you might think. If you can talk, you can write a book. Let me break this down into 8 simple steps because I believe that writing a book is one of the greatest gifts we can give the world. We talked about the concept of leaving a legacy earlier in this chapter. Writing a book certainly allows you to do that, and it also creates an opportunity for an amazing self-discovery process to unfold like none other. It is also a unique way to mentor *en masse*, which in turn teaches you yet again.

Here's the 8-step process:

1. Think of a catchy title; this can be altered, and probably will be by the time you complete your book
2. Write down the title of each chapter
3. Below the title of each chapter write 5 to 10 bullet points about the chapter title
4. Use Keynote (Apple) or PowerPoint (Microsoft) and make slides for your book, i.e., each title chapter with the bullet points below each slide
5. Record yourself giving a presentation or talking people through each slide

   Use Camtasia or ScreenFlow; you could even find an app that will help you record the audio directly to your phone
6. Go to a website such as Temi.com and have your audio file transcribed
7. Go to UpWork.com or Fiverr.com and find someone to edit your transcript
8. For the cover design, go to 99Designs.com and you'll be blown away when hundreds (and hundreds) of insanely beautiful designs are submitted for the cover of your new book

It's that simple to write a book, and it's even simpler to self-publish it on Amazon. If you really want to do this, if you really want to become an author, you will find a way. There is one resource after another (for free) on the Internet that will take you by the hand and show you every step of the way.

Remember in Chapter One how I made the "cover" of this book before I wrote a single word and pasted it to another book to render my mind's eye (mindsight) vision of the finished product? There is no greater feeling in the world than replacing the "temporary prop" with the real thing!

When you recite ("talk") your book, it gives you the audio version to sell on Audible or other similar outlets. Understand, there is no specific length to a book (I kinda over did it with this one). It's whatever you choose. You are the author. You are the designer. You call the shots. You have something to say, so say it. Out loud. Let the world hear you.

The other seldom-touted benefit of writing a book is that your descendants, even long after you're gone, are able to climb into your brain and see how you thought. What I wouldn't give to "visit" a long-gone relative and explore!

EXERCISE NO. 6: EXERCISE

You may have noticed that I continuously reinforce the extensive benefits of exercise throughout this book. Why? Because one scientific study after another has proven a crucial ingredient to increasing our intelligence (as well as overall health) can be traced back to the amount of exercise we get. Want to be smarter? Exercise. Want to solve life's toughest challenges? Exercise. Want to leave your mark on this world? Exercise. Want to live longer? Exercise.

Brain scientist Dr. Jonathan Repple states:

> *"Specifically, those who performed better on the walking test also had more white matter in their brain. White brain matter is important because it contains nerve fibers that allow signals to travel faster and more efficiently, plus protects those nerve fibers from injury."*

Science has proven that we increase the number of brain cells we have when we work out. Cardio and resistance training (weighted exercises) increases growth factors in our brain which makes it easier for our brain to form new neuronal connections.

In addition to increasing intelligence, exercise (even limited amounts) produces extraordinary health benefits. A research study that was conducted by the *British Journal of Sports Medicine* observed 232,149 people over a period of 5 to 35 years. And they discovered that the ones who made a habit of running once per week had a significantly lower mortality rate than those who didn't – as much as 27 percent less. The researchers concluded:

> *"Increased rates of participation in running, regardless of its dose, would probably lead to substantial improvements in population health and longevity. Any amount of running, even just once a week, is better than no running, but higher doses of running may not necessarily be associated with greater mortality benefits."*

Make exercise a habit in your life (see Chapter Five). Just do it.

EXERCISE NO. 7: LEADERS ARE READERS

Below is a list of 50 must-read (or listen-to) books. Many of them I've referenced throughout this book.

1. *Outwitting the Devil*, The Secret to Freedom and Success, Napoleon Hill
2. *Awaken the Giant Within*, Anthony Robbins
3. *Think and Grow Rich*, Napoleon Hill
4. *Sometimes You Win Sometimes You Learn: Life's Greatest Lessons are Gained from Our Losses*, John C. Maxwell
5. *Put Your Dream to the Test: 10 Questions to Help You See It and Seize It*, John C. Maxwell
6. *As a Man Thinketh*, James Allen
7. *Battlefield of the Mind: Winning the Battle in Your Mind*, Joyce Meyer
8. *In Search of Identity*, Anwar Sadat
9. *How We Decide*, Jonah Lehrer
10. *How the Mighty Fall: And Why Some Companies Never Give In*, Jim Collins
11. *Great by Choice*, Jim Collins
12. *Good to Great*, Jim Collins

13. *Finding the Next Steve Jobs*, Nolan Bushnell with Gene Stone
14. *Blink: The Power of Thinking Without Thinking*, Malcolm Gladwell
15. *Outliers: The Story of Success*, Malcolm Gladwell
16. *Over the Top: Moving from Survival to Stability, from Stability to Success, from Success to Significance*, Zig Ziglar
17. *See You at the Top*, Zig Ziglar
18. *Grit: The Power of Passion and Perseverance*, Angela Duckworth
19. *Predictably Irrational, Revised and Expanded Edition: The Hidden Forces That Shape Our Decisions*, Dr. Dan Ariely
20. *Poke the Box*, Seth Godin
21. *Thinking in Bets: Making Smarter Decisions When You Don't Have All the Facts*, Annie Duke
22. *Steve Jobs*, Walter Isaacson
23. *Taking People With You: The Only Way to Make Things Happen*, David Novak
24. *The Power of Habit: Why We Do What We Do in Life and Business*, Charles Duhigg
25. *The Seven Habits of Highly Effective People: Powerful Lessons in Personal Change*, Stephen R. Covey
26. *The Power of Positive Thinking*, Norman Vincent Peale
27. *The Winners Manual: For the Game of Life*, Jim Tressel
28. *The Last Lecture*, Randy Pausch with Jeffrey Zaslow
29. *The Start-up of You*, Reid Hoffman and Ben Casnocha
30. *The 50th Law*, 50 Cent and Robert Greene
31. *The 15 Invaluable Laws of Growth: Live Them and Reach Your Potential*, John C. Maxwell
32. *Failing Forward: Turning Mistakes Into Stepping Stones for Success*, John C. Maxwell
33. *The Secret*, Rhonda Byrne
34. *Night School: The Life-Changing Science of Sleep*, Richard Wiseman

35. *The Prince*, Nicolo Machiavelli
36. *Never Split The Difference: Negotiating as if Your Life Depended on It*, Chris Voss with Tahl Raz
37. *The Charge: Activating the 10 Human Drives that Make You Feel Alive*, Brendon Burchard
38. *Thinking, Fast and Slow*, Daniel Kahneman
39. *The Biology of Belief*, Bruce H. Lipton, PhD
40. *Wisdom Meets Passion: When Generations Collide and Collaborate*, Dan Miller/Jared Angaza
41. *Every Day A Friday: How to be Happier 7 Days a Week*, Joel Osteen
42. *How To Win Friends & Influence People*, Dale Carnegie
43. *The Compound Effect: Jumpstart Your Income, Your Job, Your Success*, Darren Hardy
44. *The Entrepreneur Roller Coaster*, Darren Hardy
45. *Money Master the Game: 7 Simple Steps to Financial Freedom*, Tony Robbins
46. *Man's Search for Meaning*, Viktor E. Frankl
47. *Mindset: The New Psychology of Success*, Carol S. Dweck, PhD
48. *The Slight Edge: Turning Simple Disciplines into Massive Success and Happiness*, Jeff Olson
49. *The One Thing: The Surprisingly Simple Truth Behind Extraordinary Results*, Gary Keller with Jay Papasan
50. *The Power of I Am: Two Words That Will Change Your Life Today*, Joel Osteen

Finding time to read can be difficult. However, there is such a thing as automobile university – what I call "Harvard on Wheels": listening to books in your car (or on the go) is how high-achievers continue to take it to the next level.

Conclusion: One Day or Day One, You Choose

"A mind that is stretched by a new experience can never go back to its old dimensions."

~OLIVER WENDELL HOLMES, Jr., Former Associate Justice of the Supreme Court of the United States

Success in life is often compared to a marathon. And I can certainly appreciate the rationale behind that thought process. However, I believe a better comparison would be to a boxing match: you spend a tremendous amount of time behind the scenes planning, preparing, and practicing – then life gives you those brief moments (rounds) to showcase your talents. This is precisely why Chris Voss, former FBI international hostage negotiator believes, "When the pressure is on, you don't rise to the occasion – you fall to your highest level of preparation."

Throughout this book, I've done everything I can to prepare you for the inevitable punches life is going to throw at you. Whether the blows come from depression, an addiction, a disappointment, a disease, or a divorce – know that you're continuously being battle-tested. And also know that you always have the ability to win from within. This is because the real fight takes place in your mind.

A lot of people lose the fight simply because they quit fighting. They get knocked down and they stay down. They give up and sell themselves on a lie that this is the best they can do. They walk around with smiles on their faces, pretending everything is okay. But on the inside, deep down, they know life has so much more to offer. They know this because they see it. They internalize it. But for some reason, it just does not seem tangible to them. So figuratively – and literally – they give up.

Have you ever met someone who's happy being mediocre? They're broke and they're smiling. They're nowhere close to fulfilling their potential, yet they still pretend that everything is okay. What gives? Are they delusional? Have they gone insane? No. They've sold themselves a lie. And they're doing the best they can to sell this same lie to anyone they come in contact with. But as the Indian philosopher Buddha explained:

> *"Three things cannot be long hidden: the sun, the moon, and the truth."*

The truth is we all have the ability to win the boxing matches in life. We all can become more than we currently are. But the problem is many people quit and conform when life begins to knock them around. Former heavyweight champion Mike Tyson is famous for saying, "Everybody has a plan until they get hit. Then, like a rat, they stop in fear and freeze." Each of us from the beginning of time was programed with "fight or flight" (or freeze) software. It's in our DNA. But some people, the CEOs, learn to override the program. They condition out the junk that was conditioned in. And they begin to do this when they cultivate the courage to fight back.

The only thing that will keep you from freezing (and allow you to perform at your best) when times get tough is muscle memory. And the only way to develop muscle memory is through repetition. The more you repeat something, a thought or an activity – the more you train your body how to do it better than your mind. This is why one of the best ways to reprogram your mind is through mental rehearsal (see Chapter One). When you visualize yourself overcoming obstacles that stand in your way, when you repeat the thought over and over again, the reinforcement creates the programs necessary to shatter previous false beliefs and find solutions. Once the new thought patterns have been reinforced enough, your brain is no longer a record of the past, but rather a map to the future.

> **You need to program yourself to get back in the ring and fight like your life depends on it – because it does, and quite possibly other lives as well if you have people (like your children) counting on you.**

Life is indeed like a never-ending boxing match against you and the circumstances thrust upon you. You're in for the fight of your life. And the fight is always between you and your thoughts. Since you think nearly 70,000 thoughts each day, and 90 percent of those thoughts are the same as the previous day, the most important thing you must work on (and change) is the way you habitually think. This is crucial because the same thoughts lead to the same choices, the same choices lead to the same behavior, and the same behavior leads to the results you're currently getting.

The moment you change the way you think and channel the power of mental rehearsal, you'll stop spending all of your time cringing in the corner and dodging the punches life throws at you. At this point, you'll go on the offensive and start fighting back. Now the momentum of the boxing match will begin to shift in your favor, which moves you toward a victorious outcome. You become more agile in your movements, switching from the defensive to the offensive. And as you start taking more risks with the punches you throw, you start to transform into the successful person you truly need to be to become the CEO of your life.

> **"Your results in life are a direct reflection of your choices. If you want better results, make better choices."**
>
> ~UNKNOWN

No matter where you are in life, no matter the struggles that you are going through, you are capable of stepping into the ring and winning the fight.

When you take 110 percent responsibility for your actions and the results they produce, when you stop relying on the rest of the world to give you approval and validation and, instead, decide to approve of yourself and make the deliberate choice to overcome the current circumstances you find yourself in – whatever they may be – you begin to win the fight.

THE BEACH BALL MENTALITY

"What defines us is how well we rise after falling."

~ZIG ZIGLAR

I've done the best I can to free your mind and show you the path to prosperity. But now you have to make a choice. You can choose to remain a victim of your history or, instead, choose to become a master of your destiny. It's simply a choice. And it's completely up to you what you decide. All I can do is show you the path, but you're the one who has to make the choice to walk down it. You're the one who has to take the first step.

Will letting go of all of the injustices and inequalities you've experienced be easy? Of course not. Will letting go of the bitterness you felt when others did you wrong be simple? Nope. But you need to make a conscious decision to not only let go, but – more importantly – to move on. You need to let go of the garbage that has been weighing you down. You need to stop replaying past failures over in your mind. And you need to get back into the ring. Once you permanently let go of the past and when you begin to fight for your freedom, you will rise, like a beach ball always coming to the surface, regardless of what is trying to hold it (or you) underwater.

How can I be so sure? How do you know I'm not just giving you a motivational speech as a farewell send off? Answer: because I live it! I walk the walk and I talk the talk.

Unquestionably, I'm one of the most unlikely people in the world to write a book of this magnitude – one that has the potential to make a billion lives better. There are countless reasons I can come up with about why I could be a prisoner of my past. But just like you, I had to make a choice. Do I allow my disappointments to define me? Do I let bitterness and all the indignations take root in my mind? Or do I refuse to stay down after I've been knocked down. Do I choose to rise and prosper? Either way, whatever I decide I become – it manifests as a self-fulfilling prophecy.

Let me share a final personal story with you.

August 20, 2009, police officers surrounded my home and arrested me. Two months later, I found myself in a criminal courtroom facing several prison life sentences. Without question, the pressure was on that day. I remember the district attorney looking up at the judge and informing her I had passed all my polygraph exams. My court-appointed attorney told me that passing the lie detector tests, having zero prior criminal offenses, and a stellar military background guaranteed I would go home that day. He informed me that the worst was behind me, that the charge Misapplication of Fiduciary Property was not that serious of an offense, and that I would be sentenced to something called "shock probation" because there was no room in state penitentiaries for white-collar offenders.

What I was sentenced to that day was certainly shocking, but unfortunately, probation would not be included. When the judge gave me my first 20-year prison term, it didn't even register. It was like playing a sadistic game of Simon Says, where Simon tells you to pat your head, but Simon pats his stomach. You see one thing, but you hear something completely different. I saw myself going home that day. In my mind, I believed the worst had already taken place. So when the judge gave me a second 20-year prison term, I was oblivious to that one as well. A 40-year prison sentence only happens to people without names or faces, not someone like me; that's what my mind believed.

But nothing could be further from the truth. Prison was my new reality. And no matter how hard I tried to distort reality, those thick metal bars wouldn't go away.

Shortly after I was sentenced, I was put on a bus and transported from county jail to a maximum-security penitentiary. The reality and gravity of my situation, my new environment – one I would spend many, many years – became even more real when I arrived at the Byrd Prison Unit in Huntsville, Texas. There, I went through an extensive check-in process. When that was completed, I was escorted to a six-foot by eight-foot prison cell. The guard opened the door, motioned for me to get in, then quickly slammed the metal door shut behind me. The moment I stepped in, I moved over to the steel toilet that was located in the corner of the cell. I really needed to use the bathroom and had been holding it for hours.

My cellmate was laying on the bottom bunk and barely moved as I approached the toilet. But before I could relieve myself, I noticed there were clothes (a white prison uniform) in the toilet. Befuddled, I sheepishly asked if he knew how I used the bathroom. "Grape" (the street he grew up on in Compton, which is where his prison name derived) replied, "Just doing some laundry cellie." Inmates steal bleach from the kitchen and wash their clothes in the toilet – the same place they...well, you know. Later, I learned Grape had just been sentenced to 65 years for aggravated attempted murder. I'll never forget him telling me, "People are hard to kill."

Slowly, I began to realize that my environment was not going to change, so I went to work on changing myself. I spent a tremendous amount of time replaying my life over in my mind and trying to unearth what went so wrong. The book you are reading now is the result of that forced self-reflection process. This was my attempt (and only option) to get something positive from this incredibly negative situation I had put myself in.

One day while I was writing a chapter of this book, a legal letter was slid under my prison cell door. The documents inside revealed the corporate lawyers who recommended the transactions that led to my conviction paid $1,000,000 in a confidential settlement. Euphoria flooded my mind. Instantly I thought this would lead to an early release and get me out of the nightmare I found myself in. But when the criminal court of appeals reviewed the confidential agreement they said it would have been crucial to bring up at sentencing, but now it was too late. That delivered a knockout blow – one that was not easy to recover from.

> **"Circumstance does not make the man, it reveals him to himself."**
>
> ~JAMES ALLEN

Years went by and I was sent to one prison after another – nine in total. Then, nearly half a decade later, I was provided communication that I had been given an immediate release. A prominent Texas judge went to the Board of Pardons and Paroles and advocated on my behalf.

It was finally over. I was going home. But to what? The answer was I was going home to nothing. However, nothing with freedom was significantly more than nothing with confinement. I was bussed back to the original prison that I had initially been processed into. It seemed this nightmare had come full circle. But I quickly learned that one of the worst parts of my prison process was about to take place.

> An unspoken rule in prison is you never tell anyone you're going home. Because if you do, the inmates will do everything possible to make sure that does not happen. You lie. If anyone asked where I was going I told them, "I have some fed time to go do."

Once the guards begin rounding the inmates up who were going home, the process began. In the middle of the night, about 90 of us were taken out of our prison cells and put into large metal cages. We were all corralled like cattle into these cages. Prison guards would stand by the exit door of the cages and read off names. The inmates whose names were called were quickly moved to the next cage. This process occurred over and over again, and each time anywhere from five to fifteen names were not called. This meant they would not be released. My heart continued to pound throughout this half-day long process. From cage to cage I prayed I'd go home that day.

Thankfully, my name and prison number continued to be called moving me from one cage to the next – each time closer and closer to freedom. Ninety of us started this process, but only about 25 of us made it out of the front gates of prison that day.

As I walked into freedom for the first time in years, I saw my father in the distance waiting for me. And I immediately remembered what he said when he came and visited me in prison not long after the criminal court of appeals made their ruling on the one million dollar settlement. I was at my breaking point then, and my father knew it. But he told me, "One day you'll look back on this and see it was nothing more than a blip on the radar. I believe in you son, and I know you'll find a way out."

Without question, I brought all of my hardships upon myself. But maybe you're in a situation where you had nothing to do with the dire circumstances you find yourself in. Perhaps you're in a negative environment that is not one of your creating. Let me share a story with you about someone who didn't deserve the hand she was dealt, either, yet still prospered.

Take a look at these awful circumstances which were endured by someone we all know and love:

- Born to an unmarried teenage mother
- Spent her entire childhood in extreme poverty – she was so poor she would wear potato sacks as dresses
- Did not see her mother very much due to her hectic work schedule
- Molested by her cousin, uncle, and a family friend at the age of 9
- Ran away from home at 13 after years of abuse
- Gave birth when she was 14 to a premature son who didn't survive
- Stole money from her mother before being sent to live with her father

Fortunately for this woman, living with her biological father was a blessing because he encouraged her to make education a top priority, which set her on a path toward success. In fact, she managed to land some early achievements in her career within the media and communications industry.

"If you feel like you don't fit into the world you inherited, it is because you were born to help create a new one."

~ROSS CALIGIURI

However, she continued to face constant racism and discrimination as she attempted to work in a brutally competitive environment. Many people thought she was "unfit for TV."

No one can say that this woman chose to be poor growing up, nor did she choose to suffer abuse and mistreatment at the hands of her own family. She was not responsible for the way other people treated and perceived her – that was entirely out of her control.

However, this incredible woman was eventually able to do three things:

1. She was able to put aside any bitterness, negativity, or self-doubt – leaving her private "prison."
2. With her resilience, she was able to work through her circumstances of poverty at a young age, realizing her childhood did not define her adulthood nor who she was going to be for the rest of her life.
3. She actively fought to change her environment as she gradually worked her way up a TV career, getting her own show, and eventually her own network and media empire.

Does this story sound familiar? Do you know who this is? If you guessed Oprah, you guessed right. Oprah Winfrey is arguably one of the most successful people on the planet. With hundreds of millions of dollars under her name and a reputation that will live on long after she's gone, she is a shining testament to the power you hold to prosper through unfathomable circumstances, using your inner strength to create the environment you want.

> **"You are responsible for your life. If you're sitting around waiting on somebody to save you, to fix you, to even help you, you are wasting your time. Only you have the power to move your life forward."**
>
> ~OPRAH WINFREY

Oprah Winfrey is living proof that your circumstances can change if you simply decide to view obstacles as stepping stones to be overcome. It is certainly possible for your circumstances to change, but in order for that to happen, *you need to change*, and you need to change with purpose.

Disappointments only define us if we actively hand over the power and allow them to.

Your current circumstances may be genuinely awful, and it's not uncommon to feel like they're going to control you and hold you down for the rest of your life. Many people have been conditioned to believe that they are victims of their circumstances which are out of their control. But look around: there's a wild card – and it's you!

> **Treat this very moment as day one. Day one to break out of old routines and habits. Start now, not one day, but now! Day one.**

Put one foot in front of the other and realize that your challenges must be faced head-on. Any bitterness you foster, amplified by blamelessness and not taking responsibility, only blinds you to what you need to do. Instead, allow your challenges to shift into blessings in disguise by choosing to use them to help you grow into a stronger, better version of yourself. (Remember the Bio-Dome experiment from Chapter Three?) You need challenges if you want to improve and rise to the next level. You need the mistakes. One of my favorite quotes that comes from Charles Swindoll (a quote I instructed you to memorize in the exercise section of Chapter Three) beautifully sums it up:

> *"We are all faced with a series of great opportunities brilliantly disguised as impossible situations."*

All of us go through rough patches in life. But the ones who foster the right attitude and refuse to allow their downtimes to define them are the ones who not only come out on top, but oftentimes leap ahead of those who never experience major setbacks.

By actively seeking and embracing your challenges in life, you unlock the greatness that has been lying dormant within you for as long as you've been alive. Challenges allow you to break out of your shell and evolve into the person you were meant to be. Overcoming bitterness and past indignations may be your biggest challenge, but when you do, you can emerge from your circumstances, just like a butterfly from its chrysalis.

Becoming the CEO of your life requires you to step up, so you need to admit that you are not willing to accept anything short of your dreams and your goals. Ordinary is the new mediocrity. You have gifts and talents that you want to share with the world, and you picked up this book because you want to be able to manifest them to the fullest of your ability.

> **"As I walked out the door toward the gate that would lead to my freedom, I knew if I didn't leave my bitterness and hatred behind, I'd still be in prison."**
>
> ~NELSON MANDELA

Simply acknowledging that you must change is a crucial step in erasing your present circumstances and etching new ones into your life. But where do you start?

You start by changing your universe – your vision. When you make that change, when your sight is laser-focused on your targets – your goals, your life begins to shift. Then when obstacles throw sorties of destruction your way, you engage your resilience. When you are tempted to quit, you – instead – delay instant gratification and "stay on message," remaining focused on the task at hand. You change yourself by trading away bad habits for good habits, which will help compound one successful day on top of another. You change the faulty subconscious programs that were downloaded early in your life. You create new programs through the power of repetition. Programs that will empower you and allow you to reach your full potential. You enlist high-quality people – hand-selected by you – for the best inner circle with which you can surround yourself. You maintain a student mindset, always allowing yourself to be open to new opportunities and ways of doing things.

These steps are, in essence, the chapters of this book, and they are written with the sole purpose of providing a blueprint that allows you to live your best life.

WILL YOU SOAR

> "The hardest thing about change is not making the same choices you did the day before."
>
> ~DR. JOE DISPENZA

To show you how important it is to evolve and improve on a consistent basis, I want to share one last story with you. This story is about the transformation an eagle must undergo in order to survive:

> Despite living the first 30 to 40 years as majestic creatures of flight, eagles are born with a significant threat to their lives. What, you may ask? The danger is that their beaks eventually become too dull for hunting, and their talons are no longer sharp enough to catch prey. An eagle's beak and talons are essential for hunting, so without these tools, the eagle will die of starvation.
>
> But there's a twist: when an eagle's hunting tools become useless, an opportunity exists for the eagle to expand its life for an additional 30 years, and seizing this one opportunity is a decision that literally means life or death for the eagle.
>
> To double its lifespan, the eagle must break off its old beak to form a new one and shed off all of its old heavy feathers. This process is extremely painful and it takes nearly five months to go through this transformation. If the eagle chooses to break its beak, it survives. If the eagle is unwilling to live through the challenge and the pain of doing so, it dies.
>
> In other words, the eagle must make the conscious choice to endure the pain of the only solution available in exchange for something far more significant: its very survival as one of nature's most dominant predators.

There is an ongoing debate about the accuracy of whether or not eagles go through this rite of passage, but the takeaway lesson is unmistakable: we all come to a point where we must decide whether to give up and fade away, or transform and change for the better.

This proverbial "rite of passage" implies something essential for existence. Many people who want to change, see themselves in do-or-die scenarios, eventually arrive at the realization that they don't need anyone or anything outside of themselves to succeed. It was in them all along; they just needed to tap into their inner power and truly commit to believing in themselves. They had to recognize and act upon the emergency that was right in front of them.

It's said you can't teach an old dog new tricks – but nothing could be further from the truth (and behavioral science proves it). Whether a dog, an eagle, or a human being in the December years of life – you can change. You can grow. You can evolve. You can become more than you currently are.

Be patient with yourself but also be persistent about the changes that need to be made. You're not going to get it right the first time, the second time, or perhaps even the thirtieth time. But if you never stop trying, if you promise you will not stay down when you get knocked down, you will win in the end.

It really comes down to how bad you want it. If you want it only 99 percent, that's not enough. Remember the pyramids in this book – Maslow's Hierarchy of Needs and Burch's Hierarchy of Competence? The reason the top of a pyramid is a point is because it represents that final 1 percent. If you only want it 99 percent, the remaining 1 percent – unachieved – will ensure you fail.

Winning in the end, then, means you must always fight for your freedom and firmly believe, *I am in complete control of my destiny. Only I can decide how all of this is going to end.* Such clarity and confidence will allow you to stop thinking about the things which have been trying to validate your old life and to start changing by thinking with new, positive, and empowering thoughts. And if you were successful at the beginning of this book at reverse engineering your best life, then your dreams are already in your mindsight.

Invoking the very first quote I cited in this book:

"Maybe the journey isn't so much about becoming anything. Maybe it's about un-becoming everything that isn't really you, so you can be who you were meant to be in the first place."

Source: www.americamagazine.org

In other words, you don't have to be Michelangelo to sculpt the Pietà; you only have to chip away at everything in the marble that is *not* Pietà. When you keep chipping away, you remove everything that isn't what you were meant to be. Slowly but surely, you will finally arrive at your true self: your own Pietà.

Therefore, I want to conclude this book with an invitation for you to look deep inside of yourself. Search for the reflection that is your destiny of who you will become within that vision. This self-reflection is an ambitious introspection into the highest version of yourself: the real you, the best you.

Seeking to become the best version of yourself "now" is what your future self deserves. Seeking anything less is dishonesty, and a true dis-service to yourself (and the people who are counting on you).

You are now at a crossroads where only two options remain; you can keep living as the "lying king" or you can make the necessary changes to become the Lion King:

Simba – heir to the throne but displaced and discarded in a diabolical family coup – was shown a reflection of himself in a pond. Gazing down, Simba saw his own face morph into a visage of his father, the late Mufasa. With Simba's rapt attention now in full play, his father counseled him:

> **"Remember who you are...you are more than what you have become."**

Simba's reflection – on reflection – had a purpose behind it. His reflection revealed that you should never be satisfied with the status quo and what "everyone else" wants for you. Life is a journey, and if you stand still, you are wasting both the journey and your life. And, actually, you!

And you, my friend...are a terrible thing to waste.

To your million-dollar future,

Jeremy McGilvrey

Resources

About the Author:

- https://www.vox.com/first-person/2017/8/8/16112864/recidivism-rate-jail-prostitution-break-cycle

Chapter One:

- https://blogs.scientificamerican.com/guest-blog/what-does-mindfulness-meditation-do-to-your-brain/&sa=D&ust=1571087307185000&usg=AFQjCNEUNyAPuF4lXHuH4ICMAGZq8fOjLQ
- https://www.smithsonianmag.com/innovation/how-does-human-echolocation-work-180965063/&sa=D&ust=1571087550251000&usg=AFQjCNE6sHtmnGNNxvzDccBzgepa92Ip-g
- https://www.dailymail.co.uk/news/article-2887151/Scientists-discover-just-IMAGINING-exercising-make-stronger-tone-muscles-delay-stop-muscle-atrophy.html
- https://news.stanford.edu/2018/02/15/mental-rehearsal-might-prepare-minds-action/
- https://www.nytimes.com/2014/02/23/sports/olympics/olympians-use-imagery-as-mental-training.html
- https://nuscimag.com/how-olympians-train-their-brains-bf0bd488777b
- https://www.ncbi.nlm.nih.gov/pmc/articles/PMC3662866/
- https://neurons.wordpress.com/2008/04/09/imagination-norman-doidge-others/
- https://www.ncbi.nlm.nih.gov/pmc/articles/PMC2577943/
- https://www.youtube.com/watch?v=xZbKHDPPrrc
- https://www.deseretnews.com/article/865590905/Social-media-2-why-the-medium-is-still-the-message.html
- Hodgson, R., and Stockwell, T. (1983). Cue Exposure and Response Prevention with Alcoholics: A Controlled Trial. Behaviour. Research &. Therapy, 421, 4, 435-446
- Seligman, M. E. P. (1972). "Learned helplessness". Annual Review of Medicine. 23 (1): 407–412.

- Maier, S.; Seligman, M. (July 2016). "Learned helplessness at fifty: Insights from neuroscience". Psychological Review. 123 (4): 349–367.
- Reference: Thibodeau, P. & Boroditsky, L. (2011).
- Metaphors We Think With: The Role of Metaphor in Reasoning
- Published: February 23, 2011. https://doi.org/10.1371/journal.pone.0016782

Chapter Two:

- https://www.whiskeyriff.com/2016/09/29/the-chances-of-you-being-born-you-are-1-in-400-trillion-act-like-the-miracle-you-are/
- https://www.businessinsider.com/infographic-the-odds-of-being-alive-2012-6
- http://www.normandoidge.com/?page_id=1259
- http://web.mit.edu/mcraegroup/wwwfiles/ChuangChuang/thesis_files/Appendix%20D_Artificial%20Neural%20Network.pdf
- https://www.pnas.org/content/106/25/10130.short
- https://www.sciencedirect.com/topics/neuroscience/reticular-activating-system
- https://www.sciencedirect.com/science/article/abs/pii/S1389945707000779
- https://www.sciencedirect.com/science/article/pii/B9780123868923000056
- https://www.ncbi.nlm.nih.gov/pmc/articles/PMC4526749/
- https://www.sciencedirect.com/science/article/abs/pii/S1057740810001191
- https://www.sciencedirect.com/science/article/abs/pii/S0166223699014472
- https://www.researchgate.net/publication/230652617_The_Addictive_Brain_All_Roads_Lead_to_Dopamine
- https://www.nytimes.com/2013/01/30/opinion/friedman-its-pq-and-cq-as-much-as-iq.html
- https://www.psychologytoday.com/us/blog/extreme-fear/201011/yes-you-really-can-lift-car-trapped-child
- https://www.foxnews.com/world/man-survives-6-days-in-desert-without-water-by-eating-ants
- https://www.youtube.com/watch?v=mHhrZxLWOHc

- https://www.youtube.com/watch?v=45Ph_MXIP1o
- https://www.youtube.com/watch?v=sl_kv-6-l_s
- https://psycnet.apa.org/record/2001-05428-004
- https://scholar.dominican.edu/cgi/viewcontent.cgi?article=1284&context=news-releases
- http://www.thelawofattraction.com/what-is-the-law-of-attraction/
- https://psycnet.apa.org/buy/2003-02410-012
- http://www.worldsfaircommunity.org/topic/3778-smoke-ring-button/
- https://www.mpg.de/596269/pressRelease200908171
- https://www.nbcnews.com/mach/science/einstein-showed-newton-was-wrong-about-gravity-now-scientists-are-ncna1038671
- https://joshkaufman.net/power-of-habit-charles-duhigg/
- https://www.azlyrics.com/lyrics/arloguthrie/alicesrestaurantmassacree.html
- Schultz, W. (July 2015). "Neuronal Reward and Decision Signals: From Theories to Data". Physiological Reviews. 95 (3): 853–951
- Writing to Heal: A Guided Journal for Recovering from Trauma and Emotional Upheaval. Oakland, California: New Harbinger, 2004. ISBN 978-1-57224-365-1
- Pennebaker, J. and Seagal, J. (1999). Forming a Story: the Heath Benefits of Narrative. J Clin Psychol 55: 1243–1254

Chapter Three:

- Breaking Chains: A Thirty-Day Devotional of Biblical Positive Insights
- https://www.health.harvard.edu/mind-and-mood/protect-your-brain-from-stress
- https://www.poetryfoundation.org/articles/69379/an-essay-on-criticism
- https://www.youtube.com/watch?v=YM8t29gD8J8
- https://www.franciscans.ie/a-franciscan-blessing/
- http://blogs.discovermagazine.com/neuroskeptic/2018/10/07/get-your-amygdala-removed/#.xvrwdjnkjui
- https://www.techtimes.com/articles/19283/20141101/want-to-be-fearless-get-rid-of-amygdala-neurons-in-the-brain.htm

- http://blogs.nature.com/news/2010/12/the_fearlessness_of_a_destroye.html
- https://www.thedrive.com/news/3704/first-responders-tell-us-why-drunk-people-are-more-likely-to-survive-a-collision
- https://www.nature.com/news/brain-scans-of-rappers-shed-light-on-creativity-1.11835
- https://www.semanticscholar.org/paper/Neural-Correlates-of-Lyrical-Improvisation%3A-An-fMRI-Liu-Chow/a9b73b8ce41c353156206983cfd83aaaabb0efcb
- https://onlinelibrary.wiley.com/doi/full/10.1002/hbm.22849
- Liu, S., Erkkinen, M. G., Healey, M. L., Xu, Y., Swett, K. E., Chow, H. M., & Braun, A. R. (2015). Brain activity and connectivity during poetry composition: Toward a multidimensional model of the creative process. Human Brain Mapping, 36(9), 3351-3372.
- Abraham, A., Beudt, S., Ott, DV, Yves von Cramon, D. (2012). Creative cognition and the brain: dissociations between frontal, parietal-temporal and basal ganglia groups. Brain Res 1482: 55– 70
- https://hbr.org/2010/11/why-a-happy-brain-performs-bet

Chapter Four:

- https://www.sciencedirect.com/topics/medicine-and-dentistry/pleasure-principle
- https://www.livestrong.com/article/471877-health-effects-of-doughnuts/
- https://www.mayoclinic.org/healthy-lifestyle/weight-loss/in-depth/calories/art-20048065
- https://www.psychologytoday.com/us/blog/your-emotional-meter/201712/the-benefits-delaying-gratification
- https://www.wsj.com/articles/SB100014240529702048804045772229220571408412
- https://www.30days.com/summit
- https://blogs.wsj.com/experts/2015/02/03/the-one-crucial-money-concept-children-need-to-learn/
- https://www.washingtonpost.com/nation/2019/06/20/horns-are-growing-young-peoples-skulls-phone-use-is-blame-research-suggests/?utm_term=.41cd1e50ffbd

- McClure, S. M., Ericson, K. M., Laibson, D. I., Loewenstein, G., & Cohen, J. D. (2007). Time discounting for primary rewards. Journal of neuroscience, 27(21), 5796-5804. (https://www.jneurosci.org/content/27/21/5796.short)
- https://www.cnbc.com/2019/09/15/exercise-benefits-cognitive-function-performance.html
- https://jamanetwork.com/journals/jamainternalmedicine/article-abstract/415534
- McClure, S. M., Laibson, D. I., Loewenstein, G., & Cohen, J. D. (2004). Separate neural systems value immediate and delayed monetary rewards. Science, 306(5695), 503-507. (https://science.sciencemag.org/content/306/5695/503)
- De Martino, B., Kumaran, D., Seymour, B., & Dolan, R. J. (2006). Frames, biases, and rational decision-making in the human brain. Science, 313(5787), 684-687. (https://science.sciencemag.org/content/313/5787/684.abstract)
- https://courses.lumenlearning.com/boundless-management/chapter/barriers-to-decision-making/
- https://www.washingtonpost.com/nation/2019/06/20/horns-are-growing-young-peoples-skulls-phone-use-is-blame-research-suggests/
- https://www.ncbi.nlm.nih.gov/pubmed/9858756
- https://www.npr.org/2019/08/03/747086462/lawmaker-aims-to-curb-social-media-addiction-with-new-bill
- https://www.encyclopedia.com/medicine/psychology/psychology-and-psychiatry/sensory-deprivationhttps://thebrain.mcgill.ca/flash/capsules/histoire_bleu06.html
- https://stpauls.vxcommunity.com/Issue/us-experiment-on-infants-withholding-affection/13213
- https://www.inc.com/nate-klemp/researchers-reveal-real-reason-youre-addicted-to-your-phone-and-what-you-can-do-about-it.html
- Gorospe, E. C., & Dave, J. K. (2006). The risk of dementia with increased body mass index. Age and ageing, 36 (1), 23-29
- Laurie M. Orlov. Aging in Place Technology Watch. 2016 Survey of Older Adults Conducted by Link-age Connect
- Kivimaki et al., 2017. Body mass index and risk of dementia: Analysis

of individual-level data from 1.3 million individuals. Alzheimer's & Dementia, 2017; DOI: 10.1016/j.jalz.2017.09.016

- Marlatt, G. A., & Gordon, J. R. (Eds.). (1985). Relapse prevention:
- Maintenance strategies in addictive behavior change. New York: Guilford
- https://motivationandchange.com/coping-with-after-work-drinks/
- https://www.ncbi.nlm.nih.gov/pmc/articles/PMC3900881/
- https://www.eurekalert.org/pub_releases/2019-09/econ-tfa090919.php

Chapter Five:

- https://over40healthcoach.com/wellness/
- https://www.huffpost.com/entry/compass-pleasure_b_890342
- https://en.wikipedia.org/wiki/James_Olds
- https://www.medicalnewstoday.com/articles/323483.php
- The Addictive Brain: All Roads Lead to Dopamine: https://pdfs.semanticscholar.org/1a2c/d996f2d6e7bb4d117599b67fa4612b2b1b54.pdf
- https://highlights.sawyerh.com/volumes/00f4bd57-33ab-4481-805e-8acae5ff2c87
- https://everydaypower.com/muhammad-ali-quotes/
- https://charlesduhigg.com/how-habits-work/
- https://www.sciencedirect.com/science/article/pii/S0962184905800162
- https://www.sciencedaily.com/releases/2017/06/170627105337.htm
- Grøntved, A., & Hu, F. (2011). Television Viewing and Risk of Type 2 Diabetes, Cardiovascular Disease, and All-Cause Mortality: A Meta-analysis
- JAMA. 2011;305(23):2448-2455. doi:10.1001/jama.2011.812
- Prochaska, James O.; DiClemente, Carlo C. (2005). "The transtheoretical approach". In Norcross, John C.; Goldfried, Marvin R. (eds.). Handbook of psychotherapy integration. Oxford series in clinical psychology (2nd ed.). Oxford; New York: Oxford University Press. pp. 147–171
- https://www.inc.com/jessica-stillman/new-study-sleep-is-literally-a-deep-clean-for-your-brain.html?cid=sf01002

Chapter Six:

- https://corporatefinanceinstitute.com/resources/knowledge/trading-investing/list-top-10-types-cognitive-bias/
- https://corporatefinanceinstitute.com/resources/knowledge/trading-investing/herd-mentality-bias/
- https://mailman.yale.edu/pipermail/leps-l/1999-October/017763.html
- https://www.lindahall.org/jean-henri-fabre/
- https://betterexplained.com/articles/understanding-the-pareto-principle-the-8020-rule/
- McClelland, D. C. (1987). Characteristics of successful entrepreneurs. The journal of creative behavior, 21(3), 219-233. (https://onlinelibrary.wiley.com/doi/abs/10.1002/j.2162-6057.1987.tb00479.x)
- Bruce Sacerdote. (2001). Peer Effects with Random Assignment: Results for Dartmouth Roommates, The Quarterly Journal of Economics, Volume 116, Issue 2, May 2001, Pages 681–704. (https://doi.org/10.1162/00335530151144131)
- https://www.ncbi.nlm.nih.gov/pmc/articles/PMC3817005/
- https://technology.inquirer.net/69088/good-friends-mimic-others-brainwaves-neuroscientist-claims
- https://www.ncbi.nlm.nih.gov/pmc/articles/PMC4654779/
- https://www.huffpost.com/entry/adoption-and-genetics-imp_b_4682667?guccounter=1&guce_referrer=aHR0cHM6Ly93d3cuZ29vZ2xlLmNvbS8&guce_referrer_sig=AQAAALFlA2X-14GYGX-LwpBh6BBRVvNiLlxf6XXtkRcGQUgBSZSFRc_35gcHlPCXHvpNk-qYmz-KoUtabw-WxQPalH9ZTHa79lMXl5YZm52Pj3ixFoYFwNLviOQ2-s5ZoxGIT_ctjc8rxHhnaglTiHBxz01Fhl1xgUjl9FyFcYXJNBpx
- https://jamesclear.com/book-summaries/nurture-assumption
- https://www.scientificamerican.com/article/parents-peers-children/
- Gallese, V. (2014). Bodily selves in relation: embodied simulation as second-person perspective on intersubjectivity. Philosophical Transactions of the Royal Society B: Biological Sciences, 369(1644), 20130177. (https://www.ncbi.nlm.nih.gov/pmc/articles/PMC4006180/)

- https://www.health.harvard.edu/blog/the-secret-to-happiness-heres-some-advice-from-the-longest-running-study-on-happiness-2017100512543
- https://founders.archives.gov/documents/Adams/04-10-02-0241
- https://www.marketwatch.com/story/single-digit-millionaires-like-hulk-hogan-cant-afford-justice-says-peter-thiel-2016-10-31
- van Baaren, R. B., Holland, R.W., Steenaert, B. & van Knippenberg, A. Mimicry for money: behavioral consequences of imitation. Journal of Experimental Social Psychology, 39, 393 - 398, (2003). | Article | ISI | Van Baaren, R. B., Holland, R.W., Kawakami, K.& van Knippenberg, A. Mimicry and pro-social behavior. Psychological Science, in the press, (2003)

Chapter Seven:

- https://www.moviequotes.com/s-movie/strange-brew/
- https://en.wikipedia.org/wiki/Four_stages_of_competence
- https://www.youtube.com/watch?v=MXrn5crHtx4&feature=youtu.be&t=251
- https://bible.org/seriespage/27-parable-talents-matthew-2514-30-luke-1912-28
- https://www.cell.com/neuron/fulltext/S0896-6273(17)30901-7
- https://hypnosis.edu/articles/secret-mind
- https://www.sciencedirect.com/science/article/pii/S1571064513001553
- https://europepmc.org/abstract/MED/22925839
- https://www.sciencedaily.com/releases/2002/07/020712075415.htm
- http://www.theinvisiblegorilla.com/gorilla_experiment.html
- https://www.livescience.com/6727-invisible-gorilla-test-shows-notice.html
- http://www.digitaljournal.com/tech-and-science/science/op-ed-knowledge-doubles-almost-every-day-and-it-s-set-to-increase/article/537543#ixzz5ud02uYbO
- https://www.youtube.com/watch?v=5MulMqhT8DM
- https://www.bicycling.com/news/a28981152/sleep-heart-attack-risk/

- http://darwin-online.org.uk/converted/pdf/1794_Zoonomia_A967.1.pdf (Section XXI, page 240, "On Drunkenness")
- https://www.verywellmind.com/constructive-vs-destructive-anger-in-ptsd-2797523
- https://www.reuters.com/article/us-heart-daylightsaving/daylight-saving-time-linked-to-heart-attacks-study-idUSBREA2S0D420140329
- https://www.ncbi.nlm.nih.gov/pmc/articles/PMC2740752/
- https://onlinelibrary.wiley.com/doi/full/10.1111/j.1365-2796.2004.01443.x
- https://hbr.org/2009/01/what-can-coaches-do-for-you
- http://krishnamurti.abundanthope.org/index_htm_files/Tertium-Organum-by-P-D-Ouspensky.pdf
- https://www.verywellmind.com/what-is-the-hawthorne-effect-2795234
- https://news.harvard.edu/gazette/story/2010/11/wandering-mind-not-a-happy-mind/
- http://timkastelle.org/blog/2010/06/why-is-the-retirement-age-65/
- https://www.pnas.org/content/96/23/13427/
- http://www.hiphealth.ca/blog/weight_training_improves_cognitive_function_in_seniors
- https://jamanetwork.com/journals/jamainternalmedicine/article-abstract/415534
- https://technology.inquirer.net/69088/good-friends-mimic-others-brainwaves-neuroscientist-claims

Conclusion:

- https://www.telegraph.co.uk/tv/2017/05/13/oprah-winfrey-untold-story/
- http://whatiseagle.blogspot.com/2014/02/bald-eagles-transform-their-lives-at-40.html
- https://www.americamagazine.org/faith/2019/01/01/what-michelangelos-flawed-pieta-teaches-us-about-mary

Acknowledgment

I have my son Thomas to thank for everything. You saved my life son.

Let me explain.

"High-flying financial advisor crashes" headlined the front page of the Sunday newspaper for the 7th largest city in the United States. *"Gone are the striking black Bentley convertible, the junkets to Vegas and Australia, and the photo ops with Eva Longoria and other beautiful people"* read directly below it.

Practically the entire city was buzzing about this story (my story). *Infamous*, quickly began replacing *illustrious* as the word the press used to describe my career as the chairman and CEO of the financial planning firm I founded. As the drama continued to unfold, my story drew great public fanfare while the media capitalized on my Herculean debacle. Words are hard to come by to convey how difficult it is when a personal struggle of this magnitude was thrust into the public eye for everyone to bask in.

I gave my all to building my financial planning firm. And when it died, I nearly did as well.

With each front page news story, (there were nearly a dozen) it made it extremely difficult for me to believe I had any purpose on this earth. So I devised a plan to end my life. Then I wrote out detailed instructions for my father that told him what to do with my valuables along with where to bury me.

Next I called several physicians that were clients as well as friends and told them I was going to be going on a long trip and needed extra dosages of the medications they were already prescribing me. The medications were Ambien, Xanax, and Paxil. Combined, I knew these powerful prescriptions had lethal implications.

I went to several different pharmacies to fill these prescriptions so I could get enough refills of these pills to end my life. I remember driving around to the pharmacies with tears in my eyes because I knew what I had to do.

Once I filled all the prescriptions, I headed home. When I arrived, I went into my kitchen and dumped all the bottles of pills into a large red plastic cup.

After that, for nearly 13 hours I drank vodka straight. Every now and again I'd take a few of the pills. At about four in the morning, I set a timer on my iPhone for 10 a.m. That was going to be the cue to dump all of the pills from the red plastic cup into my mouth. As I was envisioning taking the pills, I realized I needed a better way to digest them, so I went to the kitchen and poured a cup of milk. I thought that would help me swallow the pills faster, and in turn, end my life more quickly.

My plan was to take a drink of the pills in the cup and wash them down with a drink of milk in the other cup. I was going to repeat this process until all 340 pills were gone.

As I sat there on the bed in my bedroom drinking vodka, and staring at the two plastic cups, one with milk and one with pills – I thought about my two dogs Abby and Tanner that were laying in the bed next to me. I thought about how I would probably throw up after taking all the pills, and my dogs would possibly eat the vomit and die too.

So I decided to go to the bathroom, get in the shower and close the door. Sitting there on the floor, I had the plastic cup with the pills and the other plastic cup with the milk. It was time for me to end my life. As I trembled in the shower holding the cup of pills in my left hand and the cup of milk in my right hand, I began thinking about you Thomas.

I thought about the fact that I was going to become a father for the first time. And I could not stop thinking about how even though your mother Natalie was only a month pregnant, I knew I was going to have a son. All I could think about was that I have to figure this out for you. I have to get through this for you. I have to be the father you need me to be.

With a pounding heart and tears in my eyes, I slowly set the two cups down on the travertine shower floor. I opened the glass door and went back to my bed. I continued to drink vodka. And I waited. What was I waiting for? I knew the authorities were going to come and arrest me and take me to prison. I knew I was going to face several life sentences. And I knew I did not have the money to fight. I knew I was helpless and completely on my own.

But I knew because of you, that somehow, someway, I would figure this out. So that is why I say you saved my life Thomas. Because without you, I would not be here. I love you son. I did before you were born, and I do now more than ever.

About the Author

Jeremy McGilvrey is a Harvard-educated number-one bestselling author. He believes we all have a metaphorical hourglass above our heads, and that every moment of each day, our time is running out. This sense of urgency is what allows him to achieve so much so quickly.

He lives by the mantra that you don't get what you deserve in life; you get what you work for. Jeremy regularly states: Thinking life is fair is akin to thinking a bull will not charge you because you're a vegetarian. And his all-time favorite quote comes from the book *How the Mighty Fall* by Jim Collins:

> *"The signature of the truly great versus the merely successful is not the absence of difficulty, but the ability to come back from setbacks, even cataclysmic catastrophes – stronger than before. Great nations can decline and recover. Great companies can fall and recover. Great social institutions can fall and recover. And great individuals can fall and recover. As long as you never get entirely knocked out of the game, there always remains hope."*

Jeremy is someone who pours his heart and soul into everything he does. Ingrained deep in his DNA is a ferocious drive and the trait of either being all in or all out. There is no in between with him. Few people can have an effect on others like Jeremy does. If you spend more than five minutes with him, you will quickly be infected by his passion and zest for life. Understanding where his supreme self-confidence comes from is something many people are yet to discover. But most who know Jeremy know this: his ability to breakdown complex problems and provide simple solutions is second to none.

The love Jeremy has for his two boys Thomas and Tristan is

what constantly keeps him in pursuit of making a difference in this world. He tries to make every day count because it's extremely important that he leaves a legacy his children will be proud of.

In Jeremy's spare time he works. Not because he has to, but because there are few things he would rather be doing than finding ways to test new marketing strategies and improve conversions on his sales funnels. He is obsessed with getting the tiniest details right in everything he does. That's why Jeremy is currently one of the most sought after marketers in the world for helping business owners take their companies from brick and mortar to click and order.

To learn more about Jeremy visit: **JeremyMcGilvrey.com**

Today's Date: ______________

3 tasks I will complete by the end of the day tomorrow:

1. ______________________________

2. ______________________________

3. ______________________________

____

(sign above)

Be, Have, Do

"Think big. Believe big. Act big. And the results will be big."

What type of person do you want to be?

Be, Have, Do

"Think big. Believe big. Act big. And the results will be big."

What do you want to have?

Be, Have, Do

"Think big. Believe big. Act big. And the results will be big."

What do you want to do?

Track Your Money

Consciously you may be telling yourself one thing, but subconsciously (via through your actions) you may be doing the opposite. Tracking where you spend your money will reveal the facts.

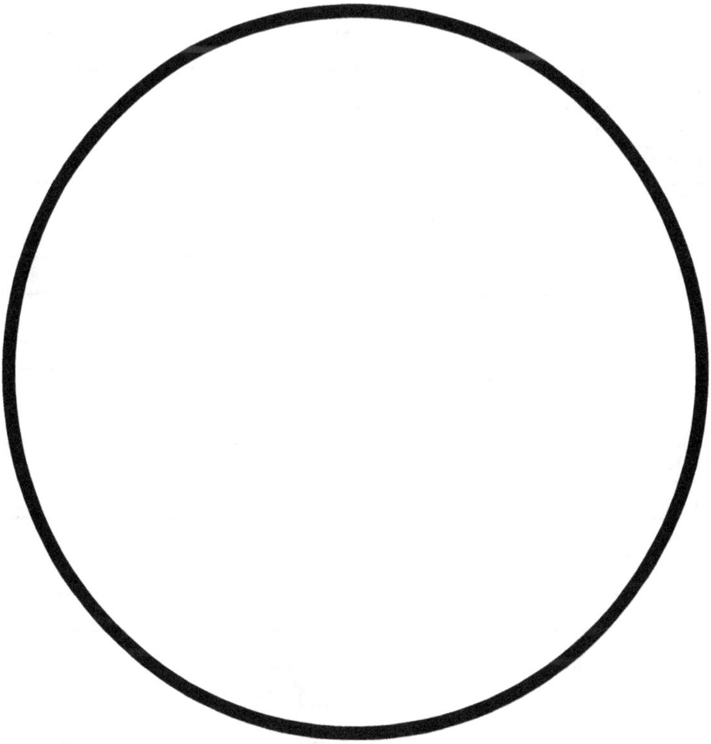

Current Expenses

Track Your Time

TIME	MONDAY	TUESDAY	WEDNESDAY
7.00 AM			
7.30 AM			
8.00 AM			
8.30 AM			
9.00 AM			
9.30 AM			
10.00 AM			
10.30 AM			
11.00 AM			
11.30 AM			
12.00 AM			
12.30 AM			
1.00 PM			
1.30 PM			
2.00 PM			
2.30 PM			
3.00 PM			
3.30 PM			
4.00 PM			
4.30 PM			
5.00 PM			
5.30 PM			
6.00 PM			
6.30 PM			
7.00 PM			
7.30 PM			
8.00 PM			
8.30 PM			
9.00 PM			
9.30 PM			
10.00 PM			
10.30 PM			
11.00 PM			

TIME	THURSDAY	FRIDAY	SATURDAY
7:00 AM			
7:30 AM			
8:00 AM			
8:30 AM			
9:00 AM			
9.30 AM			
10:00 AM			
10:30 AM			
11:00 AM			
11:30 AM			
12:00 AM			
12:30 AM			
1:00 PM			
1:30 PM			
2:00 PM			
2:30 PM			
3:00 PM			
3:30 PM			
4:00 PM			
4:30 PM			
5:00 PM			
5:30 PM			
6:00 PM			
6:30 PM			
7:00 PM			
7:30 PM			
8:00 PM			
8:30 PM			
9:00 PM			
9:30 PM			
10:00 PM			
10:30 PM			
11:00 PM			

Unfavorable Habits

"It seems ridiculously simple, but once you're aware of how your habit works, once you recognize the cues and rewards, you're halfway to changing it. It seems like it should be more complex, but the truth is, the brain can be reprogrammed. You just have to be deliberate about it."

~NATHAN AZRIN, neuroscientist who specialized in behavioral modification

Building and Removing Habits

Identify your habit loop and change the routine.

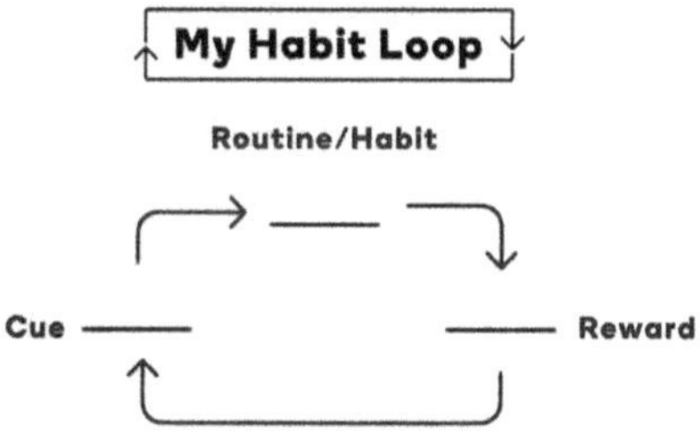

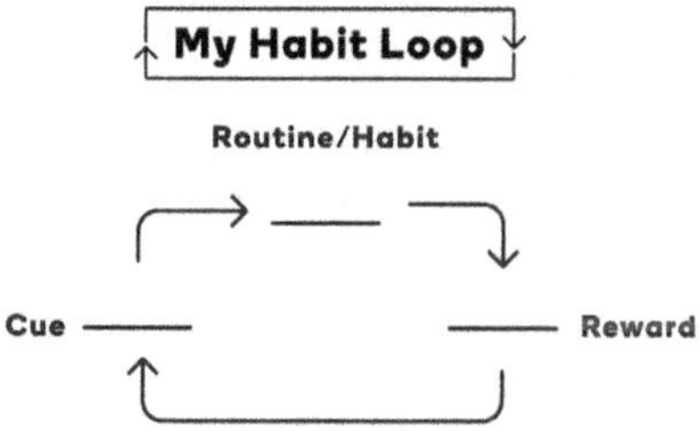

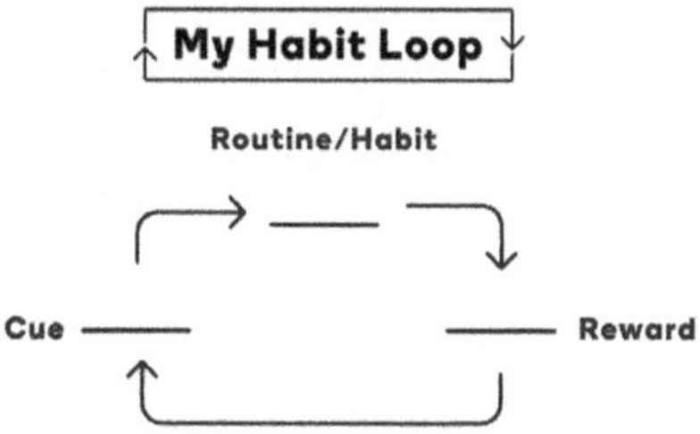

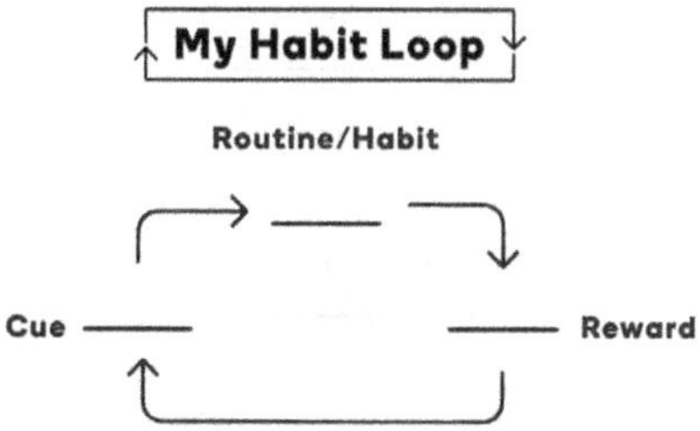

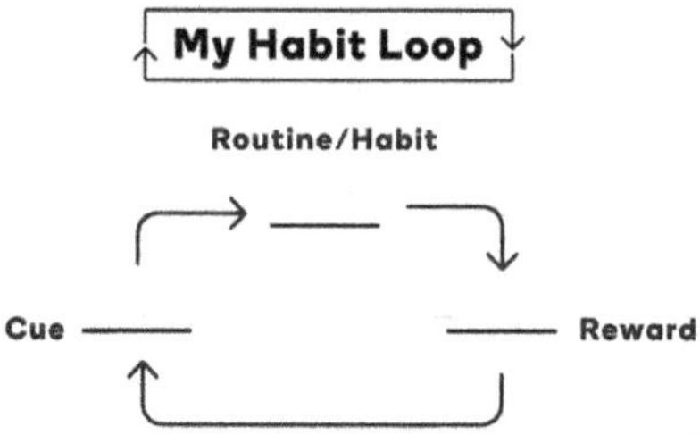

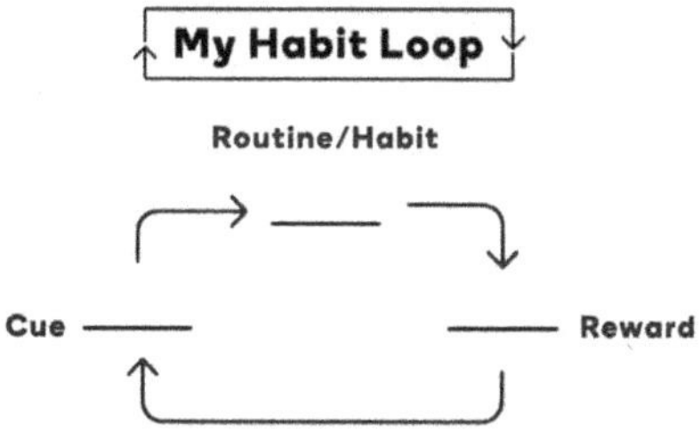

Notes

"A short pencil is better than a long memory!"